anchorites and their patrons in medieval england

anchorites and their patrons in medieval england

Ann K. Warren

University of California Press

Berkeley • *Los Angeles* • *London*

University of California Press
Berkeley and Los Angeles, California

University of California Press, Ltd.
London, England

Library of Congress Cataloging in Publication Data

Warren, Ann K.
    Anchorites and their patrons in medieval England.

    Bibliography: p.
    Includes index.
    1. Hermits—England—History.   2. Patronage, Ecclesi-
astical—England—History.   3. England—Church history—
Medieval period, 1066–1485.   I. Title.
BX2847.G7W37   1985   271'.02'042   84-24901
ISBN 0-520-05278-1

Printed in the United States of America
1   2   3   4   5   6   7   8   9

To David

CONTENTS

ACKNOWLEDGMENTS   ix

ABBREVIATIONS   xi

    Introduction   1

PART I: THE ANCHORITES

  1 The Desert   7
  2 Solitaries, Sites, and Support   15
  3 Bishops and Anchorites: Procedure and
      Protection   53
  4 Enclosure and Rule: Asceticism and
      Contemplation   92

PART II: THE PATRONS

  5 Royal Support   127
  6 Aristocratic and Gentry Support   186
  7 Merchant and Other Lay Group Support   222
  8 Clerical Support   265

    Conclusion   280

APPENDIXES

  1 Anchorite Distribution by Counties   292
  2 English Anchorite Rules   294
  3 Transference of Alms
      A: Gloucestershire 1170–98   300
      B: Surrey 1178–99   302
      C: Buckinghamshire and
          Bedfordshire 1159–97   304
  4 The Hustings Rolls   305
      D: Number of Wills Enrolled
          at the London Court of
          Husting 1271–1500   309

BIBLIOGRAPHY   313

INDEX   339

TABLES

1	Numbers of Anchorites and Sites: 1100–1539	20
2	Village, Town, and City Placements of Anchorite Cells	38
3	Transference of Alms: Herefordshire (1156–1214)	132
4	Royal Maintenance Grants: Henry II to John (1156–1216)	136
5	Transference of Alms: Winchester (1160–1215)	141
6	Transference of Alms: Essex and Hertfordshire (1160–1203)	142
7	Royal Maintenance Grants: Henry III (1216–1272)	160
8	Distribution of Alms: Gentry Wills (1301–1520)	220
9	Pious and Charitable Bequests of London Testators	227
10	Comparison of Draper Wills to All Hustings Anchorite-favoring Wills	233
11	Analysis of Wills of London Merchants Who Bequeathed to Anchorites (1420–1528)	236
12	Bequests to London Anchorites Compared to Bequests to Other Groups	237
13	Chichele Data Compared to Marche and Luffenam and Anchorite-favoring Testaments	240
14	Bequests to York Anchorites Compared to Bequests to Other Groups in York Mayoral Wills	250
15	Comparison of York and London Merchant Wills (1361–1535)	252
16	Testamentary Gifts: Exeter Recluse	270
17	Sherborne Recluses	277
18	Distribution of Gifts at Carrow Abbey by Anchorite-favoring Testators (1426–1481)	285
Appendix 3, table A: Transference of Alms: Gloucestershire (1170–1198)		300
Appendix 3, table B: Transference of Alms: Surrey (1178–1199)		302
Appendix 3, table C: Transference of Alms: Buckinghamshire and Bedfordshire (1159–1179)		304
Appendix 4, table D: Number of Wills Enrolled at the London Court of Husting (1271–1500)		309

ACKNOWLEDGMENTS

Many persons in many ways contributed to the making of this book. Lest these acknowledgments become an exercise in not forgetting, let me thank them all at once and first.

Some people and institutions were particularly involved. Without them this book would not exist in its present form or perhaps at all. Among librarians, Daniel Stabe and Jean Gastonguay of the Interlibrary Loan Department of Freiberger Library at Case Western Reserve University were of extraordinary assistance in gathering materials for me from all parts of the western world; Christopher Wood, among others at the Cleveland Public Library, graciously made available to me the extensive history and religion collections of that library; Nicholas Bennett of the Lincolnshire Archives Office gave me access to manuscripts in their holdings. Among scholars, my former mentors and now colleagues in the History Department of Case Western Reserve University nourished me in all the ways that men and women of knowledge and character can. To David Van Tassel, Carl Ubbelohde, Marion Siney, Bertram Wyatt-Brown, thank you.

Four scholars have played special roles, each of them having read the entire manuscript. Robert Lerner, a rare and intuitive medievalist, read the manuscript in an earlier version and gave me cogent (if sometimes painful) advice. Mortimer Kadish and Emilie Kadish read the work from their special vantages as philosopher and literary scholar. With precision they found its weaknesses and challenged me to overcome them. Michael Altschul, who supervised this work in its first incarnation as a doctoral dissertation, read it countless times both as a dissertation and as it later changed and matured. Teacher, critic and editor, friend and colleague, he has shared with me his superb mind and liquid imagination.

With grace and humor my children, Barbara, Mark, Lisa, Martha, Jim, and Tom, tolerated the discomforts of a preoccupied mother. More than that, they too read and corrected and encouraged. My husband's involvement in this work over years has been constant. Since there is no way I can acknowledge all of his contributions, let me just thank him for his unfailing love.

ABBREVIATIONS

BIHR D/C Reg.	Borthwick Institute of Historical Research, York. Will Registry, Dean and Chapter Jurisdiction
BIHR Reg.	Borthwick Institute of Historical Research, York. Will Registry, York Consistory Court
Blomefield, *Norfolk*	Blomefield, Francis. *An Essay towards a Topographical History of the County of Norfolk . . . and other Authentick Materials.* 11 vols. London, 1805–10.
CCR	Great Britain. Public Record Office. *Calendar of the Close Rolls.* London: His (Her) Majesty's Stationery Office 1900–.
CCW	Great Britain. Public Record Office. *Calendar of Chancery Warrants, A.D. 1244–1326.* London: His Majesty's Stationery Office, 1927.
CInqM	Great Britain. Public Record Office. *Calendar of Inquisitions Miscellaneous (Chancery).* London: His (Her) Majesty's Stationery Office, 1916–.
CInqpm	Great Britain. Public Record Office. *Calendar of Inquisitions, post mortem, and other analogous documents.* London: His (Her) Majesty's Stationery Office, 1898–.
CLR	Great Britain. Public Record Office. *Calendar of the Liberate Rolls.* London: His (Her) Majesty's Stationery Office, 1916–.
CMR	Great Britain. Public Record Office. *Calendar of Memoranda Rolls (Exchequer) . . . Michaelmas 1326–Michaelmas 1327. London: Her Majesty's Stationery Office, 1968.*

CPL	Great Britain. Public Record Office. *Calendar of Entries in the Papal Registers relating to Great Britain and Ireland: Papal Letters.* Edited by W. H. Bliss et al. London: His (Her) Majesty's Stationery Office, 1893–.
CPR	Great Britain. Public Record Office. *Calendar of the Patent Rolls.* London: His (Her) Majesty's Stationery Office, 1891–.
CR	Great Britain. Public Record Office. *Close Rolls of the Reign of Henry III.* London: His Majesty's Stationery Office, 1902–38.
CWCH	Sharpe, Reginald R., ed. *Calendar of Wills Proved and Enrolled in the Court of Husting, London, A.D. 1258–1688.* 2 vols. London, 1889–90.
CYS	Canterbury and York Society
Chichele	Jacob, Ernest F., ed. *Register of Henry Chichele, Archbishop of Canterbury, 1414–1443.* 4 vols. Canterbury and York Society 42, 45–47. 1937–47.
Clay, "Further Studies"	Clay, Rotha M. "Further Studies on Medieval Recluses." *Journal of the British Archaeological Association,* 3d ser., 16 (1953): 74–86.
Clay, *Hermits and Anchorites*	Clay, Rotha M. *The Hermits and Anchorites of England.* London: Methuen and Co., 1914.
Clay, "Northern Anchorites"	Clay, Rotha M. "Some Northern Anchorites." *Archaeologia Aeliana,* 4th ser., 33 (1955): 202–217.
Curia regis	Great Britain. Public Record Office. *Curia Regis Rolls.* London: His (Her) Majesty's Stationery Office, 1922–.
Dugdale, *Monasticon*	Dugdale, William. *Monasticon Anglicanum.* Edited by John Caley et al. 6 vols. London: 1817–30.
EETS	Early English Text Society

Foster, *Lincoln Wills*	Foster, Charles W., ed. *Lincoln Wills Registered in the District Probate Registry at Lincoln*. 3 vols. Lincoln Record Society 5, 10, 24. 1914–30.
Gibbons, *Early Lincoln Wills*	Gibbons, Alfred, ed. *Early Lincoln Wills*. Lincoln: J. Williamson, 1888.
HMSO	His (Her) Majesty's Stationery Office
LAO	Lincolnshire Archives Office
LP	Great Britain. Public Record Office. *Letters and Papers, Foreign and Domestic, of the Reign of Henry VIII*. London: His (Her) Majesty's Stationery Office, 1862–1932.
Lacy, *Exeter Reg.*	Dunstan, G. R., ed. *Register of Edmund Lacy, Bishop of Exeter 1420–1455*. 4 vols. Canterbury and York Society 60–63. 1963–71.
Nichols, *Royal Wills*	Nichols, J., ed. *A Collection of All the Wills Now Known to Be Extant of the Kings and Queens of England*. . . London, 1780.
PL	Migne, Jacques P. *Patrologiae cursus completus, series Latina*. 221 vols. Paris, 1844–64.
PR	Great Britain. Record Commission. *The Great Rolls of the Pipe for the First Year of the Reign of King Richard the First, A.D. 1189–1190*. Edited by Joseph Hunter. London, 1844.
	Great Britain. Record Commission. *The Great Rolls of the Pipe for the Second, Third, and Fourth Years of the Reign of King Henry the Second, A.D. 1155, 1156, 1157, 1158*. Edited by Joseph Hunter. London, 1844.
	The Great Roll(s) of the Pipe . . . of the Reign(s) of King Henry the Second, King Richard the First, King John . . . Pipe Roll Society Publications, 1–. London, 1884–.
Powicke and Cheney, *Councils*	Powicke, Frederick M., and Cheney, Christopher R. *Councils and Synods, with other Documents Relating to the English Church, II, A.D. 1205–1313*. 2 vols. Oxford: Clarendon Press, 1964.

RS Rolls Series: *Chronicles and Memorials of Great Britain and Ireland during the Middle Ages, published under the Direction of the Master of the Rolls,* 99 vols. London, 1858–97.

Rot. Lit. Claus. Great Britain. Record Commission. *Rotuli litterarum clausarum in turri Londinensi asservati.* Edited by Thomas D. Hardy. 2 vols. London, 1833–34.

Rymer, *Foedera* Great Britain. Record Commission. *Foedera, conventiones, litterae, et cujuscunque generis acta publica* ... Edited by Thomas Rymer. 20 vols. 1727–35.

SPCK Society for Promoting Christian Knowledge.

SS Surtees Society.

Test. Ebor. Raine, James, ed. *Testamenta Eboracensia; or Wills Registered at York Illustrative of the History, Manners, Language, Statistics, etc., of the Province of York, from the Year 1300 Downwards.* Vols. 1–5. Surtees Society 4, 30, 45, 53, 79. 1836–84.

VCH *Victoria Histories of the Counties of England.* London and Oxford, 1900–.

Wills and Inventories Raine, James, ed. *Wills and Inventories Illustrative of the History, Manners, Language, Statistics, etc., of the Northern Counties of England, from the Eleventh Century Downwards.* Vol. 1. Surtees Society 2. 1835.

INTRODUCTION

In 1914 Rotha Mary Clay published *The Hermits and Anchorites of England.* A work of impeccable scholarship, the book still stands as the only significant monograph on the reclusive life in medieval England. A subject deserving serious academic interest, eremitism as one form of the religious life of the medieval community largely has been ignored since then. Only now, more than two generations after Clay, have scholars of religious and social history again begun to examine the meaning and nature of vocations of withdrawal—this time from the perspective of the late twentieth century and its own renewed interest in religion.

Earlier disinterest in the study of the reclusive life has been costly. Not only have scholars neglected one aspect of religious life of the period but in doing so they have fostered and even encouraged antiquarian perceptions of the anchoritic vocation. To the degree that anchorites are understood at all, they are seen as exotics, deviants, or as individuals peripheral to medieval religious history. This work will argue otherwise as it shows that English anchorites were not misfits who retreated into catacombs. Conservative orthodox religious, they lived above the ground surrounded by the communities on whom they depended for support, side by side with those with whom they had formed a compact to sustain them in their chosen life of reclusion and prayer.

Two factors can be adduced to explain the undeserved neglect of the study of anchoritism as a significant form of medieval religious expression. First, at the end of the period during which anchoritic life flourished—in England at the onset of the Reformation—anchorites disappeared from the scene, leaving few physical and cultural traces. Unlike the vanishing monasteries, anchorites possessed neither extensive lands of which careful records

1

would be kept nor extensive archives from which future historians might easily reconstruct the past. Thus the recollection of
the previous existence of anchorites was relegated to folk memory
and mythology. The anchorite as exotic emerged in Elizabethan
literature and the anchorite of historical context faded away. The
anchorite as antiquarian curiosity had been born. Second, anchoritism may have been ignored by modern historians because it
stands in such contrast to the prevailing mentalities of this day.
Common is the perception of the anchorite as an aberrant personality, a person with an emotional disorder causing him or her
to flee the world. In the Middle Ages the anchorite was viewed as
living the sanest of lives, a life more perfect than any other. Far
from being neurotics, solitaries led the most authentic life considered possible for the Christian. The continuum of possible life-
styles available to medieval men and women included the active
life in the world, the secular priesthood (for men), the monastic
life, the hermit's life of separation, and the life of complete withdrawal. The anchorite, at the end of this continuum, was not considered "far out"; on the contrary, such a life was at the apex.

To study the anchoritic life as one component of the social and
religious culture of the Middle Ages is thus to study a phenomenon that lay at the heart of the religious belief of the period. To
understand it better is to enich our understanding of the times, of
the individuals who lived then, of the structures that organized
the era. The history of the religious beliefs of a people is always
central to a knowledge of those people. In the Middle Ages religious belief was quite consciously and openly proclaimed as central to existence. All aspects of this ethic deserve close attention
and analysis; its rarer expressions are as telling as its most common.
The modern historian is challenged to know medieval society better through examining a life-style undervalued in our own time.

This book is about English anchorites and the people who supported them—their patrons. It attempts to delineate a religious
phenomenon within the social context that gave rise to it and then
nourished it; to examine a widespread anchoritism supported by
all social groups for whom records exist; and to correct the cost of

neglect—the distortion in our image of the anchorite—by showing the recluse as a significant part of daily life in medieval England. Anchorites in this study emerge as carriers of the religious values of their culture and as expressions of those values in lives of exemplary form. I view recluses not as individuals whose personalities encouraged them to lead celibate lives and seek excessive privacy but as a group whose vocation was the fulfillment of lesser men's dreams. I see anchorites as high status religious because in their own time they were seen that way. While at times I have taken an anthropological, psychological, or sociological approach, this book begins and ends with the view of the anchorite in religious terms. That reading of the evidence is one of the parameters of the work.

Let me establish a few others at this point. The study begins in 1100 not because there were no anchorites before then, but because written records become available in some quantity starting in the twelfth century and at that point I could begin the kind of analysis I wanted to undertake. This book deals with anchorites not as intriguing individuals but as anonymous members of a group. Those about whom more is known become for the purposes of this study almost distractions. The focus here is on the unknown anchorite as representative, so I value the more famous figures only to the degree that their lives tell us something useful about the group. Furthermore, I study anchoritism as a nationwide phenomenon, as a religious movement having broad acceptability throughout England for the whole of the central and late medieval periods. In order to do this I have had to depend mainly on printed sources. English governmental agencies and the many English national and local historical societies have performed an invaluable service for historical researchers in making available a whole range of archival materials. The work of these societies has been in progress for nigh on to 150 years, and on the fruits of this labor I have drawn relentlessly. I have used unprinted materials when and where they seemed particularly useful, especially York wills. Extended searching of unpublished manuscripts clearly would bring some new data forward. But in the early stages of this work I determined that information to be redundant. Its great value would be in the detailed exploration of anchoritism in a local setting, a task that remains to be done.[1]

This book is divided into two parts. Part one examines the anchorite in his own world; part two explores the nature of the patronage systems that were developed to support him and the identity of some of these patrons. The interaction of the two communities—anchorites and patrons—is explored throughout, but a final chapter of conclusions brings together and puts in sharper focus the meaning and nature of those interactions and what they tell us about medieval English society. Medieval English society was enriched by the presence of recluses in its midst. This study is, in no small measure, an attempt to convey the texture and quality of that enrichment to the modern reader.

1. Norman P. Tanner's recent work, *The Church in Late Medieval Norwich 1370-1532*, Pontifical Institute of Mediaeval Studies, Studies and Texts 66 (Toronto, 1984), is an example of a local study that, while not focusing on anchorites, brings forth much new detail.

PART I

The Anchorites

1

The Desert

Anchorites were common figures in medieval England. As solitary recluses, they were dedicated to God and vowed to lifelong asceticism. As individuals, they were free of monastic obedience, subject only to a higher master. As dependents, they were asked only for their prayers by the communities on whom they relied for support. Their vocation constituted a religious phenomenon of significance in England, one that sustained both its own internal meanings and its relevance for society throughout the Middle Ages. That life-style ended abruptly, along with other forms of religious life, when Henry VIII initiated the English Reformation in the sixteenth century.

Men and women alike, most anchorites lived in cells or narrow little houses attached to parish churches. Encouraged, applauded, and supported by society and church, they undertook their solitary life by encamping in the heart of the community. Enclosed and yet exposed, hidden and yet visible, shadows behind the curtains of their access windows, medieval English anchorites were daily reminders of the proper focus of Christian existence. Martyr, *viator*, penitent, ascetic, mystic, *miles Christi*—the recluse was all of these.

Anchorites were immured, locked up, imprisoned. Once having entered the cell they could not retreat. Solitary by choice, they became solitary by law and in this way distinct from hermits. As I shall define the terms, anchorites differed from hermits in the

Middle Ages in that hermits were free to move about whereas anchorites took vows of permanent stability.[1]

In early Christian writings the two words had been synonymous. Fourth-century prototypes of the medieval anchorite belonged to that time when hermit and anchorite were one in meaning. To be an anchorite or a hermit was to withdraw (*anachōrein*) to the desert (*eremus*). Such a life could imply total seclusion and stability or considerable freedom of movement and social intercourse. The individual could live quite alone or with a group of like-minded solitaries. The recluse was *anachoreta* or *eremita* interchangeably: the Greek roots turned into first-declension Latin nouns that included both genders.

During the Middle Ages the word *hermit* continued to express the general meaning initially sustained by both words, but the word *anchorite* became more restricted in use. To be a hermit still encompassed a wide variety of behavioral patterns; to be an anchorite meant to take on a narrowly defined vocation. The anchorite was *inclusus/inclusa* or *reclusus/reclusa*, enclosed and stable with limited access to the outside world. In fact, the recluse became liturgically and psychologically dead to the world. He or she inhabited only a limited space within what was broadly considered to be an eremitic life; the hermit remained free to encounter his destiny in the remainder of that space.

Medieval English anchorites, as enclosed and incarcerated religious, lived in cells close to churches. The cell itself, that place from which the anchorite could not venture, was invested with many overlapping meanings. It was a version of the desert home of the first Christian anchorites, the arena of spiritual warfare, a place for contemplation, a representation of the prison of the early martyrs, a penitential prison, a refuge, a way station. Like in a dream, these many images condensed into a single vision, a vision that portrayed the inheritance of the past transmuted into the my-

---

1. This is a practical definition derived from medieval English usage. Scholars argue well that the two words are synonymous and should not be separated so artificially. Most cogent is Jean Leclercq, " 'Eremus' et 'eremita': Pour l'histoire du vocabulaire de la vie solitaire," *Collectanea Ordinis Cistercensium Reformatorum* 25 (1963): 8–30 (see especially p. 25). Yet in medieval England hermits and anchorites are in fact distinct from each other much of the time.

thology of the present. By a process of internalization, both the physical martyrdom of the earliest Christian centuries and the search for the desert that had followed in its wake (and which was in itself a substitute for bloody martyrdom) became mental states. What had been actual became symbolic. While the Christian goal of reliving Christ's life remained untransformed, it was to be achieved in a less extreme setting. Thus the virgin, the martyr, the repentant sinner, the ascetic and would-be mystic, the pilgrim, the soldier—all found a desert retreat as well as a deserved or necessary prison in the anchorite's cell of the Middle Ages.

The primary symbol of the cell, however, was that of the desert. The medieval anchorite's refuge, nestled against the village church, drew the recluse back in time to the desert caves of the Egyptian saints: St. Anthony, the first anchorite, St. Paul of Thebes, called the most perfect anchorite, and St. Mary the Egyptian, who provides a female solitary as archetype. These were the primitive, half-mythic, half-historic forebears of the medieval recluse, and the legends of their lives established the frame of the paradigmatic journey to heaven which found its central image in the desert motif. There the individual suffered temptation and hunger and battled against demons, ultimately to achieve total dissociation from the physical and emotional past. There the individual received his reward: the miracles of walking on water, the gift of bread from heaven, the capacity to speak with animals.

Underpinning the private obsessions of Anthony, Paul, and Mary and illuminating their private dreams was an older heritage, the wilderness theology elaborated in both Old and New Testaments. Moses and Elijah were understood as prefiguring John the Baptist and Christ. They and other men of Scripture had sought the desert, gone forth to engage the devil there. They also found in the wasteland the closest possible communion with God. These two themes would dominate the anchoritic experience. The anchorite's cell would be both the site of the devil's attack as well as the mountain of contemplation. It was a new version of the desert cave.

Anthony, Paul, Mary and many others in the early Christian centuries sought to lose themselves in the Egyptian desert. In other climates individuals retreated to islands, marshlands, woods, and forests. Bruno Bettelheim has explored the psychological meaning of being lost or self-abandoned in a wilderness:

> Since ancient times the near-impenetrable forest in which we get lost has symbolized the dark, hidden, near-impenetrable world of our unconscious. If we have lost the framework which gave structure to our past life and must now find our own way to become ourselves, and have entered this wilderness with an as yet undeveloped personality, when we succeed in finding our way out we shall emerge with a much more developed humanity. . . . It is this ancient image Dante evokes at the beginning of *The Divine Comedy*: "In the middle of the journey of our life I found myself in a dark wood where the straight way was lost."[2]

Peter Brown, who sees the desert experience of the fourth century as having its roots in social tensions, would agree:

> The total disengagement and social "death" implied in the gesture of *anachōrēsis* left the ascetics shorn of the normal social supports of identity. The hermit was regarded as a man who had set about finding his true self. By the fact of *anachōrēsis* he had resolved the tensions and incoherences of his relations with his fellow men. In the desert he was expected to settle down, in conflict with the demonic, to resolve the incoherences of his own soul. The powers the ascetic wielded came from a long process of self-discovery.[3]

Mircea Eliade sees the actual move to the desert and the cell itself in symbolic terms. In Eliade's analysis, for a man to move, to settle down somewhere new, involves making a serious decision. The physical move is an act demanding the creation of a new life. To move is not to cast off a domicile but "to abandon one's world. The house is not an object, a 'machine to live in'; *it is the universe that man constructs for himself by imitating the paradigmatic creation of the gods, the cosmogony.* Every construction and every inauguration of a new building are in some measure equivalent to a new beginning, a new life."[4]

2. Bruno Bettelheim, *The Uses of Enchantment: The Meaning and Importance of Fairy Tales* (New York: Alfred A. Knopf, 1976), p. 94.

3. Peter Brown, *The Making of Late Antiquity* (Cambridge, Mass.: Harvard University Press, 1978), p. 89.

4. Mircea Eliade, *Occultism, Witchcraft, and Cultural Fashions* (Chicago: University of Chicago Press, 1976), p. 27.

Bettelheim sees the psychological, Brown the sociological, and Eliade the anthropological meanings of these journeys away from the known. In religious terms the individual seeks the desert in order to right and extend his relationship with God, the notion of the desert containing both the positive idea of contemplation and the negative one of purgation. G. H. Williams describes the wilderness of the desert as a "place of protection, a place of contemplative retreat . . . as one's inner nature or ground of being, and . . . as the ground itself of the divine being." Negatively, the desert wilderness is understood as the "world of the unredeemed, the wasteland, and as the realm or phase of punitive or purgative preparation for salvation."[5]

Scripture developed both positive and negative constructions of the desert theme. It was in the wilderness at Mount Horeb that God first appeared to Moses (Exod. 3:1–2) and it was through the wilderness that God led the Israelites to the Red Sea (Exod. 13:17–14:22) in order to foil the Egyptians. But the wilderness was also the home of the Israelites for forty years of wandering and testing, of stress, of "murmurings," and of the defection of some. God detained his people in the desert, but he provided them with manna. He formed them into his people with hardships and trials in the desert, but the period was also a time of "redemptive, covenantal bliss."[6]

Wilderness themes entered the New Testament through the figure of John the Baptist. John appeared in the wilderness (Mark 1:4), preached in the wilderness (Matt. 3:1–3), and baptized Christ there. It was John, understood by all the Synoptists as embodying the "voice in the wilderness" prophesied by Isaiah (40:3), who prepared the way for Christ. Furthermore, as soon as Christ had been baptized, "the Spirit immediately drove him out into the wilderness. And he was in the wilderness forty days, tempted by Satan; and he was with the wild beasts; and the angels ministered to him" (Mark 1:13).

5. George H. Williams, *Wilderness and Paradise in Christian Thought* (Cambridge, Mass.: Harvard University Press, 1962), pp. 5–6. Leclercq, "Eremus," deals with similar themes, but the following takes Williams's work as authority.

6. Williams, *Wilderness*, p. 15.

11

Less concrete was Paul's conception of the desert motif as expressed in 1 Corinthians, where "he interpreted the life of Christians between the conversion and the coming of the Kingdom in power as a wilderness experience in which they would be tempted as were the Israelites of the Old Covenant in the desert, but would be sustained to the end by the eucharist bread of heaven."[7] The Epistle to the Hebrews is even more metaphysical in its interpretation of the desert experience. Here the sufferings and stages in the wilderness wanderings can be read in mystical terms as the rungs of the ladder taking the individual toward Christian perfection. With these writings the groundwork for a metaphoric comprehension of the desert was laid; the metaphoric interpretation, however, was slow to develop. The Revelation of St. John the Divine had returned the individual to the literal desert of the Old Testament where again the desert was portrayed both as a place of refuge from real physical danger and as a place of contemplation where the divine might be discerned more distinctly. It was this literal tradition that formed the core of the scriptural inheritance of the first millennium of the Christian era.

During the High Middle Ages, side by side with a continuing literal tradition, the word *desert* increasingly began to be used to imply a mental state. Desert imagery took on that psychological cast that Bettelheim describes and became invested with a range of allegorical and anagogic implications. In the mid-twelfth century Richard of St. Victor, among others, went so far as to abandon the literal meaning of *desertum* completely, using it only as a technical term to signify that point in a mystical ascent characterized by the aridity, the fears, and dangers, and the loneliness of the scriptural wilderness. For mystics of Richard's group the place where the individual lived separate from his fellow men was insignificant. The entire experience was internal.[8]

The English religious mentality did not go to such an extreme. The literal desert was not abandoned as an ideal, but at the same time the recluse in his cell in the churchyard of the medieval village was understood to be obeying a similar imperative. The me-

7. Ibid., p. 25.
8. Ibid., pp. 50–51.

dieval Englishman accommodated a notion of the desert as the actual site to which early Celtic anchorites had fled—the island wildernesses of Crowland, Farne, and Derwentwater, for example —while accepting the village anchorite as participating in this experience by passing through a mental desert in his pilgrimage toward heaven. English religious literature expressed the double focus. The Dublin Rule, a thirteenth-century rule written for anchorites living in parish cells, explained that all anchorites who live scrupulously are spiritually in the desert with Moses and Jesus; a fourteenth-century rule, the *Speculum inclusorum*, preferred that every recluse live in a remote place in a physical, not a psychological, wilderness. Richard Rolle, a fourteenth-century hermit who sought rural solitude, considered both ways valid. In his *Incendium amoris* he evoked the familiar simile of the solitary as a wild ass to whom God had given the wilderness as home (Job 39: 5–6), only to follow that passage with one explaining that the wilderness also represents the "quiet of the heart" (*quies pectoris*). Another fourteenth-century English mystic, the Monk of Farne, wrote his *Meditations* while reenacting the same wilderness experience on the island of Farne that St. Cuthbert had known in the seventh century and Bartholomew in the twelfth. But Dame Julian, perhaps the most famous of all fourteenth-century English mystics, wrote her *Showings* while living in a typical anchorite's cell attached to a parish church in the midst of thriving Norwich.[9]

The English style allowed for both inner and outer perceptions of the desert motif. The two did not compete but rather reinforced each other. That some anchorites still lived in remote places made all the more meaningful the notion of the wilderness

9. Livario Oliger, ed., "Regula reclusorum dubliniensis," in "Regulae tres reclusorum et eremitarum Angliae saec. XIII–XIV," *Antonianum* 3 (1928): 182 (hereafter cited as Dublin Rule); Livario Oliger, ed., *Speculum inclusorum: Auctore anonymo anglico saeculi XIV, Lateranum*, n.s. 4, no. 1 (Rome: Facultas Theologica Pontificii Athenaei Lateranensis, 1938), p. 70; Richard Rolle, *The Incendium Amoris of Richard Rolle of Hampole*, ed. Margaret Deanesly (Manchester: Manchester University Press, 1915), p. 182; John Whiterig, *The Monk of Farne*, ed. Hugh Farmer, Benedictine Studies (Baltimore: Helicon Press, 1961); Julian, *Julian of Norwich's Showings*, ed. Edmund Colledge and James Walsh, Classics of Western Spirituality (New York: Paulist Press, 1978).

as a way station in a mystical journey, the actualization of the hidden itinerary. Medieval Englishmen well understood that the English anchorite, most likely to be found in a cell whose door they would pass as they entered the parish church, had withdrawn as a solitary, separating himself from every goal and desire save that of total abdication to God. The anchorite had escaped into the wilderness, his life a symbol of the desert ideal of early Christianity.

2

Solitaries, Sites, and Support

The medieval Englishman who passed by the cell of the anchorite was more than a passive observer. He was part of a network of support that enabled the anchorite to exist and persist. While the individual in medieval England had the freedom to choose a reclusive life and to pursue a solitary relationship with God, his ability to make that choice was conditioned by its social acceptability. His choice implied a culture in consonance with his views, one that both sanctioned individual religious experience as an ideal (even placing a high value on it) and also encouraged it by responding to its demands. Those demands were severe and should not be underestimated. In order to become an anchorite the individual was forced to make considerable claim on the resources of the community. An anchorite was enclosed for life, a period that stretched out in some cases for forty and fifty years. During that period the anchorite needed maintenance in a home as well as food, clothes, and fuel. Unable to leave his cell, he required servants to attend him and confessors to minister to his spiritual needs. All this and more after enclosure—itself a complex process that involved members of the hierarchy, patrons both lay and clerical, guarantees of character, guarantees of support, and the finding or building anew of a reclusory. I can think of no modern equivalent with which to compare such a long-term commitment by so many to satisfy the religious compulsion of one. That commitment implies a society covenanted both to the religious values of the undertaking and to the right of an individual to make such a demand on it.

The response to that demand lies at the heart of this study. It enabled the would-be recluse to move forward in his desire, to approach the anchorhold, to be enclosed, and to begin a solitary life. It gave substance to a vision. At the same time that response left its traces in the records of its day and is the means through which we can reconstruct a distant reality. Society affirmed its commitment to an otherworldly ideal as it confirmed that commitment in the mundane world of gifts, guarantees, charters, and buildings. To trace the anchoritic life in medieval England is in large measure to trace the interaction between the people who led such a life and the society that nurtured them. To understand why people supported the solitary movements is to comprehend the awe that the asccticism of the recluse engendered within the larger community and to acknowledge the perceived value of the ascetic's intercessionary powers. Anchorites, holy men and women, repaid their patrons through prayer. Patrons earned heavenly credits with their support of recluses.

The story of a twelfth-century hermit of Gloucestershire illustrates the relationship. The king of England, Henry II, granted a hermitage-chapel in the forest of Dean, Ardland, to one "William, Solitary," at some point during his reign. It was William's responsibility to take care of the chapel as well as to maintain the road in the nearby area. He did this for a number of years, probably with the aid of some companions. After this period, and during the reign of Richard I, William decided to enter a life of greater strictness, that is, to become an anchorite (*arctiori vita, scilicet anachoritica*).[1] William, the bishop of Hereford, advised the hermit William to make an arrangement with the abbot of Flaxley by which the abbey would take over the chapel and all of William's possessions as well as his duties. In the charter the abbot, noting that he had been petitioned in this matter by many persons, promised also to provide food for William and for those with him, each day, and also to supply such clothes as were appropriate for the religious life of an anchorite (*ad religionem inclusi*) in order that William might devote himself entirely to a life of piety within

1. A. W. Crawley-Boevey, ed., *Cartulary and Historical Notes of the Cistercian Abbey of Flaxley* (Exeter, 1887), pp. 40, 78, 142.

the anchorage, praying for the "stability and peace of the realm and for the soul of King Henry from whom he had received the place and for the safety of King Richard and his subjects." Although the agreement with the abbot of Flaxley does not so indicate, the king's permission was probably sought and granted. The new arrangement changed the status of William from that of a working hermit to that of a dependent recluse, receiving the proceeds of his former endowment without doing that labor for which it was originally granted. Here is a clear substitution of spiritual work for manual work.

Medieval England, then, was an environment in which individuals chose to become religious recluses in order to assure their own salvation and in which others within the community supported these recluses the better to assure their own. The earliest clear picture of English anchoritism emerges from documents of the twelfth century. One comes upon it *in medias res*. There are anchorites in cells, liturgical forms for enclosure, episcopal regulations, letters giving advice to anchorites on how to conduct their lives, documents granting financial support. All of the mechanisms through which we can trace the anchorite movement are in place, at least in rudimentary fashion. Extant records allow us to leave the world of hagiography for the world of fact and number and to sketch a composite picture of recluse and patron in medieval English society. The sketch, like a cubist painting, will impose multiple perspectives on our vision. The anchorite will be seen not only as a unique religious of great passion but also as a carrier of the moods of contemporary society. He both shared and gave form to the values of his patrons. He acted out what was understood to be the best life for every man.

As religious history this study draws on enclosure liturgies, rules for anchorites, and ecclesiastical law and practice. As social history it reflects the charters scanned, the wills counted, the locations of cells plotted upon maps, the numbers, sex, and social class of anchorites tabulated, and the support of patrons (who made all this possible) analyzed. The data, however, do not divide so neatly. Few can be assigned solely to one category or another, whatever their ostensible original purpose. It is in the interaction between

17

the social and the religious, the institutional and the personal, that the texture of the experience is made clear. The recluse was an extraordinary individual as well as a social statistic. Much the same could be said of many of the recluse's patrons.

This chapter focuses on both anchorite and patron as social statistic. I will analyze the evidence with regard to the numbers and sex of English anchorites from 1100 to 1539, the physical characteristics of cells and their distribution countrywide, and the mechanisms of anchorite support. We turn our eyes from the desert in order to examine the social context within which anchorites flourished. When we return to the desert it will be with a greater understanding of a few of the many forces at work.

ENGLISH ANCHORITES: NUMBERS AND SEX

How many anchorites were there? The evidence implies a wide-ranging and far-reaching religious phenomenon: many anchorites all over the country. Ecclesiastical legislation of the thirteenth century addressed the priest concerning the recluse(s) in his parish, "si habeat in parochia sua." Not one in every parish, but in many. In 1245 Henry III granted a pauper's meal to all the anchoresses in London. An entry in a Bury St. Edmunds register of the early fourteenth century listed forty-two anchorholds in hamlets in the vicinity.[2] Wills in every century under review provided bequests for the anchorites of a community or shire or diocese. In the thirteenth century Agnes de Condet remembered all the anchorites of Canterbury with twelve shillings each, while Richard Elmham, a canon of St. Martin le Grand, left one pence to every anchorite in London. All female recluses of Oxford received two pence in 1231, while around 1270 all the anchorites of Oxford, male as well as female, received twelve pence. William de Beauchamp left four shillings to every anchorite in Worcester and its

<hr>

2. Powicke and Cheney, *Councils*, pp. 35, 87, 194; *CLR 1240–45*, p. 324; Antonia Gransden, "The Reply of a Fourteenth-century Abbot of Bury St. Edmunds to a Man's Petition to Be a Recluse," *English Historical Review* 75 (1960): 464.

suburbs in 1268, and Walter Suffield, bishop of Norwich in the mid-thirteenth century, left a bequest of ten pounds to be divided among all the recluses of his diocese.[3] Fourteenth-century London wills enrolled at the Court of Husting abounded in bequests bestowed generally on the anchorites of the city and its suburbs. In like manner in 1399 John of Gaunt granted every anchorite in London or within five leagues of the city three nobles in his will. A knight of Yorkshire left each recluse in his county 3s. 4d. in 1402; Ralph Neville, earl of Westmorland, left twenty shillings to each anchorite in the bishoprics of York and Durham in 1420.[4] Clearly, in towns, in villages, in cities, there were anchorites everywhere in medieval England.

Table 1 displays the statistical results of the search for data. It is the basis of the analytic work that I have done. I have assumed that this surviving evidence indicates reliable patterns of sex and locations of sites. Table 1 shows that women were anchorites more commonly than men throughout the entire period, but the degree to which this was true varied considerably from century to century. In the twelfth century there is a ratio of about five women to three men; in the thirteenth century, about four to one;[5] in the fourteenth century, about five to two; in the fifteenth, about

3. Charles W. Foster and Kathleen Major, eds., *The Registrum Antiquissimum of the Cathedral Church of Lincoln*, 11 vols., Lincoln Record Society (1931–68), 1:293; Joseph Burtt, "Will of Richard de Elmham, Canon of the Church of St. Martin le Grand, London," *Journal of the British Archaeological Association* 24 (1867): 343; Herbert E. Salter, ed., *Cartulary of Oseney Abbey*, 6 vols., Oxford Historical Society 89–91, 97–98, 101 (1929–36), 1:135; S. Robert Wigram, ed., *Cartulary of the Monastery of St. Frideswide at Oxford*, 2 vols., Oxford Historical Society 28, 31 (1895–96), 1:276; Nicholas Harris Nicolas, ed., *Testamenta Vetusta*, 2 vols. (London, 1826), 1:51; Blomefield, *Norfolk*, 3:489.

4. See CWCH, passim; *Test. Ebor.*, 1:299; *Test. Ebor.*, 1:297; *Wills and Inventories*, p. 72.

5. An Italian parallel to this lopsided ratio helps to affirm its correctness. A late thirteenth-century document in the archives of Perugia details sixty-eight local recluses of whom fifty-six were women and twelve men—a ratio of four and a half to one. See Giovanna Casagrande, "Note su manifestazioni di vita comunitaria femminile nel movimento penitenziale in Umbria nei secc. XIII, XIV, XV," *Prime manifestazioni di vita communitaria maschile e femminile nel movimento francescano della penitenza (1215–1447)* (Rome, 1982), pp. 463–464. My thanks to Professor Robert Brentano for bringing Dr. Casagrande's work to my attention.

TABLE 1

NUMBERS OF ANCHORITES AND SITES: 1100–1539[1]

Century	Sex			Totals	Sites[2]
	Female	Male	Indeterminate		
Twelfth	48	30	18	96	77
Thirteenth	123	37	38	198	175
Fourteenth	96	41	77	214	171
Fifteenth	110	66	28	204	129
Sixteenth (to 1539)	37	27	4	68	49

1. See appendix 1 for data by shires.
2. Sites are counted only once even if containing cells for more than one recluse.

five to three again; and in the sixteenth, about three to two. English anchoritism was thus a vocation that already was biased toward women in the twelfth century. It became sharply female in orientation in the thirteenth century, and then gradually reversed this trend in the succeeding years until, at its summary demise, the female/male ratio was closer to one than at any previous time.

Thirteenth-century data indicate not only many more women as recluses on a comparative basis but also many more recluses overall. This conclusion is in part a function of surviving information, but it is also true in absolute terms. Thirteenth-century anchoritism was both a growing phenomenon and one with an increasingly feminine bias. Many new anchorholds were built at the time. Henry III (1216–72) alone granted eight individuals the right to build new reclusoria at churches where he was patron, and episcopal registers, charters, and archaeological data identify additional sites as new installations.[6] Robert Bingham, bishop of Salis-

6. For Henry's installations see chapter 5, note 55. For others see J. W. Willis Bund, ed., *Register of Bishop Godfrey Giffard, Sept 23rd, 1268 to August 15th, 1301,* 2 vols., Worcestershire Historical Society (1902), 1:21; William Brown, ed., *Register of Walter Giffard, Lord Archbishop of York, 1276–1279,* SS 109 (1904), p. 108; A. Hamilton Thompson, ed., *Register of William Greenfield, Lord Archbishop of York, 1306–1315,* 2 vols., SS 145, 149 (1931–34), 2:221.

bury, was so worried about the proliferation of reclusoria around 1240 that he prohibited any new ones from being built in churchyards in his diocese and ordered old ones to be razed when the incumbents died, fearing a rash of ill-supported recluses.[7] Most data indicate that the new reclusoria were being built for women and at their requests. In one instance a patron providing both cell and endowment in perpetuity for a chaplain specified that the grant would be null if a woman were in residence. Such must have been the pressure to find accommodations for female recluses. Moreover, as the century progressed, ecclesiastical legislation increasingly addressed itself to the problems of female recluses. Whereas Stephen Langton had discussed only male recluses in his legislation dated to 1213 or 1214, only a few years later similar statutes were being broadened to include women as well and further ones were being written for women alone.[8]

That women were drawn into disparate kinds of religious lives in the thirteenth century is widely known.[9] On the Continent one discovers religious women as nuns and recluses, but also as Beguines, *Humiliati*, Franciscan tertiaries, and even heretics. English women had fewer choices. England remained in the thirteenth century a citadel of orthodoxy, a society whose religious needs were accommodated in traditional ways. Although England did welcome the mendicants—after they received papal sanction—

7. Powicke and Cheney, *Councils*, p. 379.

8. Emma Mason, ed., *Beauchamp Cartulary Charters, 1100–1268*, Pipe Roll Society, n.s. 43 (1980), p. 78, for the chaplain's cell. See my chapter 3 for comprehensive discussion of thirteenth-century ecclesiastical legislation.

9. Herbert Grundmann, *Religiöse Bewegungen im Mittelalter: Untersuchungen über die geschichtlichen Zusammenhänge zwischen der Ketzerei, den Bettelorden und der religiösen Frauenbewegung im 12. und 13. Jahrhundert und über die geschichtlichen Grundlagen der deutschen Mystik*, 2d rev. ed. with suppl., "Neue Beiträge . . ." (Hildesheim: George Olms; Darmstadt: Wissenschaftliche Buchgesellschaft, 1961), is the fundamental work dealing with the growth of female spirituality and includes the study of male spirituality as well. An excellent short article is that of Brenda Bolton, "Mulieres Sanctae," in *Sanctity and Secularity: The Church and the World*, ed. Derek Baker, Studies in Church History 10 (Oxford: Basil Blackwell, 1973), pp. 77–85, which is reprinted in Susan M. Stuard, ed., *Women in Medieval Society* (Philadelphia: University of Pennsylvania Press, 1976), pp. 141–158. Bolton not only covers the ground for the thirteenth century but her notes include most of the relevant bibliography. See also Charles McCurry, "Religious Careers and Religious Devotion in Thirteenth-century Metz," *Viator* 9 (1978): 325–333.

there was never a Beguine movement in England, and English resistance to heterodoxy remained strong. The increase in female anchoritism in the thirteenth century in England was a means of containing the explosion of spiritual enthusiasm observable throughout Catholic Europe. In a vocation of honored antiquity English women expressed current sensibilities.[10]

The vocation stabilized in English society by the fourteenth century. The recoverable numbers from this point remain fairly constant from one century to the next, a noteworthy fact for the period when the Black Death and subsequent epidemics of plague took their toll. Anchoritism continued to attract persons desiring to live an ascetic life and from the fourteenth to the sixteenth centuries the marked discrepancy between the numbers of male and female recluses began to diminish. While anchorites remained predominantly female, more men sought the recluse's cell and English anchoritism ceased to be skewed so sharply in favor of women.

Not only did male and female anchorites come to reclusion in different proportions, they also came from differing social strata. In the main, male anchorites tended to be clerical and female anchorites lay. While the male recluse was often a member of the regular clergy and frequently a priest, the anchoress was only occasionally a nun before she entered the anchorhold. The anchorite's cell provided an alternative religious vocation for women rather than the progression from an easier communal life to a harder solitary life envisioned by St. Benedict.

In its origins anchoritism preceded cenobitism. To withdraw from society was to withdraw alone, to the desert, to create a private world where no one existed save man and God. But the desert experience was too harsh, too difficult, too subject to abuse to survive as a norm. It was not long before the idea of a religious community developed. The word *monk* (meaning "he who lives alone"), initially a synonym of *anchorite* and *hermit*, became tied

10. See Brenda M. Bolton, "*Vitae Matrum*: A Further Aspect of the *Frauenfrage*," in *Medieval Women*, ed. Derek Baker, Studies in Church History, Subsidia 1 (Oxford: Basil Blackwell, 1978), pp. 253–273, on the range and interconnectedness of the varied Belgian religious movements involving women.

to the communal and conventual experience. The monastery became the haven of the first instance and the training ground for a later foray into a more fully separated existence for those who would persevere. Only the chosen few were to venture beyond the monastic walls. In the sixth century St. Benedict wrote:

> The second [kind of monks] are the Anchorites, that is, the hermits; those, namely, who not in the first fervor of their conversion, but after long probation in the monastery, have long since learned by the help of many others, to fight against the devil, and being well armed, are able to go forth from the ranks of their brethren to the singlehanded combat of the desert, safe now, even without the consolation of another, to fight with their own strength against the weaknesses of the flesh and their own evil thoughts, God alone aiding them.[11]

The Benedictine pattern became the norm in the early medieval centuries and remained the ideal in the later ones. Yet it never precluded the possibility that laymen and laywomen as well as priests and hermits might enter into an anchoritic life without prior monastic experience. Anchoritism was thus a profession that drew its candidates from three groups. Laymen and laywomen chose it in lieu of the monastery; priests, friars, secular canons, and hermits moved from a service-oriented religious profession into a contemplative one; and monks and nuns embarked on an advanced form of the regular life, taking a new and irrevocable step beyond their original vow to a greater austerity and an intensified spiritual life.

There were always considerable numbers of male anchorites who had held ecclesiastical rank in their former lives, and the likelihood that a male anchorite had once been a monk, friar, canon, or secular grew during the period 1100–1500. In the twelfth century only four of the thirty known male recluses are clearly identified as clerical before enclosure (13 percent). By the thirteenth century eighteen of thirty-seven (49 percent) are so identified. Fourteenth-century data show twenty-six out of forty-one (63 percent) in this category; in the fifteenth century we have forty-six of sixty-six (70 percent). In the sixteenth century the pattern reverses

11. *Holy Rule of St. Benedict* (St. Meinrad, Indiana, 1975), chap. 2, p. 6.

a bit, but the data still give us fourteen out of twenty-seven (52 percent) with clerical status. And these are minimal figures.

The clerical roles of male anchorites remained useful to society even after they became recluses. As priests they often continued some of their priestly functions for their patrons as well as serving as penitencers to the general public.[12] They were educated men and their talents accompanied them into their cells. Male anchorites come to our attention as copyists, as translators of Continental writings, as authors of didactic treatises. Such scholars included John Dygoun, a Carthusian anchorite at Sheen, Surrey (1438–44), John Lacy, a Blackfriar at Newcastle-upon-Tyne, Northumberland (ca. 1407–34), George Riplay, a Carmelite at Boston, Lincolnshire (ca. 1488), and Simon Appulby, a secular at All Hallows-on-the-Wall, London (ca. 1513–32). Their work was not an extension of their experience as anchorites. Rather their intellectual endeavors reflect an earlier disposition and interest, one that the anchoritic life furthered.[13]

Although male anchorites who were clerics brought that status with them into the anchorhold, whereupon they gained new status without losing the old, it was not so for women. Once a

12. A series of appointments of priest-anchorites as penitencers can be found in the registers of the bishops of Coventry and Lichfield between the years 1357 and 1374: Edmund Hobhouse, ed., "Register of Roger de Norbury, Bishop of Lichfield and Coventry, from A.D. 1322 to A.D. 1358," in *William Salt Archaeological Society* (now *Staffordshire Record Society, Collections for a History of Staffordshire*), o.s. 1 (1880), p. 286; Rowland A. Wilson, ed., *Registers or Act Books of the Bishops of Coventry and Lichfield: Book 5 being the Second Register of Bishop Robert de Stretton, A.D. 1360–1385*, William Salt Archaeological Society, n.s. 8 (1905), pp. 21, 32, 42, among other references. William Treadway, a priest-recluse at Great Torrington, Devonshire, was appointed penitencer regularly for thirty-six years (1395–1429) by Bishops Stafford and Lacy of Exeter diocese (F. C. Hingeston-Randolph, ed., *Register of Edmund Stafford, Bishop of Exeter, 1395–1419* [Exeter, 1856], p. 352; Lacy, *Exeter Reg.*, 1:24, 154, 194, 217). Priest-friar recluses at the Dominican house in Lynn were penitencers as well. One of them, in the early fifteenth century, was the confessor of Margery Kempe (*The Book of Margery Kempe*, ed. Sanford Meech, EETS, o.s. 212 [London, 1940], pp. 10, 25, 29). Benedictine monk-recluses at Westminster shrove kings in the fourteenth and fifteenth centuries (see my chapter 5).

13. Rotha M. Clay deals with such people in her work. See Clay, *Hermits and Anchorites*, pp. 167–182, "Further Studies," and "Northern Anchorites," where the more recent articles correct and add to the book.

woman became a recluse, almost never was she referred to by her former status as a nun (if she had been one). Only the original enclosure notice would have so classified her. As a group, women lost their previous identity more completely than did men. They may not have minded this. To become a recluse was to gain enormous status and this may have been enough for them. Being a former nun had no social value in the new context and so the information ceased to be of record. Only 2 of the 123 female anchorites known for the thirteenth century can with confidence be counted as former nuns. More emerge in the fourteenth and fifteenth centuries, but it is my judgment that the numbers remain too small to be considered an accurate reflection of probable lay/monastic ratios for women. While it is true that most English anchoresses came from lay society, there were always some who had followed the Benedictine ideal and it remained one aspect of the tradition. For most women, however, the reclusory provided their first experience of religious life.[14]

Unlike nuns, who would have come from purely aristocratic backgrounds, lay anchoresses came from every social group.[15] While many were upper-class Anglo-Saxons in the twelfth century and noble Normans in the thirteenth, the meager clues as to the origins of most indicate a variety of backgrounds.[16] Thirteenth-century data not only yield aristocratic women as anchoresses but

14. On anchoresses as nuns see Ann K. Warren, "The Nun as Anchoress: England 1100–1500," in *Distant Echoes: Medieval Religious Women* 1, ed. John M. Nichols and Lillian T. Shank, Cistercian Studies Series 71 (Kalamazoo, Michigan, 1984), pp. 197–212.

15. On the social class of nuns see Eileen Power, *Medieval English Nunneries c. 1275–1535* (New York: Biblo and Tannen, 1964; orig. ed., 1922), pp. 4–5. See also Janet E. Burton, *The Yorkshire Nunneries in the Twelfth and Thirteenth Centuries,* Borthwick Papers, no. 56 (York: Borthwick Institute of Historical Research, 1979), pp. 19, 24.

16. For upper-class Anglo-Saxons see Charles H. Talbot, ed. and trans., *The Life of Christina of Markyate: A Twelfth-century Recluse* (Oxford: Clarendon Press, 1959), pp. 12–13. The names of the recluses in this story attest to their origins. Reclusion can be seen in the twelfth century as an Anglo-Saxon reaction to the Normalization of the country. For noble Normans, my chapter 5 will tell of two famous sisters, one Loretta, the countess of Leicester, and the other Annora, widow of Hugh de Mortimer. Frederick M. Powicke, "Loretta, Countess of Leicester," in *Historical Essays in Honour of James Tait,* ed. J. Goronwy Edwards et al.

reveal one who was the sister of the lord of the town, another who was the daughter of a cordwainer, and another who was the niece of a yeoman.[17] A successful petitioner for an anchorhold had to have friends and patrons, but such a situation was not closed to the poorer. Servants of anchorites, themselves quasi-religious working without pay save their maintenance, at times succeeded their employers in the anchorhold, indicating that even those so lowly, when deemed worthy, could have their turn as ascetics.[18]

The social origins of male anchorites were as varied. Those who were clerics came from a wide spectrum of backgrounds. Lay male recluses too represent many classes, some of these lower ones. In fact, the modest life of the anchorhold represented a rise in the standard of living for some. Thirteenth- and fourteenth-century rules for male anchorites chided those men who desired

---

(Manchester, 1933), p. 264, says that in the thirteenth century many, if not most, recluses were of high social position. This seems unlikely. The rush of persons to become anchoresses in the century, the concern of Bishop Bingham over under-endowed cells, the lack of identification for most of these people, suggest a wider range of social background than Powicke thought. But that noble ladies, and noble Norman ladies, were part of this movement shows how far anchoritism had traveled from the twelfth century and from its anti-Norman overtones. Women of status, if not of the aristocracy certainly of the gentry, continued to be anchoresses until the Dissolution.

17. Cyril T. Flower and Michael C. B. Dawes, eds., *Registrum Simonis de Gandavo, diocesis Sarebiriensis, A.D. 1297–1315*, 2 vols., CYS 40–41 (1933–34), 2:699–700; William N. Brown, ed., *Registers of John le Romeyn and Henry of Newark, Lord Archbishops of York, 1286–1299*, 2 vols., SS 123, 128 (1913–17), 1:141; Salter, *Oseney Cartulary*, 2:483.

18. On the question of servants working without pay, see Mary B. Salu, trans., *The Ancrene Riwle (The Corpus MS.: Ancrene Wisse)* (Notre Dame: University of Notre Dame Press, 1955), p. 190. The rights of servants to "inherit" the anchorhold can be inferred from the English sources and was stated quite clearly in a German document of the fifteenth century. A servant of a Hildesheim anchoress had cared for the recluse for thirty years. After the death of her mistress the servant was considered by one authority as having a de jure right to succeed to the reclusorium: ". . . the suffragan and many other prelates did not wish that she be enclosed there on account of her age and many other reasons, but I contradicted them, saying that the sister, who had served so many years, ought not now to be put out, but that she possessed the place by the law of precedence, especially since she had so immediately begged for it" (John Busch, *Liber de reformatione monasteriorum*, ed. Karl Grubbe, 2 vols. [Halle, 1886], 2:656).

enclosure in order to alleviate the want they knew in the world.[19] Without question, for both men and women, the vocation was open to all.

Most of the women were maidens, but a share were widows who chose the reclusive life instead of remarriage. In rare instances married persons (at least one of them) sought the reclusive life. Both parties to the marriage had to accept the decision and alter their lives accordingly. A married man became a recluse at Bury St. Edmunds (ca. 1427). His wife, a woman named Emma Cheyne, took a widow's vow and moved into a reclusorium at St. Peter's, Cornhill, London, where she lived a quasi-religious life in celibacy. Twenty-two years later, at the age of sixty-eight, she successfully petitioned the king for a pension. Her husband had died recently and she was without livelihood.[20] We can reconstruct

19. Livario Oliger, ed., "Regula reclusorum Angliae et quaestiones tres de vita solitaria, saec. XIII–XIV," *Antonianum* 9 (1934): 60 (hereafter cited as Walter's Rule); Livario Oliger, ed., *Speculum inclusorum: Auctore anonymo anglico saeculi XIV, Lateranum,* n.s. 4, no. 1 (Rome: Facultas Theologica Pontificii Athenaei Lateranensis, 1938), pp. 63, 68.

20. CPR 1446–52, p. 304. Andrew Clark, ed., *Lincoln Diocese Documents 1440– 1544,* EETS, o.s. 149 (1914), pp. 19–21, discusses widows vows as they developed through church practice and doctrine. Quite commonly in fifteenth- and sixteenth-century England, the widow, on the death of her husband, made a vow not to marry again and afterward wore a dress distinctive of her status. The vow was made during the celebration of mass and in the presence of the fully robed diocesan. It was thus a ceremony of significance and solemnity. After such a ceremony these widows either entered a convent and became rather indistinguishable from the nuns or continued in a somewhat secular life, often acting as deaconesses. Some of them, Clark says, stood a "chance of obtaining a definite appointment as a paid deaconess, or an anchoress or *reclusa*." Edmund Stafford's register is illuminating. On 14 January 1396 Stafford received a letter from the bishop of London stating that Dame Katherine Brokas, a widow residing in London, had applied to him for a license to place herself in Stafford's hands. She desired to take a vow of perpetual chastity and *have some church or chapel assigned to her for her abode.* Accordingly, on 16 January Stafford received Katherine in the chapel of his London house, "juxta Temple barre," and celebrated Pontifical High Mass. Katherine took the following vow: "En le noun de Dieu ieo Katerine Brokas venevowe a Dieu perpetuel chastite en le presence de vous, Reverent Pier in Dieu Esmound, par le grace de Dieu Evesque dexcestre, et promitte establement vivere in chastite, saunz comapaignie de homme, a terme de ma vie" Hingeston-Randolph, *Reg. E. Stafford,* p. 39). For a vow in English see *Chichele* 4:221. Chichele's register also

that on her husband's decision to become a recluse pensions had been secured for both of them. Her husband's death may have terminated the arrangement and she thus threw herself on the charity of the king. Kindly, he responded with a pension of four pence daily. In another instance it was the wife who desired to become a recluse. In 1329 Bishop John Grandisson of Exeter sent this order to Sir Richard de Otery, vicar of St. Calixtus at West Down:

Beatrice, wife of Ralph Strong of our diocese, old and sterile, has come to us and showed us with supplicating prayers that for the salvation of her soul she desires to become a poor servant of Christ in solitude and poverty under a vow of perpetual continence, habit and changed life, separated from her aforesaid husband, far from carnal embraces; her aforesaid husband having given his especial consent, she supplicates us humbly that we deem her worthy for such pious work and give our consent. We, however, have some suspicion of incontinence on the part of the husband inasmuch as we are acquainted with several who have notice of it. Having heard this, we cannot with healthy conscience do what is begged, particularly since her aforesaid husband will have his hands full to remain in the world without a changed life. Wishing, however, to agree to the petition of the aforesaid woman as much as we are able to in God, we will allow for a time, that in a solitary place which she chooses, under closure, she may serve God with a pure soul and a harsh life, her husband's consent having been given, without suspending meanwhile all conjugal debts; so that if after such experience she perseveres stably in the way of life she has chosen, we will counsel the perpetual conversion of her husband fully according to the traditional canons of the married.[21]

To sever a marriage was a serious responsibility and the bishop proceeded with caution. Yet the request seems well within the

---

contains commissions to receive vows of widows (4:38, 190), and they are found in all late medieval episcopal registers. The register of a vicar-general (a bishop's general administrative deputy) of York in the mid-fourteenth century contains a letter requesting information concerning a gentlewoman who desired to take a vow of chastity (David M. Smith, "A Reconstruction of the Lost Register of the Vicars-General of Archbishop Thoresby of York," *Borthwick Institute Bulletin* 3, no. 1 [1983], no. 69). The request for information about the life and morals of the widow would have been the first step in the process.

21. F. C. Hingeston-Randolph, ed., *Register of John de Grandisson, Bishop of Exeter, A.D. 1327–1369*, 3 vols. (Exeter, 1894–99), 1:535.

boundaries of possible fulfillment and the procedural steps lack novelty. Clearly wives and husbands as well as widows, widowers, priests, nuns, monks, and maidens all could and did choose to become anchorites in medieval England. A declaration of desire was made and became the first step in a progression toward enclosure. More, however, was involved than desire. The bishop had an extensive part to play in the process and the full sweep of his role will be examined in the following chapter. On his own the potential anchorite had to secure financial support and often to find his own reclusory.

THE RECLUSORIUM

The typical English anchorite lived alone in a cell abutting or enclosed within a parish church, a chapel, or perhaps a hospital (fig. 1). The cell could also form part of a monastic complex. After the fourteenth century there was increasing likelihood that the

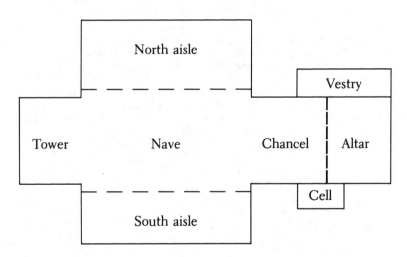

Figure 1: PLAN OF COMPTON CHURCH, SURREY: TWELFTH CENTURY. The anchorite's cell at Compton Church was the home of male priest recluses from 1185 to the early fourteenth century. Two male skeletons were found buried within it, quite possibly anchorites who had chosen to remain within their cells even after death.

anchorage might be attached to a friary. Such cells were some-times built by the recluses themselves, sometimes by their patrons —whether king, bishop, gentleman, lord, parish, municipality, or monastery. Once built, the cells were in turn inhabited by a series of anchorites, with the rights of patronage—presentation to the site—a guarded and valued prerogative in this situation as in others. The pattern of individual persons in cells designed for single occupancy remained the norm at all times from the beginning of the twelfth century.[22]

22. This in contrast to the Continent where anchorites were more likely to live in groups with some formal organization. Grimlaic, a late ninth- or tenth-century recluse monk (probably from modern-day France) who wrote the first of the surviving anchorite rules, desired that anchorites live in groups, each in a separate but connected cell, whereby they would be able to support each other ("Regula solitariorum," *PL* 103, cols. 595–596). During our period the Continental style was typically of this manner and such households were under the guidance of monasteries. For the German scene see Otmar Doerr, *Das Institut der Inclusen in Süddeutschland*, Beiträge zur Geschichte des alten Mönchtums und des Benediktinerordens 18 (Münster: Verlag der Aschendorffschen Verlagsbuchhandlung, 1934), pp. 30, 36, and passim. Louis Gougaud, *Ermites et reclus: Études sur d'anciennes formes de vie religieuse*, Moines et monastères 5 (Vienne: Abbaye Saint-Martin de Ligugé, 1928), pp. 119–127, gives the statutes that were written for a multiple reclusory at St. Reinold, Cologne, in 1448. The fact of written statutes in itself speaks to the formal arrangement of the vocation. Oliger, "Regulae tres reclusorum," pp. 166–167, notes that Italians for the most part practiced anchoritism in groups and under the guidance of a superior. Of sixty-eight anchorites scattered about Perugia in 1290, six lived singly (three men and three women) while all the rest lived in groups of from two to nine—four being the most common size (Casagrande, "Note su manifestazioni," pp. 463–464). Certainly then, this is not to say that Continental recluses never lived singly in cells attached to parish churches. F. Lemoing, *Ermites et reclus du diocèse de Bordeaux* (Bordeaux: Clèdes et Fils, 1953), pp. 130–132, cites several in that region, and Marcellin Boudet, "La Recluserie du Pont Sainte-Christine à Saint-Flour," *Revue de la Haute-Auvergne* 3 (1901): 335–355 and 4 (1902): 1–43, writes of a reclusorium that housed individual anchorites of both sexes in the fourteenth and fifteenth centuries. Others are cited by E. van Wintershoven, "Recluseries et ermitages dans l'ancien diocèse de Liége, "*Bulletin de la société scientifique el littéraire du Limbourg 23* (1906): 96–158. A general discussion of the situation in Germany in the earlier centuries is provided by Herbert Grundmann, "Deutsche Eremiten, Einsiedler und Klausner im Hochmittelalter (10.-12. Jahrhundert)," *Archiv für Kulturgeschichte* 45 (1963): 60–90, reprinted and translated into Italian in *L'eremitismo in Occidente nei secoli XI e XII: Atti della seconda settimana internazionale di studio, Mendola, 30 agosto–6 settembre 1962*, Pubblicazioni dell'Università cattolica del Sacro Cuore, Contributi Serie 3: Varia 4, Miscellanea del Centro di studi medioevali 4 (Milan, 1965), pp.

The anchorholds themselves were dwellings of variable size. Some were no more than one room, whereas others contained several; some had gardens or courts. Early rules for anchorites set out specifications: within the interior of a convent or attached to a church there was to be a room twelve feet square which communicated with the world through three narrow windows. One window was to look into the church and through it the recluse could watch mass, receive communion, speak with his confessor, and hear confession from others if he were a priest. A second window was for service: through it food and other necessities for his living were provided. A third, to allow light, was to be covered with a horn. If the recluse were a priest the cell might contain an altar. A garden was permitted.[23]

The *Ancrene Riwle*, a thirteenth-century guide for anchoresses, described the three windows as a church window, a house window, and a parlor window. The church window was for viewing the sacrament. The house window was to be used by the anchoress and her servants in the course of their daily lives. The parlor window looked outside and through it the anchoress communicated with the world: she confessed to her priest, spoke to guests, dealt with business matters. All three windows were to be kept closed, tightly shuttered, when not in use (clearly there was another source of light in this arrangement). When a window was opened, a curtain screened the outsider from visual contact with the recluse. *Ancrene Riwle* gave this advice:

Therefore, my dear sisters, be as little fond of your windows as possible. Let them all be small, those of the parlour smallest and narrowest. Have curtains made of two kinds of cloth, a black ground with a white cross showing both inside and outside. . . . The black cloth is not only symbolic, but also less harmful to the eyes than other colours and it is much stouter

---

311–329. Three Hildesheim anchoresses attached to parish churches have already been mentioned for the fifteenth century (Busch, *Liber de reformatione monasteriorum*, 2:655–659).

23. Grimlaic, *PL*, cols. 594–595; for a twelfth-century rule that is quite similar, the Bavarian Rule, see Benedict Haeften, ed., *Monasticarum disquisitionum libri XII: Quibus S. P. Benedicti regula et religiosorum rituum antiquitates varie dilucidantur* (Antwerp, 1644), 1:viii:83.

against the wind and other things. See that the parlour window is fastened and well locked on every side, and when you are near it guard your eyes.[24]

Some English anchorholds were quite restricted. One excavated at Letherhead church in Surrey was eight feet square and its window into the church was twenty-one inches square. A cell at Compton, also in Surrey, had a cubicle 6'8" by 4'4" plus a loft where the anchorite slept. Considerably larger was the cell of a fifteenth-century priest: its dimensions were twenty-nine feet by twenty-four feet. A Shropshire dwelling contained at least three rooms: one for the recluse, one for the maid, and one for guests. A house still standing in Chester-le-Street, Durham, had four rooms on two levels.[25] While guest rooms were rare, hospitality for guests was sometimes arranged even though rules discouraged and often prohibited them (this stands in sharp contrast to the absolute Benedictine obligation to provide hospitality). *Ancrene Riwle* was adamant: "Let no one sleep in your house," wrote the author, who then consented to allow guests "in great necessity," if for no longer than two nights. In Malory's *Le Morte d'Arthur* Percival spends the night in the reclusorium of his aunt. Exactly where these people were to sleep is never made clear. For Percival our imagination will do, but the *Ancrene Riwle* writer had something more specific in mind.[26]

24. *Ancrene Riwle*, pp. 21–22.
25. Philip M. Johnston, "An Anchorite's Cell at Letherhead Church," *Surrey Archaeological Collections* 20 (1907): 223, 225; J. H. Gibson, "Compton Church—The Oratory," *Surrey Archaeological Collections* 51 (1949): 154–55; for Compton, see also *VCH Surrey*, 3:21–23. A cell at Hardham church in Sussex was no larger (Philip M. Johnston, "Hardham Church, and Its Early Paintings," *Sussex Archaeological Collections* 44 [1901]: 78–81). For the priest's house see Edward Turner, "Domus Anachoritae, Aldrington," *Sussex Archaeological Collections* 12 (1860): 136 (please note that Turner misreads the evidence: the anchorhold was attached to Chichester cathedral and was not in Aldrington). The nature of the Shropshire reclusory, near Shrewsbury, can be inferred from the details of a miracle story associated with it. See Sir Herbert Maxwell, trans., *The Chronicle of Lanercost 1272–1346* (Glasgow: James Maclehose and Sons, 1913), pp. 151–156. For Chester-le-Street see Clay, *Hermits and Anchorites*, p. 83.
26. *Ancrene Riwle*, pp. 185, 191.

Several documents speak of the reclusorium by using the plural "houses."[27] How many houses and for what purpose? To domicile the anchoress? her maid? her guests? for sanitary purposes? Even accommodations for servants were by no means universal. Many servants merely shared their employers' simple room and many others went home at night. *Ancrene Riwle* tried to limit the frequency with which attendants left the premises to sleep elsewhere, especially for the younger of the two prescribed servants, but clearly it was a practice.[28] The Dublin Rule, for male anchorites, assumed that the servants would use the same outside window as other persons did when dealing with the anchorite. No antechamber for the servants is even implied.[29] Clearly, there was considerable variety in dwellings, given the limited framework. What was provided or what the recluse built was a habitation austere in aspect and sealed off from the world symbolically. If these two criteria were met, the actual design and dimensions were secondary. Rules were meant as guides and were not commands.

Establishments for more than one anchorite can be found, although they are not usual. Perhaps three or four occur in each century. Three young women lived together as anchoresses in the twelfth century (ca. 1130) at Kilburn, Middlesex. In the thirteenth century another female threesome was prominent. These were the sisters for whom the *Ancrene Riwle* was written. Each had her own cell and all three were served by two maids and a kitchen boy. More common, however, were anchorholds for two. In the twelfth century Christina of Markyate lived with a recluse named Alfwen for a period of time. In the first half of the thirteenth century two sisters lived together at St. Gregory's in Sudbury, Suffolk; Ela, the niece of Bishop Walter Suffield of Norwich, lived with a companion at Massingham; and two other women lived in Worcester priory.

27. Two in Shrewsbury, at St. George's and St. Romald's churches (Hugh Owen and John B. Blakeway, *History of Shrewsbury*, 2 vols. [London, 1825], 1:315, 2:474–475). A reclusory at Whalley, Lancashire, was also spoken of as composed of "houses": "touts les meisons, et les enclosturs" (Dugdale, *Monasticon*, 5:645).

28. *Ancrene Riwle*, p. 189.

29. Dublin Rule, p. 177.

Later in that century a reclusorium for two anchorites was built and endowed at Doncaster, Yorkshire, while in the fourteenth century one pair of male recluses lived in the parish of Worth, Somerset, and another pair was domiciled in the churchyard of St. Lawrence Jewry, London. Some of these were deliberate arrangements whereas others were brought about by the press of circumstances. Not infrequently a younger anchorite was brought into a cell to act as companion and aide to an aging recluse, with the assumption that the younger would inherit the cell as a single dwelling in due course.[30]

An anchorhold designed for more than one recluse was likely to contain separate and isolated chambers for each. When anchorholds originally built for one person were modified to accommodate two, the anchorites often shared a common room, perhaps subdivided. The data suggest that some persons were assigned to reclusoria where others already lived because there were not enough places available to accommodate each singly. Thus a nun of Arden was enclosed in a cell with another anchoress still in residence in Beverly, Yorkshire, in 1321, and Margaret Lakenby was to live with Emmota Sherman at Pontefract in 1402, if Emmota consented.[31]

Another Yorkshire pairing provides more detail. In 1314 a woman named Alice de Angrum was moved into a cell already occupied by another recluse, also called Alice. On 30 July of that year the dean of the Christianity of York had received a letter from

30. Dugdale, *Monasticon*, 3:426; Talbot, *Christina*, p. 93; *CLR 1245-51*, p. 172; Testament of Walter Suffield, Great Hospital Records 24/1/2, Norfolk and Norwich Record Office, Norwich; William H. Hale, ed., *Registrum sive liber irrotularius et consuetudinarius prioratus beatae Marie Wigorniensis*, Camden Society, o.s. 91 (1865), pp. cii, 120b, 124b; Thompson, *Reg. W. Greenfield*, 2:221; Edmund Hobhouse, ed., *Calendar of the Register of John de Drokensford, Bishop of Bath and Wells, A.D. 1309-1329*, Somerset Record Society 1 (1887), p. 284; Alfred C. Wood, ed., *Registrum Simonis de Langham, Cantuariensis Archiepiscopi* [1366-68], CYS 53 (1956), p. 192.

31. Rosalind M. T. Hill and David B. Robinson, eds., *The Register of William Melton, Archbishop of York, 1317-40*, 2 vols., CYS 70-71 (1977-78), 2:64; R. N. Swanson, ed., *Calendar of the Register of Richard Scrope, Archbishop of York, 1398-1405*, Borthwick Texts and Calendars: Records of the Northern Province 8 (York, 1981), p. 216.

Archbishop Greenfield commissioning him to inquire into the life, manners, *conversatio*, and age of Alice de Angrum, who desired to live as an anchorite in York.[32] The archbishop in this matter was responding to the supplications of no less a person than Queen Isabella. Nonetheless, the investigation was to be intensive. The dean was also to inquire of Alice "in what place in the city of York she chose to live as a recluse or anchorite, for what reason, and if she would be capable of bearing the yoke of the Lord under such an obedience." Furthermore, the dean was to determine whether the place of enclosure that Alice desired was known to be adequate for two anchorites (*pro duabus anacoritis sufficere dinoscitur*). On 4 August, only five days later, the license to enclose her was entered into the diocesan register. Citing the interest of the queen, the license granted Alice de Angrum the right to be enclosed in a house next to St. Mary's, Walmgate, where Alice le Cordwaner was already enclosed (and where she had been living for twenty years).[33] The officials of the archbishop who were to undertake the task of enclosure were to do what was necessary and suitable with regard to the site, "provided that, however, the will of the aforesaid Alice, now a recluse, does not with reason resist the desire of the other Alice."

The arrangement suggests that all the anchorite sites in York were occupied at this time, that building a new one was not considered, and that concern for the feelings of the long-term recluse already in residence was only a last-minute thought. This instance may have been unusual because of the pressure of the queen's involvement, and since there is no questioning of the adequacy of Alice de Angrum's support, usually a pro forma part of an investigation, it is possible that the queen was to be her patroness in this way too. The two-celled anchorhold was in this instance the solution to a problem and not an original conception. How frequently individual cells were enlarged in this way is hard to know, but such arrangements may have been more common than the data state. Nothing in the English perception of the appropriate form

32. Thompson, *Reg. W. Greenfield,* 2:185–186.
33. Brown, *Reg. J. Romeyn and H. Newark,* 1:141.

of the anchoritic life was inimical to the double cell. It was acceptable but not typical. In contrast, the three-cell household for which the *Ancrene Riwle* was written stands alone in the data for the period after 1200.[34] In general, then, English anchorites lived alone in cells designed for one recluse, although pairs were not so uncommon as to be rare. That cell was their home, their desert retreat, and without it they could not begin their spiritual journey.

Such cells were to be found all over England. A significant aspect of the anchorite phenomenon in England was its widespread distribution throughout the country. The evidence firmly establishes anchorites in every county of England save four: Buckinghamshire, Rutland, Cumberland, and Westmorland. Some areas contained anchorites over the entire period. Others show significant anchorite activity for periods of time, after which the vocation ceased to be important in the region. In this fashion Oxfordshire, Sussex, Worcestershire, and Hampshire exhibited notable levels of anchoritism during the twelfth and thirteenth centuries but not thereafter. Yorkshire was alive with recluses all through the thirteenth and fourteenth centuries and into the fifteenth, but by the last quarter of the fifteenth century the vocation was in decline there. Lincolnshire, in contrast, after a slower beginning, remained active throughout the period, as did Middlesex (including London) and Norfolk. Anchorites of the fourteenth to sixteenth centuries were likely to be found in the eastern portion of the country. Over half of all the sites tabulated for the fif-

34. Several writers have suggested that there were multiple households in Shrewsbury in the early fourteenth century at St. Romald's and St. George's: Owen and Blakeway, *Shrewsbury*, 2:474–475; Henrietta M. Auden, "Shropshire Hermits and Anchorites," *Transactions of the Shropshire Archaeological and Natural History Society*, 3d ser., 9 (1909): 103, who uses Owen and Blakeway as reference; *VCH Shropshire*, 2:23. This conclusion has been drawn from two sources: the use of the plural *houses* (*domibus*) to describe the reclusorium at both places (see chapter 2, note 27) and the mistranslation of a phrase in the enclosure notice of a woman who was to be placed in the anchorhold at St. Romald's. In 1314 Isolda de Hungerford was permitted enclosure in the houses of the churchyard of St. Romald's "ubi alie anacorite degebant" (where other anchorites used to live). The statement tells us not that other anchorites were currently in residence but rather that the foundation was ancient. Other reclusoria also comprised "buildings," most specifically one at Whalley that we know was just for one recluse and her servants (Thomas D. Whitaker, *An History of the Original Parish of Whalley*, ed. J. G. Nichols and P. A. Lyons, 4th ed., 2 vols. [London, 1872], 2:97).

teenth century were in five counties: Yorkshire, Lincolnshire, Norfolk, London, and Kent; moreover, these sites account for two-thirds of the anchorites of that century[35](see appendix A).

The sites themselves were dispersed among communities of every size. No community was too small and none too large to have an anchorite cell. Table 2 charts the village/town/city placements of anchorite cells.[36] Table 2 indicates that English anchorites lived primarily in village sites in the twelfth century (village to city/town ratio: 69:14). The growth of anchoritism in the thirteenth century was accompanied by a growth in the number of sites in more heavily populated areas. Cities and larger towns now took a substantial portion of the anchorite population (108:65). This pattern continued in the fourteenth century and became sharper in the fifteenth. By the sixteenth century there were more anchorites in the towns and cities than in the countryside (27:22). What had begun as a rural phenomenon had gradually changed its character, a shift that literary sources confirm. While the stories of Christina of Markyate and Wulfric of Haselbury, both twelfth-century recluses, abound with the names of other anchorites, all in rural sites and all bound together by networks of hermits and servants, *The Book of Margery Kempe*, a fifteenth-century work, takes us to Norwich and York for anchorites and only once to an anchorite living in the countryside.[37]

35. A portion of this preponderance is a factor of the high incidence of surviving wills from these areas.

36. Estimates of the sizes of communities have been made with the aid of Josiah Cox Russell, *British Medieval Population* (Albuquerque: University of New Mexico Press, 1948). Russell's population figures have been challenged as being too low. John Krause, "The Medieval Household: Large or Small?" *Economic History Review*, 2d ser., 9 (1957): 420–432, and Herbert E. Hallam, "Some Thirteenth-century Censuses," *Economic History Review*, 2d ser., 10 (1958): 340–361, discuss the question. A general exploration of population studies is made in William B. Stephens, *Sources of English Local History* (London: Cambridge University Press, 1981; rev. and enl. edition of *Sources for English Local History* [Manchester: University Press, 1971]), pp. 45–70. The argument centers around what multiplier should be used to arrive at a population figure for a community when the data represent only heads of households. The discussion affects this work only marginally, so I have deemed Russell's conclusions acceptable.

37. John, abbot of Ford, *Wulfric of Haselbury*, ed. Maurice Bell, Somerset Record Society 47 (1933). Donald Weinstein and Rudolph M. Bell, *Saints and Society: The Two Worlds of Western Christendom 1000–1700* (Chicago: University of Chi-

TABLE 2

VILLAGE, TOWN, AND CITY PLACEMENTS OF
ANCHORITE CELLS

Century	Village	Town[1]	City[2]	Total[3]
Twelfth	69	11	3	83
Thirteenth	108	39	26	173
Fourteenth	108	28	31	167
Fifteenth	71	26	33	130
Sixteenth	22	12	15	49

1. A locality is considered a town if it had a population of over 1,000 in the twelfth century and over 2,000 thereafter.

2. A locality is considered a city if it had a population of at least 4,000 in the twelfth century and 5,000 thereafter.

3. The totals column differs slightly from the figures in table 1. Sites that cannot be specifically located have been eliminated from this count. Sites that had multiple recluses have been counted repetitively.

One must be careful, however, when talking of towns and cities in England in the Middle Ages. England had only one city of any size throughout the period—London, its capital. Even that city was small (ca. 35,000 in 1377) when compared with the great cities of Continental Europe—Paris, Florence, Milan, and the commercial centers of Flanders and Germany. The second cities of the country were minor communities. The largest of them, York and Bristol (in the fourteenth century), had populations only in the 10,000–12,000 range, with Lincoln and Norwich below that. One reason that the Beguine movement may never have taken hold in England is that the country lacked the urban atmosphere in which it thrived: large communities where there was substantial imbalance between the numbers of men and women. It was from surplus women that Beguines were drawn, and the urban environ-

cago Press, 1982), pp. 211–212, note that saints became urban in the thirteenth century (along with the Franciscan movement). My data do not fully correlate with those of Weinstein and Bell, but the overlap is suggestive.

ment provided them with a range of opportunities for mutual support, work, housing, and organization.[38]

Although a true urban society did not exist in England except in London, several of the larger second-line cities as well as London supported multiple sites for anchorites. In the thirteenth century there are twelve sites known in Norwich, nine in London and its suburbs, seven in Winchester, and five in Oxford. In the fourteenth century there are twelve identified in London, eight in York, six in Norwich, four each in King's Lynn and Lincoln, and three each in Chester, Shrewsbury, and Beverly. London, York, Norwich, and Lynn continued to provide multiple residences for anchorites in the fifteenth century; only in York did the numbers decline in the sixteenth.[39]

In some measure, then, the large town provided a hospitable climate for recluses. There were more people to provide alms than in the countryside, the friars became involved with the recluses, and the merchant class was sympathetic to their needs (see chapter 7). The trend toward settlement of anchorites in towns was implicitly acknowledged in the fourteenth-century *Speculum inclusorum,* which excoriated those recluses who chose the cities to

38. The fundamental work on the Beguine movement in English is Ernest W. McDonnell, *The Beguines and Beghards in Medieval Culture* (New York: Octagon Books, 1969; repr. from Rutgers University Press edition, 1954). See also Richard W. Southern, *Western Society and the Church in the Middle Ages* (Baltimore: Penguin Books, 1970), pp. 318–331, for a study of the Cologne Beguines. Norman P. Tanner, *The Church in Late Medieval Norwich 1370–1532,* Pontifical Institute of Mediaeval Studies, Studies and Texts 66 (Toronto, 1984), pp. 64–66, discusses the brief emergence of two groups of women living a semicommunal life in fifteenth-century Norwich: quasi-Beguines. Otherwise they are unheard of in England.

39. During the fifteenth century in York at least seven anchorholds were occupied for extended periods, and wills frequently included grants for all recluses within the city. By the sixteenth century there was only one anchorhold whose occupant received the bequests of the pious. In several wills she was merely called "the anchoress" without being identified by her site—clearly she was the only one in the city. See *Test. Ebor.,* 5:177; BIHR Reg. 9, fol. 271. There is a possibility that the decline in anchoritism in York is connected to a decline in the city itself—a symptom of shifting civic fortunes, not the loss of religious fervor. On York in the later medieval period see D. M. Palliser, "A Crisis in English Towns? The Case of York, 1460-1640," *Northern History* 14 (1978): 108–125, as well as his *Tudor York* (Oxford: Oxford University Press, 1979).

better their fortunes (and those of their families): "... some recluses, these days, [live] not in the desert but in the cities, that they there may receive large alms and help and promote their kin and friends better than they might have in their former state." A fifteenth-century legal compilation actually advised that anchorites choose the city over the country because of the availability of greater monetary resources.[40]

Money alone could hardly have been the only factor impelling anchorites to take up residence in the cities. Town anchorites were supported only rarely by the municipality. They did not become civic totems. In larger communities as in smaller ones their anchorholds remained positioned next to parish churches, except in Norwich and King's Lynn where they were attached to the friaries. On a statistical basis the concentration of anchorites in the various cities that made them welcome became disproportionate even to the larger populations of these communities.[41] The shift was real. The religious climate of Western Europe was changing. The cities and towns of the fourteenth and fifteenth centuries had become the centers of the spiritual ferment of the day even as the countryside had been in the eleventh and twelfth centuries. Increased literacy, popular devotional movements, enhanced mystical expectations—these were the currents of the later fourteenth century in which the anchorite movement participated, drawing sustenance from revitalized religious expectations.[42] The fourteenth century was less ascetic in its demands and more mystical in its promises. This allowed the anchorite to experience his desert wherever he chose. Increasingly that choice led to the cities

40. Oliger, *Speculum inclusorum*, p. 70; William Lyndwood, *Provinciale ... cui adjiciuntur Constitutiones legatinae d. Othonis et d. Othoboni ... cum ... annotationibus Johannis de Anthona* (Oxford, 1679), p. 214.

41. Penelope Corfield, "Economic Growth and Change in Seventeenth-century English Towns," in *The Traditional Community under Stress* (Milton Keynes, The Open University Press, 1977), p. 39, states that as late as 1600 only about 8 percent of the population of England lived in communities of 5,000 or more—a number she finds adequate to describe an "urban" setting in seventeenth-century England.

42. For the urban reclusory on the Continent see Jean Hubert, "L'Érémitisme et l'archéologie," *Eremitismo*, pp. 485–487. (In general this volume is of great interest for students of western eremitic history.)

and the towns, especially to those centers along the eastern coast that were exposed to Continental influences.

In sum, English anchoritism was a countrywide phenomenon at all times. The movement, however, did not remain static. Different regions of the country experienced widespread anchorite activity at different times. A largely rural vocation in the twelfth and thirteenth centuries, anchoritism became increasingly urbanized in the fourteenth and fifteenth. The tenor of early English anchoritism is almost palpable as one reads the *Life* of Christina of Markyate, where hermits traverse the roads of Huntingdonshire, acting as human links between other hermits and anchorites locked in their cells. Very different is anchoritism in fifteenth-century Norwich: Julian the great mystic-anchoress just dead; her cell in a parish church now occupied by another; at least ten other cells within the confines of the crowded medieval city, three of them under the protection of the Carmelite and Dominican friars: the town a center of trade and religious enthusiasm. Such anchoritism was in some ways almost a different conception, yet it remained true to its central beliefs. The fifteenth-century phenomenon was an adaptation to a changing world and provides one mirror, albeit a limited one, into English responses to such changes in the social-religious climate of Western Europe during this era.

FINANCIAL SUPPORT

Anchoritism as a mirror reflected the financial as well as the philosophical commitment to the reclusive life. Although anchorite rules would have had the recluse have no thought for tomorrow and let God provide,[43] concern for financial stability did not degrade the vocation; financial security was the sine qua non of its existence. The degree to which money issues intrude into this discussion indicates the centrality of the subject.

43. St. Aelred, *De institutis inclusarum*, ed. Charles H. Talbot, *Analecta Sacri Ordinis Cisterciensis* 7 (1951): 178; and especially Dublin Rule, p. 172, where this issue represents the substance of the author's concern in the first chapter of his rule.

Wealthy candidates for reclusion endowed themselves. The less affluent needed a promise of support from outside sources to augment their own resources. Some anchorites earned at least a part of their support while in the anchorhold, the women doing needlework, the men working as copyists or priests, but these activities could not have guaranteed a livelihood. Thus, as their main source of income, anchorites received pensions from lay individuals, ecclesiastical officials, and religious orders or were appointed to cells already endowed by these groups. Most anchorites (certainly in the city) could expect some additional measure of support from the alms of the pious parishioner who passed his cell on entering the church. Langland would write:

> Ancres and hermytes • that holdeth hem in heore celles
> Schulen happen of myn almus • al the while I liue

and he would have put such alms in a box provided for the purpose, for "at ancres, there a box hangeth."[44] Thomas Hoccleve would report similarly some years later (ca. 1411): "To every church and recluse of the toune Bade him eeke of golde geue a quantite."[45]

Alms also were generated from bequests, anniversary arrangements, and indulgences. These could prove substantial—far beyond the needs of some recluses. In these situations the anchorite himself became the bestower of alms, recirculating grants made to him as gifts to the church, to the poor, and (as has been noted) even to his own kin. All of the rules written for anchorites urged that the recluse avoid great involvement in these matters. Aelred's rule, a twelfth-century treatise directed to women, spoke of anchoresses who accumulated too many alms and then acted as benefactresses, using these alms for orphans, widows, families, and friends and offering hospitality to fellow religious. Such anchoresses, said Aelred, fall into the most dangerous kind of sin. Aelred, who was strongly in favor of his anchoresses being self-

44. William Langland, *Piers the Plowman*, ed. Walter W. Skeat, 2 vols. (London: Oxford University Press, 1886; reprint, 1969), 1:206, 450.
45. Thomas Hoccleve, *Hoccleve's Regement of Princes*, ed. Frederick J. Furnivall, EETS, e.s. 72 (1897), p. 156.

supporting, advised them to give away the excesses of their earnings and alms through an intermediary. The only thing of value that the anchoress should give was her prayer. Let that be her offering to the poor and the dispossessed. Let that be her largesse. *Ancrene Riwle* sounded the same theme: "Courtly manners in an anchoress, openhandedness in an anchoress, have often resulted in the end in sin and shame." The anchoress was to send out any unnecessary alms from her house unobtrusively. Not for her to give ostentatiously. Nor was it otherwise expected for men. Walter too cautioned against the accumulation of alms for the purpose of appearing a great benefactor, and the *Speculum* wrote of those led by the spirit of error to live as solitaries in order that "out of the devotion and alms of true Christian people they may have more temporal goods, both for their own livelihood and to dispense, than they would have had in any other manner of living."[46]

But the rules give a misleading picture in their concern to protect the recluse from the sin of pride. Few recluses were so rich as to be burdened with these problems. Even *Ancrene Riwle* acknowledged that many anchoresses "are often afflicted with want, indignity, and vexation" with regard to so basic a need as daily food.[47] The concern of the hierarchy when enclosing recluses was not to limit their wealth but on the contrary to make sure that they had sufficient resources to sustain themselves. Clearly many anchorites must have received promises of support from friends and relatives in the first flowering of their decision to become recluses. But such support, if not well documented legally, could wane as time passed. What had begun as a spontaneous gift could become an irksome demand after years of enclosure, and payments might cease to be made. A loss of patronage could lead to disaster. Bishop Richard Swinfield of Hereford warned of that possibility when he appended this admonition to a license to enclose an anchoress in 1315: "Provided however that concerning those things which will be necessary such as food and clothes will be adequately provided for her by her friends, lest, because they

46. Aelred, pp. 179, 198–199; *Ancrene Riwle*, p. 184, also (in slightly different context) pp. 126, 127–128; Walter's Rule, p. 73; Oliger, *Speculum inclusorum*, p. 69.
47. *Ancrene Riwle*, p. 84.

are lacking, because of a lack of nourishment, she will be forced to retreat from her laudable way of life and go out, contrary to her vow, to the peril of her soul and the scandal of many."[48]

Regular alms, as distinct from occasional alms, were a substantial source of income and many alms lists survive. Anchorites appear on the lists of kings, gentle families, bishops, abbeys, and town guilds. The implication is that these were customary grants —support that the anchorite could expect year after year. Thus the prior of Holy Trinity, Aldgate, London, paid 3s. 4d. each year to the anchorites of London in the thirteenth century, and the archbishop of York placed several Yorkshire anchoresses on his rolls in 1270 and 1271.[49] Trinity Guild of King's Lynn listed several anchorites on its lists in the fourteenth and fifteenth centuries. Almoners of Edward III and Henry VIII, to name some illustrious benefactors, listed anchorites on their accounts as having received money grants. Henry III was as likely to have granted them cloaks or wood, and the great abbey at Bury St. Edmunds dispensed bread and candles to the forty-two anchorholds on its list.[50]

But such grants were not contractual and could cease without recourse. An anchoress named Miliana, enclosed at Steyning, Sussex, sued the prior of Hardham in 1279 for a regular grant she claimed she was entitled to receive from the priory. She declared she had had a charter, which she had surrendered to the former prior of the monastery, guaranteeing her two loaves of white bread

48. John Webb, ed., *A Roll of the Household Expenses of Richard de Swinfield, Bishop of Hereford, during part of the years 1289 and 1290*, Camden Society, o.s. 62 (1855), pp. 501–502.

49. Gerald A. J. Hodgett, ed., *Cartulary of Holy Trinity, Aldgate*, London Record Society 7 (1971), p. 122; Brown, *Reg. W. Giffard*, pp. 116, 123. The register shows gifts of three shillings for the *inclusa* of Elland, 6s. 8d. for the *inclusa* of Doncaster, and 2s. 6d. to the two *inclusae* of Blyth. It is possible that the scribe has confused the last two entries. There were two recluses at Doncaster and, as far as all other data show, only one at Blyth. Moreover, if the numbers were rearranged, the amounts of the grants would be more equal—ranging only from 2s. 6d. to 3s. 4d. for each individual.

50. Henry Harrod, *Report on the Deeds and Records of the Borough of King's Lynn* (King's Lynn, 1870), p. 30; Frederick Devon, ed., *Issue Roll of Thomas de Brantingham, Bishop of Exeter, Lord High Treasurer of England*, Record Commission (London: John Rodwell, 1835), p. 395; *LP*, 3:2:1545. For Henry III see my chapter 5 below.

and one of black, a gallon and a half of ale, and a mess of cooked food daily for life. The prior responded that she had never had any such charter but rather that the former prior had granted her this daily meal as alms, at his own pleasure, and that the new prior was not bound by this arrangement. The jury agreed that Miliana had never had a charter and therefore the prior was without fault. Alms were charity, not a contract. Such niceties lie behind the wording of a journal entry of a sixteenth-century prior of Worcester who several times gave attention to the needs of an anchoress attached to the monastery but was careful to note that he paid ten shillings for brick, lime, and sand to repair the "Anckras hows . . . ex devocione," that is, not by contract.[51]

Other individuals who had supported recluses in their lifetimes used their wills to continue that support. In contrast to the bequests of most wills, which are one-time grants, a few make provision for the care of anchorites over an extended period. The thirteenth-century will of a Lincolnshire woman provided two measures of wheat annually to the anchorites of Wickhamborough for as long as they lived; in the same century a bishop of Lincoln left four shillings annually for the anchoress Lina, for as long as she lived; a man in Stamford, Lincolnshire, left 20s. to an anchoress of the town in the late fifteenth century, plus twenty shillings for each of the next ten years, if there remained an anchoress living at the site. In this way regular grants of alms were continued beyond the lifetime of the donor.[52]

The kind of contract Miliana claimed to have possessed was called a corrody. It provided for a fixed share in the common goods of a religious house. Some corrodies were granted to anchorites as alms of the religious house itself. Some were bought by patrons for recluses as one way to guarantee a regular gift of alms.

51. L. F. Salzman, "A Litigious Anchorite," *Sussex Notes and Queries* 2 (1928/29): 135–137; William More, *Journal of Prior William More*, ed. Ethel S. Fegan, Worcestershire Historical Society (1914), p. 136.

52. Will of Agnes de Condet (Foster and Major, *Registrum antiquissimum*, 1:294); will of Bishop Henry Lexington (ibid., 2:117–118); will of William Brown (Charles W. Foster, ed., "Lincolnshire Wills Proved in the Prerogative Court of Canterbury," *Reports and Papers of the Architectural and Archaeological Societies* 41 [1932–33]: 206).

The patrons would make a grant of land or rents in perpetuity to the religious house under the condition that during the life of the recluse the proceeds of the grant (or a portion thereof) were to be given to the anchorite. Corrodial arrangements for the maintenance of anchorites were fairly common in the thirteenth century. They fed one anchoress at St. Albans, two at Worcester priory, and others in Berkshire, Norfolk, Sussex, and Nottinghamshire. A woman named Childlove, anchoress of Faringdon, Berkshire, was supported by a corrody purchased for her by her brother from Oseney abbey. Margaret of St. Edward's, Norwich, purchased her own. Richard, the anchorite of Hardham (probably the former prior of Hardham who had been Miliana's benefactor), held two corrodies in the priory, while the anchoress of Blyth, Nottinghamshire, received a conventual loaf and an allowance of food from the kitchen of Blyth priory at the instance of Queen Eleanor, wife of Henry III, and their son, the future Edward I.[53]

The simplest and best way for an anchorite to secure both home and material needs at the same time was to be appointed to a cell that carried its own endowment. A thirteenth-century bishop of Exeter built a cell for an anchorite in Devonshire. He appointed one Brother Nicholas to it as "first anchorite" (*primus inclusus*) after endowing the cell with proceeds from certain lands owned by the diocese amounting to eight shillings annually. By his charter he bound his episcopal successors as well as himself to perpetual maintenance. More richly endowed was the Pontefract cell established by the Lacy family in 1240. Its occupant received nine quarters of corn plus one-half mark (6s. 8d.). By 1320 the endowment had risen to ten quarters, three bushels of grain, plus the

53. Henry T. Riley, ed., *Chronica monasterii S. Albani: Gesta abbatum monasterii sancti Albani, a Thoma Walsingham, regnante Ricardo secundo, ejusdem ecclesiae precentore, compilata*, 3 vols., RS 28, part 4, (1867–69), 1:305; William H. Hale, ed., *Registrum sive liber irrotularius et consuetudinarius prioratus beatae Marie Wigorniensis*, Camden Society, o.s. 91 (1865), pp. cii, 120b, 124b; Salter, *Oseney Cartulary*, 1:31; Clay, *Hermits and Anchorites*, p. 111; Salzman, "A Litigious Anchorite," pp. 135–136; Reginald T. Timson, ed., *The Cartulary of Blyth Priory*, 2 vols., Thoroton Record Society 27–28 (1973), 2:508. On royal corrodies see the informative John H. Tillotson, "Pensions, Corrodies, and Religious Houses: An Aspect of the Relations of Crown and Church in Early Fourteenth-century England," *Journal of Religious History* 8 (1974–75): 127–143.

half-mark in money. In contrast, a site at Richmond, also in York-shire, brought only two quarters of wheat to its occupant from its inception in 1274. In the fifteenth century, when the obligation devolved on Henry VI, the endowment was reckoned at twenty shillings yearly, it having been converted to a cash equivalent in the recent past.[54]

Endowed cells represented a commitment to support a recluse at a particular place in perpetuity and differed from corrodial ar-rangements and other pensions that were tied to the life of a par-ticular individual. An endowed cell was the most secure kind of support available to an anchorite. The value of the written charter was immediately clear when payment was slow in forthcoming. The continuing saga of an endowed reclusorium of the thirteenth century makes the point. The reclusorium was established at Don-caster Bridge, near Sprotburgh, Yorkshire, around 1270 by the gentle Fitzwilliam family as a home for two anchoresses. Within ten years of the foundation, sometime around 1280, William Fitz-william was sued by the "community of the chapel of St. Edmund, 'extra Doncastr,'" for arrears of twenty-four quarters of wheat—a full three years' grant.[55] The indebtedness is a good indication of what could happen to commitments to anchorites. When financial obligations pressed from many sides, even sympathetic lords might allow their alms payments to take second place to more insistent creditors. No question here of cancellation, just of temporary delay that could stretch into years. Legal service was necessary to prod and remind the lord of his good intentions and promises. And Fitzwilliam did pay up.

Thirty-five years later, in 1315, the grant was again being with-held. Archbishop Greenfield intervened, perhaps on supplication

---

54. F. C. Hingeston-Randolph, ed., *Registers of Walter Bronescombe (A.D. 1257–1280), and Peter Quivil (A.D. 1280–1291), Bishops of Exeter, with Some Records of the Episcopate of Bishop Thomas de Bytton; also the Taxation of Pope Nicholas IV, A.D. 1291 (Diocese of Exeter)* (London and Exeter, 1889), p. 5; CR 1237–42, p. 258; CMR 1326–27, no. 2167; CPR 1436–41, p. 289.

55. Norman Smedley, "An Incised Stone from the Free Chapel of Ancres, near Doncaster," *Yorkshire Archaeological Journal* 37 (1948–51): 503–513, has gathered considerable information concerning the reclusorium. See also Thompson, *Reg. W. Greenfield,* 2:221.

of one of the anchoresses. Greenfield wrote to one Thomas de Cresacre, who was at that time holding the lands and tenements (perhaps as agent) that his ancestor Lord William Fitzwilliam had entailed to provide for the two anchoresses, a provision now stated to be worth *ten* quarters of wheat annually. Greenfield warned Cresacre:

Being unwilling that such exceptional and such pious alms so healthfully ordained for the sustenance of two poor women should cease in our time, we instruct you, uninterruptedly and without delay [to provide] in so far as the aforesaid Lady Beatrice is concerned, whilst the same shall remain, five quarters of grain for her portion, and for the other anchoress, five, in order that the said ordinance and foundation, and approved usage shall be maintained effectively each year, under severe canonical penalty, so that if you do not effectively carry out this order against you, as against the strong who are contemptuous of ecclesiastical discipline, we shall be mindful to exercise the former justice.[56]

Cresacre must have taken heed, for thirteen years later he was still in control of the Doncaster lands. The legality of the written commitment had been affirmed, the possibility of judicial action threatened, and the anchoresses began regular receipt of grain once more.

Two elaborate foundation charters survive to provide a good indication of the organization of an anchorite household of the thirteenth and fourteenth centuries. In 1237 a cell was endowed by a knight of the Beauchamp *familia*. The charter stated that Peter of Wick-by-Pershore, Worcestershire, had received permission to build a new reclusory in his own courtyard (next to his chapel) and to enclose his own chaplain within it. Each year the anchorite-chaplain was to receive thirteen crannocks of wheat, four of mixed rye and wheat, one-half crannock of peas, one of farina, a crannock of salt, eight bundles of firewood, and 6s. 8d. in cash plus an additional three shillings for the specific purchase of candles. Two shillings were to provide candles for nighttime lighting and one for the mass. The grant was payable quarterly, in almost equal

---

56. Smedley, "Incised Stone," p. 512; James Raine, ed., *Historical Papers and Letters from Northern Registers*, RS 61 (1873), pp. 196–197.

portions, with all the wood and the extra crannock of wheat disbursed during the winter term. To this agreement Peter bound himself and his heirs in perpetuity, for the health of his soul, that of his wife, and those of his antecedents and successors. While the agreement was nullified if the recluse were a woman or anyone else save a chaplain who would serve the chapel, Peter acknowledged that his rights of presentation were limited by the overview of the bishop and the bishop's successors.[57]

A mid-fourteenth-century indenture establishing a cell at Whalley in Lancashire is similar. No less a personage than Henry, duke of Lancaster, granted two cottages and extensive lands to Whalley abbey in return for which the monks were to take care of the reclusorium and its occupants according to the terms of the charter. The recluse (a woman) and her servants (two women) were to live in the churchyard of the parish church at Whalley and pray for the souls of the duke, his ancestors, and his heirs. Each week the abbey was to provide the recluse and her servants with seventeen conventual loaves of bread plus seven more of a poorer quality, eight gallons of the better conventual beer, and three pence in cash to purchase food to eat with their bread. Once a year on the feast of All Saints (1 November) the recluse household was to receive ten hard fish called stockfish, a bushel of oatmeal, a bushel of rye, two gallons of oil to light their lamps, a weight of tallow for candles, plus ten loads of turf and one of faggots as fuel. The monks of Whalley were bound further to maintain the buildings inhabited by the recluse and her servants and to repair them when necessary. Finally, the abbey was to provide the household with a monk of honest conversation to serve the women as chaplain and the monk was to be given a clerk to assist him in administering the mass. The duke and his heirs retained the right of nomination to any vacancies through death or any other cause.[58]

57. Mason, *Beauchamp Cartulary Charters*, p. 78.

58. The summary of the indenture's provisions is drawn from the document printed in Dugdale, *Monasticon*, 5:645–646. Whitaker's discussion of this agreement (*Whalley*, 1:96–97) makes several corrections of the Dugdale transcription which I have incorporated here. For example, *ten* (*dys*) is printed in Dugdale as *six* (*sys*). Also, the house was for *one* recluse, not for two, as is stated in some editions.

49

The Wick-by-Pershore and Whalley arrangements are paralleled in the provisions of a royal foundation of the fifteenth century. In 1417 Henry V established a reclusorium at the Carthusian monastery of Sheen and granted it twenty marks yearly (a very large sum), the monastery holding the lands that provided the endowment. The occupant was to be a chaplain who would pray for the royal family. He was provided with two servants, food, and clothing, the costs of this maintenance to come from the endowment. If the support payments were in arrears beyond forty days the monastery was fined one hundred shillings. Beyond this the expenses of repairing the reclusory were to be borne by the Carthusians of Sheen. At some later date the monks added a garden to the reclusorium, perhaps at the request of a subsequent anchorite. The anchorite paid an annual rent of eight pence for a garden "newly walled." This must not have been considered a necessary condition of the royal grant if the anchorite had to sustain the costs.[59]

Wick-by-Pershore, Whalley, and Sheen—the endowments of all of these were adequate to support their anchorites. A recluse living in any of these cells needed to go no further in the search for funding. Bread and beer would be the major fare; the quantities of lighting fuel were sufficient considering the daylight regimen prescribed for anchorites. The detailed descriptions provided by the Wick-by-Pershore and Whalley charters are probably good indicators of the ideals of the time, ideals that were no doubt shared by other patrons as well.

The typical royal rate for an anchorite pension during the twelfth century and into the thirteenth was one penny per day (30s. 5d. per annum) and it was adequate to sustain an anchorite household. In the twelfth century this was the wage of an ordinary manual laborer and would thus have sufficed for the necessities of an ascetic's life. In the thirteenth century Henry III granted an occasional penny and a half daily, but any rise in the pension rate was slow. When in the late fourteenth century Richard II took

59. CPR 1413-19, p. 114. E. Margaret Thompson, *The Carthusian Order in England* (London: SPCK, 1930), pp. 241–242.

over an obligation of his first wife's it was still only at the rate of two pence per day. While Henry V's grant to the Sheen recluse was an extraordinary eight and a half pence daily, the more typical recluse under royal support even in the late fifteenth century received at best a grant of six marks (just a bit more than two and a half pence per day).[60]

"Royal rates" were granted by members of the aristocracy and by the episcopacy as well. In general, the farther down the social scale the anchorite went in search of patronage the more likely his or her endowment would be more modest or pieced together from several sources. Such an endowment would call on the joint resources of family, friends, and patrons. The recluse's local community would know that the endowment was weak and be more liberal in its almsgiving. The bishop might grant an indulgence for those who benefited the recluse.

Inhabitants of the reclusorium established at Doncaster in Yorkshire about 1270 were aided by many of these methods: secondary support enabled a foundation of only moderate resources to survive from its inception to the Dissolution. Its initial endowment was for four quarters of grain annually for each anchoress (worth twenty to twenty-six shillings). The sum was increased to five quarters in the fourteenth century, when it had a value of about forty shillings per year, still a modest rate. Almost immediately on foundation of the site the anchoresses living there received alms from Archbishop Walter Giffard. A few years later, in 1284, Edward I provided alms of forty shillings "duabus reclusis ... ad earum sustentacionem" (for the two recluses ... to their sustenance). In 1294 Archbishop John Romeyn issued an indulgence of twenty days for those who contributed to the upkeep of the household. Wills record bequests to the anchoresses there in 1348, 1360, 1382, and 1403. In all these ways the larger community responded to the needs of the Doncaster recluses.[61]

60. See my chapter 5 for further elaboration of these data.
61. Smedley, "Incised Stone," pp. 503–513; Brown, *Reg. W. Giffard*, p. 116; Thompson, *Reg. W. Greenfield*, 2:221; Arnold Taylor, "Royal Alms and Oblations in the Later 13th Century: An Analysis of the Alms Roll of 12 Edward I (1283–84)," in *Tribute to an Antiquary: Essays Presented to Marc Fitch by Some of His Friends,*

The medieval English anchorite was not an entity unto himself. He walked the path of salvation hand in hand with his patrons. He carried their spiritual burdens even as they carried his worldly concerns. Both parties considered it an eminently satisfactory relationship. Time and again throughout the Middle Ages cells were endowed. Time and again lifetime grants of support were made. Anchorites might remain thirty, forty, fifty years within their cells. A lifetime promise was not a sometime thing.

Later chapters will examine in detail the nature of anchorite support by social group. For now it will be profitable to turn our attention to the man and the office governing both the anchorite and his relations with the outside world, including his own patrons. That man was the bishop. Through his person and his diocesan authority he established the parameters of the reclusive life in medieval England. He was father and judge, friend and chastizer, and, most of all, lawful guardian of all individual religious. These were obligations to which the English bishops responded both willingly and well.

ed. Frederick Emmison and Roy Stephens (Leopard's Head Press, 1976), p. 123; Brown, *Reg. J. Romeyn and H. Newark*, 1:141; *Test. Ebor.*, 1:51; Richard S. Ferguson, ed., *Testamenta Karleolensia: The Series of Wills from Pre-Reformation Registers of the Bishops of Carlisle, 1351–1386*, Cumberland and Westmorland Antiquarian and Archaeological Society, Extra Series 9 (1893), p. 30; Foster, *Lincoln Wills*, 1:17; Gibbons, *Early Lincoln Wills*, p. 103.

3

Bishops and Anchorites:
Procedure and Protection

Legal responsibility for recluses was vested in the bishop. It was a fivefold charge. The bishop, usually through a commission set up for this purpose, first ruled on the personal credentials of the candidate—on his fitness for such a life—sometimes ordering a probationary period before permanent enclosure. Second, the bishop determined if the financial support was adequate to sustain the recluse for his or her lifetime. Third, he aided in the finding of a suitable reclusorium. Fourth, he performed (or ordered performed) the rite of enclosure. And finally, he entered into an extended period of supervision of the recluse for the years of his confinement, a supervision that might bring in its wake the appointment of confessors, gifts of alms, grants of indulgences to others who supported the recluse, legislation to correct abuses, visitations, and a general paternal involvement. Some prelates further undertook to support recluses as a diocesan responsibility; others remembered anchorites in their wills and anniversary arrangements. But this was beyond the range of their formal requirements. To investigate, to enclose, and to ensure that the recluse's life remained true to its purpose— this was the canonically instituted role of the English bishop.

Episcopal responsibility had developed over centuries. Some of the earliest Continental church councils and synods (held between 465 and 794) dealt with problems relative to ecclesiastical control of the solitary life. Out of these councils came a series of canons ratifying the authority of the bishop (sometimes in conjunction with that of an abbot) over anchorites, establishing a policy of probationary periods before enclosure, and declaring that the vow of the anchorite was permanent and irrevocable. The Council of Vannes mandated in 465 that persons desiring a solitary life should first prove themselves in a monastic setting. At Agde in 506 and Orleans in 516 it was stated that no monk might construct a cell for himself without permission of the bishop or the approval of his abbot.[1] Councils at Toledo (646), Constantinople (*in Trullo*) (692), and Frankfurt (794) added that probationary periods were necessary and that once finally enclosed the anchorite was never to leave his cell. The Trullan synod decreed that any person desiring to be an anchorite, whether he wished to be enclosed in a city or a village, must first enter a monastery. There he would spend a period in an anchoritelike setting, separated from the other monks (*separatus ac semotus*) but under the obedience of a master. Probation would last for three years while he considered if his commitment was sure and his motivations pure and not the product of a vain and empty search for glory. If on examination the anchorite was found worthy, he was to be returned to the *communal* monastic setting for another year during which his resolve would be further tested. Only then, his determination still unwavering, was he to be granted permission to be enclosed. The enclosure was to be made with the benediction of the diocesan after it was well understood that enclosure was inviolable. Once enclosed, the recluse could not leave, save under sentence of eternal damnation, unless such action were necessary for the common utility or when life itself was threatened.[2]

These early laws anticipate a degree of cooperation between abbot and bishop: in canons promulgated at Agde and Orleans, either the bishop or (*vel*) the abbot had to give permission; at

1. Johannes D. Mansi, ed., *Sacrorum conciliorum nova et amplissima collectio*, 31 vols. (Florence, 1759–98), 8:331, 347, 953. For the sixth-century Franco-Gallic councils a better edition is Carlo de Clercq, ed., *Concilia Galliae, a. 511–a. 695*, Corpus Christianorum, Series Latina, vol. 148a (Turnhout, Belgium, 1963).

2. Mansi, 10:769; 11:963; 13:908.

Frankfurt, both (*atque*) had to consent; at the Trullan synod, the extensive procedure provides for the interaction of both arms of control. Of such interaction, there is little evidence in early medieval England, although Bede did speak of the monastic probation of one recluse.[3] Abbots, however, exerted controls both on their own monks and on others who entered their domains. Wulfa, a Benedictine of St. Albans in the late ninth century, received license from his abbot to build an oratory where he lived as a solitary in extreme austerity. So famous was he that bishops, among other important men, lay as well as secular, came and confessed to him, and when he died he was buried among the abbots.[4] Abbots themselves are found "retiring" to the solitary life during these early centuries. After years of service they surrendered the reins of their monastery and withdrew to a hermitage, presumably on their own responsibility and having made their own arrangements.[5] In the early twelfth century St. Henry of Coquet, a Dane of noble birth, fled from home and an arranged marriage in order to live as a recluse. He arrived on the island of Coquet, which was owned by the priory of Tynemouth, and there received the prior's consent to build a small cell within which he might live alone. In these same years Geoffrey, the abbot of St. Albans, took two women (who had encamped near the monastery) under his protection, building a house for them in lieu of the rough shelter they had provided for themselves.[6]

These stories come to us from monastic annals, a source not likely to remark on episcopal supervision. If the bishop participated in any of these enclosures, the annals do not mention it.

3. Venerabilis Bedae, *Opera historica*, ed., Charles Plummer, 2 vols. (Oxford: Clarendon Press, 1899), 1:168 (book 3, chapter 19 of the *Ecclesiastical History of the English People*).

4. Henry T. Riley, ed., *Chronica monasterii S. Albani: Gesta abbatum monasterii sancti Albani, a Thoma Walsingham, regnante Ricardo secundo, ejusdem ecclesiae precentore, compilata*, 3 vols., RS 28, part 4 (1867-69), 1:21-22.

5. Ibid.; William H. Hart and Ponsonby A. Lyons, eds., *Cartularium monasterii de Rameseia*, 3 vols., RS 79 (1884-93), 3:173.

6. Carl Horstman, *Nova Legenda Angliae*, 2 vols. (Oxford: Clarendon Press, 1901), 2:22-26; Riley, *Gesta abbatum*, 1:80-82.

Some bishops, however, were playing their appointed roles with respect to solitaries, and from the twelfth century on there is evidence in archiepiscopal letters, hagiobiographic literature, and royal records. In these documents the function of the bishop begins to be noted, even if sometimes seen in the breach. St. Anselm, in his capacity as archbishop of Canterbury, wrote a letter of advice (ca. 1102) for two lay anchoresses under the guidance of a priest named Robert. Anselm had learned of them from William (probably William Giffard, the newly elected bishop of Winchester), who had described their "holy love, religious conversation, heavenly way of life and spiritual intention." A few years later St. Godric was installed in his hermitage at Finchale under the auspices of the bishop of Durham, Raoul Flambard.[7] A liturgical service for enclosing anchorites is contained in an extant bishop's manual of the twelfth century.

At mid-century John of Ford wrote a biography of the priest-anchorite Wulfric of Haselbury. He remarked that when Wulfric was enclosed in a house attached to the parish church in Haselbury Plucknett, Somerset, in 1125, it was "without bishop or benediction . . . under the authority of the Holy Spirit" and the protection of the local lay lord, William Fitzwalter. In noting the absence of canonical enclosure John implied that such enclosure was irregular, yet he mentioned it only in passing. Moreover, Wulfric's relationship with the bishop was in no way affected by the absence of episcopal participation at the time of his enclosure. Their intercourse was cordial for the entire thirty-year period of Wulfric's life in the cell.[8] It is clear, then, that the mechanisms of episcopal control existed and were known at this time. Compliance, however, was only occasional and noncompliance still acceptable.

<hr/>

7. St. Anselm, *Sancti Anselmi opera omnia*, ed. Franciscus S. Schmitt, 6 vols. (Edinburgh: Thomas Nelson and Sons, 1946–61), 4:134–135; Reginald, *Libellus de vita et miraculis S. Godrici, heremitae de Finchale, auctore Reginaldo monacho Dunelmensi*, ed. Joseph Stephenson, SS 20 (1847), p. 66.

8. John, abbot of Ford, *Wulfric of Haselbury*, ed. Maurice Bell, Somerset Record Society 47 (1933), p. 15, and passim.

Pipe Roll evidence of the second half of the twelfth century demonstrates an increasing involvement between bishop and recluse: the episcopacy of London supported one male recluse (ca. 1160), the episcopacy of Ely seven recluses (ca. 1168), the episcopacy of Salisbury four recluses (ca. 1185), the episcopacy of Worcester an indeterminate number (ca. 1195), the archiepiscopacy of York a male recluse at the same time.[9] Although the fact of support does not guarantee that these recluses were canonically enclosed, it is a reasonable assumption. Anchorite and bishop were each accepting their mandated association.

The position of the bishop solidified in the thirteenth century. Church legislation of the period provides one measure. All such legislation that concerned anchorites was diocesan and related to postenclosure problems. The episcopal right and role with regard to anchorites seems to have needed neither confirmation nor elaboration. Archbishop Stephen Langton, for example, issued two sets of statutes for the diocese of Canterbury. Whereas both sets of these decrees touched on anchorites, those emanating from the great provincial council held at Oxford in 1222 did not. The provincial canons were involved neither with the regulating of recluses nor with any definition of the responsibilities of bishops to them. The correction of anchorites was left to the bishop as anchorites were implicitly acknowledged to fall under episcopal jurisdiction.[10]

Diocesan legislation was not comprehensive and tended to focus on one or two concerns. It was remedial, not systematic.

9. *PR 8 Henry II* (1162), p. 73; *PR 16 Henry II* (1170), p. 96; *PR 31 Henry II* (1185), p. 205; *PR 8 Richard I* (1196), pp. 207–208; *PR 7 Richard I* (1195), p. 31.

10. The work of Christopher R. Cheney forms the basis of what follows on the legislation of the English episcopate. Specifically it may be found in his "Legislation of the Medieval English Church," *English Historical Review* 50 (1935): 193–224, 385–417; "The Medieval Statutes of the Diocese of Carlisle," *English Historical Review* 62 (1947): 52–57; "The Earliest English Diocesan Statutes," *English Historical Review* 75 (1960): 1–29; "The So-called Statutes of John Pecham and Robert Winchelsey for the Province of Canterbury," *Journal of Ecclesiastical History* 12 (1961): 14–34; and *English Synodalia of the Thirteenth Century* (London: Oxford University Press, 1941; reprint, 1968); Powicke and Cheney, *Councils.*

Through it abuses may be glimpsed but the structure is left to inference. Issues addressed included sexual incontinence (both in anchorites and the clergy who served them), the practice of unlicensed individuals (anchorites and others) hearing confessions and granting penances, the depositing of valuable objects in anchorites' cells, and the enclosure of anchorites without sufficient endowment. All these problems can be identified in legislation of the first half of the thirteenth century.

The earliest intact set of statutes written for an English diocese is the first set of Archbishop Langton, dated 1213 or 1214.[11] The statutes were written in the interval between Langton's return from exile and the suspension of the interdict. In them Langton addressed the parish priest concerning his anchorites. He was brief and to the point: let the priest warn his *inclusum*, if he has one in his parish, that he is not to receive any woman into his household by night.[12] Langton's statute was soon borrowed by Bishop Richard Poore when he issued a series of synodal statutes (1217 x 1219) for the diocese of Salisbury. Poore took Langton's admonition concerning recluses, made it relevant to women anchorites as well as to men (*similiter nec mulier masculum*), and further expanded it by adding a clause stating that "no things were to be deposited with recluses without the testimony of the priest and of faith-worthy men."[13] The Salisbury statutes were destined to be among the most significant legislative decrees of medieval England, and they were widely copied both in whole and in part by other episcopal legislators of the post-Fourth Lateran period. First Langton himself took Poore's statutes and reissued them almost verbatim under his own name as his second compilation (1222 x 1228) for Canterbury diocese (including the expanded version of his own original statute concerning recluses).[14] Poore's

11. Cheney, "Earliest Statutes," pp. 2–18; Powicke and Cheney, *Councils,* pp. 23–24. For the earlier period see Dorothy Whitelock et al., eds., *Councils and Snyods with Other Documents relating to the English Church I, A.D. 871–1204,* 2 vols. (Oxford: Clarendon Press, 1981).

12. Powicke and Cheney, *Councils,* p. 35.

13. Ibid., p. 86. The practice of using the anchorite's cell as a repository for valuable objects may have been widespread. See my chapter 4 for discussion.

14. Powicke and Cheney, *Councils,* pp. 165–166.

work next traveled verbatim to Durham (1228 x 1236) when Poore, translated to Durham, reissued his Salisbury statutes without change for his new diocese. There they also took root and some years later were again issued largely intact—this time to serve the peculiars of the church of Durham in the diocese of York (1241 x 1249?).[15] Moreover, Poore's successors, both at Salisbury and at Durham, also took care to note in the prologues to their own sets of synodal statutes that Poore's legislation remained in effect.[16] While here overtly stated and so emphasized, this was true for all legislation. Once canonically enacted, legislation was binding for all time. Future legislation largely clarified, expanded, and reiterated, occasionally addressing new problems.

Not all sets of statutes derivative of Poore contained his anchorite chapter. One such set (perhaps written for Hereford diocese) included only the first part of Poore's canon on anchorites (the sexual prohibition) in its series,[17] while bishops at Winchester, Exeter, and London who had Poore's statutes in front of them ignored his legislation for anchorites, though each bishop had recluses in his diocese during the thirteenth century. In the Synodal Statutes of Unknown Province (1222 x 1225), also derivative of Poore, Poore's admonition concerning recluses again went unmentioned, but here recluses were included in a mandate firmly prohibiting religious from action as confessors—and specifying that category as including monks, canons, anchorites, and hermits.[18] Statute making, then, in this early period, was clearly a combination of the borrowing of appropriate materials, the discarding of irrelevant or unnecessary sections, and the framing of new statutes when no old and authoritative ones existed to make the necessary point.

Three sets of mid-century statutes contained mandates concerning anchorites which were individually written and more specific in their exposition. Sometime between 1238 and 1244 Robert

15. Ibid., pp. 201, 442.
16. Ibid., pp. 366, 423.
17. Ibid., pp. 182, 194.
18. Ibid., pp. 145–146. Some manuscripts add "without license of his own prelate. . . ."

Bingham, bishop of Salisbury, who had already confirmed that Poore's statutes were still in force in the diocese, wrote a chapter in his own series dealing with the question of inadequate endowments. Within the context of an order relating to the enclosure of churchyards to protect the hallowed ground from the ordure of animals, he went on to instruct the parishioners who were to do the work to demolish anything extraneous found in the churchyard "unless it was of use to the church or deputed for recluses." Bingham continued: "We prohibit new reclusoria to be made, ordering old ones to be demolished as the anchorites die, those being excepted that were constructed by the authority of bishops of old, having certain and sufficient grants for the sustenance of recluses."[19]

Richard Wich, bishop of Chichester, issued further proscriptions (1245 x 1252):

We order anchorites not to receive or have any person in their houses concerning whom sinister suspicion may arise. Also, they shall have windows that are narrow and true. We permit them to have private conversations with only such persons as whose gravity and honesty admit of no suspicion. The custody of the vestments of the church shall not be handed over to female recluses; but if necessity demands this, we command that they be delivered cautiously so that the *inclusae* are not seen in the delivering.[20]

Finally, a Norwich statute, possibly issued by Walter Suffield, bishop from 1244 to 1257, addressed the issue of improper behavior with respect to anchorites as a problem of the chaplaincy:

Sorrowing we note that our subjects have not observed our synodal statutes, that they have ensnared themselves and not feared that we would condemn them. Since, therefore, breaking our law, parochial chaplains are frequently chatting with anchorites in their own houses under the pretext of questioning them, their maids having been sent outside in scandal to the church of God and with not a little cost of souls, we enjoin each

19. Ibid., p. 379.
20. Ibid., p. 465. The use of the reclusorium for the custody of vestments is a variation of the problem expressed by Poore (see my chapter 3, note 13, above). Naturally, the persons who would hand over the vestments to the anchoresses would be clergy. It is from such clergy that the anchoresses must be guarded.

of our deans by virtue of their obedience that, wherever anchorites live serving churches they shall bind all chaplains with an oath: that they shall not speak with them [the anchorites] within the enclosure of their houses, but shall seek them out only at their windows that turn to the church, having honest conversation, unless sickness clearly requires some other arrangement. We command also, that they expedite themselves quickly and talk with them chiefly concerning those things that pertain to the health of souls.[21]

Although the sexually indeterminate *anachorita* is employed in the above passage, the feminine form *earundum* is the possessive in each context (their maids, their houses). Clearly the anchorites for whom the statute was framed were all women. If indeed this was a statute of Bishop Suffield, we may be seeing evidence of avuncular concern, for his niece Ela was among the anchorites of his diocese.[22] But, more generally, these statutes indicate what other evidence further confirms: that anchoritism was growing in the thirteenth century, giving rise to a profusion of quickly erected cells, some underendowed, and that many of the anchorites then enclosed were women (who needed some protection from their protectors).

Such were the problems attacked by thirteenth-century episcopal legislators through synodal statutes. Their decrees were copied and recopied throughout the Middle Ages. Most of these series exist in many manuscripts and were included in various canon law texts and compilations. But the routine responsibility of the bishop went beyond these monitions. His major role was to place the seal of approval on those who chose the reclusive life. It was a role that had become sharply defined—a far cry from its anomalous position in the twelfth century—although challenges to episcopal authority would still be seen.

In 1237, the same year that Peter of Wick-by-Pershore acknowledged the bishop's right of overview to appointments made to his endowed cell, a woman was enclosed in Bristol in a procedure involving only herself and her lay supporters. That event had repercussions, but it was not the episcopal arm that flexed its muscle

21. Ibid., p. 359.
22. Blomefield, *Norfolk*, 3:489.

and called the lady into court. The annals of Tewkesbury report that "the townsmen of Bristol, as well as the *inclusa* who had been thrust into the reclusorium of St. Michael on the hill without Bristol, confessed that they had done so *contra justitiam* and they begged mercy from Robert, the lord abbot."[23] The issue at law was the violation of the patronage rights of the abbey with respect to the reclusorium. The informal nature of the enclosure and the lay usurpation (as with Wulfric) of an episcopal prerogative were not under attack here. But times were changing. When in 1269 the bishop of Worcester discovered one Juliana living as a recluse in an anchorage that she herself had built without any sort of episcopal permission or liturgical sanction, he proceeded to ordain and confirm the situation, regularizing the irregular after the fact.[24] It was no longer an acceptable deviation, for, as has been shown, during the thirteenth century entrance into the solitary life had become conditioned by episcopal practice as ecclesiastical law had made itself felt more firmly and more consistently. The bishop's responsibility for the anchorites of his diocese had developed into a continuum that began with the request for enclosure and ended with the death of the recluse. The performance of the bishop's fivefold charge became customary as the power of his office was expressed through his person, his delegates, and his diocesan statutes.

The earliest extant episcopal registers contain commissions to investigate potential candidates for enclosure as anchorites. In 1267 Walter Giffard, archbishop of York, wrote to the archdeacon of the East Riding concerning the petition of Alice de Folkton, who desired to live as an anchorite in the churchyard of St. Nicholas of Hedon, in a house yet to be built:

But, because we know nothing concerning the *conversatio*, the condition, and the mores of the aforesaid woman, whether she has adequate sustenance, and whether it is practicable, both with regard to the place and to the parish, we send this notice to you, commanding that you make inquiry as far as it is suitable, concerning the foregoing matters, so that we will be

23. Henry R. Luard, ed., *Annales monastici*, 5 vols., RS 36 (1864–69), 1:105–106.
24. J. W. Willis Bund, ed., *Register of Bishop Godfrey Giffard, Sept. 23rd, 1268 to August 15th, 1301*, 2 vols., Worcestershire Historical Society (1902), 1:35.

able to see from it what is best done about the said petition when we have been made certain through you.[25]

If Alice passed her review a license would be issued. In 1286 such a license was granted for a woman named Agnes Muscegros. Her petition to be enclosed in the churchyard at North Cave, Yorkshire, had been made through the good offices of John of Melsa and his wife Beatrice (probably the patrons of the church) and of Gilbert, the church rector. Her desire to live there "chastely and honestly" was examined and approved and the archbishop, John Romeyn, gave his permission. A later entry in Romeyn's register finds him not only granting license to yet another Agnes, a virgin and the daughter of William of Burton, but also delegating the responsibility of her liturgical enclosure to the abbot of Roche abbey.[26]

The bishop delegated this responsibility to others frequently. In fact, a service in which the diocesan actually presided was the exception rather than the rule. Most licenses to enclose were in the form of commissions to various clergy to perform the rites. Such commissions were directed to abbots, priors, church officials, deans, canons—any priest could say the mass and accept the vows. The power of enclosure was one of the rights of office routinely delegated to a suffragan bishop by his superior. Some combination of high status of the postulant and/or his patrons, coupled with the availability of time in a busy bishop's schedule, was probably necessary for a full episcopal ceremony. Certainly the bishop did not travel about his diocese to induct anchorites into their vocation. The full episcopal ceremony was rare.[27]

25. William N. Brown, ed., *Register of Walter Giffard, Lord Archbishop of York, 1276-1279*, SS 114 (1907), p. 108.

26. William N. Brown, ed., *Registers of John le Romeyn and Henry of Newark, Lord Archbishops of York, 1286-1299*, 2 vols., SS 123, 128 (1913-17), 1:196, 126.

27. For examples of the delegation of the rights of enclosure to the suffragan, see Rowland A. Wilson, ed., *The Registers or Act Books of the Bishops of Coventry and Lichfield: Book 5 Being the Second Register of Bishop Robert de Stretton, A.D. 1360-1385,* William Salt Archaeological Society, n.s. 8 (1905), pp. 131, 199-200, 356. For examples of enclosures delegated to abbots or priors: 1294, the abbot of Kirkstall enclosed Sybil of Insula (Brown, *Reg. J. Romeyn and H. Newark*, 1:121); 1300, the abbot of Roche enclosed Beatrice, daughter of Thomas de Hodesack (ibid.,

The procedure by which one secular priest became an anchorite in the early fifteenth century can be deduced from three
memoranda entered in the register of Bishop Robert Reade of
Chichester. William Bolle, the rector of the parish church of Aldrington, Sussex, desired to become a recluse and made contact
with the dean and chapter of Chichester cathedral, which offered
both to sponsor him and to grant permission for him to build an
anchorhold attached to the cathedral church. The first recorded
document establishes that on the last day of May 1402 Bishop
Reade granted permission for Bolle to become an anchorite and
build a habitation for that purpose next to the northern side of
the church. The building was to be twenty-four feet wide and
twenty-nine feet long; after the withdrawal or death (*post recessum
vel decessum*) of Bolle the anchorage was to revert to the church
at Chichester. Two days later the dean and chapter added their
license to that of the bishop. Their letter to Bolle states that the
width of the house was to be twenty-six feet and that it was to
have access (*cum ingressu et egressu*) to the Lady Chapel, which it
would abut, in order that Bolle might celebrate mass there during
his life in the cell. The actual notice of enclosure is dated 20 December 1402, more than six months after these entries. It states
that Bolle's resignation of his benefice had been duly notarized

---

2:322–323); 1332, the abbot of Newnham enclosed Beatrice of Colyford (F. C.
Hingeston-Randolph, ed., *Register of John de Grandisson, Bishop of Exeter, A.D.
1327–1369*, 3 vols. [Exeter, 1894–99], 2:650); 1363, the prior of Birkenhead enclosed
Brother John de Chorleton, a Domincan (Rowland A. Wilson, ed., *The Registers or
Act Books . . . and the First Register of Bishop Robert de Stretton, 1358– 1385*,
William Salt Archaeological Society, n.s. 10, part 2 [1907], p. 162). Diocesan offi-
cials were appointed by Simon of Ghent in 1308 (Cyril T. Flower and Michael
C. B. Dawes, eds., *Registrum Simonis de Gandavo, diocesis Sarebiriensis, A.D. 1297–
1315*, 2 vols., CYS 40–41 [1933–34], 2:699–700); by Richard Swinfield in 1315 (John
Webb, ed., *A Roll of the Household Expenses of Richard de Swinfield, Bishop of
Hereford, during Part of the Years 1289 and 1290*, Camden Society, o.s. 62 [1855],
pp. 213–214); by Adam de Orleton in 1321 (Arthur T. Bannister, ed., *Registrum
Ade de Orleton, episcopi Herefordensis, A.D. 1318–1327*, CYS 5[1908], p. 205). Clay,
"Further Studies," p. 82, speaking of the enclosure of Master Simon Appulby in
1513, says that "the bishop would inevitably preside when a priest was to be
solemnly set apart in so important a city church [All Hallows, London Wall]." If
that was the case in London, we have little notice of it elsewhere, but see the text
immediately below and the next footnote for the episcopal enclosure of Sir
William Bolle.

and that the bishop had conducted the investiture of the priest into his new status as anchorite.[28]

Central to the acceptance of Bolle's petition for enclosure was the mutual consent of the three parties involved: the bishop, the dean and chapter, and Bolle himself. Had Bolle chosen to be enclosed in a parish church, the third party to the consent would have been the parish priest along with his parishioners. If the indicated cell had been under the control of a local or other patron, that person would also have had a primary right of approval in any enclosure, adding a fourth element to the transaction.

The process that was used to investigate individuals who wished to migrate from a monastery to an anchorage was similar to that already described, save that the monk also needed permission of the abbot or prior to release him from his monastic vows.[29] On occasion that release was waived by the intercession of the pope.

28. Edward Turner, "Domus Anachoritae, Aldrington," *Sussex Archaelogical Collections* 12 (1860):134–136. One month after Bolle's enclosure Bishop Reade's register notes the appointment of a new rector at Bolle's resigned church in Aldrington (Cecil Deedes, ed., *Episcopal Register of Robert Rede, ordines predicatorum, Lord Bishop of Chichester, 1397–1415*, 2 vols., Sussex Record Society 8, 11 [1908–10], 1:276–277).

29. For an example of such a license: "Margaret H., by the sufferance of God Prioress of the priory of Stainfield, of the order of St. Benedict, of the diocese of Lincoln, to our beloved daughter and sister, sister Beatrice Franke, fellow nun and sister of us and our said priory, publicly and expressly professed in the same. With much approval in the Lord of your purpose which as we stedfastly believe, has been divinely inspired in you, wherewith not lightly or recklessly, but out of an honest heart and faith unfeigned, and to win the fruit of a more holy life, you desire to change your condition to a stricter life under the rule or order of an anchorite, and to be shut up in a building adjacent to the parish church of Winterton, of the said diocese of Lincoln, where you may have more freedom to contemplate your Creator, we grant you special licence by the purport of these presents to have power to remove to such life and be shut up in the said building, as it has oft-times been asked of us by you to this end, with the will and consent of the most reverend father in Christ and lord, the lord William, by the grace of God bishop of Lincoln, diocesan of such places, and after sufficient deliberation, and we release you by these presents from the bond of the obedience wherewith you were and are bound to us and our said priory, to the effect of the removal and inclosure aforesaid, and not for any other purpose or in any other manner. In witness of the which thing the seal of our office is attached to these presents. Given in the chapter house of our priory aforesaid, etc." (A. Hamilton Thompson, ed., *Visitations of Religious Houses in the Diocese of Lincoln*, 3 vols., CYS 17, 24, 33 [1915–27], 1:115).

Papal letters written between 1399 and 1424 show Rome granting permission to three male religious to become anchorites without license of their superiors. One was an Augustinian canon, the two others friars. Whether papal involvement was necessary for these men to achieve their ends or was rather a sign of status is a tantalizing question. All three were to live as anchorites beyond the confines of their own houses, one in a cell "which has been built for one religious near the church of the Hospitallers' house in Bokland in the diocese of Wells" and the other two in any fit place "in the realm."[30] Typically, however, religious who were leaving the confines of their own community received the permission of their superior and passed under episcopal jurisdiction.

An exchange of letters between a bishop and an abbot allows us to see one such migration in its entirety. On 3 January 1436 Bishop William Gray of Lincoln requested that the abbot of the Augustinian house of Thornton examine a Benedictine nun who desired to become an anchoress. John Hoton, the abbot, was to proceed in four stages. First, he was to satisfy himself that the nun's resolve in this matter was in no way capricious; next, he was to examine the premises of the suggested reclusorium, a small house attached to the parish church at Winterton; third, he was to survey the attitudes of the general community; and, finally, if reassured that all was in order, he was to perform rites of enclosure in the name of the bishop, reporting back to him the details of the investigation and its outcome. The entire process was delegated to the abbot as agent for the bishop. There is no question of shared responsibility but rather of the assignment of a task belonging to a busy diocesan to a trusted and capable second-in-command, his "lowly and devoted John."[31] John's subsequent letter to the bishop related that he had arrived at Winterton on the twenty-first of January. The nun, Beatrice Franke of Stainfield priory, was waiting for him on his arrival. He examined her with

30. CPL 5 (1396–1404): 200; CPL 7 (1417–1431): 180, 368.
31. Thompson, *Visitations of Religious Houses*, 1:112–116. Nor was this infrequent. See, for example, Lacy, *Exeter Reg.*, 2:158–159, 394–396, where he on two occasions designates officials of the cathedral at Exeter to undertake the entire responsibility.

regard to the length of time during which she had persisted in desiring to make such a move and the peril in which she placed herself should she fail. Satisfied that she neither wavered nor faltered in any way and that she had desired to become an anchoress almost from the time of her childhood, he released her from her bond of obedience to the prioress of Stainfield and enclosed her on the next day in a ceremony in which during the mass she publicly made her new profession, reading it "openly and clearly," and promised obedience and chastity to John (standing for the bishop).[32] The letter from Hoton to Gray, signed and dated on the twenty-third of January, when the abbot was already back home at Thornton, is followed in the register by the prioress's license to Beatrice. Noting, as had Hoton, the extended duration of time during which Beatrice had persevered in her resolve to become a recluse, the prioress, Margaret Hulle, cited the episcopal decision to allow Beatrice to become an anchoress and gave her own permission. The monastic license of release was necessary but secondary.

The dates suggest that the whole process of Beatrice's migration was perfunctory. The abbot received Gray's letter some time after the third of January. On the twenty-first he arrived at Winterton, where the nun awaited him. It is unclear whether she was already living in the cell, but without formal approval and liturgical enclosure, or had been brought to the site from the convent by prearrangement on that day. Whatever the sequence, her presence at the site, already beyond the confines of her cloister, indicates that the process was expected to go forward. In fact, the busy abbot examined her on that day, enclosed her on the next (the twenty-second), and was sufficiently reestablished at home to take up his correspondence on the twenty-third.

Clearly much had been arranged in advance. The site was accounted for and all seem to have been of one mind that Beatrice Franke's commitment to become a recluse was neither lightly embraced nor likely to be transitory. Enough time elapsed between the third of January and the twenty-first for some correspondence

---

32. Thompson, *Visitations of Religious Houses*, 1:114–116.

between John at Thornton and Margaret at Stainfield, establishing that this was to be an uncomplicated procedure. That the anchoress-to-be had followed the most cautious of paths leading to the anchoritic life certainly made the appropriateness of this enclosure easy to confirm. In general, however, the seeming haste with which this and other enclosures (such as Alice de Angrum's) were undertaken probably indicates that by the time even a first notice appeared in an episcopal register the process had almost been completed and only formalities remained. Exceptions frequently involved situations in which a reclusorium was not immediately available. Thus a nun of Arden had to wait six months between the first notice of her request for enclosure and the act itself,[33] and an equal time was needed for Sir William Bolle to build his new anchorhold at Chichester cathedral. All of the evidence implies that bishops considered the task of assessing the suitability of prospective anchorites a serious responsibility.

Some religious may have become anchorites without episcopal license. Certain conventual houses contained a reclusorium within or near their confines, a reclusorium in which one of the monks or nuns of the house lived. Westminster had a long tradition of such recluse-monks who remained under the discipline of the abbey but lived as anchorites in the abbey anchorhold. Monastic pensions were granted to them as well as allowances of candles and fuel.[34] The nunnery at Polesworth, Warwickshire, also contained a cell for a recluse where one of the nuns of the convent lived.[35] A fourteenth-century letter indicates a similar situation at Bury St. Edmunds. The letter is a reply of a Bury abbot to the request of a monk to live as an anchorite in a cell near the abbey church. The abbot responded: "First we concede to you that you may live perpetually in the cell assigned to you in the manner of

33. VCH Yorkshire, 3:113.

34. Ernest H. Pearce, The Monks of Westminster (Cambridge: Cambridge University Press, 1916), pp. 33, 95, 115. See also David Knowles, The Religious Orders in England, 3 vols. (Cambridge: Cambridge University Press, 1948–59; reprint, 1971), 2:219–222, for discussion of the Westminster anchorites and chapter 5 of my work for Henry V's relationship with them.

35. For a discussion of one of these anchoresses see Clay, "Further Studies," pp. 79–80.

an anchorite, from which cell you are never to exit nor have discourse with anyone, whether regular or secular, except for the confessor and the servant assigned to you, save by the license and express will of the abbot or prior, or in their absence the sub-prior or third prior. . . ."[36] This seems to have been an internal private arrangement not involving episcopal overview, much less control. The anchorite would remain supported by the monastic treasury, subject to monastic obedience; he might not even write a letter without abbatial license. It is even possible that there was more than one cell available for such purposes at Bury St. Edmunds. The document reads "within the cell assigned to you" (*intra cellam tibi assignatum*), which could indicate that there was more than one cell available, especially when read with the parallel passage "except for the confessor and the servant assigned to you" (*excepto confessore et famulo tibi assignatis*), which surely implies a choice.

Other instances of "internal" recluses can be found at several Dominican houses. John Lacy lived at the reclusorium of Newcastle-upon-Tyne's Blackfriary circa 1400–34; Richard Pekard was enclosed at the Blackfriars in Lancaster in 1390; Margery Kempe's favorite confessor was one of a string of recluses who lived in the anchorhold of the Dominican house of Lynn, Norfolk, in the fourteenth and fifteenth centuries. All of these men were priests and members of the house in which they were enclosed. All almost surely acted as confessors to lay persons outside their community. Archbishop Scrope's appointment of Pekard as confessor is on record; John Lacy, who was a writer, warns of the "perils that belong to the shrift" in his work, implying that he experienced them; Margery Kempe's anchorite-confessor was famous in Lynn.[37] The

36. Antonia Gransden, "The Reply of a Fourteenth-century Abbot of Bury St. Edmunds to a Man's Petition to Be a Recluse," *English Historical Review* 75 (1960):464–467.

37. For Lacy, see Clay, "Northern Anchorites," pp. 210–212 and Clay, "Further Studies," pp. 75–78; for Pekard, see *VCH Lancashire*, 2:103; for Lynn Dominican anchorites, see C. F. R. Palmer, "The Friar-Preachers, or Blackfriars, of King's Lynn," *Journal of the British Archaeological Association* 41 (1884): 79–86, and Margery Kempe, *The Book of Margery Kempe*, ed., Sanford Meech, EETS, o.s. 212 (London, 1940), pp. 17, 33, 37, 43.

commissioning of these men as confessors indicates that bishops knew of their enclosures and in fact sanctioned them by this further honor. What, if any, episcopal presence had been deemed necessary in converting these men from friars to anchorites is unclear, but the anchorites' status was acceptable. The Westminster anchorites also functioned as confessors—to kings.

Certainly no religious could leave his own convent for a distant cell without episcopal or papal consent. A document concerning one John Bourne, also a Blackfriar, makes this clear. Initially Bourne may have been enclosed without episcopal license in a procedure similar to those described for anchorites at other Dominican friaries. A papal indult describes him as a man "who formerly, fired with devotion, with license of his superior and after long remaining in his order, had himself enclosed in a cell in the house of his order at Arundel in the diocese of Chichester. . . ."[38] The purpose of the indult, however, is to allow him to change his place of enclosure: ". . . to transfer himself to another fit and honest place of the same or other order mendicant or non-mendicant, with his clothes, books and other things conferred upon him as alms, and, under like enclosure, to remain there perpetually." Although the circumstances of the original enclosure remain unclear, save that he had license of his own superior, he could not change his cell and leave his convent without permission, and in this case papal authority was brought to bear. Other examples deal with initial states of enclosure and with episcopal license but reemphasize that migration meant the leaving of abbatial (or other communal) authority. Margaret de Kirkeby, the anchoress for whom Richard Rolle wrote the *Form of Living*, received episcopal permission in 1348 to transfer from Hampole, where she was a nun, to a cell attached to a chapel in East Layton, Yorkshire.[39] In 1409 Archbishop Arundel mandated the enclosure of a Chertsey monk (of Winchester diocese) in a cell at Broughton

38. *CPL* 5 (1396–1404): 470.

39. Hope Emily Allen, *Writings Ascribed to Richard Rolle, Hermit of Hampole, and Materials for His Biography* (Modern Language Association of America, 1927; reprint, New York: Kraus, 1966), p. 502.

(in Lincoln diocese).[40] Norton priory, an Augustinian house, itself petitioned Roger Northburger, bishop of Coventry and Lichfield, in 1356 to admit one of their brethren as an anchorite to the reclusorium of the collegial church of St. John, Chester. The site of St. John's was the home in turn of at least three male recluses during the mid-fourteenth century, each of whom was from a different order: a Cistercian monk, an Augustinian canon, and a Dominican friar.[41]

Dom Robert Cherde, a Cistercian of Ford abbey, appeared personally in 1402 before Richard Prates, the Vicar General in Spirituals of Henry Bowet, bishop of Bath and Wells, carrying with him his letters of discharge from the abbot of Ford. Prates examined Dom Robert, questioned corroborating witnesses under oath, and, satisfied as to the seriousness of his purpose, accepted his petition in the name of the bishop. Three local priests were delegated to undertake his enclosure in the churchyard of the parish church of Crewkerne, Somerset, an enclosure that was not to permit any egress whatsoever (*absque egressu quocumque*).[42]

None of these examples demanded or even suggested a period of probation. Probationary periods are in fact quite uncommon in these documents. Only occasionally were they required. In all known instances probation was ordered for women who were proceeding to the anchorite life without having been nuns. I noted above the case of Beatrice Strong, the married woman of West Down. She was to be enclosed "for a time" to see if she would persevere in her decision. In the fifteenth century Edmund Stafford, bishop of Exeter, arranged for the probation of "one Cecilia Moys, desiring to lead the contemplative life of an anchorite in a

40. "Anchorites in Faversham Churchyard," *Archaeologia Cantiana* 11 (1877): 36–37.

41. Edmund Hobhouse, ed., "Register of Roger de Norbury, Bishop of Lichfield and Coventry from A.D. 1322 to A.D. 1358," *William Salt Archaeological Society*, o.s. 1 (1880): 283; Wilson, *Reg. R. Stretton*, 1:162; Clay, "Northern Anchorites," p. 209.

42. John de Trokelowe, *Annales Edwardi II*, ed. Thomas Hearne (Oxford, 1729), 2:263–265. Note that the procedure here has been reversed. Prates has been discharged by his abbot before being accepted by the bishop.

certain House in the Cemetery of Marhamchurch . . . [and] commissioned Philip, abbot of Hartland, and Walter Dollebeare R[ector] of Southhill, to place her there under proper protection, assigning her till Christmas as a time of probation," a period of seven and one-half months.[43] Elizabeth Elltoft, a widow, was assigned a probationary period of a year, after her enclosure at the Doncaster reclusory in 1484; Archbishop Rotherham commissioned the dean of Doncaster to oversee that responsibility.[44] In 1418 Edmund Lacy, as bishop of Hereford, appointed two of his officials to investigate the resolve of Margaret Shipster to live as an anchoress. If satisfied, they were to enclose her in a dwelling next to St. Peter's Church, Hereford, but only after an indeterminate period of probation during which she was to deliberate carefully on her desire to be a recluse and her capacity to sustain such a life.[45] Unlike the Exeter and York probations, the anchoress was not to enter the cell until after the probation was over. She was prescribed a period of reflection as opposed to a trial run.

An anchorite had to muster approval not only for his personal qualifications but also for the surety of his endowment. In 1267 Alice de Folkton's investigator had been reminded that "we know nothing about . . . whether she has adequate sustenance." Concern for ample endowment was constant throughout the Middle Ages. Robert Bingham ruthlessly attacked the problem of inadequate support in his Salisbury statutes, ordering the destruction of underendowed anchorholds as the anchorites died. But anchorites still living in cells often watched their support fade away. Miliana was not alone in going to court to redress a failed promise. Such promises were usually tied to the rents and proceeds of land. As lands changed hands through death, marriage, escheat, or the succession of new ecclesiastical officials, persons other than those who had made these grants became responsible for their payment.

43. F. C. Hingeston-Randolph, ed., *Register of Edmund Stafford, Bishop of Exeter, 1395–1419* (Exeter, 1856), p. 251.

44. Eric E. Barker, ed., *Register of Thomas Rotherham*, vol. 1, CYS 69 (1976), no. 1646.

45. Joseph H. Parry, transcr., and Arthur T. Bannister, ed., *Registrum Edmundi Lacy, episcopi Herefordensis, A.D. 1417–1420*, CYS 22 (1918), pp. 34–35.

Miliana failed in her attempt to recover her loss. Others, like the recluse at Doncaster, were more successful—but the necessity of seeking legal resolutions to quarrels over support must have caused prolonged periods of tension for the recluses, whose very existence was at stake. In 1203 a dispute between Hugh of Adinton, a clerk, and the recluse of Brampton, Northamptonshire, over the ownership of half a virgate of land and its appurtenances was settled when Hugh came to court and agreed that the anchoress was to receive its proceeds during her lifetime and only after her death would it revert to Hugh and his heirs. The anchoress of St. James, Colchester, took the abbot of St. Osyth's to court in 1272 and negotiated a settlement with him whereby he promised to pay her five quarters of wheat annually as well as arrears already accrued.[46] The anchoress of Wigan, Lancashire, had to beg Edward II to restore a pension that had ceased when her patron became involved in the Lancastrian rebellion of 1322 and lost his lands. Her petition reached Edward in Holland and he returned this message to England:

The king sends enclosed a petition of Alyne, recluse of Wygan. Mandate to ordain a remedy for her according to right and reason.

Aline, the poor recluse of Wygan, prays the king that she may have restitution of a rent of 30s. yearly, which Sir Robert de Holand gave her in the towns of Wygan and Schevyngton when she was enclosed, for her maintenance for life. Sir John Travers, steward of Lancaster, took it when Sir Robert was taken, so that she has had nothing since and is dying for lack (*dount ele ne ad ren eu pus en sa par quay qe ele moert presdelock pour defaute*).[47]

---

46. *Curia regis 1201–03*, pp. 205, 255–256; *VCH Essex*, 2:158, among other legal actions involving recluses. A woman known as Margery the Anchorite (Margeria le Auncre) was involved in a court case in which she was sued for possession of land, land that she said was her dower. She did not come to court when summoned in Michaelmas Term, 1234, sending word that she was enclosed and not able to go out. In rebuttal it was argued that she sometimes went into her garden (!) and so did go out. She was summoned again to appear in three weeks time. Typically, recluses appeared in court through an attorney, but some (Miliana among them) do seem to have pled their own cases. For Margery's case see *Curia regis 1233–37*, p. 98. The resolution is not known.

47. *CCW 1244–1326*, p. 544.

The king's involvement was sufficient. Aline received fifty-nine shillings for years 17–18 Edward II from "a moiety of 5 messuages, 36 acres land and 8½ acres meadow in Wygan and Schevyngton,"[48] and this anchoress was saved from disaster.

All recluses had to have guaranteed support and no circumstances were considered so pressing as to allow suspension of that requirement. Christine Holby's story serves as example. Christine was a canoness of Kildare whose convent dispersed when raiding Irish foresters "destroyed and devastated" it. She came to Edmund Lacy, then bishop of Exeter, seeking a reclusorium. She brought with her letters of consent from her prioress and letters recommending she be accepted by the bishop as an anchoress. But enclosure was not so easily done. The bishop handled her petition as he would have any other, the fact of her convent's dispersal serving only as explanation for her presence and not as reason for special treatment. On 14 September 1447 Lacy commissioned the precentor of the cathedral, Walter Collys, to examine her with regard to her desire to enclose herself as an anchoress in the churchyard of St. Leonard's, Exeter. Collys was to look into her heart and to make sure that Christine was indeed ready to make this new vow and that Satan had not transformed himself into an angel of light leading Christine to her downfall. All persons connected to St. Leonard's were to have their right to discuss her acceptability as a candidate. Finally, Collys was to "make sure that she had secure and certain sustenance, and who will bestow it and sustain it to the end of her life, and of how much, where, and of what things this manner of dowry ought to consist, *so that we and our successors in this place shall never be burdened by this reclusion.*" Lacy demanded a fixed endowment *before* reclusion, lest "in opprobrium of this work, she is forced fearfully to violate her solemn vow because of the failure of her fixed endowment."[49]

An anchorite fallen on hard times would indeed become the responsibility of the local community and ultimately of the diocesan authority. Archbishop of York William Wickwane rose to the occasion in 1281 when an aging anchoress who had partially

48. CMR 1327–28, no. 2180.
49. Lacy, *Exeter Reg.*, 2:394–396 (italics mine).

supported herself in her younger days was found ill and in want in her cell at Blyth, Nottinghamshire.[50] Bishop Poore, when at Durham, probably did so as well. A 1237 notice referring to an anchoress at Durham ordered the guardian of the bishopric of Durham "to find the woman-recluse of Durham necessaries . . . in the same way as R[ichard] late bishop of Durham was wont to find her necessaries in his time."[51] This is in contrast to the commands issued to the same guardian concerning a female recluse at Gateshead, a woman whose support was guaranteed by charter. The guardian was informed "to cause the woman-recluse of Gateseyed to be maintained . . . in accordance with what R[ichard] late bishop of Durham granted to her by his charter and by the confirmation of the chapter of the church of Durham, which charter is in her possession."[52] The Durham anchoress seems to have been without charter and her support was at the level of "necessaries." That Bishop Poore would respond to the needs of an anchoress abandoned by others is not surprising considering his general concern for recluses. But the reactions of others were cooler. Bishops tried to prevent the situation from developing. They did not want to encourage any recluse who might become dependent on the diocese. It is hard to imagine an anchorite "put out onto the street," as Bishops Swinfield and Lacy threatened, but the caution and the warnings indicate that many anchorites may have become a financial burden that was quite unwelcome to those unprepared to sustain it and that the bishop was responsible for anticipating that problem before enclosure.

Most anchorites seem to have made their own arrangements for a cell. Commissions usually indicate the cell to be entered if the candidate received approval. A vacancy was probably a precondition of application in many cases. At other times new cells were built and licenses of the bishop are found granting that permission.[53] Sometimes the petitioner proposed himself for enclosure

50. William Brown, ed., *The Register of William Wickwane, Lord Archbishop of York, 1279–1285,* SS 114 (1907), p. 74.

51. CLR 1226–40, p. 272. See also ibid., pp. 388, 408, 503.

52. Ibid., p. 283.

53. Willis Bund, *Reg. G. Giffard,* 1:21, 2:99; Sir Thomas D. Hardy, ed., *Registrum palatinum Dunelmense, the Register of Richard de Kellawe, Lord Palatine and Bishop of Durham, 1314–1316,* 4 vols., RS 62 (1873–78), 3:300–301.

but without an assured dwelling place and the bishop delegated his dean or other officials to locate a suitable anchorhold.[54] All this accomplished, the ritual act of enclosure was finally performed and the solitary life begun in earnest.

Enclosure ceremonies are contained in extant pontificals from the twelfth to the fifteenth centuries and in the first published manuals of the sixteenth.[55] They are of varying length, complexity, and drama. The actual service will be described in the following chapter, which in part deals with the psychological implications of enclosure and asceticism. Here let me say that a pontifical contains the peculiar church services assigned to the episcopal office. The pontifical of Lacy, for example, contains *ordines* for reconciling churches, cemeteries, and penitents, for consecrating virgins,

54. Brown, *Reg. W. Giffard*, p. 185; A. Hamilton Thompson, ed., *Register of William Greenfield, Lord Archbishop of York, 1306-1315*, 2 vols., SS 145, 149 (1931-34), 2:185-186.

55. The earliest has been published as an appendix to Henry A. Wilson, ed., *The Pontifical of Magdalen College*, Henry Bradshaw Society 39 (1910), pp. 243-244. William G. Henderson, ed., *The Liber pontificalis Chr. Bainbridge archiepiscopi Eboracensis*, SS 61 (1875), pp. v-xliv, gives a list of pontificals of English and Scottish use, several of which contain *ordines* for anchorite enclosure. Walter H. Frere, *Pontifical Services Illustrated from Miniatures of the XVth and XVIth Centuries* I, Alcuin Club 3 (1901), corrects Henderson's dating in several instances and provides a more complete list, explaining as well "that pontificals do not belong to any diocesan use but represent the personal use of the bishop to whom they may happen to belong" (p. 89). Henderson, *Liber pontificalis . . . Bainbridge*, pp. 81-86, contains an anchorite *ordo* from the thirteenth century (Frere correcton, p. 104) that Bainbridge was using in the sixteenth. Ralph Barnes, ed., *The Liber Pontificalis of Edmund Lacy, Bishop of Exeter* (Exeter, 1846), pp. 131-137, contains a fourteenth-century service for anchorites that Lacy was using in the fifteenth century. In William G. Henderson, ed., *Manuale et processionale ad usum insignis ecclesiae Eboracensis*, SS 63 (1875), pp. 36-42, 108-109, two completely different services for anchorite reclusion are printed, both of Sarum usage. Clay, *Hermits and Anchorites*, prints a translation of the longer of these two services, pp. 193-198. A new edition of the Sarum Manual, A. Jefferies Collins, ed., *Manuale ad usum Percelebris Ecclesie Sarisburiensis*, Henry Bradshaw Society 91 (1958), pp. 74-81, contains a version similar to that translated in Clay. In manuscript are services in the Pontifical of Richard Clifford, bishop of Worcester (1401-07) and London (1407-21), CCCC MS 79, Corpus Christi, Cambridge, fol. 72; The Pontifical of Henry Chichele, archbishop of Canterbury (1414-43), MS B. 11. 9, Trinity College, Cambridge, fols. 98v-116v; and the Pontifical of John Russell, bishop of Rochester (1476-80) and Lincoln (1480-94), MS Mm. 3. 21, Cambridge University Library, fols. 189v-190v.

for accepting the vows of widows and hermits, and for many other offices in addition to the *reclusio anachoritarum.* The enclosing of anchorites was an occasional task in the life of a busy prelate, and nothing makes this so clear as the long list of other services and benedictions given in the pontifical. Many of these services, however, required only a one-time involvement on the part of the episcopal office. In contrast, the service enclosing an anchorite brought the candidate into episcopal jurisdiction and episcopal care. The enclosure ceremony was the beginning, not only for the anchorite but also for a new pattern of ecclesiastical paternalism.

A fairly regular postenclosure task was the granting of licenses to anchorites to choose their own confessors—a welcome privilege to most, for save for servants the anchorite's confessor was his or her only routine contact with the outside world. One "Lucie" Moys received such a license in 1405 from her bishop. She is almost certainly the Cecilia Moys who was given a probationary period in 1403, now enclosed and being granted this favor.[56] Papal authority also granted this right to some anchorites, whose confessors were further enjoined that the recluses might receive plenary remission, once, at the hour of death.[57] Bishops are found appointing confessors for some and also licensing priests to celebrate in an anchorite's oratory or adjoining chapel.[58] Papal permission was granted to some recluses to leave their cells for a period for the purpose of pilgrimage, then to be allowed to return;[59] both pope and bishop sanctioned changes in cells, if the circumstances warranted it. One papal mandate did both:

---

56. Hingeston-Randolph, *Reg. E. Stafford,* p. 251, for Lucie. For other examples see ibid., p. 20; Wilson *Reg. R. Stretton,* 2:29; Margaret Archer, ed., *Register of Bishop Philip Repingdon, 1405–1419,* 2 vols., Lincoln Record Society 57–58 (1963), 1:51.

57. *CPL* 5 (1342–1362): 504; *CPL* 9 (1431–47): 241; *CPL* 12 (1458–71): 699.

58. Hingeston-Randolph, *Reg. E. Stafford,* p. 132; Hingeston-Randolph, *Reg. J. Grandisson,* 2:653; Clay, "Further Studies," p. 79. The recipient of the Grandisson license was a woman named Alice who was enclosed at Pilton, Devonshire. Her license was to allow private masses. Three years earlier, in 1329, Grandisson (1:538) had granted her permission to choose her own confessor. These licenses usually were for fixed periods of time, often two years, and then had to be renewed.

59. *CPL* 5 (1396–1404): 249; *CPL* 13:2 (1475–84): 625.

To Emma Scherman, of the diocese of York. Indult to her—who formerly took a vow of a recluse, and has had herself for many years enclosed in a cell in the place of Pontefract, with a little garden (*ortulo*) contiguous thereto for the sake of taking fresh air (*refrigerum aeris recaptando*),—on account of the tumults and clamours of the people in the said place, to transfer herself to a more suitable place, to have there another cell with a like garden, and to leave her cell yearly for the purpose of visiting churches and other pious places, and of gaining the indulgences granted there, without requiring license of the diocesan or other.[60]

In 1340 Richard Bury, bishop of Durham, gave license to choose a new site for the reclusorium at Gateshead, situated at St. Mary's church there. The new house was to be placed in a suitable area of the churchyard, next to the church, as long as the rector and parishioners were willing and there remained sufficient place to bury the dead. The old anchorage there was still inhabited by a female recluse but was obviously in need of such repair as to make a new dwelling more reasonable. So permission was granted by the bishop to build anew and then, we infer, to move the anchoress into the new cell.[61]

Individual problems demanded individual responses. In 1328 John de Drokensford, bishop of Bath and Wells, wrote to the vicar of Muchelney, Somerset: "Brother Thomas, lately '*inclusus*' in the hermitage of Oth (Worth), in Aller parish, petitions to have a door to admit you or another confessor, also to have choice of burial at Aller, or elsewhere." Drokensford directed the vicar to make the door and keep the key in hand for his visits to the recluse. In the late fifteenth century Bishop James Goldwell of Norwich

---

60. *CPL* 5 (1396–1404): 471. See also ibid., p. 470, for the transfer of John Bourne, a Friar Preacher, because of the inconvenience of his cell and the penury of his house, to the Dominican friary at Arundel, Sussex. See Allen, *Writings Ascribed to Richard Rolle*, p. 502, for the move of Margaret de Kirkeby to a cell at Ainderby, Yorkshire, from one at Layton, so that she may see and hear mass. Margery Pensax, anchoress at Hawton, Nottinghamshire, received permission in 1399 to choose a new cell and a prelate to seclude her (R. N. Swanson, ed., *Calendar of the Register of Richard Scrope, Archbishop of York, 1398–1405*, Borthwick Texts and Calendars: Records of the Northern Province 8 [York, 1981], p. 483); she turned up at a London cell with a royal pension of forty shillings yearly six months later and lived there for at least eighteen years (*CCR 1399–1402*, p. 35).

61. Hardy, *Reg. pal. Dunel.*, 3:300–301.

permitted an old and ill anchoress of Lynn to leave her cell for an infirmary bed in Denney abbey, Cambridgeshire.[62] Similarly, in 1459 Thomas Beckington, bishop of Bath and Wells, issued a dispensation

for Joan an anchorite enclosed within the parish church of Crukern,—on representations by her that she has for many years observed the injunction to abstain from eating flesh which she took on herself by the authority of John Stafford, the bishop's predecessor, but that owing to age and occasional infirmity she cannot any longer continually observe the same, —to eat flesh on every day of the year on which such eating is allowed by the Church.[63]

In a harsher vein, fourteenth-century bishops investigated three anchoresses for heretical views. Little is known of one case, save that Bishop Bek of Lincoln diocese inquired as to the behavior of the recluse at the church of St. John the Baptist, Huntingdon, who had "introduced doctrines contrary to the Catholic faith."[64] The year was 1346 and the Lollard heresy had yet to infect England. The anchoress's error may have been a private one. Lollardy was the issue in the cases of two other anchoresses, one of whom was domiciled at St. Peter's, Leicester, and the other at St. Peter's, Northampton. Their stories depart from the secure orthodoxy that characterizes the anchorite movement throughout its whole life cycle in England.

The anchoress at Leicester was a woman named Matilda. She became something of a cause célèbre. Knighton wrote of her and John Foxe included her in his *Book of Martyrs*.[65] In 1389 she was

---

62. Edmund Hobhouse, ed., *Calendar of the Register of John de Drokensford, Bishop of Bath and Wells, A.D. 1309-1329,* Somerset Record Society 1 (1887), p. 284; Norman P. Tanner, *Popular Religion in Norwich with Special Reference to the Evidence of Wills, 1370-1532* (Ph.D. diss., Oxford University, 1973), p. 124 citing Goldwell's register, NNCO Reg.7/12, fol. 245d.

63. Sir H. C. Maxwell Lyte and Michael C. B. Dawes, eds., *The Register of Thomas Bekynton, Bishop of Bath and Wells, 1433-1465,* 2 vols., Somerset Record Society 49-50 (1934-35), 1:333.

64. *VCH Huntingdonshire,* 1:361; *VCH Leicestershire,* 1:367.

65. Henry Knighton, *Chronicon Henrici Knighton, vel Cnitthon, monachi Leycestrensis,* ed. Joseph R. Lumby, 2 vols., RS 92 (1889-95), 2:312; John Foxe, *The Acts and Monuments of John Foxe,* ed. Josiah Pratt, 4th ed., 8 vols. (London: Reli-

examined, along with other persons accused of Lollardy in the city of Leicester, by Archbishop William Courtenay. She was reported to have answered his questions "non plene . . . sed pocius sophistice":[66]

> . . . it was declared and showed to the said archbishop that there was a certain anchoress, whose name was Matilda, inclosed within, in the churchyard of St. Peter's Church in the said town of Leicester, infected, as they said with the pestiferous contagion of the aforesaid heretics and lollards: whereupon, after the said archbishop had examined the aforesaid Matilda, touching the aforesaid conclusions, heresies, and errors, and found her not to answer plainly and directly to the same, but sophistically and subtilely.[67]

The anchoress was removed from her anchorhold and placed in a real prison at St. James, Northampton, while Courtenay moved on with his visitation entourage. Returning five days later, he examined Matilda again, and she, having had time to reflect on her errors, answered his questions more humbly, retracting any unorthodox opinions she had held. Courtenay then not only reenclosed her in her reclusorium but also issued a mandate "pro anachorita reducta ad viam veritatis" (for an anchorite returned to the true way), offering forty days' indulgence to those who should come to her assistance.[68]

---

gious Tract Society, n.d.), 3:198–199. Matilda is the only anchorite included in Foxe's work, which speaks to the rarity of anchorite involvement in heretical movements. In general, Foxe's work places anchorites *within* the religious establishment. The testimony of William Thorpe says: "And in all these ungrounded and unlawful doings, priests are partners, and great meddlers and counsellors; and over this viciousness, hermits and pardoners, Ankers and strange beggars, are licensed and admitted by prelates and priests, to beguile the people with flatterings and leasings slanderously against all good reason and true belief; and so to increase divers vices in themselves, and also among all that accept them, or consent to them" (p. 284). See James Crompton, "Leicestershire Lollards," *Leicestershire Archaeological and Historical Society, Transactions* 44 (1968–69): 11–44, for the atmosphere in Leicester and pp. 23–24 for brief discussion of Matilda.

66. Thompson, *Visitations of Religious House*, 1:xxix. For full Latin original see Joseph H. Dahmus, ed., *The Metropolitan Visitations of William Courteney, 1381–1396: Documents Transcribed from the Original Manuscripts of Courteney's Register, with an Introduction Describing the Archbishop's Investigations* (Urbana: University of Illinois Press, 1950), p. 166.

67. Foxe, *Acts and Monuments*, 3:198–199.

68. Dahmus, *Metropolitan Visitations*, pp. 49, 169.

Such a happy resolution is not documented in the case of Anna Palmer, an anchoress whose heresy may have been stimulated by the "pestiferous contagion" of Matilda in prison at Northampton.[69] Bishop Buckingham was the prelate who pursued Anna. He accused her not only of heresy but also of incontinence, since she had allowed a group of male heretics into her anchorhold at night for secret meetings. She denied only incontinence and held firmly to her beliefs. She spent the winter of 1393/94 in Banbury episcopal prison and then was remanded to London for further examination. Here we lose sight of her.

It would be comforting to conjecture that Anna was ultimately restored to her cell at St. Peters and received, like Matilda, the reward of reconciliation, an indulgence. Such a use for an indulgence was but one of several. Whereas Matilda's indulgence takes on the tone of a proclamation to the community of how completely she had been restored to favor by her submission to Courtenay, most indulgences were related to financial need. Bishops used the indulgence to raise immediate funds or to create a financial base for the anchorite. In general, however, indulgences for the benefit of anchorites were not common and the rarity with which they occur (especially compared to the frequency with which they were provided for hermits) indicates that the processing of anchorites with regard to financial security may have been a fairly successful undertaking.[70]

---

69. For the story of Anna Palmer in its larger Lollard context see A. K. McHardy, "Bishop Buckingham and the Lollards of Lincoln Diocese," in *Schism, Heresy, and Religious Protest*, ed. Derek Baker, Studies in Church History 9 (Cambridge: Cambridge University Press, 1972), pp. 131–145, esp. pp. 138–140.

70. Indulgences for hermits were common. A few examples from the fourteenth century: forty days indulgence were granted to the benefactors of St. Wynennus Chapel, Dalston, Cumberland, and its hermit, and those who contributed food for the hermit were considered benefactors of the chapel (*Historical Manuscripts Commission, Ninth Report*, 3 vols. [1883–84], 1:189); a similar indulgence for those who contributed to the maintenance of the hermit of Wragmire, John of Corbridge, who spent his time maintaining the road between Carlisle and Penrith (ibid., p. 192); an indulgence for the repair of the the the bridge and causeway between Great and Little Shelford and for the relief of John Lucas, hermit there (Alfred W. Gibbons, ed., *Ely Episcopal Records* [Lincoln: James Williamson, 1891], p. 400). Fifteenth- and sixteenth-century indulgences were similar.

One anchoress received the proceeds of an indulgence immediately on her enclosure in a new cell in 1337. The indulgence of ten days to all who would contribute to her support was in the nature of a house-warming present and for the purpose of establishing a fund that would support her in the future (*ad subvencionem ejusdem Sibille infra sanctarium ut premittitur incluse de bonis sibi*). Similar in tone was a forty-day indulgence granted for the benefit of Beatrice de Hotham in 1340. She lived in the same cell at St. Peter's, Leicester, from which Matilda would be summarily ejected almost fifty years later. Her indulgence was to provide for her maintenance and for the repair of her house. Two anchorites living together in the churchyard of St. Lawrence Jewry, London, received the proceeds of indulgences in 1368 and 1370. Forty days were remitted both by Archbishop Simon Langham and by the bishop of Winchester, William of Wykeham, for those who helped Richard Swepestone, priest, and Walter Richard, lay, "poor anchorites" (*pauperes anchorite*). Indulgences that did not cite or imply that the anchorites were needy (although they may have been) were granted for the benefit of two women who lived successively at Holy Trinity, Huntingdon, in the early fourteenth century. Another recluse, Edmund Arthur, at St. Mary le Bowe, Sherborne, Dorset, benefited from an indulgence granted by the bishop of Salisbury circa 1396, the same year that he received a substantial bequest in the will of Archbishop Courtenay.[71]

Indulgences, like alms, could help the needy and at the same time indicate to the community the anchorite's value. Using this mighty power, the bishop both accepted and glorified the anchorite. This was one level of a relationship that was complex and multidimensional. A pair of episcopal letters of the early four-

71. Thomas S. Holmes, ed., *The Register of Ralph of Shrewsbury, Bishop of Bath and Wells, 1329–1363*, 2 vols., Somerset Record Society 9–10 (1896), 1:303; LAO Register 5, Burghersh Memoranda, fol. 585v; Alfred C. Wood, ed., *Registrum Simonis de Langham, Cantuariensis Archiepiscopi* [1366–68], CYS 53 (1956), p. 192; T. F. Kirby, ed., *Wykeman's Register*, 2 vols., Hampshire Record Society 9–10 (1896–99), 2:122–123; LAO Register 3, Dalderby Memoranda, fol. 258, fol. 403v; Christopher Wordsworth, "Wiltshire Pardons or Indulgences," *Wiltshire Archaeological and Natural History Magazine* 38 (1913/14): 31. For Arthur's relationship with Courtenay see this chapter below and its note 78. Arthur is one of two specifically named recluses in Courtenay's will.

teenth century brings to light the story of one archbishop and an anchoress in his charge and indicates how personal, how continuing, and how all-embracing such a relationship might be. The anchoress at issue lived in the endowed reclusorium at Doncaster, where she had been enclosed just a few years after an indulgence for the benefit of that reclusorium had been granted. But her needs were of a different sort.

In 1300 an entry in the *sede vacante* register of the see of York noted a request that the abbot of Roche enclose at Doncaster Beatrice, the daughter of Thomas de Hodesack. Her credentials had been formalized and the consent of all who had interest in the matter received. Ten years later Beatrice became the subject of a letter written by Archbishop William Greenfield to the bishop of St. Andrews. Here she was identified as a former nun of Coldstream (in the Scottish diocese of St. Andrews). She had lived in the convent for many years, had run away from it when war seemed imminent in that part of Scotland, and had no wish to return there. Yet she remained without license to have withdrawn: license either of her prelate or her prioress. She lived now in the anchoress's house at Doncaster. Greenfield's tone now turned conventionally philosophical as he mused on how all good shepherds have wandering sheep who escape from their flocks and how zeal must be tempered with compassion to help the erring quiet their fear and return to the sheepfold. The bishop, William de Lamberton, was asked to look into the matter, Greenfield pledging to be guided by his decisions.[72]

Five years later, in 1315, Beatrice was again the subject of a Greenfield letter. This one was addressed to Thomas de Cresacre who was holding the lands and tenements provided for support of the endowed reclusorium at Doncaster. As we have already seen, Thomas was in arrears with his payments to the two anchoresses in residence. After Greenfield admonished Thomas for recalcitrance in paying what was owed, he moved on to describe Beatrice's history and current status. Greenfield wrote that she left Coldstream with the license of her prelate, the diocesan bishop

---

72. Brown, *Reg. J. Romeyn and H. Newark*, 2:322–323; James Raine, ed. *Historical Papers and Letters from Northern Registers*, RS 61 (1873), pp. 196–198.

(William de Lamberton), as well as that of her prioress; that there was just and reasonable cause that she did so; that she entered the Doncaster reclusorium with the license of Thomas Corbridge, formerly archbishop of York, and continued there with his (Greenfield's) permission; and that the convent at Coldstream had been devastated and despoiled during the Scottish wars and was now dispersed, so that Beatrice could no longer return, even had she so desired.[73]

This is a complicated story in which the bishop played many roles—all bearing on his sense of the seriousness of Beatrice's enclosure. We see his desire that it be made ecclesiastically proper, if indeed it was not, and his concern for her physical as well as her spiritual welfare. The letters cover a span of fifteen years. Other sources affirm that Beatrice lived in the cell until 1328.[74] Whatever the initial forces motivating Beatrice to seek the reclusorium, once within it she remained for over a quarter of a century, until her death, and the bishop remained her true friend and concerned spiritual father.

In general, a positive view of the relationship of solitaries to the ecclesiastical network emerges from the registers. Reinforcing that perception are those data indicating the degree to which bishops and other clergy went beyond their mandated responsibilities to anchorites and provided them with pensions and regular support and mentioned them in their wills and testaments. In the twelfth and thirteenth centuries bishops supported recluses in the dioceses of London, Ely, Salisbury, Worcester, York, Exeter, Norwich, Durham, and Canterbury. A reclusory at Loose, Kent, was maintained by the archbishops of Canterbury throughout the thirteenth century. Stephen Langton had granted a charter for corn and "other things" to one Sara de Assinis during his tenure as archbishop. Sara survived Langton and Langton's successor, Richard Grant. Sometime during the tenure of Edmund Rich, the cell at Loose became the retreat of a male recluse, Sara having died. When the archbishopric fell into the hands of the king dur-

73. Raine, *Historical Papers and Letters*, p. 196-198; see also Thompson, *Reg. W. Greenfield*, 2:221.
74. Clay, *Hermits and Anchorites*, p. 94.

ing the vacancy caused by Edmund's death, Henry III paid to that recluse "8 quarters of wheat out of the corn of the manor of Maydenestan and 2 marks of the king's gift yearly for his maintenance as long as the archbishopric is vacant." In 1272 the recluse at Loose was again a woman, her allowance was forty shillings per year out of the fixed alms of the archbishopric, and it was again paid by permission of the king during the vacancy between the incumbencies of Boniface of Savoy and Robert Kilwardby.[75] Although the original grant was probably only a lifetime promise of support for Sara, in effect the cell itself became an endowed entity and the pension transferable to successive anchorites. Each bishop in turn took over the obligation when it devolved on him and then continued the pattern by appointing new anchorites to the site when it became available. In this way the archbishops both honored the appointments of their predecessors and provided obligations for their successors. None, however, terminated the expense when an opportunity arose.

The wills of bishops and other clergy give us a more personal sense of their care and concern for anchorites. The will of Richard Wich, bishop of Chichester 1245–53 and one of the bishops who legislated for anchorites in the thirteenth century, is extant. Written in 1253, it provided bequests for five named anchorites, two male and three female, bequests ranging from forty shillings to five. Close in time and personality to Wich's will was that of Walter Suffield, bishop of Norwich, a friend of Wich's and himself a legatee in Wich's will. Like Wich, Suffield also may have been a legislator for anchorites. Certainly his will shows him as involved with recluses, both as individuals and in general. Suffield left money to six specific anchorites, one of whom was his niece Ela. Another anchorite mentioned was one at Thornham, who held a charter from him. Both of these were probably in his regular gift. His niece received one hundred shillings from him to provide herself with sustenance in her cell; the male anchorite at Thornham received "what had been promised to him by charter." Anchorites

---

75. CR 1227–31, p. 73; ibid., pp. 563–564; CR 1231–34, p. 104; CLR 1240–45, p. 130; CLR 1267–72, p. 239.

at Suffield, Stratton, and Massingham (Ela and her associate were there) received further disbursements ranging from a pound to a mark. Every poor recluse (*inclusus*) in the diocese shared in a gift of ten pounds, and the anchorites of Norwich each received an additional gift of six pence beyond their share of the common legacy on the day of Suffield's burial.[76]

Other bishops left bequests for anchorites as well. Some were diocesan in scope; some contained only specific grants. Thus Bishop Anian II of St. Asaph, Wales, left a hundred cows for pious uses in his 1288 will, defining "pious uses" as those responding to the needs of monasteries, lepers, and anchorites (*inclusi*). John Wakering, bishop of Norwich 1416–25, left an indeterminate sum up to the value of one thousand marks to be shared by anchorites, recluses, and other needy poor throughout his dominion—especially those in rural areas where they might be most indigent. In contrast, Robert Reade, bishop of Chichester 1396–1415, earmarked money for only two anchorites in his will, one an anchorite at Steyning, Sussex (perhaps living in the cell once inhabited by the ill-fated Miliana), and the second none other than that Sir William Bolle whose transfer from the rectory of Aldrington church to a new reclusory at Chichester cathedral has been described. Walter Lyhert of Norwich (1446–72) granted a sum only for one anchoress in Norwich, at a time when there were many other anchorites in that city alone, not to mention the rest of his diocese. A bishop's will was a unique document and one that expressed his own predilections. He clearly was not bound by precedent in this area. His grants could be personal. He could leave bequests to individual anchorites with whom he had a personal

---

76. W. H. Blaauw, "Will of Richard de la Wych," *Sussex Archaeological Collections* 5 (1848): 164–192, esp. 175–177; Blomefield, *Norfolk*, 3:486–492. Father Michael M. Sheehan of the Pontifical Institute of Medieval Studies has generously provided me with a corrected reading of the manuscript of Suffolk's will in which Ela, Suffield's niece, is described as living at Massingham with her *companion* (singular), not *companions* (plural, as Blomefield transcribed [p. 489]). In general on episcopal bequests see Joel T. Rosenthal, "The Fifteenth-century Episcopate: Careers and Bequests," in *Sanctity and Secularity: The Church and the World*, ed. Derek Baker, Studies in Church History 10 (Oxford: Basil Blackwell, 1973), pp. 117–127.

relationship (if indeed he left money to any anchorites at all) or he could remember them in a general way, as a group worthy of some portion of his final alms. He could leave them much or little. The anchorite of Steyning received 6s. 8d. from Robert Reade but William Bolle more than four pounds.[77]

The liberty allowed to bishops in the making of their wills was fully enjoyed by William Courtenay when it came time for him to write that document. Archbishop of Canterbury, a man of importance in the last quarter of the fourteenth century, he had saved Matilda (as well as others) from heretical error. She was then included in his general bequest for anchorites when Courtenay wrote a will that expressed both the wide scope of his office and his choices within it. Leaving aside his gifts to his king, Richard II, his *familia*, and his friends, Courtenay's provincial status was displayed through his gifts to cathedral churches in Exeter, London, and Hereford and to bishops there and in other diocesan seats within his jurisdiction as well as to the archbishop of York. His gifts to convents and friaries were diocesan, with rare exceptions. Every mendicant house in the diocese was granted five marks (66s. 8d.); convents, individually named, received grants of from five to forty pounds, and only two of fifteen were from without the diocese. Paupers coming to his funeral were to get a penny each and ten marks were reserved for the poor in two Canterbury parishes. In this context Courtenay's bequest of forty shillings to every anchorite in his province is remarkable. He further singled out two individual recluses who received additional grants of five marks and forty shillings. Courtenay's will was thus provincial with respect to his bishops and his anchorites, diocesan with respect to convents and friaries, and "parish level" with respect to the poor. His will expressed both his freedom of testamentary distribution and his high regard for the anchorites of his time.[78]

---

77. C. Eveleigh Woodruff, ed., *Sede Vacante Wills*, Kent Archaeological Society, Records Branch 3 (1949), p. 116; *Chichele*, 2:311–314; ibid., pp. 36–41; Blomefield, *Norfolk*, 3:535–538.

78. Leland L. Duncan, "The Will of William Courtenay, Archbishop of Canterbury," *Archaeologia Cantiana* 23 (1898): 58–67.

The bishops and archbishops of medieval England had accepted that responsibility for anchorites demanded by canon law. In many instances they went even further and expressed their esteem for anchorites through their wills and through the support of recluses with diocesan funds. We know that anchorites were only of occasional importance and concern in the overall activity of the industrious medieval bishop with his widespread range of involvements, yet the registers, the wills, and the rolls offer a caring and harmonious picture of the inner workings of these procedures. The problems, sexual and otherwise, that surfaced in the thirteenth-century legislation rarely make their way into the registers, save for the continuing concern over endowments. Anchorite and bishop were secure in a relationship that satisfied the needs of the one and the accountability of the other.

A "canon" ascribed to St. Edmund (Edmund Rich, archbishop of Canterbury 1234–40) which was included in William Lyndwood's fifteenth-century compendium of provincial statutes, the *Provinciale* (ca. 1430), exemplifies the solidification both of the role of the bishop and of the canonical rulings that established that role. Edmund's so-called canon elaborated and defined the contours of episcopal practice with regard to anchorites. It found its way into the *Provinciale* because of its archiepiscopal attribution, but it was written neither by Edmund Rich when archbishop of Canterbury nor, as far as is known, by any other metropolitan legislating for a province, including "Stephen" Mepham to whom it also has been attributed.[79] Unknown before the late fourteenth century, despite its "date" (ca. 1234), its origins remain unidentified. An equal mystery is where Lyndwood found an "Edmund" attribution for this canon, for it does not even appear in any of the manuscripts of "Edmund's *Constitutiones*," which themselves are little more than late fourteenth-century copies of the diocesan

79. William Lyndwood, *Provinciale . . . cui adjiciuntur Constitutiones legatinae . . . Johannis de Anthona* (Oxford, 1679), pp. 214–215 (book 3, title 20), where it is ascribed to Edmund, and *Constitutiones legitime seu legatine regionis anglicane cum subtilissima interpretatione domini Johannis de Athon . . . necnon et constitutiones provinciales . . .* (Paris, 1504), fol. 164va, where it is attributed to Mepham. See Powicke and Cheney, *Councils*, pp. 100–104, 121n, 139–140; Cheney, "Legislation," pp. 389–394; Cheney, "Earliest Statutes," pp. 18–23.

legislation of Bishop Richard Poore. The canon is first found in-
terpolated into various late fourteenth-century texts of Langton's
Oxford Council of 1222, as if emanating from that council, and
subsequently it surfaces in all the fifteenth-century texts of a
series of statutes attributed to Mepham. The Mepham texts,
Christopher Cheney has shown, are late renditions of a set of
synodal statutes written for an unknown English diocese (1222 x
1225) and were formerly known as the *Legenda*. Although at the
present state of scholarship the statute cannot even be considered
legislation, its wide dissemination as such after the late fourteenth
century makes it of considerable interest.

Unlike diocesan statutes that were directed toward the allevia-
tion of specific ills, "St. Edmund's canon" was a summary of good
episcopal procedure and in a general way reflects diocesan problems as articulated in true thirteenth-century legislation. The
canon reads: "We strictly command that neither men nor women
be shut up in any place without special license of the diocesan,
the place, the way of life, the quality of the persons diligently
considered, and from whence they shall be sustained. Moreover, no secular persons shall be received in their houses without
honest and manifest cause."[80] That Lyndwood chose to include
this canon in his compilation is indicative of its importance to
him, for he did not include all the materials that were available.
Moreover, he did not include all the statutes that form the texts,
however spurious, of the *Constitutiones* of Edmund. Thus, the
Edmund attribution alone was not enough to ensure the canon's
inclusion in the *Provinciale*. The gloss Lyndwood provided, of
course, was written in the fifteenth century as exposition of a sup-
posed thirteenth-century statute. On the one hand, the gloss em-
phasizes the continuity of the tradition; on the other, it gives us
an essentially fifteenth-century view of process.

The gloss begins by clarifying that *inclusi* are those commonly
called "anchorites," as that word had become the common one by
the fifteenth century. With respect to the licensing power of the
bishop to create an anchorite, Lyndwood asserted that no one

80. Lyndwood, *Provinciale*, pp. 214–215.

below the rank of a bishop might give such license. Specifically, Lyndwood, citing authorities, stated that no abbot might give license to his own monk to be enclosed (*nec Abbas potest licentiare Monachum suum ut includatur*), although he might (even must: *nec obstat*) give license for a monk's transference to the solitary life. (Was the situation at Bury St. Edmunds and elsewhere under attack here?) With regard to the place of enclosure, of concern was whether it was near or far from a church and whether in the city or the country—it was easier to provide necessities in the city where there were many people than in the country where there were few and where people were commonly poorer and less able to succor such as anchorites. Another kind of place to be considered was one near a monastery, from whose alms an anchorite might be sustained. As to the way of life of the petitioner, his *mores*, Lyndwood encouraged the bishop to investigate whether he was shameful or virtuous, constant or changeable, and whether he had been perfect in the active life: for the contemplative life is harder than the active life, and if the candidate cannot do perfectly what is easier let him not begin what is more difficult. Let the bishop also consider if such candidates may be religious or seculars, clerks or lay, men or women, already expert in a life of austerity or inexpert, young or old.

Lyndwood discoursed extensively on the word *sustenari*. The problem of the sustenance of anchorites was always a primary concern. Lyndwood had already touched on the subject in his analysis of the best sites for reclusoria, but in this gloss he dealt with the problem directly. Anchorites might be enclosed, he explained, if they had their own resources, because, like hermits, they were allowed to have possessions. Lyndwood recommended that others, without such sufficiency, ought not to be enclosed unless they shared certain goods in common, as for example, a monk shared in the goods of the monastery which would perhaps support him in reclusion. Mendicants, Lyndwood noted, have special problems with the idea of guaranteed support. They should be released from the jurisdiction of the bishop in this matter (but only in this one area) and allowed to resolve the issue within their own order. Most particularly, Lyndwood urged that clerics, already subject to episcopal obedience, not be allowed to be enclosed without their own property or the promise of some community to support them, because for them to fall into need would reflect badly on the episcopate: "for precarious mendicity seems to be reprobated in law . . . the reason is that the mendicity of clerics is the ignominy of bishops" (Incerta namque mendicitas videtur in Jure reprobata . . . Ratio est, quia mendicitas Clericorum est ignominia Episcoporum).

Finally Lyndwood addressed the question of who is meant in the phrase "secular persons," those persons who are not to stay or tarry within the confines of the anchorhold. He concluded that it was clerics and not lay persons who were to be understood here. The admonition, then, is a variant of that expressed at Norwich, two hundred years earlier.[81] Lyndwood's gloss is a mirror of fifteenth-century episcopal practice with regard to recluses: such practice had been essentially constant over a two-hundred-year period and would continue for yet another century. St. Edmund's canon was wrongly dated and wrongly ascribed, but it correctly described the English episcopal obligation to anchorites throughout the Middle Ages.

81. Such problems surely had not ended in the thirteenth century. John Mirk's fifteenth-century *Instructions for Parish Priests*, ed. Gillis Kristensson, Lund Studies in English 49 (Lund, 1974), pp. 138–139, inveighs against the parish priest: "Hast thou sinned in lechery, tell me son, how badly . . . and if you have known anchoresses or nuns, widows or wives or any that were vowed to chasity" (my free rendering).

4

Enclosure and Rule: Asceticism and Contemplation

English medieval enclosure ceremonies varied in length and complexity. Some were more dramatic than others, but all concluded with the sealing of the door of the anchorhold after the anchorite had entered. The psychological impact of the walling up of the recluse forces the modern mind to thoughts of incarceration as punishment, the cell as a prison, and the anchorite existence as a living death. All of these themes were in fact accepted and even utilized in the medieval period. It is the modern reaction of bewilderment and even horror that a person could elect such a fate that manifests the cultural distance from the medieval era to our own.

Let it be established at the outset that immuring—the walling up of a live person—was never a form of capital punishment in the Middle Ages. Legends and romantic literature aside, all reasoned and reasonable evidence indicates otherwise. When words and phrases such as *immurata* or "incarcerated between two walls" are used in medieval documents, they describe the strictness of punishment and narrowness of the confinement cell, not a death sentence.[1] Such confinement could be at the hand of the civil or the ecclesiastical judge, and in fact abbots and prioresses "immured" the disobedient in cells deeply imbedded within the convent.[2] It is

1. On this whole subject see Frederic W. Maitland, "The Deacon and the Jewess," *Law Quarterly Review* 3 (1886): 153–165, reprinted in F. W. Maitland, *Roman Cannon Law in the Church of England* (London: Methuen, 1898), pp. 158–79.
2. For such a prison see the story by St. Aelred about the disobedient (and pregnant) Gilbertine nun who was placed in one, chained and fettered: *De sancti-*

solitary confinement that is meant here, not real death—a solitary confinement, however, that was a punishment.

The voluntary solitary confinement of the anchorite could well be likened to a self-imprisonment but was not confused with an actual death sentence by the medieval person; and the ritualistic "dead to the world" mentality the anchorite assumed in the rite of enclosure was not a substitute for physical death.[3] The cell of enclosure, however, was equated with a prison into which the anchorite propelled himself for fear of hell and for love of Christ. The eternal punishment of hell might be escaped by the lifetime refusal of escape from the anchorhold. At the same time union with Christ might be achieved even in this life.

As Jean Leclercq has shown, imprisonment symbolism was widely used in discussions of religious life from the patristic period onward.[4] The martyrs of the first Christian centuries suffered actual imprisonment at the hands of the Romans. Tertullian made a virtue of their sentences, seeing in their enforced separation from the world all the values that ascetic and contemplative life patterns would make their own. As recluses avoided the temptations of the world by enclosure, they at the same time were given the opportunity of extended leisure—an opportunity for prayer. The prison of the martyrs could thus easily be equated with the desert of the prophets and of Christ.

By the seventh century the monastery also was understood as a symbolic prison to which the monk condemned himself. The words *carcer* and *claustrum* were often used as synonyms. To be imprisoned and to be enclosed were linked grammatically, philosophically, and emotionally.[5] If Jerome considered the monastery a provisional

---

moniali de Wattun, PL 195, cols. 789–796. For further discussions of the poor nun, see Giles Constable, "Aelred of Rievaulx and the Nun of Watton: An Episode in the Early History of the Gilbertine Order," in *Medieval Women*, ed. Derek Baker, Studies in Church History, Subsidia 1 (Oxford: Basil Blackwell, 1978), pp. 205–226.

3. *The Ancrene Riwle (The Corpus MS: Ancrene Wisse)*, trans. Mary B. Salu (Notre Dame: Notre Dame University Press, 1955), p. 47, ". . . an anchoress, anointed and buried—for what is her anchor-house but her grave?"

4. Jean Leclercq, "Le cloître est-il une prison?" *Revue d'ascétique et de mystique* 47 (1971): 407–420.

5. In the story of Christina of Markyate (Charles H. Talbot, ed., and trans., *The Life of Christina of Markyate* [Oxford: Clarendon Press, 1959], p. 102), the hidden place where the hermit Roger secretes the anchoress is called a prison: "In hoc

paradise, and in the eleventh century the hermit Guillaume Firmat would repeat that theme, Firmat would also say that when one yielded to temptation the paradisiacal cloister became a prison.[6] The cloister, and more strongly, the anchorite's cell, was designed not only as a place of contemplation but also as a prison. It would ward off the outside world and its temptations as well as punish the individual for the devil's victories over his or her conscious efforts.

Rules for anchorites and enclosure ceremonials employed prison terminology. *Prison* is a pejorative in these documents.[7] The word conjures up the penitential aspects of the dual theme. The emphasis on punishment as opposed to glorification of the rewards of reclusive life is a mark of the Western tradition of Christianity with its strong Celtic influences. George Williams remarks, "Instead of the contemplative cave, for the Celtic monks it was the penitential mission that was most characteristic."[8] The

---

ergo carcere Rogerus ovantem socium posuit." The juxtaposition of the words *prison* (*carcere*) and *happy companion* (*ovantem socium*) makes the dramatic contrast. Robert Hanning, *The Individual in Twelfth-century Romance* (New Haven: Yale University Press, 1977), pp. 223–224, comments on the fundamental polarity of chivalric as opposed to ascetic literature with regard to imprisonment themes. Speaking of the chivalric hero Hanning says, "Imprisonment is especially inimical to the human condition considered as personal quest, for it denies the hero the possibility of seeking the goals that proceed from his private awareness of his current situation and of its distance from his equally personal vision of eventual self-perfection, the final attainment of his greatest desires. . . . This, incidentally, is the key distinction between the inner vision of the romance hero and that of the mystical or devotional experience in the twelfth century: the latter need not find fulfillment in the world outside, indeed cannot."

6. Jean Leclercq, "L'exhortation de Guillaume Firmat," *Analecta Monastica 2, Studia Anselmiana* 31 (1953): 41.

7. See Livario Oliger, ed., "Regula reclusorum angliae et quaestiones tres de vita solitaria, saec. XIII–XIV," *Antonianum* 9 (1934): 56 (Walter's Rule); *Ancrene Riwle*, p. 62; and Leclercq, "Cloître," p. 412, where he summarizes several of Oliger's references.

8. George Williams, *Wilderness and Paradise in Christian Thought* (Cambridge, Mass.: Harvard University Press, 1962), p. 46. Giovanna Casagrande, "Note su manifestazioni di vita comunitaria femminile nel movimento penitenziale in Umbria nei secc. XIII, XIV, XV," *Prime manifestazioni di vita comunitaria Maschile e femminile nel movimento francescano della penitenza (1215–1447)* (Rome, 1982), pp. 462–464, writing of the thirteenth-century Umbrian penitential movement and of the recluses who were part of it, says, "La terminologia usata per qualificare questi *fratres* e *sorores* è quella di *incarcerati* e *religiosi*." A document of 1290 listing sites

penitential mission as a traditional focus is evident in all the sources concerning anchorites until the mid-fourteenth century, when a more positive and mystical wind began to blow.

Enclosure as imprisonment was but one aspect of the enclosure ceremony. The rite of enclosure heralded the beginning of a new life for the postulant. Unlike other rites of passage, however, this was one from which the participant would not reemerge into society. The alteration of self, which the rite both acknowledged and produced, would be wholly internal, not social. As Victor Turner has suggested and Christopher Holdsworth more fully developed,[9] the recluse (as other enclosed religious) entered into a liminal phase, a threshold existence in which he would continue for the remainder of his life.

Initiatory states are typically temporary. They serve to move the individual forward in status or occupation on reintegration into the community. The recluse, however, would fully "cross over" into a new stage and a new status only at death. Denied individuality, sexuality, rank, money, will, and speech—psychologically he became a nonperson rather than a new person. His "conversion" (and the many implications of the word are telling) was profound. The sociologist Erving Goffman, writing about entrance into monasteries (as well as prisons and mental hospitals), says:

The recruit comes into the establishment with a conception of himself made possible by certain stable social arrangements in his home world. Upon entrance, he is immediately stripped of the support provided by these arrangements. In the accurate language of some of our oldest total institutions [monasteries], he begins a series of abasements, degrada-

---

where anchorites were living singly and in groups described its purpose as "pro infrascriptio carceratio seu recluxis." Fourteen of fifty-six women are designated as "in carceribus" at four different sites, perhaps actually using vacant prison cells for their voluntary incarceration. English anchoritism remained much tamer than this, leaving the prison cell to symbolic representation.

9. Victor Turner, The Ritual Process (Ithaca: Cornell University Press, 1969), pp. 94–108, where he ascribes these characteristics to monastic lives in general. Christopher Holdsworth, in an unpublished paper which he has been kind enough to share with me, "Hermits and the Powers of the Frontier," points out that Turner's criteria fit no one so clearly as the recluse.

tions, humiliations, and profanations of self. His self is systematically . . . mortified.[10]

Goffman then goes on to note that the first curtailment of self is induced by the physical barrier of the enclosed situation, which the inmate may not abandon at will.

The recluse, like the monk, welcomed this mortification and this distancing from society and all previously known social roles and experiences. He moved into a new and shadowy existence in which those things most highly valued in secular states would now be denied. As Turner writes, his liminal position prescribed that he had

> no status, property, insignia, secular clothing indicating rank or role, position in a kinship system. . . . It is as though [he were] being reduced or ground down to a uniform condition to be fashioned anew and endowed with additional powers. . . . What is interesting about liminal phenomena for our present purposes is the blend they offer of lowliness and sacredness. . . . Liminality implies that the high could not be high unless the low existed, and that he who [would be] high must experience what it is like to be low.[11]

These are precisely the realities of the solitary and (to a lesser degree) monastic life. Although theoretically the rewards of the contemplative life belong mainly to the next world, entrants into the religious life (in all its manifestations) did undergo a rise in status even though they did not reenter society in a manner that enabled them to use it competitively. The permanent institutionalization of the liminal state (which in tribal society was a temporary condition) should have eliminated all social rewards resulting from change in status. But in fact some of these rewards were garnered by the person who was forever to deny his personality. If his whole life was to be a transitional stage, its realization only in the next world, the recluse was understood to have guaranteed his celestial future. He may have been a nonperson, but he was also a future saint. Like Peter Brown's "holy man,"[12] who shares many

10. Erving Goffman, *Asylums* (Chicago: Aldine, 1962), p. 14.

11. Turner, *The Ritual Process*, pp. 95–97.

12. Peter Brown, "The Rise and Function of the Holy Man in Late Antiquity," *Journal of Roman Studies* 61 (1971): 80–101.

of these liminal characteristics, the anchorite in his cell was revered in his lifetime and financially supported by those who desired to share in his holiness. Knowledge of the reverence with which many of these people were treated was surely a factor in the decision of some to undertake such a life. Walter, in his *Rule*, speaks more than once of the *nomen reclusi*, of the high value placed on it, and of hypocrites who without vocation become recluses to augment their self-esteem. Every recluse, says Walter, is greater than anyone placed in the world or in the cloister, and they who were despised in the world as insignificant are, after their enclosure, venerated and loved as excellent and strong.[13]

Clearly there were psychological rewards available on this earth which made imprisonment and self-effacement palatable for many anchorites. It goes without saying that anchorites would be warned in rules and letters that God's gifts were inversely proportional to those engendered by men's approval and that the devil was likely to be more at home in some cells than Christ. Men could and did become anchorites for less than pure motives. But this is not to deny the true meaning of the life for many individual recluses. A penitential journey was begun but its destination was paradise.

The earliest extant pontifical service for enclosing anchorites dates from the twelfth century and follows this form:[14] The barefoot postulant lies prostrate in the church (in the west end if female, at the entrance to the choir if male, and in mid-choir if a cleric). Two clerks recite the litany while the bishop (or his appointed delegate) and his entourage bless the candidate with holy water and incense. The postulant then receives two lighted tapers. One is given to him by a priest, the other by someone whom he himself has chosen. The tapers and their bestowers represent the love of God and of one's neighbor. There is a scriptural reading. Then, while the sponsors of the postulant lead him to the foot of

---

13. Walter's Rule, p. 71: "The name of the recluse is great beyond that of all other religious." Also pp. 53, 75, 83.

14. Henry A. Wilson, *The Pontifical of Magdalen College*, Henry Bradshaw Society 39 (1910), pp. 243–244. This *ordo* is similar to that found in Lacy's pontifical. These services, as was appropriate in an eternal and catholic church, were not time-bound.

the altar, the clergy chant the *Veni creator*. Kneeling at the altar the postulant recites the verse *Suscipe me Domine* three times and then places his tapers in a candelabra on the altar. Following an explication of the scriptural text by a priest, the congregation is invited to pray for the individual who is about to become enclosed, the *recludendus*. A mass of the Holy Spirit is then celebrated. If the postulant is himself a priest, he may be the celebrant. After the mass the recluse is conducted to his reclusorium while the entourage chants antiphons and psalms drawn from the Office of the Dead; the reclusorium is sanctified with holy water and incense. The officiant then proceeds with the Office of Extreme Unction followed by prayers for the dying. Now the recluse enters the house; the officiant sprinkles him with a little dust to the continued singing of antiphons and psalms; all then withdraw save the priest, who remains with the recluse to tell him to rise and to live by obedience. On the emergence of the officiant the command is given to block up the door of the house: *Obstruant hostium domus*.[15] Two final prayers are said and all then depart in peace.

It was such a rite that Wulfric (the twelfth-century priest-anchorite of Haselbury) had avoided when he entered his cell without episcopal confirmation, but others were more receptive to the ritual formalizing of their new life. Ecclesiastical law prescribed it and the great solemnity of the performance provided a fitting climax to the long process that brought the anchorite to this desired moment. The twelfth-century rite detailed above was but

15. The blocking of the door was a symbolic act. The door remained in most cases the point of access for servants, clergy, and other visitors, all of whom did enter the cell from time to time. Though rules imply that the recluse would communicate with the world solely through his or her windows, I have noted in my discussion of the cell that visitors were permitted when necessary. Bishop Wich (Powicke and Cheney, *Councils*, p. 465) ordered anchorites not to receive persons in their cells whose presence might breed suspicion—implying that others were acceptable—while the bishop of Norwich (ibid., p. 359) decried the practice of clergymen's speaking to anchorites within their cells, again implying a commonplace. Cells with access to an adjoining church may have had two doors; those with gardens needed to provide access to that facility. The situation of Brother Thomas, enclosed at Worth, Somerset, in a cell without a door is unusual (see my chapter 3, p. 78).

one of many used in England during the Middle Ages. Services from later centuries vary considerably both in length and order and project further elements into the ceremony.[16] Some add a requiem mass to the service, reinforcing the dead-to-the-world psychology appropriate to the anchorite[17] and expressing that permanent liminality discussed above. In several rites a habit is granted and blessed; an altar may be consecrated in the reclusorium; the anchorite may be offered communion. In some the anchorite makes a profession of desire: "I, brother or sister N., offer and present myself to the goodness of God to serve in the order of an anchorite; and according to the rule of that order I promise to remain henceforward in the service of God through the grace of God and the guidance of the church and to render canonical obedience to my spiritual fathers."[18]

The Sarum Manual, first published in 1506, contains a preface to its office for the enclosing of anchorites. Touching on many of the themes that are central to this analysis, it is worth reading in full:

In what manner those who approach the order of anchorites ought to approach and to order themselves, that which follows according to the Use of Sarum will make clear. No one ought to be enclosed without the advice of the Bishop: but let him be taught and warned by the Bishop or some other presbyter that he must devoutly examine his own conscience, and in particular whether he desires holiness with a good or bad purpose; if he desires it to please God or to attain wealth or the praise of men; lastly, whether he have strength and endurance of mind to avail against the crafts of the evil enemy and against manifold mischiefs of that sort. When he shall have promised to bear such things for the kingdom of God, and to set his hope on God alone, let the Bishop, or a presbyter by command of the Bishop, enclose him. But, let the one who is enclosed learn

16. Otmar Doerr, *Das Institut der Inclusen in Süddeutschland*, Beiträge zur Geschichte des alten Mönchtums und des Benediktinerordens 18 (Münster: Verlag der Aschendorffschen Verlagsbuchhandlung, 1934), pp. 42–53, discusses and compares several of these services, as well as some Continental ones. He includes Magdalen, described above, both Sarum rituals, and that of Bainbridge.

17. Ralph Barnes, ed., *The Liber Pontificalis of Edmund Lacy, Bishop of Exeter* (Exeter, 1846), p. 136, calls the cell a "sepulchre" as the anchorite enters it.

18. From the Sarum Manual (Clay, *Hermits and Anchorites*, p. 195).

not to think highly of himself, as though he deserves to be set apart from the mass of mankind; but let him rather believe that it is provided and appointed for his own weakness that he should be set far from the companionship of his neighbors, lest by more frequent sin he should both himself perish and do harm to those who dwell with him, and should thus fall into greater damnation. Let him therefore think that he is convicted of his sins and committed to solitary confinement as to a prison, and that on account of his own weakness he is unworthy of the fellowship of mankind. This rule must be observed with both sexes.[19]

With these warnings the recluse was enclosed. At the moment, sure of purpose and carried forth by the inexorable rhythm of the proceedings, he approached his future with love and longing. The sealing of the entrance, however, would bring him to an emotional climax. Then, alone save for his servants, he would begin his new life.

Enclosed in his cell the anchorite had achieved a desired goal. Ideally he was now placed in a setting free of all personal and practical entanglements in which he might wholeheartedly and continuously contemplate God. The contemplation of God is fundamentally the purpose of the solitary life, the penitential aspects of such a life being the preparation for a journey toward a heightened consciousness.

The word *contemplative* has many meanings.[20] In general parlance the contemplative life is juxtaposed to the active life. In scriptural terms it is the choice of Rachel over Leah, of Mary over Martha. The contemplative life can theoretically be led anywhere but is usually identified with the monastery. The monastic life,

19. Ibid., p. 193.
20. For some help in sorting them out, see Jean Leclercq, "Etudes sur le vocabulaire monastique du Moyen Âge," *Studia Anselmiana* 48 (1961): 80–144; Louis Gougaud, "La *Theoria* dans la spiritualité médiévale," *Revue d'ascétique et de mystique* 3 (1922): 381–394; Jean Leclercq, "La contemplation dans la littérature chrétienne latine," *Dictionnaire de spiritualité, ascétique et mystique* (Paris, 1960), cols. 1911–1948; J. M. Déchanet, "La contemplation au XIIe siècle," ibid., cols. 1948–1966; Paul Philippe, "La contemplation au XIIIe siècle," ibid., cols. 1966–1988; and François Vandenbroucke, "La contemplation au XIVe siècle," ibid., cols. 1988–2013.

then, vis-à-vis the secular life, is a contemplative life. Within the monastery itself cloistered monks are "contemplatives" as contrasted to those who are involved in the business of administering the monastery and its resources, here perceived as living an "active" life. In another definition, Carthusian monks are considered "contemplatives" in contradistinction to Benedictines, while yet other scholars and practitioners, narrowing the definition still further, define contemplation only as that experience leading to the mystical state.

Common to all these frames of reference is the perception of the solitary life as providing the greatest opportunity for pursuing the contemplative ideal. Stripped (theoretically) of human contact, dead to the world, the soul would be freest to find its home. The anchorite, enclosed in perpetuity, dedicated to penitence and prayer alone, had elected the purest form of a contemplative life. The recluse, however, would quickly learn that his vocation too was composed of the two ways. The contemplative life of the enclosed anchorite began only after an "active" life during which he accomplished the work of climbing the low, purgative rungs on the ladders of perfection designed for this use. Such activity represented the battle against instinct and demon, the fight against the internal evils of lustful thought and lack of humility and the struggle to overcome the external danger of the powers of the devil.[21] The active life of the anchorite represented the *askesis* that gives its name to a large class of theological literature.

Writings for anchorites are classified as ascetic treatises. They give practical instruction for achieving ultimate Christian goals in this world and the next. Unlike monastic rules, which are demands, rules for anchorites are suggestions and supports. The solitary vocation was always a choice, an individual embrace of a

---

21. For discussion of the devil as the personified and externalized force of evil, see Jeffrey Burton Russell, *The Devil: Preceptions of Evil from Antiquity to Primitive Christianity* (Ithaca: Cornell University Press, 1977), pp. 32–35. See also Russell's second volume on the subject, *Satan: The Early Christian Tradition* (Ithaca: Cornell University Press, 1981), especially chapter 6, "Dualism and the Desert," as well as the recent *Lucifer: The Devil in The Middle Ages* (Ithaca: Cornell University Press, 1984), pp. 290–293.

most difficult choice. One of the manifestations of that choice was its freedom from institutionally imposed restraints. This freedom was also perceived as one of its dangers. "Woe to him who is alone when he falls and has not another to lift him up," said Solomon (Eccles. 4:10). St. Basil, writing for Eastern monks, would repeat the caution in the fourth century. Nine hundred years later Walter would begin his treatise with the same warning.[22] The anchorite was dependent on his own inner strength to sustain his fidelity to his goal. Anxiety about the capacity of a man to persist in his vocation and remain faithful to his vow when freed of the primary Benedictine responsibility of obedience goes far to explain the cautious and even negative attitudes of some ecclesiastical figures toward the solitary life.[23] That anxiety also lay behind the awareness of many anchorites—alone in their cells, exposed to the seduction of anarchy, the perils of hypocrisy, and the risks of heresy—of their need for private works of guidance, a need fulfilled in England many times over.[24]

22. W. K. Lowther Clarke, ed., *The Ascetic Works of Saint Basil* (London: SPCK, 1925), pp. 163–166; Walter's Rule, p. 53.

23. While most medieval writers expressed the notion that the solitary life was superior to the monastic, a few did not. Peter the Venerable, in the Cluniac tradition, was very positive about hermitism; but the Cistercians, St. Bernard especially, and to a lesser degree St. Aelred himself, were unsure, thinking that most individuals were best served in a strict conventual setting. Aelred's ambivalence is expressed both in his letter to his anchorite sister and in a sermon he gave in which he argued against hermitism (*PL* 195, cols. 241–243). For the views of other English Cistercians see the sensitive article by Derek Baker, " 'The Surest Road to Heaven': Ascetic Spiritualities in English Post-Conquest Religious Life," in *Sanctity and Secularity: The Church and the World*, ed. Derek Baker, Studies in Church History 10 (Oxford: Basil Blackwell, 1973), pp. 45–57. For some of the other literature on this subject see D. G. Morin, "Rainaud l'ermite et Ives de Chartres: Un épisode de la crise du cénobitisme au XIᵉ–XIIᵉ siècles," *Revue bénédictine* 40 (1928): 99–115; Jean Leclercq, "Pierre le Vénérable et l'érémitisme clunisien," in *Petrus Venerabilis 1156–1956: Studies and Text Commemorating the Eighth Centenary of his Death*, ed. Giles Constable and James Kritzeck, Studia Anselmiana 40 (1956): 99–120; Jean Leclercq, "Deux opuscules médiévaux sur la vie solitaire," *Studia Monastica* 4 (1962): 93–109; and, for an overview, Pierre Doyere, "Érémitisme en occident," *Dictionnaire de spiritualité, ascétique et mystique* (Paris, 1960), cols. 953–982.

24. Such rules are generally lacking for the Continent. Doerr, *Institut*, and F. Lemoing, *Ermites et reclus du diocèse de Bordeaux* (Bordeaux: Clèdes et Fils, 1953), both attribute their absence to Continental recluses' use of the monastic rule of the convent on which they were dependent, an indication of the different

Writings for anchorites range from the briefest of hortatory and didactic epistles to major ascetic and mystical treatises. Extant English works include the *Liber confortatorius* (ca. 1080), by Goscelin, a Benedictine monk and well-known hagiographer, written for Eve, a former nun of Wilton; two letters of St. Anselm (ca. 1103–1107); Aelred's letter to his sister (ca. 1162); a short treatise by Robert, a priest, for Hugo, an anchorite (between 1140 and 1215); *Ancrene Riwle* (ca. 1220); the Dublin Rule, an anonymous treatise for male anchorites (thirteenth century); Walter's Rule (ca. 1280); the Lambeth Rule, anonymous, for male lay anchorites (thirteenth century); the letter of the fourteenth-century abbot of Bury St. Edmunds; the anonymous *Speculum inclusorum* (early in the second half of the fourteenth century); *The Form of Living* (ca. 1348), by Richard Rolle; and two works by Walter Hilton: *The Scale of Perfection* and a letter for a priest who had become a solitary (both second half of the fourteenth century). (See appendix 2 for specific bibliographic data.)

Often written in epistolary form, most of the major works, no less than the minor ones, seem to have been genuine responses to requests for such a guide. The use of the letter form was of course often no more than a rhetorical device in the Middle Ages, and it is clear that all of the major works were expected to reach a larger audience than the lone anchorites (or three in the case of the *Ancrene Riwle*) to whom they were addressed. Nonetheless, the works of Goscelin and Aelred, the *Ancrene Riwle*, the *Form of Living* by Rolle, and the *Scale of Perfection* by Hilton were created for specific women with whom the writers had previous relationships and the writings carry the meanings of those relationships forward. The tone of these works is personal, individual, and often loving. The five treatises just named compose the major works among the anchoritic writings in length, literary quality, and fame. The three Middle English rules (*Ancrene Riwle*, the *Form*, and the *Scale*) are the central works around which theories of the continuity of Middle English prose have been developed. This literature represents almost an embarrassment of riches, yet that

---

face of English anchoritism. Lemoing says: "La claustration totale était pour elles [the Bordelaise recluses] un supplément de pénitence, non un changement d'idéal monastique" (p. 115).

the heights of the vernacular prose literary tradition in medieval England were reached in writings for anchorites is of major significance in this study.[25]

Whether a brief letter or a two-hundred-page *libellus*, all of this literature directs itself to the proper ordering of the life of the anchorite, and through this literature we can construct a model of the anchorite's life (albeit an idealized one). The writings offer explicit pastoral instructions on daily household routines (Aelred, *Ancrene Riwle*, Lambeth, the Bury St. Edmunds fourteenth-century letter), suggestions and support for the struggle against temptations (Anselm, Goscelin, *Ancrene Riwle*, Aelred, *Speculum*), meditations (Aelred, Walter), and further directions as aids leading to the mystical state (*Speculum*, Rolle, Hilton). This material is usually organized into what was called the outer rule (the formal daily regimen) and the inner rule (the guide to the achievement of that inner purity for which the outer rule existed). In beautiful literary form the outer rule consists of the first and last chapters of the *Ancrene Riwle*[26] and physically surrounds the remaining chapters that deal with inner asceticism.

The shorter works usually limit themselves and do not try to cover the whole ground. Thus Anselm, when asked for advice,

25. Mary Byrne, *The Tradition of the Nun in Medieval England* (Washington, D.C., 1932), pp. 56–67, notes from another point of view that in the thirteenth century Latin didactic literature praising perfect feminine behavior ceased to center on the "ideal nun" as exemplar and that the English anchoress replaced the nun as the model of chastity and virtue in that literature.

26. The literature on the *Ancrene Riwle* is vast and no attempt will be made to summarize it here. Geoffrey Shepherd's introductory remarks in his edition of the work, *Ancrene Wisse: Parts Six and Seven* (New York: Barnes and Noble, 1959), remain an excellent analysis. A more recent work by Janet Grayson, *Structure and Imagery in Ancrene Wisse* (Hanover: University Press of New England, for the University of New Hampshire, 1974), also is worthwhile. Linda Georgiana, *The Solitary Self: Individuality in the Ancrene Wisse* (Cambridge, Mass.: Harvard University Press, 1981), takes a new perspective. Alexandra Barratt, "Anchoritic Aspects of Ancrene Wisse," *Medium Aevum* 49: 1 (1980): 32–56, picks up on some of Dobson's points. Let me note that "Ancrene Riwle" means "Rule for Anchoresses," "ancrene" being the genitive form of the Middle English word for anchoress. "Ancrene Wisse" means "Guide for Anchoresses," and it was, as is noted in my appendix 2, the title given to the work in one of its main revisions. "Ancrene Wisse" is considered by many authorities to be the "correct" title, the one indicated by the author himself.

directed his remarks to the inner life and temptation. He wrote to the women under Robert's care:

Most beloved daughters, all action is laudable or reprehensible as it possesses praiseworthiness or evil qualities from the manner in which it was willed. For truly indeed, the root and origin of all acts that are in our power is in the will; and if what we wish is not possible, one is still judged before God according to one's volition. Therefore, be unwilling to consider so much what you may do, but what you should desire; not so much what should be your tasks, but rather what is your inclination. . . .[27]

With regard to temptation of thought, Anselm then wrote:

Be unwilling to dispute with perverse thoughts or perverse desires; but when they have infested you, occupy your mind, most rigorously, with some useful thought or desire until these others disappear. For a thought or desire will never be expelled from the mind if not by another thought or another wish that is not in harmony with it. . . . When, however, you wish to pray or to turn to some good meditation: if unsuitable thoughts that you ought not to hold are yet with you, never on account of the unsuitableness of these do you wish to bring down the good that you have in hand, lest the instigator of these things, the devil, rejoice because he has caused you to break loose from a good beginning. . . . Neither shall you be sad or suffer concerning the infestation of these things, as long as you offer to them, as I have said, no approbation along with your despising, lest they return to memory once more on an occasion of sadness and renew their importuning. For the mind of man has this habit, that when either happy or sad, it often returns to a memory that it felt or thought to be negligible.[28]

And with regard to temptations of the flesh:

One ought to regard oneself as a zealous performer in a holy way of life in coping with any indecent impulses whether of the mind or of the body, whether it is a stimulation of the flesh, or of anger, or of envy, or of empty glory. For then they will be extinguished more easily, since we refuse to be willing to feel them, or think about them, or to enhance their importance by means of persuasion. . . .[29]

27. Anselm, *Sancti Anselmi opera ominia*, ed. F. S. Schmitt, 6 vols. (Edinburgh: Thomas Nelson and Sons, 1946–61), 5:360, lines 13–18.
28. Ibid., pp. 360–361, lines 35–52.
29. Ibid., p. 361, lines 53–57.

In contrast to this kind of spiritual letter, that of the abbot of Bury St. Edmunds to his male recluse was a purely formal summary of rules and regulations to govern daily routine. The recluse was to say the hours; read, meditate, and pray in lieu of manual work; practice silence from compline to sunrise; eat no flesh; and in general obey what was a standard set of directions that parallels Aelred in most instances but is less demanding. The abbot, after counseling moderation, finally concluded:

Beyond this, for the conquering of your flesh, especially when you feel the law of your members which is repugnant to the law of your mind, we concede to you the faculty of afflicting your body with a hairshirt. So, dearest brother, this conversation of the outward man, not for the fervid ones of antiquity but for the lukewarm men of this modern time, we hand over to you at your instance and request, for your obedience.[30]

The outer rule in this and in the major works of Aelred and *Ancrene Riwle* details a complete, Benedictine-based regimen for daily life. The outer rule describes appropriate dress, food, time and manner of sleeping, fasts, vigils, the saying of the canonical hours, and the alternation of prayer, reading, and work.[31] It can proclaim the size of the cell, the meanness of its decoration, the open sepulchre within it.[32] It decrees silence. It limits the number of the recluse's servants and describes his proper relations with them. It prohibits the recluse from teaching children. It warns him against receiving the care of secular things. Hair cutting, blood letting,

30. Antonia Gransden, "The Reply of a Fourteenth-century Abbot of Bury St. Edmunds to a Man's Petition to Be a Recluse," *English Historical Review* 75 (1960): 467.

31. Neither the Bury St. Edmunds letter nor Walter's Rule demands work. Walter specifies prayer, reading and meditation as his trio (p. 75).

32. Aelred, *De institutis inclusorium*, ed. C. H. Talbot, *Analecta Sacri Ordinis Cisterciensis* 7 (1951): 196–197; Walter's Rule says: "The sepulchre of the recluse shall always be open so that day and night he may see where he will go" (p. 68). The practice of an open sepulchre within the cell was more severe than the symbolic "anchorhold as grave" expression of the *Ancrene Riwle*, and although it was common in early extant Continental rules, this is the sole English rule that assumes this will be the situation. Where the practice was followed, the anchorite often used the sepulchre as a bed. A cell excavated at Compton, Surrey, held the skeletons of two males, probably thirteenth-century anchorites who had been buried in their anchorhold (*VCH Surrey*, 3:21–23).

frequency of confession and receiving of the Eucharist—all these are in the province of the outer rule.

Aelred, *Ancrene Riwle*, the Dublin Rule, and Walter's Rule were written between 1160 and 1280. Two composed for women, two for men, they cover the themes that are central to the vocation. *Ancrene Riwle* is gentler than Aelred, more celebratory of female recluses. Dublin is more matter-of-fact than Walter, who like Aelred is harsh and critical of improper hypocritical anchorites. But if for the purpose at hand an attempt is made to read out the passion and the bias of the individual writers, the rules tell much the same story. Moderation is the major theme. Great asceticism is neither desired nor desirable: it leads to pride. Moderation, an even keel, and perseverance are to be sought. Moderation in food: fish is allowed and wine tolerated; moderation in dress: linen is allowed for underclothing and hair shirts only tolerated; moderation in speech: silence is preferred, but speech is accepted under controls.

Speech is to be controlled by two methods: positively, through establishing a Benedictine schedule that sets out in detail when each anchorite may or may not speak; negatively, by impressing the anchorite with the dangers of frequent and loose conversation. So important an issue was the regulation of speech to Aelred that he addressed it in the first chapter of his letter to his sister from both positive and negative directions.[33] Advising the anchoresses who would use his rule to organize their day about the monastic *horarium*,[34] Aelred prescribed that they rise before dawn but remain silent until after prime (about 6:45 A.M. in the winter *horarium*). After prime the recluse might speak to her servants briefly concerning the needs of the day; then she was to remain silent until after terce (8:00 A.M.). Between terce and none (1:30 P.M.) she was allowed to speak with visitors and deal further with her servants. Dinner came after none when speech was further

---

33. Aelred, *De institutis* pp. 179–183.

34. For a description of the monastic *horarium* (from which I have marked approximate hours in the text), see David Knowles, *The Monastic Order in England: From the Times of St. Dunstan to the Fourth Lateran Council, 940–1216*, 2d ed. (Cambridge: Cambridge University Press, 1966), pp. 714–715.

proscribed until vespers (4:15 P.M.). Between vespers and collation (6:00 P.M.) she was again allowed to speak with her attendants. During Lent the recluse was to speak with no one, if possible, but certainly only to her servants and confessor, except if some notable person had come from a considerable distance. And so on. The times allotted to speech, however, were not to be spent that way unless necessary. Speech took the anchorite away from the process of internalization that was the major concern of contemplative life.

Speech was more than just an intrusion in a contemplative life. It was a true danger, a cancer that could eat away the individual's will; it could expose the recluse to that repressed sexuality constantly striving to reemerge as well as to more commonplace evil. In the opening remarks of his letter Aelred attacked the gossiping anchoress, already a stereotype in 1160 and one of his prime concerns:

It is rare these days to find any recluse alone before whose window does not sit an old garrulous woman, often a rumor-monger, who occupies the anchoress with stories and feeds her with scandal and slander. The old woman describes the form, the face, and the mannerisms of this or that monk or cleric, or of a man of any other order. Interspersing every allurement, she depicts the lasciviousness of girls, the liberty of widows who are allowed whatever they desire, the sly wife who deceives her husband, blinding him to her voluptuous behavior with other men. Meanwhile, the recluse is dissolved with raucous laughter, which, like a drug that has the sweetness of drink, is then diffused throughout her whole body. So, when the hour compels them to leave each other, the recluse withdraws, burdened with her sensual thoughts; the old woman, burdened with victuals. Quiet returns. The anchoress, wretched, draws in those things that she has heard. She turns over their images in her heart; she rekindles the fire ignited by her previous conversation. As if intoxicated, she staggers during psalms, she is dazed during reading, she sways during prayers.[35]

Ancrene Riwle is less dramatic but no less passionate in its defense of the virtues of silence: An anchoress ought not to chat with her visitors, setting herself up as a scholar, "teaching those

35. Aelred, *De institutis*, p. 178.

who have come to teach her, and [wishing] to be soon recognized and known among the wise . . . she is foolish, for she is looking for esteem and instead she incurs blame."[36] The anchoress is urged to keep silence on every Friday, with greater restrictions in weeks with ember days and in Lent. She is to stop her ears against evil speech, the worst forms of which are heresy, downright lying, backbiting, and flattery, though, thanks to God, heresy is not a problem in England. Backbiting and flattery are the worst of these kinds of "venomous speech" and constitute a genuine danger to anchorites:

The flatterer's work is to cover the privy-hole; he does this whenever, by his flattery and praise, he conceals people's sin (than which nothing stinks worse) from themselves; he hides it and covers it in this way, so that the sinner does not smell it. The backbiter uncovers it and so lays open the filth that it stinks far and wide. And so they are always busy about this foul work, and each works against the other.[37]

Repeating Aelred's stereotype, the *Riwle* concludes its long section on the virtues of silence: "It is said of anchoresses that almost every one of them has some old woman to feed her ears . . . so that there is now a saying: 'From mill and from market, from smithy and from anchor-house one hears the news.'"[38]

Aelred's imagery is genital, *Ancrene Riwle*'s is anal; both are horrified by the excitement engendered by oral communication. In contrast, the Dublin Rule takes a pragmatic tone: moderate the tongue against foolishness, two-facedness, anger, sinful talk, deceit, sexual innuendo, backbiting; love silence, fear to speak, be wholly silent three days of the week. Walter's concern is minimal, but even he expects restricted speech at all times, including during meals, and in this all his fellow authors agree.[39]

The concern over the danger of speech demonstrated in each of these rules takes us to the heart of many of the problems the

36. *Ancrene Riwle*, pp. 28–29. In general, pages 28–39 deal with the problems of speech.
37. Ibid., p. 37.
38. Ibid., p. 39.
39. Livario Oliger, ed., "Regulae tres reclusorum et eremitarum Angliae, saec. XIII–XIV." Antonianum 3 (1928): 176–178 (Dublin Rule); Walter's Rule, p. 67.

outer rules seek to define. Essentially the rules address the issue of how the recluse deals with the outside world—a world that constantly impinges on his reclusion. It is paradoxical that so much energy needed to be directed to this problem when in theory the recluse was beyond this world. In fact, the recluse remained part of the fabric of the community in which he or she lived and sometimes of the larger world as well. The rules thus sought to control and organize the anchorite's intercourse with that community—not because intercourse should have existed but because it did. Walter describes the frequent interaction between an anchorite and the parishioners of the church in which he was enclosed. Making his favorite comparison of false anchorites with hypocrites, Walter derides those who would pray standing in the corner of the streets (Matt. 6:5) for "what is a house of enclosure if not a street corner since all of every age and sex have constant recourse to the church."[40]

Anchorites could and did serve many purposes within their communities beyond the purely intercessionary one that was their raison d'être. Henry Mayr-Harting has analyzed the functions of the famous Wulfric of Haselbury in his setting: he was an arbitrator, a healer, a prophet, a dispenser of poor relief, perhaps even a primitive banker.[41] All of these roles were common to other anchorites as well, female as well as male. They gave excess alms to the poor. Their cells were used to harbor precious goods. Their visions were interpreted to clarify the future. Some anchorites were active as patrons to others, using their influence to gain them favors, aiding them in lawsuits. Some were in touch with the currents of their day: Loretta of Hackington supported the mendicants when they first arrived in England in the early thirteenth century; Matilda of Leicester was contaminated by heresy in the fourteenth century; in the sixteenth century Katherine Mann of Norwich was a correspondent of Thomas Bilney, and Christopher

40. Ibid., p. 58.
41. Henry Mayr-Harting, "Functions of a Twelfth-century Recluse," *History* 60 (1975): 337–352.

Warner of Canterbury found himself drawn into the Nun Barton episode. Westminster anchorites advised kings.[42]

While all of these roles brought anchorites into contact with the world (and such contact was to be avoided), some roles had more redeeming value than others and these were tolerated, even exploited. Most acceptable was the use of priest-anchorites as confessors. Less acceptable and of great concern to the rule writers (as it was also for the legislators) was the use of the anchorhold to store valuables. Walter wrote:

> Let no one receive the care of secular things, because they draw much to one's perils. For certain men were killed by robbers for the valuables left in their care; the robbers were overcome with desire for these things and carried them off. Indeed, the responsibility for such things is exceedingly incongruous for a holy man, for he who is anxious over his responsibility of protecting money will not be without reproach.[43]

Anchorholds were an ideal place to store precious goods, money, and papers in an era when there were no banks and few places for the safekeeping of valuables. The sanctity of the reclusory made it a place beyond easy access (the depositor hoped). The cell of Joan, the anchoress of Blyth who was to have a difficult old age, was used as a safe deposit in 1241. In a complicated situation involving a theft, she became the intermediary through whom the stolen goods were retrieved and delivered to the king. But the reclusorium was not sufficiently sacrosanct to some whose concern for their souls was at best second to their lust for treasure. Walter's knowledge of robbers who had broken into the cells of anchorites is but an echo of an entry found in the annals of Tewkesbury, where in 1226 the chronicler noted a breaking into the reclusorium of Ashurst, Gloucestershire. Bishop Richard Wich disallowed

---

42. For Loretta and Christopher Warner, see text below and chapter 4, notes 64–66. Matilda has been discussed in the previous chapter. For Katherine Mann, see James Gairdner, "A Letter concerning Bishop Fisher and Sir Thomas More," *English Historical Review* 7 (1892): 712–715; John Foxe, *The Acts and Monuments of John Foxe*, ed. Josiah Pratt, 4th ed., 8 vols. (London: Religious Tract Society, n.d.), 4:642; and Clay, "Further Studies," p. 79.

43. Walter's Rule, p. 77.

(save in necessity) even the keeping of church vestments in the anchorholds of women, but clearly this was common. Both *Ancrene Riwle* and the Dublin Rule addressed the issue of the care of things, the *Riwle* saying: do not keep other people's things in your house, dear daughters, possessions, clothes, chests, deeds, accounts, indentures, the church vestments or vessels, unless necessity or violence compels it, or great fear. The Dublin Rule *commanded* (a word of unusual intensity) that no anchorite put his "own warranty between men as security or as pledge or as witness" and furthermore threatened the anchorite that God would punish him with death if he sheltered the money of another or anything of value, even the church vestments.[44]

The use of anchorhold as treasury was a natural social response to the pressures for finding safe places and originated out of its simple convenience. In the same way, the use of the anchorite as schoolteacher was reasonable, especially in an age when few were literate and such resources not likely to be squandered. This concern dates from the earliest days (even Grimlaic had discussed it),[45] and Aelred, *Ancrene Riwle*, and Walter all argued against the involvement of anchorites with children. "An anchoress must not turn into a schoolmistress, nor turn an anchorhouse into a school for children ... an anchoress ought to give her attention to no one but God," says the author of the *Riwle*.[46] Walter too saw the care of children as a danger to a life of discipline. Care of boys will cause the recluse to weaken his high resolve. He will be drawn into the cares of his students, into their difficulties. He will become angry at their dissolute behavior. His mind will be distracted from its fundamental purpose.[47] Aelred is the most poignant of all in his analysis:

44. CR 1237–42, p. 282; Reginald T. Timson, ed., *The Cartulary of Blyth Priory*, 2 vols., Thoroton Record Society 27–28 (1973), 1:cx–cxi; Henry R. Luard, ed., *Annales monastici*, 5 vols., RS 36 (1864–69), 1:68; Powicke and Cheney, *Councils*, p. 465; *Ancrene Riwle*, p. 185; Dublin Rule, pp. 177, 179–180.

45. Grimlaic, *PL*, col. 644.

46. *Ancrene Riwle*, p. 188.

47. Walter's Rule, p. 78.

Concerning boys and girls, let none have access to you. There are some recluses who are kept busy teaching girls and they turn their cell into a school. The anchoress sits at her window. The girls stay on the porch. She looks upon them, one by one, and watching the interactions among them, now she is angry, now she laughs, now she threatens, now caresses, now strikes, now kisses, now she calls forth tears with her own words. She caresses the face, she touches the neck, and falling into embrace now calls one daughter, and friend. Where is the thought of God in all this . . . ?[48]

Boys are considered too bad to be safe, girls too good and loving. Both took the anchorite's mind from where it belonged: focused on God alone. Both exposed the recluse to worldly and sexual feelings, feelings that needed to be controlled.

The discipline of the outer rule is presented as a guide and a protection. Both the recluse's own physical desires and drives and the demands of the community are to be rejected in favor of a format for a daily life whose rhythms, once established, will be the first step in the process of the chastisement and subjugation of the body—the ultimate purpose of which is to free the soul. Outer rules attempt to control social behavior in order to free the anchorite from the accustomed patterns of his life, to break down the social man and release the spiritual man within. Outer rules deny to the recluse those social amenities that create normal personal and communal relationships and help him to channel his energies inward. Outer rules try to protect the anchorite from the lures of the secular world and then teach the active life of the solitary *conversatio.*

Ascetic disciplines—hunger, fatigue, self-flagellation, hair shirts —are embraced and have multiple purposes. Primarily, the systematic and routine denial to the body of its instinctual satisfactions has as its goal the transformation of carnal desires into spiritual ones. At the physiological level, the purgative process may debilitate the body to the point that at least temporarily it no longer responds as before to instinctual stimuli.[49] In addition, the *askesis*

48. Aelred, *De institutis,* p. 180.
49. Ibid., pp. 190–193. Aelred says in these chapters that such deprivation is purposeful and good with this end in mind. Psychologically, sublimation should be

113

supports that penitential mentality made evident in the ritual for the enclosing of anchorites. Finally, the punishing process called purgation is likened to self-martyrdom, a reliving and a sharing of Christ's agony through the individual's own. All of these levels of meaning interact and reinforce one another. In some rules penitential aspects are much the strongest motif. In others, which focus more on spiritual rewards, the purgative theme fades from central view and its impact is softened. Whatever the major emphasis of the particular work, however, all of these themes are present in some measure.

The outward aspects of conduct, subject to verbal control and observation, concerned with behavior and discipline, form the topical material of the outer rules. The inner rules direct themselves to the struggle against vice and temptation. Interior prayer and meditation are their techniques and the nature of the approach to God their ultimate lesson. The purpose of all these rules, inner and outer, is to aid in effecting that transformation of self that, with God's grace, will take the recluse up the ladder that reaches to Him. But the documents written in the eleventh, twelfth, and thirteenth centuries approach the ascent of that ladder only in a tentative and furtive manner. In such works as Goscelin's *Liber*, Aelred's *Letter*, and the *Ancrene Riwle*, the achievement of the mystical moment is mentioned only in passing and is cloaked in obscure language or hidden in a cipher of didactic discourse. The mysticism is there, but the verbal key must be known, for the words describing the ultimate human experience are so understated as to blur their own meaning. At most Aelred, *Ancrene Riwle*, and Goscelin offer the barest suggestion of a chaste happening. They do not proclaim an ecstasy.[50]

---

a mental process made in health. Aelred here takes away mental achievement as a method of control over the individual's desires and substitutes a body so exhausted that of its own it will not desire.

50. See Charles H. Talbot, "Godric of Finchale and Christina of Markyate," *Month* (May 1963): 26–31, for discussion of these themes. The question, however, that Talbot does not discuss is why this literature is so ambiguous. In the twelfth century there was much overt mystical writing. Yet when it came time to direct a work to anchorites, or at least to female anchorites, the tone is penitential and only minimally mystical. In contrast, a work such as *The Golden Epistle* of William of St. Thierry (*The Works of William of St. Thierry*, Cistercian Fathers Series [Kalama-

1. ENCLOSURE OF AN ANCHORESS. By permission of Corpus Christi College, Cambridge. The Pontifical of Richard Clifford, CCCC MS 79, fol. 96a (formerly fol. 72a). An anchoress receives the final benediction of the bishop.

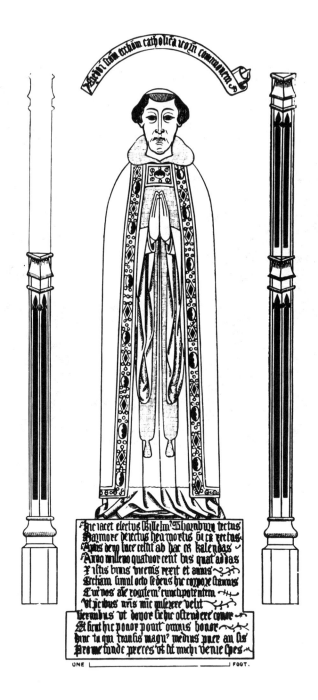

 One |_____| Foot.

2. BRASS OF WILLIAM THORNBURY, PRIEST-ANCHORITE, FAVERSHAM, KENT.
  Here William Thornbury, the elect, lies hidden,
  Cast 'neath the stone, and by death's might o'er ridden.
  On March the twenty-third he life gave o'er,
  The fourteen hundredth year with eighty more.
  Years twenty two his rule this church invested,
  Years eight, in cells hard by, his limbs he rested.
  Now to th' Almighty let our prayers be said,
  That on his soul He mercy deign to shed.
How I to worms am given a prey, I thus endeavour to display;
And as I here am slowly laid, lowly must every glory fade.
O thou, in passing pilgrimage, in youth, in manhood, or in age,
Pour, for my sake, a prayer of thine that hope of pardon may be mine.

(Trans. from "Anchorites in Faversham Churchyard," *Archaeologia
Cantiana* 11 [1877]).

3. SIR PERCIVAL ARRIVES AT HIS AUNT'S RECLUSORIUM. By permission of
the British Library. *Roman du Saint Graal*, B.M. MS Royal 14 E. III, fol. 101v.

4. A Fourteenth-Century Reclusorium. By permission of the British Library. Marginal drawing from B.M. MS Royal 10 E. IV, fol. 181.

5. The Pageant of Richard Beauchamp. By permission of the British Library. The Pageants of Richard Beauchamp, BM Cotton MS Julius E. IV. The text of this pageant, number 47, reads: Here shewes howe Kyng Henry was after crowned Kyng of Fraunce at Seynt Denys besides Parys. Of the which coronacion in Fraunce and also the said Erle to haue the rule of his noble persone vnto he were of the age of xvj. yeres, it was the will and ordenaunce of Almyghty God, as our blessed Lady shewed by revelacion vnto Dam Emme Rawhton, Recluse at all halowes in Northgate strete of York; and she said that thorowe the Reame of Englond was no persone, lorde ne other, like to hym in habilite of grace and true feithfulnesse to vertuously norisshe and gouerne his noble persone accordyng to his Roial astate. Also she put greet commendacion, by the ordenaunce of God, of his greet benefytes in tyme to come of devowt commers to þe place of Gye clif, oþerwise called Gibclyff, which in processe of tyme shal growe to a place of greet worship, oon of þe moost named in Englond.

Here shewes howe kyng Henry was after crouned kyng of Fraunce at Seynt
Denys besyde parys. Of the whiche coronacion in Fraunce and also that sayd
Erle to haue the rule of his noble psone vnto he were of the age of xxj yeres
it was the will & ordenince of almyghty god and is blessed lady shewed by Relacion
vnto Dame Emme Raldhood Recluse at att hulswre in Northgate strete of york
and she sayd that there was the Reame of Englond was no psone to do in othe-
like to hym in habilite of grace and true fauthfulnesse to vertuously worsshp & gouerne
his noble psone accordyng to his Royal astate Also thys pute great commendacion by
the ordenance of god of his great benefitts in tyme to come of Robert conuert to ye place of

Rye clif enprwse called Cukclyff whiche in
passe of hyme shal growe to a place
of great Worshyp and ye
moost in mid in Englond

6. Brass of Dame Joan Clopton, Anchoress, Quinton, Gloucester-shire. The brass of Lady Joan Clopton at Quinton Church who became an anchoress upon the death of her husband, Sir William Clopton, ca. 1420. She herself died in December 1430. The legend surrounding the brass states that her husband desired her to become an anchoress upon his death: *"Que tibi sacrata clauditur hic vidua milite defuncto sponso pro te ihu fuit ista."*

7. JOHN LACY IN HIS RECLUSORIUM. By permission of the Bodleian Library. John Lacy's codex, MS St. John's College 94, fol. 16v. In a self portrait, Lacy shows himself dressed in a Dominican habit, leaning through the grille that bars the doorway of his reclusory. Rapt in a vision of the Passion, the Virgin Mary and a Disciple on either side of the Rood (partially defaced), Lacy exclaims "*Christe, lacy fratris animae misere.*"

In marked contrast to this early literature, the works of the second half of the fourteenth century, most notably Rolle's work and Hilton's *Scale* but including also the anonymous *Speculum*, lead the anchorite toward mystical union with God in explicit and joyous terms. Here the purgative way is clearly only a beginning. The teaching of the outer rule has effected transformation. Purification now overtly leads to illumination and then to union. The goal of the contemplative life is stated and embraced.

Anchorites in the eleventh, twelfth, and thirteenth centuries were described as ascetics in their own literature and it was only with the flowering of mysticism in the fourteenth century that this focus changed. Soon a similar change can be noted in a strikingly different group of sources. The shift of emphasis in the literary tradition—the expectation that the anchorite will be a contemplative as well as a penitential ascetic—is paralleled in the episcopal registers and the royal rolls of the fifteenth century. The change is one of nuance and vocabulary. A different mood is projected. Whether the change of emphasis in the sources represented a fundamental change in the absolute reality of the anchorite life is an open question, but for the moment let us trace this transformation.

The entries in the rolls and registers that delineate the procedural steps necessary to become an anchorite are verbal expositions of the social and hierarchal mores of the period. They define not only what is expected of recluses but also what is proper to express concerning those expectations at any particular moment in time. They create a perceptual base against which other indicators of change can be measured.

In the thirteenth century both rolls and registers note transactions concerning anchorites in forms that are brief and legalistic. Henry III's rolls abound in references:

1234—The Lord king concedes and gives license to Emma of Skepeye to enter into the reclusorium next to the church of St. Mary, within the Dover Castle, and to cause herself to be enclosed (*recludi*) in it.[51]

---

zoo, Mich.: Cistercian Publications, 1976]), written for Carthusian monks, takes one directly to the mystical after the purgative is done.
51. *CR 1231–34*, p. 473.

1242— . . . yielding to the prayers of Alice, the bearer, who has made a vow to serve God in some solitary place, the king has granted that on the north side of the church of St. Budhoc, Oxford, she may build herself a cell (*reclusorium*) where she may for her life serve God and the Blessed Virgin.[52]

1241—The king gives to Br. Nicholas a pension of two pence per day . . . out of the fixed alms of the king, to sustain him in divine service (*obsequio*).[53]

1250—The king concedes, in the name of charity, to Christine, daughter of Henry of Sumerford, that reclusorium which is under the town wall of Malmesbury; so that in that place she may stay as an anchorite (*inclusam*) perpetually.[54]

1267—Whereas Maud Malet desires to serve God perpetually in a cell (*reclusorio*) under the church of St. Dunstan, which church belongs to the House of Converts without London, the king, thinking it to be pious to accede to her wishes, commands Adam de Cestreton his clerk, master of the said house and the converts inhabiting there, that having first received security for their indemnity, and for the preservation of the said church, they shall assign to her there some fit place which she can build upon and inhabit, provided that she bears herself honourably.[55]

Two entries in the register of Walter Giffard, archbishop of York, also in the year 1267, establish the ecclesiastical tone. Giffard will allow the construction of a house for Alice de Folkton in the churchyard of St. Nicholas of Hedon "in qua vitam anacoritam ducere possit" (in which she can lead an anchoritic life). The second entry is slightly more expansive. An anchoress is described as seeking a hermitage in Nottingham and the archdeacon there is enjoined by the archbishop to aid her to find one in which "she will be able to lead an anchoritic life in perpetuity, thus serving God more freely (*liberius*)."[56] The vocabulary of these entries is

---

52. CPR 1232-47, p. 275.
53. CR 1237-42, p. 296.
54. CR 1247-51, p. 314.
55. CPR 1266-72, p. 84.
56. William N. Brown, ed., *Register of Walter Giffard, Lord Archbishop of York, 1276-1279*, SS 109 (1904), pp. 118, 108.

limited. The participants desire to become anchorites, which is equivalent to serving God, under closure, and in perpetuity.

The registers of subsequent archbishops of York provide additional terms in their entries about anchorites, demonstrating that while we are dealing with legal forms and legal formalities the language is not completely fixed. In 1280 Lady Joan was described as leading a "religious life as a solitary." Six years later Agnes Muscegros received a license from Archbishop Romeyn to live "honestly and chastely . . . under closure." And, in a somewhat more somber tone, in 1293 Romeyn gave permission to another Agnes, "a virgin, . . . to enter into an honest cell, next to the church [at Kirkburton, Yorkshire], having cast away worldly pleasures, where she, as a solitary anchorite, desires to attend divine service, and to live as a penitent of God." Solitary, chaste, penitent: the new words reinforce but do not move forward or alter the simple ascetic conception.[57]

Few verbal elements enter episcopal or royal notices for the next fifty years. The phrase *affectat Domino famulari* or its equivalent *cupit Altissimo famulari* (he or she desires to be a servant of God) becomes routine during this period, not only among the registers of York archdiocese but also in the dioceses of Hereford, Exeter, London, and elsewhere as well. The "servant of God" motif was strong during the first half of the fourteenth century, and when a nun petitioned Archbishop Melton in 1320 to be enclosed "in a proper and worthy place," it was yet only "so that she might serve God *more strictly* by leading the solitary life."[58] In general, notices of the early fourteenth century tended to be more amplified than those of the thirteenth, but they achieved this by the use of repetitive ideas, not new ones. For example: the proposition of Beatrice de Meaus to live as a solitary and (*et*) anchorite near the church of St. Peter of Cornhill, London, was considered laudable by Bishop Baldock. In this place where anchorites had

---

57. William N. Brown, ed., *Register of William Wickwane, Lord Archbishop of York, 1279–1285*, SS 114 (1907), p. 74; William N. Brown, ed., *Registers of John le Romeyn and Henry of Newark, Lord Archbishops of York, 1286–1299*, 2 vols., SS 123, 128 (1913–17), 1:196, 126.

58. *VCH Yorkshire*, 3:113 (italics mine).

lived before, he gave her license to enter and remain perpetually, leading there an anchoritic life and serving God in a praiseworthy manner.[59]

A few anchorites are described as poor, as living in solitude and poverty, or as being a poor servant of Christ. The idea of poverty is the only newly expressed idea that surfaces during these years, and it is still very much in the purgative mode here being elaborated. From 1230 to 1350 then, in these legal compendia, both lay and clerical, the life of the anchorite is essentially defined as solitary and perpetual and having as its purpose the service of God. The sources deal with the reclusive life in terms of its demands, not in terms of its expectations, gifts, or rewards.

In the midyears of the fourteenth century a new cell was built for a chaplain at a church in Coventry, Warwickshire, for the "purpose of [his] serving God ... having spurned worldly pleasures, and with contempt for meaningless wanderings ... and in this reclusorium [he] would remain, and be enclosed, and lead [his] life in praise of his Redeemer." In the same period Margaret de Kirkeby was enclosed and the archbishop's register notes the confirmation of her petition saying that she greatly desired the anchoritic life "in order that she might fashion herself as a servant of God more freely and more quietly with pious prayers and vigils." A few years later, in 1360, the prior of Maxtox, in Staffordshire, was commissioned to enclose an anchorite, one Fr. Roger de Henerebarwe, "who desires to retire from the world and pass his life in devotion ... in the building assigned for this purpose."[60] In 1371 the Patent Roll of Edward III registered "protection for John Ingram of Wroxston, sometimes monk of the monastery of

59. Robert C. Fowler, ed., *Registrum Radulphi Baldock, Gilberti Segrave, Ricardi Newport, et Stephani Gravesend, episcoporum Londoniensium, A.D. 1304–1338*, CYS 7 (1911), p. 54.

60. Sir William Dugdale, *The Antiquities of Warwickshire*, 2d ed., 2 vols. (London, 1730), 1:193; Hope Emily Allen, *Writings Ascribed to Richard Rolle, Hermit of Hampole and Materials for His Biography* (Modern Language Association of America, 1927; reprint, New York: Kraus, 1966), p. 502; Rowland A. Wilson, ed., *Registers or Act Books of the Bishops of Coventry and Lichfield: Book 5 Being the Second Register of Bishop Robert de Stretton, A.D. 1360–1385*, William Salt Archaeological Society, n.s. 8 (1905), p. 193.

Medmenham, of the Cistercian diocese [*sic*], who, withdrawing from the society of men and choosing to live a solitary life in a cavern or hidden place called 'Swannesnest' by the Tower of London, where he waits upon the Most High in quietness, has been disturbed by the ordinary."[61]

The jurisdictional dispute that prompted the royal intervention does not concern us here. This entry and the three preceding ones interest us because they take us into a different psychological world. There is a personal, celebratory element in these items. The purpose of reclusion here is not only to serve but also to praise and even to receive. The word *quiet* is twice employed. There is an affective implication that might pass unnoticed but actually serves as a bridge to the next century: for at the onset of the fifteenth century a new word appears in that limited vocabulary that has thus far been encountered. That word is *contemplative*.

In 1403, in the register of Edmund Stafford, Cecilia Moys was described as "desiring to lead the contemplative life of an anchorite." In 1405 Isolda N. was admitted to the cell at St. Peter's, Leicester, which formerly had housed the anchoress whom Courtenay had examined for Lollard errors in 1389. No less a person than Philip Repingdon, then bishop of Lincoln, accepted Isolda's petition—Repingdon himself was one of the earliest of Wyclif's supporters and one of the first to withdraw his support. Repingdon's register records Isolda's request as follows: ". . . desiring to [cast off] secular pomp and illicit worldly life in order to earn the riches of eternal wealth, she chooses a spiritual mansion by being enclosed in an anchorite's cell perpetually, scorning worldly pleasures, the more freely to contemplate her Creator."[62]

A 1417 Patent Roll entry marking the appointment of the chaplain John Kyngeslowe to the reclusory Henry V had established at Sheen quoted from the indenture instrument in similar terms. By virtue of Henry's endowment Kyngeslowe and his successors in

---

61. *CPR 1370–74*, p. 51.

62. F. C. Hingeston-Randolph, ed., *Register of Edmund Stafford, Bishop of Exeter, 1395–1419* (Exeter, 1856), p. 251; John Nichols, *History and Antiquities of the County of Leicester*, 4 vols. (London, 1795–1815), vol. 1, part 2, p. 65.

the anchorhold were made free for "orisons, and divine praises, and holy contemplation." A 1418 entry in Bishop Lacy's register is more sober but still holds to the word *contemplation*. Combining both earlier and newer elements, the register describes the anchoress Margaret Shipster as desiring to lead the contemplative or/ and anchoritic life (the connective *seu* equating the two terms) in order to "serve God more freely and to hold herself immaculate from the sins and wickednesses of this world." And in 1436 Beatrice Franke, the nun of Stainfield, was allowed her Lincolnshire anchorhold "to win the fruit of a better life, to change her condition to a stricter life under the rule or order of an anchorite . . . [to] have more freedom to contemplate her Creator." Three years later in 1439 another religious, the canon Richard Lyle, was granted enclosure in a new cell built for him in his priory, whereby he might gain the "fruits of a better life . . . through a life more holy and more strictly contemplative and [*et*] anchoritic . . . and in humility of spirit, serve God more devotedly."[63]

The word *contemplative* first appears in these documents in the fifteenth century and with it comes the suggestion (at least for migrating religious) that anchorites will "win the fruits of a better life." The word "contemplative" and the phrase "to win the fruits of a better life" combine to produce an image of recluses as experiencing their reward both in this life and in the next. The anchoritic life is seen as enhanced by its solitude and quiet, not endangered by it; the cell is seen as a spiritual mansion as well as a prison; the anchorite will be a contemplative, not merely an ascetic. God is nearer. Much more dramatic than the earlier notices, those of the fifteenth century take for granted a mystical expectation barely hinted at in the thirteenth century. Clearly there had been a change in the attitude of society toward anchorites.

A final journal entry comes from a moment so late in the history of English anchoritism as to sound a note of pathos. In 1533 a man named Christopher Warner was the anchorite within the

63. *CPR 1413–19*, p. 114; A. Hamilton Thompson, ed., *Visitations of Religious Houses in the Diocese of Lincoln*, 3 vols., CYS 17, 24, 33 (1915–27), 1:113–15; Lacy, *Exeter Reg.*, 2:158–159.

house of the Blackfriars of Canterbury. He became involved in the controversy that arose over the revelations of the nun Elizabeth Barton, who had declared that Henry VIII would not be king a month after he married Anne Boleyn. Warner was questioned many times concerning what he knew of the situation. The state papers of Henry VIII contain this communication:

From Christopher Warner to Cromwell,
The official to the archdeacon of Canterbury has been with me and said it was your pleasure that he should examine me of certain matters concerning Dr. Bocking, cellarer of Christchurch, and the Nun. They have often times come to visit me of their charity, and so have others because I am a prisoner. . . .[64]

Warner then goes on to give his testimony and finally concludes: "You may learn more of the truth by the people of the world. It is to me a great hindrance to my contemplation that I should have in Almighty God."[65]

In this letter Warner expressed the paradox of the anchorite's life. On the one hand, he is a prisoner. If someone desires to speak to him, that person must come to him. On the other hand, his is a great freedom and its purpose is to contemplate his Lord. It peeves him to be called on to give worldly testimony, even for Henry VIII, his temporal lord.

In 1265 Henry III had desired information from Loretta, onetime countess of Leicester and now the recluse of Hackington, Kent. He, no less than his more imperious namesake, felt no compunction about disturbing the religious solitude of an anchorite.[66] Like Christopher, Loretta had entertained many visitors in her cell and did in fact allow her "contemplation" to be disturbed by the demands of others. And yet, *mutatis mutandis*, we cannot imagine that Loretta would ever have used Christopher's words to express irritation over the royal intrusion into her quiet.

64. *LP*, 6 (1533): 1336.
65. Ibid.
66. *CR* 1264–68, pp. 115–116. On Loretta, see also Frederick M. Powicke, "Loretta, Countess of Leicester," in *Historical Essays in Honor of James Tait*, ed. J. Goronwy Edwards et al. (Manchester, 1933), pp. 247–271.

Loretta belongs to the time of the *Ancrene Riwle.* The verbalized perception of the life she had chosen as a vocation, even when associated with so great a lady, was limited, austere, and understated. The late fourteenth century seems to have wrought a change in the emotional climate that had decreed this restraint. With the English Reformation almost at hand (one wonders what became of him a few years later), Christopher Warner wrote of both the prisonlike and the contemplative aspects of his life in a most natural, forthright, even offhand manner. What had intervened in the time between Loretta and Christopher was not necessarily a change in the demands of the anchoritic life or in its experience. But surely a new mental climate now warmed the anchorite in his dank cell. Perceived in terms of asceticism in the twelfth and thirteenth centuries, anchoritism in the fourteenth and fifteenth centuries had come to be seen as a fully contemplative vocation. It drew its coloring from the wider spectrum that had been released by the popular piety movements. Although the formal structure of the anchorite's life remained constant, its more purely ascetic and somewhat archaic vestiges were allowed to fade from primary view. Now anchoritism epitomized a new religious mentality and society responded afresh. Anchorites in the late fourteenth and fifteenth centuries became perfect vehicles for the expression both of orthodox varieties of the "Lollard" mentality of self-abnegation and of its positive underside, the mystical expectations of Rolle and Hilton.

Whereas the asceticism of the anchorite stimulated the imagination of English society in the twelfth century, the more literate populace in the fourteenth and fifteenth assumed recluses were climbing ladders of perfection. In a significant reversal the anchorite became the fulcrum around which mysticism turned. Works for and by solitaries, written in Middle English, dominated the English mystical movement. Other people, lay as well as religious, shared these works by identifying with the anchorite, drawing from these treatises their own fulfillment according to the dimensions of their own interests and capabilities. The mystical literature of the second half of the fourteenth century, although mainly written by clergy, responded to the change in the popular perception of anchorites and satisfied popular devotional needs.

Anchorites of the later period approached their cells with long-ing and desire and more conscious expectation of the mystical experience. The fire of love that Rolle openly beheld always had smoldered in the hearth of the anchorhold, but its flame had been banked and hidden from view along with the anchorites who tended it. Late medieval anchorites may have been no greater mystics than those of the twelfth and thirteenth centuries, but as the anticipation of mystical experience came to be deemed appro-priate, they probably felt freer to abandon themselves to it.

Throughout the Middle Ages in England there were individuals who chose to live alone and live a life dedicated to God. The lapses from grace, the prohibitions against wicked speech, the re-lease from vows for travel or pilgrimage, the dispensations from abstinence, the move to a more comfortable cell—these limita-tions and accommodations mark the vocation as living and true. They impart a sense of honest adjustment to human frailty and human need. They make it understandable that the individual recluse could carry on past moments of despair. They help us to remember that we are talking about persons, and not icons. They are indicators of vitality, not subversion.

Persons in medieval England chose, desired, even pleaded to be allowed this opportunity to serve God in loneliness. Men and women alike sought the privilege and understood it as such. It is true that a woman might have wanted to become an anchorite to escape an unattractive marriage, to avoid the dangers of child-birth, to have a private home, because she had no husband, be-cause there was no place for her at the local nunnery. It is true that a man might have desired to become an anchorite because of the competitions of communal or secular life, because he was poor, because of a desire to have more free time (if only to spend it in virtuous pursuits such as writing or copying manuscripts). It is true that a man or a woman might have wanted to become an anchorite to be transformed into an object of veneration and bear the *nomen reclusi*. But these were secondary gains and perhaps unconscious desires.

It was hard to be an anchorite. Most deadly was the boredom, the repetition, day after day, week after week, year after year without alteration. That so many sustained this endless pattern without failure is notable and speaks to the efficacy of the screening process. But it speaks even more clearly to the true commitment of English anchorites. They were *anchoretae*, withdrawn from society, begun on that ladder that reached to heaven. They had abandoned self to find self and to participate in the community of saints. The world could be forsaken that God might be seen for a fleeting instant. Yet the world refused to be discarded and the anchorite still had need of it. Who existed for whom?

In this book thus far the anchorite has held the core of our attention. Although his life has been described as liminal our eyes have been on him. We have seen him both deeply tied to and sharply separated from the larger world that surrounded him and on which he depended for sustenance. But it is that world that has faded in and out of our view, that world that has had a threshold existence. It is time to reverse the field of inquiry: to place the patron in the center of the canvas; to view the phenomenon from the social perspective; to take the measure of men and communities that created the environments in which anchoritism could flourish; to examine how anchorites participated in the English patronage system. At the apex of that system stood the king, so it will be well to begin with him.

PART II

The Patrons

5

Royal Support

The ninth-century *Liber Vitae* of Durham listed anchorites after kings and queens but before abbots, priors, and priests. The kings and queens who preceded anchorites in the Book of Life were their protectors in real life. For the early British days legend survives to tell this tale; for the England immediately after the Conquest, the Lives of Wulfric of Haselbury and Christina of Markyate affirm that Henry I and Stephen knew and respected their reclusive subjects. In the second half of the twelfth century these relationships become tangible and quantifiable as the extant Pipe Rolls, the records of the accounts of the king's private lands, begin their notation of day-by-day financial support of anchorites by the monarchy. The earliest consecutive records of this kind show that the king, by his support and by his example, was committed to the anchoritic vocation of self-imposed asceticism. The commitment varied in degree from monarch to monarch, but no English king, including Henry VIII, failed to respond in some measure. Each tied his future salvation to benefits accrued from his support of anchorites. When English kings wanted to prove their virtue or restore their reputation (whether before God or their fellow men), support of anchorites was one natural response, even as the endowment of a monastery, the gift of an altarpiece, or the foundation of an almshouse might serve the same purpose. To focus on the gifts of kings and others to anchorites, then, is not to suggest that anchorites were unique recipients of this kind of largesse. On the contrary, the purpose of this and the following chapters is to place anchorites within a framework that binds them to other individuals and entities found worthy of medieval charity. These chapters seek to strip anchorites of mystery and to show them as seen by their contemporaries—rather common-place and almost ordinary as they lived out their lives within the limits of a *conversatio* that had become an accepted and routine aspect of medieval society. Anchorites were special only to the degree that they carried a medieval message: a difficult life could be borne in return for an easier eternity. Anchorites carried that burden both for themselves and for their patrons. Royal families, like other patrons, attended to their recluses' physical needs and so participated in the exaltation of their spirit.

THE EARLY PLANTAGENETS: 1154–1216

The Pipe Rolls are the source of most of the available informa-tion on royal support of anchorites for the period through the reign of King John. These rolls generate a body of hard and con-tinuous data recording the payments of Henry II and his sons Richard I and John for maintaining anchorites out of the issues of specific farms. The rolls mark commitments that were either life-time grants to discrete individuals, lapsing on the death of the re-cipient, or long-term commitments to a site, continuing through the lives of many anchorites and often through many reigns as well. Grants originating in one reign were invariably honored at the succession of a new monarch, at least for the duration of the life of the incumbent anchorite. All grants were vulnerable to ter-mination, however, when an anchorage fell vacant during a reign other than that in which it had been endowed. A cell at Writtle, Essex, had three different occupants between the years 1185 and 1201 (spanning three reigns as well) before its support was ended by John;[1] in contrast, a cell at Severn Stoke, Worcestershire, was continuously supported from 1171 to 1264, and when it finally dis-

---

1. PR 31 *Henry II* (1185), p. 12, to PR 1 *Richard I* (1189), p. 20: male recluse; PR 2 *Richard I* (1190), p. 103, to PR 5 *Richard I* (1193), p. 1: female recluse; PR 6 *Richard I* (1194), pp. 28, 29, to PR 3 *John* (1201), p. 58: male recluse.

appeared from the royal records (although not necessarily from the royal coffers) it had known ninety-three years of royal support.[2]

A pension grant to an anchorite was a grant of royal alms. These alms were fixed alms (*elemosinae constitutae*) and once established by writ they continued year after year, at the pleasure of the king, without further authorization. Unlike gifts (*donae*) and other random payments for which the sheriff had to provide warrants at the exchequer, fixed alms, along with fixed tithes and fixed payments (*decimae, liberationes*), were relatively permanent expenses of the farm and allowances routinely were made for them. Only when a change occurred in one of these payments was a writ issued by the king, produced at the exchequer by the sheriff, and duly entered onto the roll.[3] A change could be a new grant, a "new penny" expanding the alms base of the shire or town, or the substitution of one recipient of an established commitment for another. Generally a substitution would occur at the death of a recipient, at which time a new individual or group would be designated to receive the released funds.

The distinctions between fixed alms, fixed tithes, and fixed payments were not rigidly observed on the rolls. Although most grants for anchorites were listed under fixed alms, as was appropriate, when anchorites entered the rolls by taking over the grants of others, they took over their place in the roll as well. Thus the pension of the recluses of Writtle was listed under fixed payments because earlier that penny had been distributed in turn to Harvey the vintner and Gilbert the chaplain. In another instance the grant to the anchorite at Severn Stoke, a new penny that was called a grant of fixed alms in the enabling writ, was listed under tithes all through the reigns of Henry II, Richard I, and John. It

2. This grant is absolutely continuous and appears in every Pipe Roll that is complete and printed from 17 Henry II (1171), p. 97, to 26 Henry III (1242), p. 96. The anchorite was female from 1171 to 1202, male from 1203 to 1219, female again in 1230 (14 Henry III, p. 30) and 1242. The last notice appears in *CPR 1258-66*, p. 355, where the anchorite is female. Payments also are recorded in *CLR 1226-40*, pp. 197, 238.

3. *Introduction to the Study of the Pipe Rolls*, Pipe Roll Society 3 (London, 1884; reprint, 1966), pp. 45-48, 77.

was finally moved into the alms column in Henry III's reign—perhaps by a bookkeeper tidying up.

However categorized, a grant of the king for the support of an anchorite was a gift of royal alms, a charitable grant for an indefinite period of time and one that was listed along with similar grants of modest pensions to other individuals (mostly lay) and to such groups as the "infirm of Windsor" (or Maldon or St. Albans), the Templars, the Hospitallers, and conventual houses. In almost all cases these grants were for small amounts of money—one to two pennies per day—and for most of the individuals, including the anchorites, the grant probably represented the bulk of their livelihood.[4]

The amount of money available for these disbursements remained stable after the first years of Henry II's reign. In his early years Henry expanded the number of such grants, after which time little or no change took place. New individuals rarely entered the pension list save when funds were released by someone else's death. If a larger pension was desired for an individual it was created not by the appropriation of new funds but by combining the former grants of two or more individuals, resulting in a contraction in the number of people receiving such payments. If a large pension was vacated it could be divided and spread more thinly but the amount of money was quite constant. Table 3 indicates the process in Herefordshire.

The substantial tithes to the monks of Lyre and Cormeille and the minimal alms grants to the priory, the infirm, and the churchyard of Hereford most probably predate Henry II's reign. In 2 Henry II (1156) the gift to the Templars is called *new* and fits into a pattern of similar grants to Templars in other shires and towns—

4. A few individuals can be found on the membranes of more than one shire—doubling or even tripling their endowments. For example: Wulstan, *caretarius*, received one pence per day from the receipts of the city of Winchester (*PR 32 Henry II* [1186], p. 177) and two pence per day from the issues of Wiltshire (ibid., p. 159), and he did so each year from 1186 to 1200. Moreover, both of these grants had previously been received by Harvey, *focarius*. Svein, *valtrarius*, received one pence each from Surrey and Essex (*PR 15 Henry II* [1169], pp. 166, 122) between the years 1169 and 1197, when both pennies were transferred to William de Stiviton (*PR 10 Richard I* [1198], pp. 147, 125).

the grants were routine and ranged in amount from one to four marks. During the third accounting year Henry added two men to his alms list, one at a penny per day (30s. 5d. per annum) and one at two pennies. The next year shows five more individuals pensioned by Henry. Four of them, including the anchorite of Newnham, received a penny per day; the fifth received the munificent sum of four pence per day. There were no further expansions in the amount of money available for penny alms of this type until 18 Henry II (1172), a period of fourteen years, and that expansion was the last to be made. It is satisfying for this study that the recipient of that final new penny was another recluse, Richard of St. Sepulchre.

Table 3 also shows how new persons or corporate entities entered the rolls on the deaths of former recipients and how the amount of individual pensions was altered without enlarging the base. Robert, *sumetarius* (groom of a packhorse), received two pennies per day for eleven years beginning in 1180. Those two pennies earlier had supported two people and after Robert's death were divided again. Subsequently they came to rest on yet another recluse and the Hospitallers. In another example the unusually large grant of four pennies instituted in the fourth year of Henry II's reign soon became enlarged to five. Returned to the treasury for an extended period of time at the end of Henry's reign, the grant was activated again in the fourth year of Richard's reign and granted to Gerald, archdeacon of Breknow.[5] The five pennies were then subdivided in 5 John (1203) and became the grants of Simon, *pictavensis* (the Poitevin), and Roger, chaplain, each of whom received two and a half pence per day. In 1230 Simon was still in receipt of his grant, but the prioress of Boclaud was receiving that of the chaplain. She was also receiving two pennies that formerly had been individual pensions. Such is the continuity and conservatism that can be observed within each accounting unit. When anchorites and others supplicated their kings for support it was within this context of a fixed amount of

5. The roll actually states that the five pence per day are part of a seven-pence-per-day grant of which Adam of Newnham takes two pence daily (*PR 5 Richard I* [1193] p. 88).

131

TABLE 3

TRANSFERENCE OF ALMS: HEREFORDSHIRE (1156–1214)

Year	Priory. Hereford 60s. 10d.	Infirm. Hereford 12d.	Churchyard 7s.	Templars 13s. 4d.	Tithes: Monks of Lyre and Cormeille £24	Walter Coterellus 14s.[1]	Durandus de Roth 7s.[1]	Hugh Schin 30s. 5d.	Robert Contreunt 30s. 5d.	Recluse: Newnham 30s. 5d.	Ralph, nephew of Thomas le Brun £6. 1. 8.	Rand Lucan 30s. 5d.	Recluse: St. Sepulchre 30s. 5d.
Henry II 1156													
1157	"	"	"	"	"								30s. 5d.
1158	"	"	"	"	"	60s. 10d.	30s. 5d.	30s. 5d.				"	"
1159	"	"	"	"	"	"	"	"		"		"	"
1160	"	"	"	"	"	"	"	"	Osanne, wife of Robert Contreunt 30s. 5d.	"	Thomas le Brun, almoner of the King £7. 12. 1. (five pence per day)	"	"
1161–70	"	"	"	"	"	"	"	"	"	"	"	"	"
1171	"	"	"	"	"	"	"	"	15s. 2½d. ǀ Baldwin 15s. 2½d.	"	"	"	"
1172	"	"	"	"	"	"	"	"	Baldwin 30s. 5d.	"	"	"	"
1173	"	"	"	"	"	"	"	"	"	"	"	"	"
1174	"	"	"	"	"	"	"	"	15s. 2½d.	"	"	"	"
1175	"	"	"	"	"	✕	✕	"	✕	"	"	"	"
1176	"	"	"	"	"	✕	✕	"	✕	"	"	"	"
1177	"	"	"	"	"	Robert Broszart 60s. 10d.	22s. 9d.	"	✕	"	"	"	"
1178	"	"	"	"	"	✕	✕	"	✕	"	"	"	"
1179	"	"	"	"	"	✕	✕	"	✕	"	"	"	"
1180	"	"	"	"	"	✕	Robert, sumetarius 30s. 5d.	"	Robert, sumetarius 30s. 5d.	"	76s. ½d.	✕	"
1181–88	"	"	"	"	"		"	"	"	"	✕	✕	"
Richard I 1189	"	"	"	"	"		"	"	"	"	✕	✕	"
1190	"	"	"	"	"	✕	"	"	"	"	✕	✕	"

Year	Adam of Newnham / John Braz	Recluse: St. Audoneus	Rohesius, costumer / Obert, Queen's man	Brothers of Hospital	Robert Chester	Simon, Poitevan (76s. ½d.)	Gerald, archdeacon / Brian, clerk of Ely	Recluse: Margaret
1191	Adam of Newnham 60s. 10d.	..	..	Brothers of Hospital 30s. 5d.	..	..	✗	..
1192	✗	..	..	..	..	..	Gerald, archdeacon of Breknow £7.12.1.	..
1193	..	..	..	..	..	..	..	..
1194	..	Recluse: St. Audoneus 30s. 5d.	..	..	..	..	..	..
1195	John Braz 45s. 2½d. / John Braz 15s. 2½d.	..	..	..	..	..	..	..
1196	John Braz 60s. 10d.	..	Rohesius, costumer 15s. 2½d.	..	..	..	..	..
1197	..	..	Rohesius, costumer 30s. 5d.	..	..	..	..	..
1198	..	..	..	..	..	..	..	..
John 1199	..	..	..	..	..	..	..	..
1200	..	..	..	..	Robert 7s. 7d. / Robert Chester 22s. 10d.	..	..	..
1201	..	..	Obert, Queen's man 15s. 2½d.	..	Robert Chester 30s. 5d.	..	..	..
1202	..	Obert, Queen's man 30s. 5d.	..	..	..	76s. ½d.	✗	..
1203	..	..	..	..	..	Simon, Poitevan 76s. ½d.	Brian, clerk of Ely 76s. ½d.	Recluse: Margaret 15s. 2½d. / 15s. 2½d.
1204	..	..	..	..	..	..	Roger, chaplain 76s. ½d.	Recluse: Margaret 30s. 5d.
1205–10	..	..	..	..	..	..	..	..
1211	..	..	..	..	William, herald of Prince 15s. 2½d. / 15s. 2½d.	..	..	..
1212	..	..	..	..	William, herald of Prince 30s. 5d.	..	..	..
(missing) 1213	(-)	(-)	(-)	(-)	(-)	(-)	(-)	(-)
1214	..	..	..	..	..	..	..	Simon de Cambrai 30s. 5d.
Henry III 1230	Legenda, wife of Semayne 60s. 10d.	John de Lisewys 30s. 5d.	Prioress of Boclaud 30s. 5d.	Prioress of Boclaud 30s. 5d.	Prioress of Boclaud 30s. 5d.	Prioress of Boclaud 76s. ½d.	Prioress of Boclaud 76s. ½d.	✗
1242	..	Norman, herald 30s. 5d.	..	✗	..	Mag. Ely, cocus 76s. ½d.	..	William le Engleys 30s. 5d.

1. Represents a partial payment: instituted after beginning of accounting year.

available resources, for after the third or fourth year of Henry II's reign a new penny became very infrequent. Anchorites had to compete for appointment to vacated alms slots.

The chancery rolls identify seventeen sites inhabited by anchorites receiving royal pensions from Henry II. Most of the anchorites received that typical penny per day, but an occasional one received additional allowances or a larger grant. The male recluse of St. Mary of Bedford received thirty-two pennies for clothes during his first year of enclosure (perhaps to help him purchase a suitable habit for his vocation); the anchorite at Randleston, Suffolk, was allowed 12s. 8d. yearly in addition to his maintenance penny; Adam, the recluse of Gloucester, received sixty shillings (almost two pence per day) for each of the almost twenty-five years that he lived in his cell (1171–96).[6]

One penny, however, was generally considered ample and was standard for royal anchorites during the twelfth century. When a grant varies from that pattern it is usually a signal that the grant was instituted by someone other than Henry II. The two recluses who appear on the rolls in the first year for which there are consecutive records, 2 Henry II (1156), the anchorites of *Pevesia*, Berkshire, and Colchester, Essex, were paid 15s. 7½d. per annum out of the issues of their respective farms.[7] This rate, a half-penny per day, suggests that their financial arrangements and their enclosures belong to an earlier reign (Stephen's?) and that a half-penny was the royal rate in that period. Lower rates also can indicate that the recluse had been in the gift of a member of the nobility whose lands had escheated to the king. Thus, the recluse of Stedham, whose maintenance was dependent on the receipts of the honor of Petworth, continued to receive only the two pence per week she had been promised by the earl of Arundel even after Henry II reasserted his title to those lands; the recluse of Maldon, who initially was in the gift of Henry's brother William, was confirmed of a grant of 8s. 8d. per year by the king after William died and his lands and the charges on them reverted to Henry.[8]

6. *PR 31 Henry II* (1185), p. 130; *PR 4 Henry II* (1158), p. 125, to *PR 28 Henry II* (1182), p. 64; *PR 17 Henry II* (1171), p. 84, to *PR 8 Richard I* (1196), p. 101.
7. *PR 2 Henry II* (1156), pp. 19, 21.
8. *PR 27 Henry II* (1181), p. 146; *PR 10 Henry II* (1164), p. 38.

These examples show that rates of individual grants did not change. Payments to the recluses of Colchester can be followed well into the reign of Henry III. In 1242 the anchorite of Colchester was still receiving a pension at the half-penny rate,[9] although by then some anchorites at newer sites were being granted a penny and a half per day by the king. The king's promise was modest, then, but it was likely to be sustained, and in any particular year these small amounts were multiplied many times by the sizable number of anchorites on the rolls. Table 4 explores the royal commitment as detailed in the Pipe Rolls.[10]

Table 4 indicates that Henry began his reign by inheriting an obligation to support two anchorites from lands on the Pipe Roll accounts. In 1158 Henry assumed responsibility for two additional anchorites, one at Newnham (actually in Gloucestershire but part of the Herefordshire farm) and another at Randleston, Suffolk. Each was to receive a penny per day, with the recluse at Randleston accepting that additional 12s. 8d. yearly. The recluse at Newnham was a woman who would live in her cell for forty-four years, her life spanning three reigns; the recluse of Randleston was a man who would live enclosed for twenty-five years, dying before Henry in 1182.[11]

No further additions of anchorites to Henry's alms lists appear in the Pipe Rolls for the next ten years, save for a two-year period

9. PR 26 Henry III (1242), p. 222.

10. The number of anchorites on the royal rolls in any one year might reflect more than just the monarch's commitment to recluse support because the rolls also included those anchorites whose maintenance was dependent on lands, both lay and episcopal, that had escheated to the crown. Table 4, which graphs the royal commitments to anchorite support, does not include this escheat information. I have kept it separate from data on the king's own gifts because the assumption of these obligations does not reflect the royal will. Nonetheless, in a feudal society a shifting percentage of nonroyal lands was always in the hands of the king. That some of these lands bore a charge to the king for the maintenance of recluses for the duration of the escheat period was a fact of which the king would be aware. These recluses too would become part of his own commitment to such support. Although many years brought no additional anchorites onto the rolls via escheats, other years brought many. During 1171, 1172, and 1173 there were seven episcopally endowed recluses on Henry's rolls; in 1177, again seven anchorites, four from noble endowments and three from episcopal; in the last four years of Henry's reign, 1185–88, an average of nine each year.

11. For Newnham, consecutively from PR 4 Henry II (1158), p. 144, to PR 3 John (1201), p. 265. For Randleston, see chapter 5, note 6 above.

TABLE 4
Royal Maintenance Grants: Henry II to John (1156–1216)

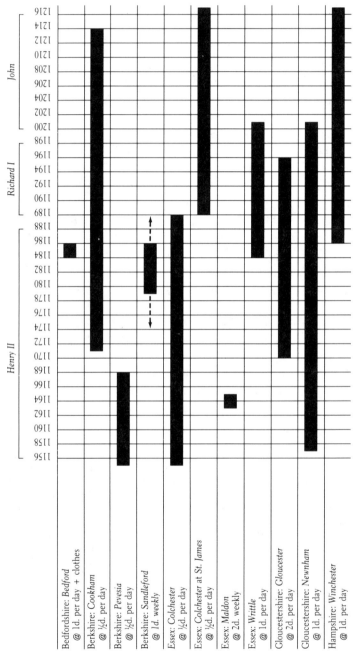

Hampshire: *Isle of Wight* @ 12s. yearly for corn

Herefordshire: *Hereford* @ 1d. per day

Herefordshire: *Hereford at St. Audoneus,* @ 1d. per day

Herefordshire: *Hereford at St. Sepulchre,* @ 1d. per day

Lincolnshire: *Belshford* @ 1d. per day

Nottinghamshire: *Higham Ferrers* @ 1d. per day — to escheat

Somerset: *Crewkerne* @ 39s. 7d. yearly — to escheat

Suffolk: *Randleston* @ 1d. per day

Sussex: *Stedham* @ 2d. weekly

Wiltshire: *Marlborough* @ 1d. per day

Wiltshire: *Marlborough at St. Mary's,* @ 1d. per day

Wiltshire: *Preshute* @ 1d. per day

Worcestershire: *Severn Stoke* @ 1d. per day

Totals: 2 4 4 5 5 4 3 7 8 9 10 9 8 8 8 11 9 9 5 5 5 5 5 4

- - - - - ▶ indicates the likelihood that the grant was paid in these other years (though data are lacking).

(1164 and 1165) when the male recluse of Maldon appeared on his accounts. The Maldon recluse, mentioned earlier as having been in the gift of Henry's brother, William, count of Poitou, disappears from the rolls in 1166. The presumption is that he died. If he did not die but rather lost his support, this would be meaningful, if negative, evidence. But nothing in the data suggests that possibility. We assume that an obligation Henry had inherited on his brother's death was terminated by the death of the recluse, and the episode created only a ripple in the essentially stable line of Henry's support of anchorites for the eleven-year period that had begun in 1158.

The only other variation in these years was caused by the death of the *Pevesia* recluse in mid-1163. In that year she received only half her accustomed alms, the other half remaining in the treasury.[12] The following year another female recluse took her place on the roll and received the pension for five successive years, the last of which was 1168. Gone from the roll of 1169, the alms of the *Pevesia* anchorite and her accustomed place in the order of the list of fixed payments of the Windsor farm were taken by two "groups" of people: the "infirm of Windsor" and the "nuns of the forest" (a community that has not been identified). These two newly constituted recipients of the royal largesse split the former anchorite's daily half-pence almost equally.[13] They continued to receive their doles throughout the remainder of Henry's reign and through Richard's and John's. In the Pipe Roll of 1230 the "nuns of the forest" were no longer in receipt of a gift but the "infirm of Windsor" were still in their slot and receiving 7s. 7½d. per annum, exactly one quarter of a penny per day.[14]

12. This is not evident in the table, where a gift for part of the year is shown as equal to that for a full year.

13. *PR 15 Henry II* (1169), p. 135, awards the whole gift of 15s. 2 1/2d. to the "nuns of the forest." The "infirm" are marked down for 7s. 2 1/2d. but the entry is deleted. During the following two years (*PR 16 Henry II* [1170], p. 73, *PR 17 Henry II* [1171], p. 125), the nuns get 8s. 2 1/2d. and the infirm seven shillings. By 18 Henry II (1172), p. 16, grants are fixed for the remainder of these reigns at eight shillings per annum for the nuns and 7s. 2 1/2d. for the infirm. Was there a fight for funds here? At the least, this kind of manipulation of a very small amount of money is an indication of the conservatism and limitations on alms expenditures discussed above.

14. *PR 14 Henry III* (1230), p. 5.

When the second recluse of *Pevesia* died, as with the Maldon recluse, Henry seems to have terminated a grant probably not of his own foundation. But unlike the Maldon circumstances, in which the alms gift reverted to the income of the farm, here the money was redistributed. Perhaps no other recluse came forward immediately to take the place of the deceased anchorite. Perhaps the cell was no longer habitable. In any case, whether or not it was a question of several entities vying for his gift, the half-penny per day that had gone to anchorites at *Pevesia* was more or less permanently bestowed on two alternate groups. The new grants did retain the "religious" quality of the gift to the anchorites, that is, they were *alms*, not secular pensions or gifts. By 1169 there remained only three anchorites on Henry's rolls.

In 1171 and 1172 Henry added four new anchorites to his alms lists, more than doubling his ongoing commitment. One of these, the recluse of Cookham, probably was a replacement for the *Pevesia* recluse and like the *Pevesia* recluse a charge against the Windsor farm. In the Pipe Roll of 1172 she took over both the place on the list and the half-penny formerly bestowed on Ralph, *apostolicus*.[15] The half-penny grant, atypical for Henry at a new foundation, suggests that the cell at Cookham was a replacement for the one at *Pevesia* and the half-penny that had become available by Ralph's death (which grant may as well have originated in Stephen's reign) provided an easy means by which to continue the former obligation. The Windsor account now bore charges for the nuns, the infirm, and the new recluse.

The other three new commitments of 1171–72 were additional alms expenditures. In 1171 Henry endowed the long-lived cell at Severn Stoke at a penny a day, and the recluse of Gloucester was granted his pension of sixty shillings per annum. In the following year Henry granted a pension to Richard, the anchorite of St. Sepulchre. The addition of Richard to the Herefordshire account meant that there were now two anchorites being supported out of those revenues: the anchoress of Newnham and Richard.[16]

The final years of Henry's life saw another influx of anchorites on his rolls, at least one anchorite representing a new penny, an

15. *PR 18 Henry II* (1172), p. 16.
16. *PR 17 Henry II* (1171), pp. 97, 84; *PR 18 Henry II* (1172), p. 1.

unusual occurrence at this time.[17] Others received grants that formerly had gone elsewhere. Thus, the priest recluse Godwin, who was enclosed at St. Aedred's outside Winchester, was granted a penny that previously had supported Stephen the Saracen; the anchorite of Writtle received a penny that had been the pension of Gilbert, a chaplain.[18] In neither of these two cases, however, was the transference of alms from one individual to another accomplished directly. Rather, the alms were first granted elsewhere on a temporary basis before a permanent new commitment was made. Because these transactions offer a clue to the attitudes and patterns of the almsgiving of Henry's final years, they are worth studying in some detail. Tables 5 and 6 trace the movement of these fixed grants and are excellent indicators of a process that developed in the later years of Henry's reign.

Table 5 indicates that grants of fixed alms remained absolutely constant for over twenty years in the city of Winchester. Along with other typical grants to the Templars, the infirm, the almoner, three men each received a penny per day each year until 1181. The rolls record their names as Stephen the Saracen, Burguignon, and Paucamatus. The death of Paucamatus eight months into the fiscal year 1181 set in motion a complicated series of transactions not finally resolved for eleven years. During all that time at least one of these pennies, and sometimes two or even all three, were in a state of flux. At the death of Paucamatus in 1181 his penny was granted to Harvey, *focarius* (hearthkeeper, stoker). Harvey lived less than a calendar year after receiving his grant. His alms then "floated about" for the next three and a half years, enjoyed by three different groups of nuns, the sick *super montem*, and William, *arbalastarius* (crossbowman) before they were regranted on a permanent basis to Wulstan, *caretarius* (carter). In 1184 both Burguignon and Stephen the Saracen died. In neither case were their pennies immediately regranted. During the intervals in which the alms were free at least seven different groups of nuns, three clerics (Peter, Marius, and Reginald), and William the crossbowman received parts of their proceeds. Ultimately these pennies

17. The anchorite of Bedford, PR 31 *Henry II* (1185), p. 130.
18. PR 33 *Henry II* (1187), p. 200; PR 31 *Henry II* (1185), p. 12.

TABLE 5
Transference of Alms: Winchester[1] (1160–1215)

Henry II 1160-80	Robert, almoner 40s.	Paucamatus 30s. 5d.		Burguignon 30s. 5d		Stephen, Saracen 30s. 5d	
1181	"	" 20s. 2d.	Harvey 10s. 3d.	"		"	
1182	"	Sick, super montem 11s. 10d.	Nuns: Wintney 11s. / " 7s. 7d.	"		"	
1183	"	Nuns of St. James, Westminster 30s. 5d.		"		"	
1184	"	" 15s. 2½d.	William 15s. 2½d.	" 19s. 5d.	William 11s.	" 27s. 6d.	Nuns: St. James, Westminster 2s. 11d.
1185	"	Nuns of Ickleton 30s. 5d.		Peter, priest 11s. 3d.	" 22s. 2d.[2]	Nuns: Cheshunt 15s. 2½d.	Nuns: Wintney 15s. 2½d.
1186	"	Wulstan, carter 30s. 5d.		Nuns: Davington 15s. 2½d.	Nuns: Wintney 15s. 2½d.	"	Nuns: Kilburn 15s. 2½d.
1187	"	"		Nuns: Coeford 15s. 2½d.	Marinus, clerk 15s. 2½d.	Recluse: St. Aedred 30s. 5d.	
1188	" 30s. / Silvester, chaplain 10s.	"		Nuns: ? 15s. 2½d.	?[3] 15s. 2½d.	"	
Richard I 1189	Silvester, chaplain 40s.	"		Recluse: St. Aedred 30s. 5d.		Reginald, chaplain 15s. 2½d.	Nuns: Garing 15s. 2½d.
1190	Henry Joseph, chaplain 40s.	"		"		Nicholas, ostiary 30s. 5d.	
1191	"	"		"		Reginald, chaplain 30s. 5d.	
1192	"	"		"		Nicholas, ostiary 30s. 5d	
1193	"	"		"		"	
1194	"	"		"		"	
John 1201	"	William f. Edric 30s. 5d.		"		"	
1207	"	"		"		Walter Long 30s. 5d.	
1215	"	"		"		"	

1. Alms of sixty shillings per year to the sick "super montem" and of one mark per year for the Templars are constant throughout the period and not shown on the table.

2. There is an extra three shillings granted in this one instance.

3. Defective roll.

TABLE 6

Transference of Alms: Essex and Hertfordshire (1160–1203)

	Henry II 1160	John Adulbedent 30s. 5d.	Terricus, almoner 30s. 5d.	Berardus 30s. 5d.	Richard f. Ruald 45s. 7½d.	Roger, falconer 30s. 5d.	Aeline 30s. 5d.	Angus of Cambridge 30s. 5d.	Turstinus, sick 30s. 5d.	Richard Sazun 30s. 5d.	William, infant 60s. 10d.	Ralph, parter 45s. 7½d.	William, potter 30s. 5d.	f. Aelard 30s. 5d.	William Capun 30s. 5d.	Robert de Lazi 30s. 5d.	Durandus, sick 30s. 5d.	Sick Maldon 30s. 5d.	Roger Taillefions 42s. 7½d.!
1161–62																Gunnor 30s. 5d.			
1163								Robert Fergant 30s. 5d.									William Sarraganella 30s. 5d.		
1164							15s. 2½ ☒											Sick Maldon 30s. 5d.	
1165					Roger Taillefions 30s. 5d.! / 15s. 2½d.		Harvey, virtuer 30s. 5d.												
1166					Richard f. Ruald 45s. 7½d.		☒	22s. 10d. ☒				Walter f. Ralph 45s. 7½d.							
1167								☒					7s. 8d. ☒						
1168																			22s. 7½d.
1169					Richard (Cocher) 45s. 7½d.			Swen, keeper 30s. 5d.					Baldwin, owear 30s. 5d.		7s. 7½d.				
1170									Robert f. Turstinus 30s. 5d.										
1171		26s. 4d.	Magister Elerardus 4s. 1d. + 30s. 5d.							15s. 2½d. / John, chaplain 15s. 2½d.					Robert de Toka 15s. 2½d.				
1172			Magister Elerardus 60s. 10d.				Gilbert, chaplain 30s. 5d.												
1173																			
1174																			
1175		☒	15s. 2½d. / Richard Malhanch 30s. 5d.																
1176			Richard Malhanch 60s. 10d.																
1177–78																			
1179			Walter le Megre 30s. 5d.																
1180–81																			
1182						Nuns: Kilburn 30s. 5d.													

A tabular chart of annual disbursements, with years listed down the left column (1183–1203). Selected legible entries by row:

Year	Entries (left to right)
1183	—
1184	Nuns: Marrick 90s.[2]; Nuns: Kilburn 90s.[2]
1185	90s. 5d.; Nuns: Kilburn 90s. 5d.; Philip, armiger; Nuns: Marrick 15s. 2½d.; Sick Dunstaple 15s. 5d.½; Robt. f. William 15s. 2½d. 45s. 7½d.
1186	Canons: Greencroft 15s. 2½d.; Nuns: St James 90s. 5d.; Nuns: Ankerwyke 90s. 5d.; Robert f. William 60s. 10d.
1187	Sick Dunstable 90s. 5d.; Nuns: Stratford 15s. 2½d.; Nuns: Cockhill 15s. 2½d.; Nuns: Ankerwyke 15s. 2½d.; Nuns: Kilburn 15s. 2½d.
1188	Marinus, clerk 90s. 5d.; Nuns: Littlemore 15s. 2½d.; Nuns: Stratford 15s. 2½d.; John, convert 15s. 2½d.; Nicholas, convert 15s. 2½d.; Peter, convert 15s. 2½d.; William Harerng 90s. 5d.[1]
Richard I 1189	John, convert 15s. 2½d.; Nicholas, convert 15s. 2½d.; Nuns: Ankerwyke 15s. 2½d.; Nuns: Kilburn 15s. 2½d.; Hugh, cleric 15s. 2½d.; Canons: Gisgas 15s. 2½d.; John f. Alfred 45s. 7½d.; John of Damascus 45s. 7½d.
1190	Fernandus, clerk 60s. 10d.; William Paneslawe 90s. 5d.; Robert Schanke 90s. 5d.[1]; New Recluse: female 90s. 5d.; William Purchaz 90s. 5d.
1191	—
1192	Peter Pollard 15s. 2½d.
1193	Peter Pollard 90s. 5d.; Robert Tempurnouse 90s. 5d.
1194–95	New Recluse: male 90s. 5d.
1196	Walter London 15s. 2½d.
1197	Walter London 90s. 5d.
1198	Gilbert Surdus 11s. 5d.; Godfrey Spigernel 45s. 7½d.; Godfrey Spigernel 34s. 2½d.; 15s. 2½d.; Chamberlain 7s. 7d.; William Stiviton 7s. 7d.; William Stiviton 90s. 5d.; Hamelinus, herald 90s. 5d.
John 1199	Andr. chaplain 25s.; Andr. chaplain 90s.[1]
1200	—
1201	Andr. chaplain 20s.[1]
1202	Waiwanus, herald 90s. 5d.[1]; Philip Russel 45s. 7½d.; Philip Russel 45s. 7½d.; 15s. 2½d.; Walter London 15s. 2½d.; Robert Schanke 90s. 5d.; Waiwanus, herald 7s. 4½d.; Chaplain: Hertford 50s.[1]
1203	Waiwanus, herald 90s. 5d.; Philip Russel 60s. 10d.

1. Individual is receiving funds from more than one column.

2. Five pence not used in 1183 is used in 1185.

3. Extra shillings available from William Capum column.

were settled on the recluse Godwin and one Nicholas, an ostiary, where they remained fixed for many years until the natural deaths of these individuals.[19]

The Essex and Hertfordshire membranes, table 6, are even broader in scope and indicate not only that this pattern is in evidence elsewhere but also that it was something new (which the unusual continuity of the Winchester grants for the years 1160–80 obscures). In the early years of Henry's reign it was not at all uncommon for him to return alms to the treasury for a short period of time before regranting them to someone else. Some pennies were immediately re-presented, especially when they were given to the wife or the child of the former recipient. Others rested for a year or two (or longer) in the royal treasury. Thus Angus of Corbridge's penny was passed directly to Richard Fergant but was only given to Svein, *valtrarius* (keeper of the greyhounds), after a hiatus of more than two years; the penny of William, *pottarius* (potter), was detoured for twenty-one months before it was given to Baldwin, the blind man. Similar instances can be seen in table 3 and throughout the rolls. In these documents Henry appears somewhat penny-pinching and the generosity of his right hand seems diminished by the penuriousness of his left.

The pattern changed abruptly in 1182 (28 Henry II), and there is even an intimation of this change in Surrey in the preceding year.[20] Beginning in 1181–82 most monies that became available for redistribution were immediately circulated. Either a new permanent recipient was announced or a series of temporary grantees (as already shown in Winchester) took possession of the alms.

---

19. It is peculiar that the recluse first receives Stephen the Saracen's penny and two years later is recorded as receiving that of Burguignon. In addition, the roll for 1186 (p. 177) introduces a further confusion. It grants Harvey's penny to Wulstan and in the next sentence grants Paucamatus' penny to two groups of nuns (see table 5). But Harvey's penny and that of Paucamatus are one and the same. The confusion is clearly clerical error. Four individuals had died in fairly rapid succession and "who" was receiving "whose" penny became difficult to keep straight. Thus the recluse is first seen as receiving one man's pension and subsequently that of another.

20. See appendix 3, table B, *Transference of Alms: Surrey*, where the infirm of Gildford receive the alms released by the death of Gilbert de Moretano in the year 1181.

144

In the Essex account no fewer than six pennies were subject to this manipulation between 1182 and Henry's death in 1189. One penny stayed in flux for seven years, others for four or five. The penny subsequently granted to the anchorite of Writtle was withheld for the shortest interval—only six months—possibly because the new recipient was such an estimable religious: for the temporary grants were all religious in orientation. Receiving temporary grants were eleven groups of nuns who shared twenty-three gifts, Kilburn receiving six of them and Ankerwyke, Cheshunt, and Stratford-at-Bow three each. Three converts each received two gifts, as did the sick of Dunstable. Two clerics and two groups of canons also had a share of these proceeds.

Four other accounting units exhibit the same process of making temporary grants to nunneries, converts and clerics, or the sick and the poor: Surrey, Buckinghamshire and Bedfordshire, Cambridgeshire and Huntingdonshire, and Gloucestershire.[21] Counties that do not show this pattern are frequently those where there was no movement of alms during this period—so Herefordshire (table 3), Worcestershire, Yorkshire, Kent, Devonshire.[22] Female conventuals were the major although not the exclusive recipients of these temporary benefactions, a preference not discoverable in the grants of Henry's earlier years. Save for the king's extensive commitments to Fontevrault, both abroad and in his foundation of Amesbury at home, Henry's routine involvement with nunneries was minimal throughout his reign.[23] In the same years when

21. See appendix 3 for extensions of Surrey, as above; table A, Gloucestershire; table C, Buckinghamshire and Bedfordshire.

22. Herefordshire is constant because there were no deaths among alms recipients during this interval and so no possibility of this kind of transference. Other shires lack movement because they are almost completely lacking in this type of alms commitment. Southampton and Yorkshire had an alms allowance only for the Templars; Devonshire and Nottingham and Derbyshire for the Templars and a house of canons; Kent for the Templars and the infirm of Rochester (listed under tithes); Worcestershire for the Templars and the anchorite of Severn Stoke (also listed under tithes).

23. Only three Benedictine nunneries received permanent alms grants instituted by Henry II: Moxby, Yorkshire, in 1159, thirty shillings yearly; Thetford, Norfolk, in 1177, 30s. 5d. yearly; Polsloe, Devonshire, in 1178, one hundred shillings yearly. Canons and nuns at Haverholm received a grant. The nuns of Carrow,

temporary grants to nunneries became common, however, many other houses of nuns garnered small gifts, mostly as pardons of fines and ranging in amount from five pence to forty shillings. The increase in the number of anchorites on the rolls in the final years of Henry's life was thus paralleled by heightened alms activity to other religious as well. Many groups shared in this wider distribution of Henry's wealth.[24]

The foregoing analysis answers one question and raises another. Clearly anchorites were considered by Henry to be worthy of his alms. Nonetheless, adding an anchorite to the rolls was by no means an automatic process. It came only at the end of a decision-making procedure during which many claims were put forward and only few could be granted. Although the amounts of money involved remained small, the disposition of that money was a serious matter. The king bestowed his pennies neither casually nor frivolously, even on a temporary basis, and the permanent grant required by the anchorite represented a true commitment. That as late as 1185 anchorites were being granted new pennies is an indication of the high regard accorded them by Henry II. So much the analysis answers.

The question raised is why the level of Henry's response to anchorites varies during his lifetime and what this variation tells us about Henry and his attitudes toward recluses? Henry's support of anchorites was a continuous element within the framework of his almsgiving and it was an element that grew. The first real increase

---

Norfolk, routinely received twenty-five shillings, initiated by Stephen. The minister of Sheppey, Kent, received 39s. 5d. each year from the king after the lands supporting it escheated to the crown (*PR 17 Henry II* [1171], p. 137).

24. Pardons and temporary grants represent ways to bestow small gifts to many houses without precluding future options. Pardons were offered for payments of Danegeld, murder, and forest infractions in most instances. In general, the groups of nuns who received the pardons might be the same as those who were in Henry's gift previously—Fontevrault, Amesbury, and Polsloe—but were different from the groups who were receiving temporary grants from the released alms. In sum, seventeen nunneries shared more than fifty-six temporary grants of alms: Ankerwyke and Kilburn each received nine; St. James, Westminster, eight; Cheshunt, six; Stratford-at-Bow, four. Two nunneries received outright gifts: Clerkenwell and Godstow. Nineteen received relief by way of pardons. There was little overlap between the two groups—they represent thirty-six different institutions.

in the level of that support was concurrent with the Becket episode and may represent an announcement or expression of Henry's piety and orthodoxy. In the 1180s another, more gradual, rise in the level of anchorite support began, and it was coupled with the bestowing of small gifts to many other religious entities as well. I suggest that the behavior of Henry in the 1180s was connected to his anxiety about death, that there was a direct relationship between his concern about death (which he may have felt was imminent) and his seeking of the goodwill and prayers of anchorites and others. If this was so, the facile identification of the king's almsgiving in 1171 and 1172 with the Becket trauma seems less sure.

The data relative to the distribution of alms breaks with the past quite sharply in 1181/82. In that year Henry wrote his will.[25] Medieval men, even medieval kings, typically wrote their wills in close anticipation of death.[26] Save when a will was composed by a man about to leave on crusade, medieval wills most often bear a probate date that is separated from the date of writing only by months. Henry's will was written long before his death in 1189. Such an act implies a fear and sense of foreboding that probably colored his final years. The death of Young Henry in June 1183 must have sharpened those fears. The new anchorite foundations of the later years come after that event.[27]

But what of the Becket years? Is it an error to tie all events of 1171 and 1172 into that frame of reference? In 1170 Henry had

25. Henry's will is undated but internal evidence assigns it to 1182. It is printed in Nichols, *Royal Wills*, pp. 7–10.

26. Alone among the early monarchs, Henry III wrote his will a full twenty years before his death (Nichols, *Royal Wills*, pp. 15–17). A great benefactor to anchorites in his lifetime, Henry III left no bequests for them in his will. See also Joel T. Rosenthal, *The Purchase of Paradise* (London: Routledge and Kegan Paul, 1972), p. 23.

27. For an excellent discussion of some aspects of the dating of Henry's charitable foundations, see Elizabeth M. Hallam, "Henry II as a Founder of Monasteries," *Journal of Ecclesiastical History* 28 (1977): 113–132. Hallam, however, gives more credence to a long-term involvement with the Becket penance than I consider justifiable. The major new monastic foundations of Henry's later life come after 1182 and fit this analysis closely. For a basic study of Henry see Wilfred L. Warren, *Henry II* (Berkeley, Los Angeles, London: University of California Press, 1973).

thought he was dying and had made plans to be buried at Grand-mont.[28] His gratitude on being spared death then could explain the increase of anchorite support on his rolls in these years and may be the link between those two periods of his life when anchorites were more frequently endowed. The evidence within Henry's will points in the same direction. The generosity of his final gifts for anchorites indicates his belief in the value of their vocation and in the efficacy of their intercession. Their prominence in the will indicates how central that belief was to his religious perception.

Henry's will elaborated a distribution of alms from a portion of his estate: ". . . feci divisam meam de quadam parte pecuniae meae in hunc modum. . . ." His gifts were for the defense of Jerusalem and the military orders there as well as to all religious houses in Jerusalem, Normandy, England, and Anjou. In addition, he separately bequeathed money to the Carthusians, the Cluniacs, the Grandmontines, the Cistercians, the Premonstratensians, and to individual houses of nuns on the Continent, most generously of course to Fontevrault. He left money for the marrying of poor maidens: three hundred gold marks for those in England, one hundred marks for those in Normandy, and one hundred further for the poor maidens of Anjou on the lands of his father. Not least, he left money for anchorites and hermits. Five thousand silver marks were bequeathed to religious houses in Jerusalem and to the lepers, anchorites, and hermits of that land (*leprosis et inclusis et heremitis ejusdem terrae*); five thousand marks were bequeathed to the religious houses of England and to the monks, canons, nuns, lepers, anchorites, and hermits of that land; three thousand silver marks were bequeathed to the religious houses of Normandy and to the anchorites and hermits of that land.

Sharing their place of honor and need with conventuals, lepers, and poor maidens (in a pattern that will be seen to be common), anchorites were to profit on Henry's death. In death he would re-

28. William Stubbs, ed., *Gesta regis Henrici secundi Benedicti abbatis*, 2 vols., RS 49 (1867), 1:7. For some of the ramifications and meanings of this decision with respect to the order, see Elizabeth M. Hallam, "Henry II, Richard I, and the Order of Grandmont," *Journal of Medieval History* 1 (1975): 168–169.

main the benefactor he had been in life. He would continue to purchase their prayers. One wonders if the recluses of Cookham and Writtle, of Gloucester and Winchester, of Hereford and Stedham received their royal bequest and how many others there were in England (and elsewhere) whose petition was put forth to participate in the royal grant. The royal will embraced them all. It verified that daily penny in a final act of faith and supplication.

Richard I inherited the throne in 1189 and with it the responsibility for at least nine anchorites on his lands in England (see table 4). Two of them died during the first year of his reign. One of these, the recluse of Stedham, had been receiving a grant not originally of royal foundation, and, like Maldon, this money was reabsorbed into the treasury at the death of the recluse.[29] The other recluse to die in this year was the male recluse at Writtle, succumbing after five years in his cell. Richard first permitted a female recluse to take his place, then four years later she was in turn succeeded by a male anchorite.[30] Also in 1194 Richard accepted the charge of a new recluse against the receipts of the Herefordshire farm. The anchoress of St. Audoneus was granted a daily penny as a gift of the king and joined two other recluses already supported by that farm. In 1195 Richard added two more anchorites to his rolls at the same penny rate, one at Marlborough and one at Higham Ferrers, Northamptonshire, bringing royal support of anchorites as indicated in this one source to its highest totals for the reigns of Henry II and his sons.[31]

The Marlborough anchorite died in the middle of the second year of his enclosure. His grant was temporarily bestowed on some poor men (*pluribus pauperibus*). The anchorite of Gloucester, the long-term beneficiary of Henry II's most generous anchoritic endowment, also died at this time. His decease in the middle of the 1196 accounting year released sixty shillings annually. Thirty shillings, the money for the remaining half of 1196, was granted

29. *PR 1 Richard I* (1189), p. 215.
30. See chapter 5, note 1, above.
31. *PR 6 Richard I* (1194), p. 136; *PR 7 Richard I* (1195), pp. 151, 34.

to Thomas, a chamberlain, by writ of Hubert, archbishop of Canterbury, pending a subsequent order of the king. The next roll indicates that Thomas received another thirty shillings in the first half of 1197, and then, by writ of the king, the money was transferred permanently to Harvey Freschet, a layman.[32]

There seems to have been no clear policy regulating the disposition of anchoritic pension grants after the death of the initial recipient during Richard's reign. When Richard was on crusade and in captivity the tendency was to mirror behavior of Henry II's reign. Later decisions seemed to be made on an ad hoc basis, Richard once returning the money to the treasury, once continuing support for a cell by allowing a change in occupants, once granting the alms to "paupers" in a holding pattern that resembles Henry's grants to nunneries, and once giving the money to a lay individual. That Richard had a positive attitude about anchorites can best be inferred from the numbers on his rolls, from his response to the petition of William, the hermit of Ardland, to become an anchorite,[33] and from the new installations he supported, all of which belong to the period after he returned from captivity and perhaps are reflections of his own personality and tastes.[34] I say this with caution considering Richard's minimal personal involvement in the day-to-day affairs of his realm. Certainly, however, there is no contradiction in proposing that the flamboyant Crusader king would have felt concern and respect for the withdrawn religious ascetic undertaking his own interior pilgrimage.

32. *PR 9 Richard I* (1197), p. 216; *PR 10 Richard I* (1198), p. 71; *PR 8 Richard I* (1196), p. 101; *PR 9 Richard I* (1197), p. 120; *PR 10 Richard I* (1198), p. 1.

33. See chapter 2 and its note 1 for discussion of this change of vocation by William. The survival of William's charter makes clear that the Pipe Rolls are providing only one class of information. How many other anchorites might be outside its range is unanswerable.

34. The role of Hubert Walter, virtual regent during these years, has been considered. See Christopher R. Cheney, *Hubert Walter* (London: Thomas Nelson, 1967), p. 90. There is no way to be sure that what we ascribe to Richard truly belongs to him and not to Walter or lesser men. Walter was, of course, also chancellor during John's reign, when, as shall be seen, a very different set of circumstances for anchorites existed. For Walter's roles see Austin L. Poole, *From Domesday Book to Magna Carta, 1087–1216*, 2d ed. (Oxford: Clarendon Press, 1955), pp. 442–443, and John Gillingham, *Richard the Lionheart* (New York: Times Books, 1978), pp. 244–245.

The extroverted Richard may have viewed the recluse with awe: Richard's acts always demanded a public stage. Social values coupled with his father's explicit commitments and final testament would have reinforced Richard's own romantic projections. Together they would assure a stable period for royal recluses, and this is what the data indicate.

John's reign changed the picture. In the third year after his succession three cells fell vacant and in all three instances were terminated. The anchorites of Writtle, Newnham, and St. Audoneus died and were not replaced. The following year the responsibility for the anchorite at Higham Ferrers moved to the earl of Derby when certain lands were transferred to him. Thus, at the onset of the year 1203 John was carrying only five anchorites on his rolls, a number that would not rise during the remainder of his reign and represented less than half of the eleven found only seven years earlier. In the year 1203 the recluses of Severn Stoke, Cookham, and Hereford died. While all were replaced, at least temporarily, we are witnessing a trimming down of a particular kind of almsgiving for which John's enthusiasm was limited. Although John was not necessarily hostile to anchorites, their life-style may have failed to capture his imagination. Not until the sixteenth year of his reign did he found an anchorite cell on his own, and he did this in the wake of the lifting of the interdict and the religious excesses accompanying that event.

This is not to say that John was not generous in traditional ways or even in support of that other class of recluses, hermits. Hermits, in fact, seem to have been more to his taste than anchorites. Anchorites must be viewed as dependents, their value to society determined less by their activity than by their representation of a Christian exemplar that pointed toward a threshold of perfection. As a vocation, the anchoritic life represented the ultimate in withdrawal in a society that perceived withdrawal as the ultimate good. Alms support for an anchorite bought prayers for the soul but also bought identification with a value system honoring passivity and self-denial. Hermits, however, retained the option to participate fully in their own support and maintenance and to set for themselves a social task if it did not violate their own consciences. Their freedom of movement, denied to the anchorite, allowed for a very different set of conditions and mentality.

The Pipe Roll for 1205 notes John's initiation of an alms gift of forty shillings per annum for the hermit of St. Edwin's in Sherwood Forest: the roll notes that he sings in the chapel of St. Edwin's in the woods of Birchwood and celebrates divine service there for the king's soul and the souls of his ancestors. Thus it was to a chapel-hermit, not a remote solitary, that John was willing to grant a pension during this period when no new commitments to anchorites were being made and the anchorite ranks already had been thinned.[35] John's involvement with the well-known hermit St. Robert of Knaresborough is similar in tone, for Robert was not a recluse either, at least by the time he came to John's attention. Rather, in reversal of the pattern of William, hermit of Ardland, Robert began as a solitary and ended as the head of an outreaching household which included a fellow hermit named Ivo and four servants, two of them tilling the land, while the third did general chores and the fourth aided Robert and Ivo in their self-appointed task of collecting alms.[36] In 1216 John found himself at Knaresborough and paid Robert a visit. Chronicles reporting that event tell a didactic story that portrays John as first ignored by the hermit, who was at his devotions when the king arrived. Then Robert, rising from his prayers, imperiously challenged his sovereign. He

---

35. *PR 7 John* (1205), pp. 220–221; *Rot. Lit. Claus.*, i, 20a. Several other chaplains made their way onto the rolls in John's reign. See Herefordshire (table 3), where Roger, the chaplain, receives two and a half pence per day and Essex (table 6), where both Andre and the chaplain at Hertford castle receive fifty shillings annually.

36. For data on St. Robert's life *VCH Yorkshire*, 3:296–297, summarizes well. See also John R. Walbran, ed., *Memorials of the Abbey of St. Mary of Fountains*, I, SS 42 (1863), pp. 166–171n; and Hubert Dauphin, "L'érémitisme en Angleterre aux XIe et XIIe siècles," in *L'eremitismo in Occidente nei secoli XI e XII: Atti della seconda settimana internazionale di studio, Mendola, 30 agosto–6 settembre 1962*, Publicazioni dell'Università cattolica del Sacro Cuore, Contributi Serie 3: Varia 4, Miscellanea del Centro di studi medioevali 4 (Milan, 1965), pp. 293–294.

> toke ane ere of corne
> And sayd, standard the kyng byforne,
> Yff thou be kynge, sir, kand ou oght
> Off corn maike slyke ane ere of noght?[37]

Was it Robert's impertinence that captured John's imagination? On the spot he granted Robert "half a caracute of land in the wood of Swinesco as near to his hermitage as possible." It is possible that John's sense of value was directed to the active and to the tangible, even in religious phenomena.[38]

Supporting these observations is evidence from the honor of Gloucester. These lands were in John's control for the decade preceding his accession to the throne by virtue of his marriage to Isabella, the heiress. At the time the lands were delivered to him there were multiple female anchorites in the gift of the earldom and charged against the revenues of the farm.[39] Eleven years later when the accounts reappear on the royal rolls in the wake of John's divorce from Isabella and his accession to the throne, there is only one female anchorite still receiving a pension, a grant of 10s. 10d. yearly. Also on this roll is an entry noting a grant to a hermit named Godwin to whom John had awarded twenty-two shillings yearly.[40] On the lands of his earldom as on his regnal lands he had reduced anchorite support and advanced that for hermits.

Most typically, however, John used vacated anchorite slots to provide pensions for laymen. When the Writtle anchorite died, that penny was granted to one Havise de Burdell. The Marlborough penny, which was being given to paupers when John ascended the throne, was granted first to a leper and then permanently to a man called Adam le Cat.[41] The Herefordshire account had three different recluses and the monies of each of them

37. Joyce Bazire, ed., *The Metrical Life of St. Robert of Knaresborough*, EETS, o.s. 228 (1953), p. 65.

38. *Rot. Lit. Claus.*, i, 247.

39. *PR 33 Henry II* (1187), pp. 14–15: ". . . et in liberationibus inclusarum et prebendarium xli s. et viij d"; and a similar entry in the next year's roll, (*PR 34 Henry II* [1188], p. 13), where the dative case is used.

40. *PR 1 John* (1199), p. 36.

41. *PR 4 John* (1202), p. 259; *PR 1 John* (1199), p. 174.

ultimately became the pension of a lay individual. Let us examine that process in greater detail.

No accounting unit in the data supported more than one recluse at a time except for Herefordshire. The Herefordshire membranes continually detail an obligation to at least one recluse from 1158 to 1212, but for forty-two years of that interval it supported two and for eight years it supported three (see table 3). In 1201 three of the nine recluses on the royal rolls were concentrated in this one shire and give evidence of the unusual local commitment to this type of spirituality. That these were the lands where the *Ancrene Riwle* would be written twenty years later is not surprising. In 1201 two of the three Herefordshire sites became vacant. The *inclusa* of Newnham died after a tenure of forty-four years. Her penny was granted to Robert Chester. The *inclusa* of St. Audoneus died after a seven-and-a-half year enclosure. Her penny was granted to Osbert, *homo regine*. Only Richard at St. Sepulchre remained on the rolls. When he died during the first half of 1203 after thirty-one and a half years as a recluse his alms were granted to Margaret, *inclusa*. To terminate royal support of three anchorites within two years in this one region perhaps seemed excessive. Thus Margaret may have gained her penny. She continued on the rolls until 1212. The roll for 1213 is missing. In the roll for 1214 Margaret is gone and in her place is Simon of Cambrai, *inaneus* (destitute).[42]

Doris Stenton has noted King John's generosity to his friends, his gifts to nunneries too poor and obscure to have any effect on public opinion, and his purchase of "a quiet conscience for hunting in a prohibited time" through gifts of food and drink for poor men.[43] Sidney Smith, analyzing the contents of the Pipe Roll for 1205, noted John's thoughtfulness and concern for his servants. The Pipe Roll for 1208 records that a woman named Elena de Papworth of Cambridgeshire held certain lands for the service of feeding two paupers, every day in perpetuity, for the soul of the king and the souls of his ancestors.[44] Friends, servants, hermits at

---

42. *PR 3 John* (1201), p. 265; *PR 5 John* (1203), p. 55; *PR 16 John* (1214), p. 135.
43. *PR 6 John* (1204), pp. xxxvj–xxxvij. See also Poole, *Domesday*, p. 428.
44. *PR 7 John* (1205), p. xl; *PR 10 John* (1208), p. 188.

work, poor nuns, poor men, the destitute Simon de Cambrai—
these were the recipients of John's alms. Anchorites were only
nominally served during his reign.

It is possible that the interdict interfered with the establishment
of new anchorites after 1208 and that this accounts for the lack of
data of such activity on John's part until 1214. Although details of
the interdict are not precisely known, they seem to have involved
a suspension of most ecclesiastical rites,[45] the enclosing of anchorites surely among them. But the patterns described for John were
established before the interdict began and provide the more
forceful argument for his seeming lack of interest in recluses. In
1214 or early 1215 John may have instituted a recluse at Marlborough. Although nowhere mentioned in the Pipe Rolls for those
years, the fragmentary Close Roll for 1215 provides information
that Eve of Preshute, Wiltshire, *inclusa*, who was to receive a daily
penny of the king's alms beginning in May 1215, was to take over
that penny from the former alms of the male recluse of St. Mary
of Marlborough.[46] Thus John did accept at least one new recluse
gift on his rolls. But, conveniently for him, it happened in the
year when he gave up Margaret's grant in Herefordshire.

FROM HENRY III TO HENRY VIII

In his support and regard for anchorites Henry III was more the
child of his grandfather, Henry II, than of his father, John. The
Patent, Close, and Liberate Rolls of Henry III's reign document a

45. Poole, *Domesday*, pp. 445–446; W. L. Warren, *King John* (Berkeley and Los
Angeles: University of California Press, 1961), p. 164.
46. A 1215 notice in the Patent Roll (*Rot. Lit. Pat.*, p. 152a) states that Eve, the
recluse of Preshute, has received a grant of one pence per day from the king. The
fragmentary Close Roll of 1215 (R. Allen Brown, ed., *The Memoranda Roll . . .
together with . . . fragments of the Close Rolls of 16 and 17 John, 1215–16*, Pipe Roll
Society, n.s. 31 [1957], p. 139) says ". . . de Prestchet' quem reclus' Sancte Marie de
Merleb' habuit de dono nostro. . . ." Drawing from these two refernces I assume
that John had earlier (1214?) established a male recluse at St. Mary's Marlborough
and that Eve of Preshute was now to receive his penny. Neither of these grants
surfaces on the Pipe Roll accounts.

wide range of royal gifts and involvements. Henry III granted pensions both in money and kind, domiciles, land to plough and land to build upon, wheat, robes, and most commonly wood—and these to many anchorites. While that splendid sense of continuity which the Pipe Rolls established for the earlier reigns is here more difficult to obtain, the wider range of evidence available for this period, including such nonroyal sources as bishops' registers, monastic charters, court proceedings, and wills, gives us a broader social context within which to examine the royal commitment. Of over 150 persons known to have been anchorites during Henry III's reign (1216–72), 48 received some kind of direct support from the king.[47] Thus, one-third of all tabulated data reflects Henry's positive attitudes toward anchorites. Given that an anchorite could exist only through a conjunction of his own inner propulsion and a social acquiescence that most often included financial support, royal benevolence during this reign was a meaningful factor and perhaps an exemplar as well.

47. All figures of royal support presented in these pages are minimal, even within their own narrow parameters. As has been indicated above, it is a problem of the evidence that certain grants that should be listed are nowhere to be found on the rolls. For example, a grant of one and a half pence per day for the recluse of the castle of Dover was already of long standing in 1232 according to the Close Roll of that year which ordered Simon de Greneweye to pay it to her: ". . . sicut eos [iij obolos] percipere consuevit de dono predecessorum regis vel ipsius regis" (CR 1231–34, p. 105). Yet it appears on no previous rolls of any of Henry III's predecessors, nor of Henry III previous to 1232, nor in the Pipe Roll for 1242. But we know that there was a recluse in the reclusorium attached to the church of St. Mary within the castle during Henry's reign—at least until 1265. One possible answer is that certain gifts are lost in detail because they were reported on the Pipe Rolls as a lump sum. This is true for the Windsor account starting in 9 John (1207) and continuing throughout the remainder of John's reign. See also the Wiltshire membrane 33 Henry II (1187), p. 173, and Yorkshire membranes beginning 5 Henry II (1159), p. 29, and continuing for years. Another possibility is that payment was made through an intermediary—such as the abbot who assumed responsibility for William at Ardland, or a smith who was paid 38s. 10d. of the king's money for the anchoress of St. Margaret Pattens (CLR 1245–51, p. 47). Gifts also were made through almoners. Others are simply lost because of faulty accounting procedures and scribal error. For the purposes of this study no assumptions have been made and all figures represent hard data, but that these numbers are too low is without question.

Henry's gifts could take the form of lifetime commitments, occasional grants *de dono regis,* or one-time responses to immediate needs, but the most privileged anchorites were those who received a maintenance grant from him. At least twenty-seven anchorites at twenty-two sites received that promise during his long reign. The usual grant of these maintenance pensions was still for a penny or a penny and a half per day, but there was less consistency in this pattern than there had been in the earlier reigns. Christiana, the recluse of Market Harborough, Leicestershire, and Alice, at Hereford, each received one mark (13s. 4d.) per year; Sarah, enclosed at Hecham, Norfolk, received twenty shillings yearly;[48] a succession of women enclosed at Dover Castle received 45s. 7½d. (a penny and a half per day), and the recluse of Dublin Castle in Ireland received a yearly clothes allowance of ten shillings in addition to his daily penny and a half.[49] Grants in kind were for fixed amounts of wheat or firewood. The *inclusa* of Wotton, Oxfordshire, received a quarter of wheat from the proceeds of the king's manor there beginning in 1252. In 1264 she was still receiving it. Earlier, in 1236, Robert, nearby at Dornford, had been promised three cartloads of firewood yearly from the wood of Wotton.[50]

In addition to their regular stipends many persons who received a maintenance grant from the king were awarded occasional gifts of wood, robes, or other necessities. These ongoing involvements imply that Henry's commitment was personal and continuous, that these people were not given a pension and then forgotten save as a ledger entry. The recluse of Bristol Castle was to have a tunic and cloak (*pallium*) with a coarse fur lining (*grossa penula*) of lambskin, priced at twelve pence per yard, in 1226, 1227, and 1228—clearly a yearly gift. The recluse of St. Margaret Pattens,

48. *CLR 1251–60,* p. 232; *CLR 1226–40,* p. 289; *CLR 1251–60,* p. 406.
49. *CR 1231–34,* p. 105; *CR 1254–56,* p. 272; *CLR 1251–60,* pp. 323, 324, 446, 490; *CPR 1258–66,* p. 63; *CPR 1232–47,* p. 428.
50. In 1230 a quarter of wheat cost from four shillings to half a mark (*PR 14 Henry III* [1230], p. 11). For the recluse of Wotton, *CLR 1251–60,* p. 24; *CLR 1260–67,* p. 119; *CR 1261–64,* p. 55; *CR 1264–68,* pp. 9–10; for Robert, *CPR 1232–47,* p. 138.

London, who regularly received a grant of 38s. 10d., was pardoned of a debt of twelve shillings owed to Sclune and Pyum, Jews of London, in 1236.[51] Nineteen years later the sheriffs of London were ordered "to go in person to the anchoress of St. Margaret Pattens to review her buildings and the defects thereof, and repair them where necessary."[52] Juliana of Worcester received a license to widen her courtyard "on the street side" in 1256. In 1264 she received two good oak stumps for her hearth, besides her regular gift of thirty-one shillings per year. The male recluse who lived in the Tower of London received a robe "suitable for him" (*sibi convenientem*) in 1252, in addition to his daily penny; and the recluse of Dover received forty shillings *de dono regis* while staying at Roche abbey in Yorkshire, a notice that defies casual explanation.[53]

An examination of Henry's further donations to anchorites enlarges this framework for his giving and concern. During his reign Henry granted reclusoria in his gift to nine anchorites.[54] To eight others he granted the right, and sometimes the wood, to build a new reclusorium at a church or a hospital of which he was patron. For this purpose one Alice received three oaks in 1245. In 1235 Joanna of Farlington had received five oaks to rebuild her reclusorium damaged by fire.[55] Ten years before that, when Payne

51. *Rot. Lit. Claus.* ii, 158a; *CLR 1226–40*, pp. 52–53, 113; *CLR 1245–51*, p. 47; *CR 1234–37*, p. 30.

52. *CLR 1251–60*, p. 200.

53. *CPR 1247–58*, p. 492; *CR 1264–68*, p. 7; *CPR 1258–66*, p. 546; *CR 1251–53*, p. 291; *CR 1259–61*, p. 223. Their vows of stability notwithstanding, some anchorites certainly did move about from time to time. They changed cells, went on pilgrimage, occasionally went to court. In 1491 a Norwich anchorite who was a Carmelite friar was one of twenty-four priests (dressed in red and white vestments) who walked in procession on the festival day of St. George's Guild (Mary Grace, ed., *Records of the Gild of St. George in Norwich, 1389–1547*, Norfolk Record Society 9 [1937], p. 18). In my chapter 6, I mention an anchoress brought to London from her Winchester cell for a consultation with Richard Beauchamp, earl of Warwick. All of these activities seem to have been generally acceptable to society.

54. *CR 1227–31*, p. 31; *CR 1234–37*, pp. 424, 467; *CR 1237–42*, p. 273; *CR 1247–51*, pp. 292, 314; *CR 1251–53*, p. 412; *CR 1254–56*, p. 265; *CPR 1258–66*, p. 118.

55. For Alice: *CR 1242–47*, p. 368. For Joanna: *CR 1234–37*, p. 211. See also *Rot. Lit. Claus.*, ii, 44a, 181b; *CR 1234–37*, p. 296; *CR 1237–42*, p. 325; *CPR 1232–47*, p. 275; *CPR 1266–72*, p. 84.

de Lench had requested and received royal permission to live in the forest of Dean at Ardland, the king granted her two oaks for a new dwelling plus four acres for her sustenance.[56] Other anchorites received wood for their hearths: Mathilda de la More received an oak in 1237; the recluse of Windsor an oak stump in 1247; the recluses of Britford, Wiltshire, at least one stump each year for a period of over thirty years; the recluse of Iffley, Oxfordshire, a gift of wood every year for nine consecutive years.[57]

In 1245 all the anchoresses in London received a special gift from Henry. His father-in-law, Raymond, the count of Provence, had died and Henry directed his London sheriffs "to feed 10,000 poor for the soul of the count of Provence, besides the friars preachers and the friars minors, the sick in hospitals, and the anchoresses in and about London, who are also to be fed, as William de Haverhull and Edward de Westm' will tell them from the king."[58] In his role as pious son-in-law Henry was to be second to none. In fact, as Matthew Paris stated, the king's most excellent behavior was quite in contrast to that of his brother-in-law, Louis IX of France, who had responded to the news of Raymond's death by marching his soldiers into Provence.[59] Grouped with the absolute poor, the voluntary poor, and the sickly poor, Henry included the female recluses of London in his memorial gesture.

Henry was most involved with anchorites during the middle thirty-five years of his reign. The period of Henry's minority shows mainly the continuation of inherited obligations. The last ten years of his life show almost nothing in the way of new commitments (quite in contrast to Henry II). For purposes of comparison, table 7 projects that in 1230 eight anchorites were

56. William the Solitary had died by 1225 when Henry granted the location to Payne. Sixteen years later the new reclusorium was regranted to another woman named Juetta de Wiz (CR 1237-42, p. 273). In the sixteenth century the hermitage again was being lived in by chapel-hermits and was again in the possession of Flaxley Abbey (Arthur T. Bannister, ed., *Registrum Caroli Bothe, episcopi Herefordensis, A.D. 1516-1535*, CYS 28 [1921], pp. 355, 358).

57. For Mathilda: CR 1234-37, p. 489; for Windsor: CR 1242-47, p. 499; for Britford, see my chapter 5, note 60; for Iffley, see my chapter 5, note 66.

58. CLR 1240-45, p. 324.

59. Matthew Paris, *Matthaei Parisiensis, monachi sancti Albani, chronica majora*, ed. Henry R. Luard, 7 vols., RS 57 (1872-83), 4:485.

TABLE 7
ROYAL MAINTENANCE GRANTS: HENRY III (1216–1272)

Chester: *Frodsham*
@ 1d. per day

Essex: *Colchester* at St. James
@ ½d. per day

Gloucestershire: *Ardland*
house + 4 acres land

Gloucestershire: *Bristol Castle*
@ ? (data lacking)

Herefordshire: *Alice*
@ 13s. 4d. yearly

Kent: *Dover Castle*
@ 1½d. per day

Kent: *Sutton*
@ 1d. per day

Leicestershire: *Market Harborough*
@ 13s. 4d. yearly

London: *Charing Cross*
@ 60s. yearly

London: *St. Margaret Pattens*
@ 38s. 10d. yearly

London: *Tower*
@ 1d. per day

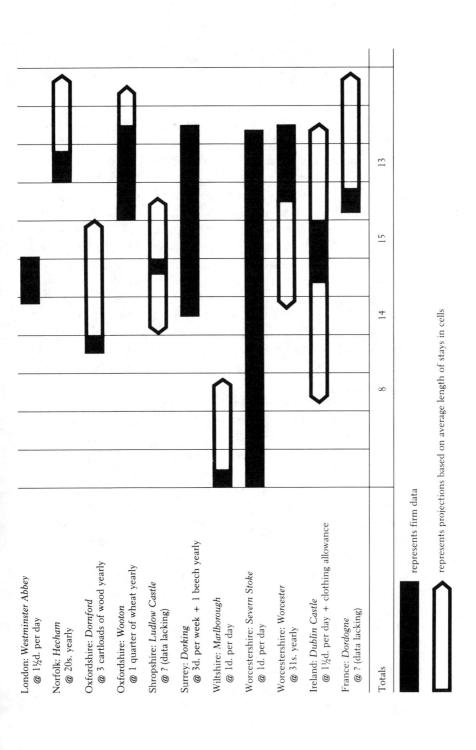

London: *Westminster Abbey*
@ 1½d. per day

Norfolk: *Hecham*
@ 20s. yearly

Oxfordshire: *Dornford*
@ 3 cartloads of wood yearly

Oxfordshire: *Wooton*
@ 1 quarter of wheat yearly

Shropshire: *Ludlow Castle*
@ ? (data lacking)

Surrey: *Dorking*
@ 3d. per week + 1 beech yearly

Wiltshire: *Marlborough*
@ 1d. per day

Worcestershire: *Severn Stoke*
@ 1d. per day

Worcestershire: *Worcester*
@ 31s. yearly

Ireland: *Dublin Castle*
@ 1½d. per day + clothing allowance

France: *Dordogne*
@ ? (data lacking)

Totals

13   15   14   8

represents firm data

represents projections based on average length of stays in cells

possibly in Henry's regular gift; perhaps fourteen in 1240; fifteen in 1250; thirteen in 1260. But these represent only a portion of his involvements.

Some recluses seen to have been special favorites of Henry III. The anchoress Joan Malewn, who lived at the reclusorium at Britford, was one. In receipt of a pension of one mark yearly from nonroyal sources, she became in 1226 the regular recipient of the king's wood. His orders specified that the gift be delivered to her house. The grants were for variable quantities: in 1226 she received two oak stumps; in 1231 and 1232 one; in 1238 three. In some other years cartloads of brushwood were delivered, in 1244 as many as ten. During these years the king also caused the courtyard extending around her house to be enclosed with a stone wall. In the early 1240s, after more than twenty years of known royal gifts, Joan died. A male recluse may have taken her place briefly and then in 1246 a new female recluse is mentioned by name in the Close Roll. She received *unum robur*, one oak stump, each year until 1255, when these gifts ceased.[60] The continuity of this relationship is not typical. It leads one to suspect that Joan Malewn was a person significant to Henry and that the king's patronage to the cell had become so well established by the time of Joan's death that it maintained its rhythm throughout the tenure of her successors.

Another anchorite who had unusual status with Henry was Nicholas at Westminster. Brother Nicholas was an anchorite there only for seven years, but his story, better documented than most, is rich in detail. He is first mentioned in a Close Roll writ of 28 April 1241 granting him a pension of two pence per day, formerly the pension of John Blundus, onetime messenger to the king. This writ, however, was immediately cancelled "quia prius data fuit alii." A month later, on 25 May, Nicholas's name appeared on the roll again. Having lost the first pension because it had been promised elsewhere, he was now to be given the pension of John de la Tudel, newly deceased.[61] Sadly for Nicholas, this latter pension

60. *Rot. Lit. Claus.*, ii, 92b; CR *1227–31*, p. 482; CR *1231–34*, p. 176; CR *1237–42*, p. 83; CR *1242–47*, p. 169; CLR *1226–40*, p. 273; CLR *1240–45*, p. 209; CR *1242–47*, p. 400; CR *1247–51*, pp. 20, 145, 462; CR *1254–56*, p. 88.

61. CR *1237–42*, pp. 296, 303.

had been only for one and a half pennies per day, and so this amount became his grant. It would seem that Nicholas, approved for a grant, had to wait to receive it until funds were released by the death of another pensioner and he received only the amount that had been granted previously.[62] Given the laissez-faire nature of this transaction the quality of Nicholas's relationship with the king seems casual. Yet three years later in 1244 Nicholas is found securing the release of Gilbert de Hoton from his outlawry for rape. In 1246 the king arranged for a tun of wine to be given to the abbess and convent of Romsey against the day when Nicholas's niece would be veiled there. In September 1247 Henry, responding to Nicholas's request, granted Stephen of Twye a pension of three and a half pence per day (with a promise of more to come). This is an unusual series of examples of personal prestige and power for a recluse at this time, made even more curious because he did not seem of consequence earlier. Perhaps Nicholas had grown in importance to the king during his tenure. In future years the anchorites of the cell at Westminster would participate in English history because of the respect of the monarch for the reigning anchorites. Richard II and Henry V each consulted a Westminster anchorite at crucial moments in their lives. Nicholas, titled "brother" in some of the documents, may have been a Benedictine and a priest and an occasional confessor to the king. In this way he could have gained both the king's ear and his respect while still enclosed in his cell in the abbey cathedral. However Nicholas's rather unusual influence was achieved, it was not to last. In January 1248, less than four months after he had arranged for Stephen's future, his own time had come; the calendar informs us that after his death his daily penny and a half was granted to Alice, the widow of Master David, former surgeon to the king.[63]

---

62. That this was not always the case is indicated by the following notice in which Henry states that the pension he is granting is to be in the amount of twelve pence per day and is to come "de primis escaetis ad elemosinam regis assingnatis habeat . . ." (CR 1251–53, p. 131). The same limitation of alms expenses noted for the earlier reigns is in evidence in these transactions.

63. CPR 1232–47, p. 429; CLR 1245–51, p. 78; CR 1242–47, p. 535; CPR 1232–47, p. 509. In 1381, just before Richard went out to meet Wat Tyler, he confessed to Dan John Murymouth, resident anchorite in Westminster Abbey (David

It is clear that Henry's gifts to anchorites were part of the broad sweep of his patronage style. Medieval monarchs dispensed that patronage widely and any page of a mid-thirteenth-century Close Roll will detail the process for Henry's reign in a half-dozen entries that conclude *de dono regis*. Granted to many individuals and religious houses were wood, robes, linen and canvas, stags, does and fawns, wine, and live fish for stocking fish ponds. Recorded also were pensions of one pence per day for a groom of the king's chapel, of approximately three and a half pence per day for Petronilla, Prince Edmund's nurse, and of twelve pence per day for Henry of Winchester, a convert. The prior of Lessingham received a cape of samite with a broad gold fringe. Randomly chosen, these writs lifted from the rolls of 1252 and 1253 give some sense of the nature of Henry's routine patronage at the lowest level.

More specifically, Henry's support of university students has been studied as a function of his overall patronage policies, and Franklin Pegues's analysis[64] provides both a useful parallel to my own enumeration of Henry's gifts for anchorites and a confirmation of the range and nature of Henry's grants seen in the randomly selected entries. During his reign Henry gave stipends to young clerics attending universities or supported them with gifts in lesser ways. Just as with anchorites, he sometimes assumed their total support, sometimes added to that with further gifts and attentions, and sometimes provided only occasional offerings that added an element of luxury to a poor student's life. Annual stipends (for those who received them) were in the range of £20 per year and were paid either through the exchequer or by presentation to one or more ecclesiastical livings. Additional gifts were

---

Knowles, *The Religious Orders in England*, 3 vols. [1948–59; reprint Cambridge: Cambridge University Press, 1971], 2:220); for Henry V, see below, this chapter. Whether anchorites made places famous or places gave anchorites renown is not clear; I suspect some of both. Walter's Rule (Livario Oliger, ed., "Regulae reclusorum Angliae et quaestiones tres de vita solitaria, saec. XIII–XIV," *Antonianum* 9 [1934]: 58) speaks of "the hypocritical anchorite" who "desires to be enclosed in a famous place, so that he can be considered better."

64. Franklin Pegues, "Royal Support of Students in the Thirteenth Century," *Speculum* 31 (1956): 454–462.

for wine, firewood, venison, and other sundries, the venison frequently granted for banquets celebrating the granting of a degree.

Thus the gifts Henry provided for recluses were gifts he gave to others as well and the patterns of support similar to the patterns by which he supported others. What is different are the restrictions placed both on the nature and the amounts of those gifts when granted to anchorites. The evidence implies that Henry respected the asceticism of the recluse. His favorite gift for anchorites was wood, *ad focum suum,* for their hearth—even ascetics needed a fire against the English winter.[65] And that even the limited gifts he bestowed do not seem to have been granted indiscriminately adds to the picture of Henry as a benefactor. A comparison of Henry's relationship with two famous anchorites of the thirteenth century supports the perception that the king was drawn to true religious commitment. The two recluses, sisters, were the daughters of William de Braose, a marcher baron of great power in the early years of the century. One was Annora, first wife and then widow of Hugh de Mortimer; the other was Loretta, countess of Leicester.

Annora had been a great lady. Eric J. Dobson, in his recent work on the *Ancrene Riwle,* considers it likely that she and her husband were the patrons of the three sisters for whom the *Riwle* was written and that the French version of that work was created for Annora at the time of her reclusion. She became an anchoress in the autumn of 1232, having made arrangements, by consent of the king, to retain an annual income of one hundred shillings from her *maritagium.* Once enclosed, she completely disappeared as a personality. The recluse of Iffley in Oxfordshire now began to appear on the public records. Within a nine-year period ten royal writs concerned her. There were yearly grants of large quantities of wood, a "suitable" robe was provided one year, six quarters of wheat in another. It can be assumed that she had died when these

65. A typical example, this one for the recluse of Britford, reads as follows: "Mandatum est custodi foreste de Clarendon' quod faciat habere recluse de Bretford' unum robur ad focum suum in foresta predicta, de dono regis" (CR 1234-37, p. 241).

grants ceased abruptly in 1241.[66] Given her known income of one hundred shillings per year, she was guaranteed more than three pence per day at a time when the average recluse was content with less than half that amount. The royal gifts, then, must be understood not in terms of absolute need but as a voluntary response to a high-born lady who withdrew from the world completely when she became an anchoress. That Annora's husband, Hugh de Mortimer, had been a loyal supporter of Henry's father would not have been forgotten. That Annora herself had been imprisoned by John because she was the daughter of William de Braose would also have been known to Henry. Religious perception, royal generosity, royal gratitude, and royal guilt may have found mutual accommodation within the accustomed forms of royal patronage.

Henry's relationship with Loretta was of a different order. Loretta was a recluse for more than forty-five years (1219–65 +). During that entire period, as far as the records show, Henry never made her a gift of his own choice. Doubtlessly well supported by her own preenclosure financial arrangements (not discoverable on the rolls, however), she was nonetheless in the gift of her friend Alice, the countess of Eu, whose customary alms to her included wheat, barley, and oats, in addition to two sides of bacon. While the countess's grants were acknowledged by Henry and allowed to continue when Alice's lands escheated to the crown, that was the extent of his concern for Loretta's physical needs. Loretta nevertheless appeared in the records frequently. Thomas de Eccleston reports that she was an early supporter of the Franciscans in England, using her influence with magnates and prelates even though she was already in her cell at the time of their arrival in the country. A bit later her male servant was excused from jury duty. For a female recluse to have a male servant was contrary to ecclesiastical policy, but it spoke in all probability of her involvement in affairs of the world, not of the flesh. The extent of those affairs began to be chronicled in the fifties when Loretta is found

66. Eric J. Dobson, *The Origins of Ancrene Wisse* (Oxford: Clarendon Press, 1976), pp. 307–309; *CPR 1225–32*, p. 501; *CR 1231–34*, pp. 230, 421, 500; *CR 1234–37*, pp. 128, 299; *CR 1237–42*, pp. 44, 66, 269 (*bis*); *CLR 1226–40*, p. 429.

using her influence to promote friends. The nuns of St. Sepulchre were aided once and then again in an interminable lawsuit over land; William le Jay and Martha, a widow, were quit of their assessed tallage at her instance; another William was pardoned the death of his brother in an inquest first achieved through Loretta's efforts, the results of which were to be reported to her; a woman named Agnes was pardoned of outlawry; Peter of Ockam was relieved of indebtedness on the death of a London Jew. In 1265 the king himself wrote to Loretta, desiring and commanding her recollection concerning the rights and liberties pertaining to the earldom and honor of Leicester. She must have been eighty years old by then. She seems to have been a good lady but a rather worldly anchorite. Her capacity to control the affairs of others from her anchorage is unmatched in the sources. Henry was clearly respectful to her and responsive to her requests. She was part of his world. But he did not send her wood.[67]

Evidence of royal involvement with anchorites falls off sharply with the accession of Edward I, giving notice again that while royal support of anchorites continued without break until the Reformation, it was more pro forma in some reigns than in others. Available data suggest that Edward I and Edward II had minimal involvement with anchorites, that royal interest quickened in the mid-fourteenth century (along with the mystical-devotional movement of that time), and that such interest continued and grew during the Lancastrian era, after which it declined to polite levels for the remainder of the medieval period. It is possible that this brief overview expresses fluctuations in the number of people interested in becoming anchorites rather than in the royal response to the vocation; in keeping with this possibility we remember that the final years of Henry III's reign showed no new anchorite foundations. The problem, of course, lies in the nature of the evidence.

67. CCR 1242-47, p. 425; CLR 1251-60, p. 27; Thomas of Eccleston, *Tractatus de adventu Fratrum Minorum in Angliam,* ed. Andrew G. Little (Manchester: Manchester University Press, 1951), p. 20; CPR 1232-47, p. 133; CPR 1247-58, p. 502; CPR 1258-66, pp. 10, 23, 51, 350-351; CPR 1266-72, p. 727; CR 1254-56, p. 48; CR 1261-64, p. 343; CR 1264-68, pp. 115-116.

During a period when royal data provide a high percentage of that evidence, the loss of them creates a serious void. This is the situation in the years between 1275 and 1350, after which large quantities of will evidence fill in many gaps and the royal presence does not loom so large. Nonroyal evidence extant for the period 1275–1325 gives us a sense that anchorites did remain part of the local scene in late thirteenth- and early fourteenth-century England. The will of an Oxford man, Reginald the Mason, circa 1270–75, provided a shilling for all the anchorites of Oxford in the same years that another Oxford man, the burgess Nicholas de Weston, left bequests of from one to three shillings to nine specific anchorites in the Oxford area; the Bury St. Edmunds register indicates the presence of thirty-seven anchorholds in Suffolk, three in Norfolk, and two in Cambridgeshire.[68] The anchoritic way of life was an ongoing religious phenomenon at least in these two regions during the reigns of the first two Edwards and I take the absence of evidence in the printed rolls of these reigns at face value—to imply essential indifference on the part of these monarchs to anchorites.

But essential indifference was not total disregard. Edward I, in addition to those anchorites whose support he inherited along with the throne, maintained two recluses on those lands where he was earl of Chester.[69] Late in his father's reign he also joined with his mother to "persuade" the monks of Blyth priory to give support to the aged and needy anchorite Joan: "Note that Prior William and the monks gave from their house to Joan the recluse of the chapel of St. John the Evangelist outside Blyth, *at the instance of the queen and her firstborn son* [Edward], a livery—namely a conventual loaf, a gallon of conventual wine, and a general allow-

68. Spencer R. Wigram, ed., *The Cartulary of the Monastery of St. Frideswide at Oxford*, 2 vols., Oxford Historical Society (1895–96), 1:276; Herbert E. Salter, ed., *Cartulary of Oseney Abbey*, 6 vols., Oxford Historical Society 89–91, 97–98, 101 (1929–36), 2:563; Antonia Gransden, "The Reply of a Fourteenth-century Abbot of Bury St. Edmunds to a Man's Petition to Be a Recluse," *English Historical Review* 75, (1960): 464n.

69. CCR 1272–79, p. 209; R. Steward Brown, ed., *Cheshire in the Pipe Rolls, 1158–1301*, Lancashire and Cheshire Record Society 92 (1938), pp. 113, 115, 118, 123, 135.

ance of food from the kitchen, every day for her lifetime."[70] It is hard to determine whether the needs of the recluse or the pleasure of the royal family was being served. But the Blyth priory notice does show that royal attitudes toward recluses were expressed in ways other than direct support. Both this notice and the response of Edward to anchorites in his appanage may suggest that his support for recluses was "local"—a function of lordship rather than kingship.

Edward II allowed Catherine de Audley, later to be immortalized in Wordsworth's sonnet, to keep thirty pounds per year out of the issues of her dead husband's lands as a recluse's pension, just as his grandfather had allowed Annora de Braose a hundred shillings per year a hundred years earlier.[71] In another intervention indicative of moral support, Edward II interceded in behalf of the anchoress Aline whose nobly endowed pension had ceased being paid as a result of the Lancastrian rebellion of 1322.[72] Edward's wife Isabella was a patron in the requests of anchorites for enclosure and for access to scarce cells both as queen and later as queen mother in the reign of her son Edward III. Edward III himself granted a reclusorium to a woman in 1339 at a hospital in Lincoln which was of his foundation; in 1353 Alice de Latimer received twenty shillings "of the king's alms in aid of her support"; in 1370

70. Reginald T. Timson, ed., *The Cartulary of Blyth Priory*, 2 vols., Thoroton Record Society 27–28 (1973), 2:508 (my italics).

71. Clay, *Hermits and Anchorites*, pp. 74–75; *CCR 1323–27*, p. 19. Lady Audley, the recluse of Ledbury, Herefordshire, was widowed in 1299. In 1312, presumably when her two sons and daughter were grown, she became a recluse after making provisions for her unusually large endowment. She was still alive in 1327 (*CMR*, no. 476; I. J. Sanders, *English Baronies* [Oxford: Clarendon Press, 1960], p. 36n, errs in dating her death to 1322). She was half-sister to Margaret, de jure countess of Salisbury, who married Henry de Lacy, earl of Lincoln. The Lacys were longtime supporters of anchorites. Wordsworth's poem about Catherine is witness to the legend that grew up around her.

72. For Aline see my chapter 3 and its note 47. As with other monarchs, records indicate Edward II's support for hermits. See Hope Emily Allen, *Writings, Ascribed to Richard Rolle, Hermit of Hampole, and Materials for His Biography* (Modern Language Association of America, 1927; reprint, New York: Kraus, 1966), p. 128, for William the hermit of Dalby, and *VCH Yorkshire*, 3:91, for a group of six hermits at Knaresborough (where Robert had lived) to whom Edward was very generous.

three hermits and eight anchorites, "recluse persons within the city of London and the suburbs thereof," each received one mark, in a notice that, like Alice's, sounds as if it were a regular commitment.[73] During these same years the register of the Black Prince, Edward's son and presumed heir, notes his involvements with solitaries in the Cheshire lands. In 1358 he ordered fuel (two leafless trees) for the anchorite of Chester and four shillings as a gift of charity for Robert de Shefeld, hermit there. Four years earlier his auditors in Cornwall had been instructed with regard to Sir William Pruet, chaplain, who "has promised the prince that he will stay for life at the hermitage within the park of Rostormel to sing masses there for the prince's ancestors, and the prince for that reason has promised that he will grant him 16s. 8d. yearly in addition to the 50s. yearly which he already receives as his salary . . ." Other hermits, in Dorset, Oxfordshire, Wiltshire, and York, received hermitages in Prince Edward's gift, two of them receiving oaks fit for timber as well.[74]

When Richard II inherited the throne he inherited these obligations and enough of a sense of deference to recluses to choose the anchorite at Westminster as his confessor at a critical moment in his life. In 1381, just before Richard went out to meet Wat Tyler, he confessed to Dan John Murymouth, resident anchorite in the abbey.[75] Richard's wife Anne established an anchorite named Joan de Ayleston at Nottingham, unquestionably with Richard's knowledge and consent. When Anne died in 1394, Richard assumed the obligation of Joan's two-penny-per-day grant. In turn, Henry IV quickly accepted his cousin's responsibility as his

73. A. Hamilton Thompson, ed., *Register of William Greenfield, Lord Archbishop of York, 1306–1315*, 2 vols., SS 145, 149 (1931–34), 2:185–186; Sir William Dugdale, *The Antiquities of Warwickshire*, 2d ed., 2 vols. (London: J. Osborn and T. Longman, 1730), 1:193, where the 1362 date must be wrong since Isabel died in 1358; CPR 1337–39, p. 318; Frederick Devon, ed., *Issues of the Exchequer, King Henry III–King Henry VI*, Record Commission (London, 1837), p. 160; Frederick Devon, ed., *Issue Roll of Thomas de Brantingham, Bishop of Exeter, Lord High Treasurer of England*, Record Commission (London, 1835), p. 395.

74. Great Britain, Public Record Office, *Register of Edward the Black Prince*, 4 vols. (London: HMSO, 1930–33), 3:309, 310; 1:94; 4:48, 85, 380, 518; 2:63.

75. Knowles, *Religious Orders*, 2:220.

own on his assuming his cousin's throne and, in an unusual act, raised Joan's grant to three pence per day.[76] Perhaps the behavior of a guilty man, this generosity can also be explained by the positive attitude of the Lancastrians toward anchorites.

The Lancastrians came to the English throne with a double commitment to support the ascetic life. On the one hand, ascendance to the throne meant that Henry IV assumed the ongoing commitments of Richard II; on the other, Henry brought with him to the crown a sympathy and a sense of responsibility of his own toward anchorites, one born out of his own twofold inheritance as a Plantagenet and a Lancastrian (fig. 2). Both inheritances exposed Henry to a value system that respected the solitary tradition, but while the responses of the later Plantagenets seem to have become routine, the Lancastrian tradition remained fervent and intense.

The Lancastrian connections to the solitary movements can be traced back in the records to the twelfth century and the Lacy family. This orientation was still in sharp focus in the fourteenth century in the time of Henry, duke of Lancaster, who may have given it some of its most meaningful elements. Duke Henry, who died of the plague in 1361, came as near as any man to achieving the romantic ideal of his time.[77] A fighting knight when the occasion demanded, he was even more valued by his cousin and friend Edward III as a diplomat and advisor. One of the first Knights of the Garter, Henry appears on the list of members in third place, his name preceded only by those of Edward himself and Edward's son, the Black Prince. Henry preferred the tournament to the battlefield, but even in the midst of war he was famed for his courtesy and chivalry. Two further attributes of the perfect knight were ascribed to him—grandeur and generosity. His London

---

76. CPR 1391–96, p. 503; CPR 1399–1401, p. 183; CCR 1402–05, p. 243.

77. The following draws from both Émile J. F. Arnould, "Henry of Lancaster and his *Livre des Seintes Medicines*," *Bulletin of the John Rylands Library* 21 (1937): 352–386, and from Margaret Wade Labarge, "Henry of Lancaster and *Le Livre de Seyntz Medicines*," *Florilegium* 2 (1980): 183–191. The standard biography of Henry of Lancaster is Kenneth Fowler, *The King's Lieutenant: Henry of Grosmont, First Duke of Lancaster 1310–1361* (New York: Barnes and Noble, 1969).

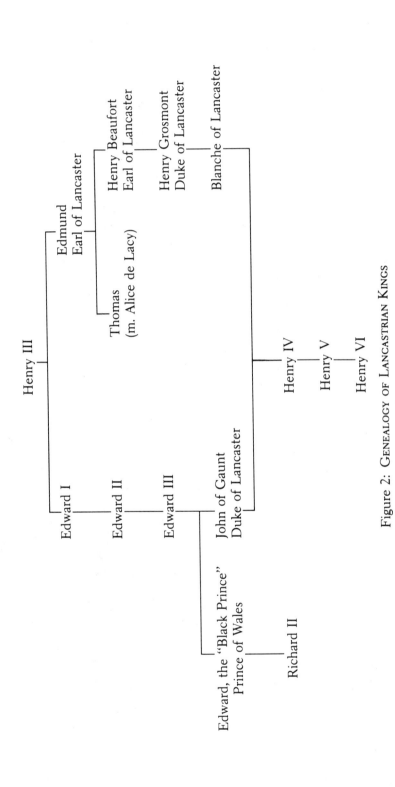

Figure 2: GENEALOGY OF LANCASTRIAN KINGS

home was one of the great houses of England and his retinue was numerous and magnificently clad. His giving was as expansive as his graciousness. He was generous to his men in the name of chivalry; he was generous to many religious establishments in the name of God. Such sentiments were not mere formality. A unique man, he wrote a unique work, *Le Livre de Seyntz Medicines*. In the confessional genre, the work is "ingenuously humble and sometimes crudely frank . . . the utterance of a soul deeply conscious of the vanity of worldly things and of the spiritual perils inherent in a life of pomp and luxury." Malcolm Vale speaks of the "self-denigrating, contemptuous, penitential" tone of the work, remarking on how that motif runs through much of the upper-class piety of the time. Lancaster wrote of himself as a "pauper, destitute of all goods and sorely wounded in seven wounds so repulsive . . . my wounds are so horrible and so full of venom from the evil smelling infection . . . my whole body is full of sores." He compared himself to a fox who will be dug out of his subterranean lair by his shrift-father: "one pulls out the fox with great joy, however stinking he may be."[78] The conflict of his life was expressed in this work. His career was an example of the active life played to its ultimate perfection: he was a good man by every definition. Yet his literary work was an expression of the inherent sinfulness of that life, a sinfulness from which there seemed no escape, save perhaps for the religious and certainly for the recluse. Henry's endowments of religious institutions were not the attempts of a wicked man to redeem his way into heaven but vicarious acts completing his life.

When in 1345 Henry became the earl of Lancaster at the death of his father, "blind" Henry, there were many commitments to solitaries guaranteed by the lordship, some of them already ancient. The Pontefract reclusorium in the chapel of St. Helen near the castle had been established sometime before 1240.[79] Then in

78. Malcolm G. A. Vale, *Piety, Charity, and Literacy among the Yorkshire Gentry, 1370–1480*, Borthwick Papers, no. 50 (York: St. Anthony Hall's Publications, 1976), p. 2; Arnould, "Henry of Lancaster," pp. 365, 378. Arnould has edited the complete work: Henry of Lancaster, *Le Livre de Seyntz Medicines: The Unpublished Devotional Treatise of Henry of Lancaster*, ed. Émile J. F. Arnould, Anglo-Norman Text Society (Oxford: Basil Blackwell, 1940).

79. CR 1237–42, p. 258.

the gift of the Lacys, the anchorage passed to the Lancasters in 1311 when Henry de Lacy died leaving no male heirs. His daughter and heiress Alice married Thomas, earl of Lancaster, bringing the Pontefract lordship into the Lancastrian demesne. Lancaster was executed in 1322 during the conflicts of Edward II's reign and the confiscation of his lands brings this royal accounting to light: "Paid to an anchoress living in Pontefract for the latter half of 15 Ed. II, all 16 Ed. II and part of 17 Ed. II partly in cash and partly in corn of the allowances [*super illo certo*] that she used to receive in the time of the earl of Lancaster, *viz.* 1 qr. 7 bush. each of wheat, rye and barley, 4 qrs. 6 bush. oats and 6s. 8d. cash: £8. 15. 20½."[80] The cash value of the grant on a yearly basis was about £4. 8s., quite a large sum, and women continued to live at Pontefract all through the fourteenth and fifteenth centuries. In 1359 Henry of Lancaster received a license to assign a livery to the anchorites at Pontefract to support a chaplain who would celebrate divine service daily for them in the chapel. There were probably two women there at the time, and this notice indicates that Henry's involvement with them was personal (license is granted to "the king's kinsman") and that he was expanding the limits of his support. Not long after this, Henry made provision for a new reclusorium of his own foundation at Whalley, Lancashire.[81]

Henry's daughter Blanche was the first wife of John of Gaunt. Both the Lancastrian lands and the dukedom became her inheritance on the death of her father and of her sister who had first shared that inheritance with her. It was through marriage to Blanche that Gaunt became duke of Lancaster as he took possession of his wife's patrimony. Gaunt was a more complicated figure than his father-in-law. As son of Edward III, brother to the Black Prince, and later uncle and advisor to the young Richard II, his fortunes were tied to those of the crown. His advocacy of Wyclif brought him danger, and his response to that danger was belligerent and autocratic. His patronage of Chaucer was another side of

---

80. CMR 1326–27, no. 2167.
81. CPR 1358–61, p. 246, for Pontefract anchorites (note plural); for Whalley see my chapter 2 and its note 58 and also text below and chapter 5 notes 99–100.

his personality, his capacity to love women yet another. He seems to have been genuinely devoted to Blanche of Lancaster during the nine years of their life together. She died of the plague in September 1368 at the age of twenty-seven. She was buried at St. Paul's in London, where Gaunt erected an expensive tomb in her memory and chose to be buried next to her.[82]

A man whose motives often have been questioned, Gaunt was traditionally religious and a benefactor to recluses.[83] His will provided three nobles (twenty shillings) to every poor hermit and recluse having a house in London or within a radius of five leagues of London. This testamentary bequest honored a group of solitaries outside the range of his regular commitments to recluses in Yorkshire, Lancashire, Leicestershire, and elsewhere. The grant provided a stipend for enclosed anchorites, for hermits living solitary lives in the manner of anchorites but without formal permanent enclosure, for hermits who were serving isolated chapels, and for working hermits (those mending bridges and roads). Gaunt's registers note his involvement with all these kinds of recluses on his own lands. Specifically, there were anchorites in the gift of the duchy at Beverly, at Pontefract, at Whalley, at Snaith (near Pontefract), at Richmond, at Bishop's Lynn, and at Leicester.[84]

82. Blanche, of course, is the "Duchess" in Chaucer's *Book of the Duchess*. J. J. N. Palmer, in "The Historical Context of the *Book of the Duchess*: A Revision," *Chaucer Review* 8 (1974): 253–261, establishes her death as occurring in 1368, not in 1369 as had been thought previously.

83. See James Crompton, "Leicestershire Lollards," *Leicestershire Archaeological and Historical Society, Transactions* 44 (1968–69): 19, for Gaunt's patronage of the hermit William Swinderby (who later was accused of Lollardy). Crompton comments, "Gaunt seemed to enjoy contact with such religious enthusiasts though his way of life seems to have shown little change therefrom."

84. Gaunt's will, written in 1398, is printed both in *Test. Ebor.*, 1:223–239, and in Nichols, *Royal Wills*, pp. 145–173. A noble (6s. 8d.) was a new coin first minted by Edward III and equivalent to one-half mark. The will provides grants only to London recluses. As such it supplements Gaunt's more permanent and ongoing commitments and identifies him with the capital city where he chose to be buried. Both Gaunt's will and that of Henry of Lancaster indicate how partial a piece of evidence a will may be. Henry's will is bare of reference to anchorites; Gaunt's notes only London ones. Both documents are thus in themselves lacking for my purposes. I have considered will evidence of anchorite support only in posi-

All this was the inheritance of Henry IV when he came to the throne in 1399. Commenting on Henry's wide support of anchorites during his reign, James H. Wylie remarked that Henry was "only continuing payments which had been made by his father before him." It would be more correct to say that Henry was part of a tradition that respected recluses and that he participated in that custom fully and willingly as he assumed control of both the royal and the family inheritances. Sir Walter Besant wrote that Henry IV endowed a cell for an anchorite in a Lancashire village before his accession. This is not a surprise. Within six weeks of his accession he granted a new pension to a woman named Margery Pensax. Margery was to live as an anchoress in the cell at St. Botulph's without Bishopsgate, London, and to receive forty shillings yearly which "the king of his alms granted her for life . . . of the farm of the city of London." The same year another woman, Maude Wardesale at St. Peter's, Leicester, was in receipt of a pension for six marks per year (eighty shillings) paid from the accounts of the Duchy of Lancaster; she may have been that Matilda whose orthodoxy Courtenay questioned.[85]

One result of Henry IV's dual inheritance was that royal largesse to anchorites became more widely dispersed. In the reign of Henry III anchorites in Middlesex (including London) and Oxfordshire accounted for 40 percent of his involvements, and all of his gifts were within a hundred-mile radius of London. The north of the country was thus excluded from Henry's grants as were the southwest counties. With the accession of Henry IV, Yorkshire, Northumberland, Lancashire—the northern counties—entered into greater community with the London center and royal recluse support took on a more national tone.

---

tive terms. The presence of such evidence is useful, but I do not consider its absence interpretable unless supported by other data. See my chapter 6 for further discussion of these issues. See James H. Wylie, *History of England under Henry IV*, 4 vols. (London: Longman's Green, 1884–98), 4:145, for references to unpublished Lancastrian documents.

85. Wylie, *Henry IV*, 4:145; Sir Walter Besant, *Survey of London*, 10 vols. (London: Adam and Charles Black, 1902–12), 2:175; *CCR 1399–1402*, p. 35; Clay, *Hermits and Anchorites*, p. 143: "nostre bienaimé Maude Wardesale *Ankores* recluse en leglise de saint pierre."

The amount of money granted was as variable as the places, but the range remained close to what it had been 150 years earlier in the time of Henry III. The remove of five generations had not altered the parameters that guided the notion of appropriate levels of royal (or great-noble) support. The anchorite at St. Helen's in Pontefract received 30s. 2d. per annum, which was the lowest grant at slightly less than a penny per day. The anchoress Joan de Ayleston in Nottingham, expansively raised to three pence per day (91s. 3d. per annum), received the highest. All other grants fell into the intermediate range. By way of comparison, six marks was an average salary for a chantry priest after 1378. In Henry III's reign it had been closer to four marks, fifty to sixty shillings being a more likely payment.[86] Thus, anchorite support had followed the slight rise in the general level of payments for low-level ecclesiastics. Henry's grants remained firmly in the context of appropriate support for the anchoritic vocation: moderate asceticism but protection from serious need.

Henry V, the son of Henry IV, grew up in an environment in which recluses were revered. It is little wonder that he is reported to have spent the evening after his father's funeral with an anchorite of Westminster to whom he made a general confession and from whom he received penance and absolution.[87] In all probability that anchorite was William Alnwick, a Benedictine monk of St. Albans, now enclosed in one of two recluse cells at Westminster.[88]

86. Katherine Wood-Legh, *Church Life under Edward III* (Cambridge: Cambridge University Press, 1934), pp. 120, 121; *CLR 1240–45*, p. 149; *CLR 1245–51*, p. 112 (*bis*); *CLR 1251–60*, p. 375.

87. The funeral night story originates with the anonymous biographer of Henry V whose chronicle was edited by Thomas Hearne as *Tomae de Elmham Vita et Gesta Henrici Quinti* (Oxford, 1727), p. 15. Later in his reign Henry reportedly asked the Westminster anchorite to pray for his success in battle. See Frank Taylor and John S. Roshell, eds. and trans., *Gesta Henrici Quinti: The Deeds of Henry the Fifth* (Oxford: Clarendon Press, 1975), p. 147: "In order that, by increasing the number of those making intercession, he might better obtain from God's bountifulness a favourable outcome to his prayer, he [Henry] sent word on the following morning to the man of God, the hermit at Westminster [*ad virum dei reclusum Westmonasterii*] and to the saintly monks of the London Charterhouse and his own house at Sheen. . . ."

88. The identification of the anchorite as William Alnwick was first made by James H. Wylie, *The Reign of Henry V*, 3 vols. (Cambridge: Cambridge University

Scholars have conjectured that William reminded Henry of his father's unfulfilled promise to Pope Gregory XII to found three religious houses under strict rule, a promise Henry IV had made in 1408 when exonerated of responsibility in the death of Archbishop Scrope. Whether or not William pressed Henry IV's unredeemed pledge on him, Henry V did move swiftly to found these new monasteries, and although the third, a Celestine foundation, was never built, the Bridgettine house of Syon and the Carthusian monastery of Sheen were the last two religious institutions established in England during the Middle Ages. Both were mighty houses, of strict rules, of superior and ascetic members, and connected to recluses in several ways.

At Sheen, soon after its foundation in 1414, Henry endowed a permanent reclusory.[89] His generous endowment of twenty marks (£13. 6s. 8d.) was equaled in a lifetime grant to another recluse, Matilda Newton, a former nun of Barking and briefly the abbess of Syon.[90] The saga of Syon includes the stories of recluses migrating both ways—from their anchorholds to Syon and from Syon to a previous or new cell. So rare was this as to be curious,

Press, 1914–29), 1:119. Margaret Deanesly, in the "Introduction" to the *Incendium Amoris of Richard Rolle of Hampole* (Manchester: Manchester University Press, 1915), pp. 100–130, deals with the question of the identification of Alnwick, which is complicated by the existence of several contemporary William Alnwicks as well as two Westminster recluses during this period. Knowles, *Religious Orders*, 2:220–222, 367–368, separates four William Alnwicks, one of whom was the bishop of Norwich and later of Lincoln, one a Premonstratensian canon, one a monk of St. Albans and later prior of Wymondham and Belvoir, and one a recluse and first confessor-general of the Bridgettines at Twickenham. Knowles also details the now considerable evidence for two cells at Westminster. C. Peers and Lawrence E. Tanner, "On Some Recent Discoveries in Westminster Abbey," *Archaeologia* 93 (1949): 151–164, cover similar ground with respect to the two cells, having identified the sites of both. William Alnwick was the second recluse in the time of John London, who was himself well known and received many bequests, most notably from Henry, Lord Scrope of Masham (see my chapter 6). London, a monk of Westminster, lived in the cell near the infirmary that had once housed John Murymouth, Henry IV's confessor. Alnwick lived in a cell built in the fourteenth century. It was placed in the external angle between the south transept and St. Benedict's chapel, with a door cut through the south wall of the chapel to give access to it. Such a cell would have been available to a penitent seeking advice or counsel.

89. See my chapter 2 and its note 59.
90. CPR 1416–22, p. 102. Confirmed by Henry VI (CPR 1422–29, p. 43).

and although the severe and disciplined structure of the Bridgettine establishment offers some explanation, such movement is puzzling, forcing us to ponder the possible role of the king. Matilda's story is fairly direct. She had been appointed abbess by the king, but lacking the talent (personal? administrative?) to succeed she was rather quickly removed from office. What to do with her became a problem. She did not want to remain as nun where once she had ruled as abbess, and it was not considered proper that she return to the lax Benedictine life after having migrated to the stricter rule of Syon. Thus the reclusory was a resolution of a troubled situation, and Henry V provided her with a pension of twenty marks yearly, perhaps patterned after his Sheen grant.[91]

Several other recluses left the cell for Syon. One was a woman named Margaret, a recluse at Bodmin, Cornwall. She received permission from her bishop, Edmund Stafford, to join the Bridgettines on 10 March 1416. Bridgettines were often described as "enclosed" and Stafford may have felt that the order was sufficiently austere to be an acceptable alternative for Margaret.[92] More significant than Margaret's migration were those of William

91. The anchorite's cell was considered as possible solution for the problems of a Carthusian monk who left the charterhouse at Kingston upon Hull in 1477 "on account of the persecutions which he suffered therein" and took his case directly and in person to the Roman curia. In this case the monk was granted a choice between returning to Kingston or transferring to another Carthusian monastery and his petition for a license to become a recluse denied. See *CPL* 13:1:55.

92. F. C. Hingeston-Randolph, ed., *The Register of Edmund Stafford, Bishop of Exeter, 1395–1419* (Exeter, 1856), p. 25. She had received a will bequest as an anchoress in 1406 (ibid., p. 394). John Amundesham, *Chronica monasterii S. Albani, Annales monasterii S. Albani, a Johanne Amundesham, monacho,* ed. Henry T. Riley, 2 vols., RS 28, pt. 5 (1870–71), 1:27, describes Matilda Newton as living in "reclusionem" at Syon. A Carthusian monk was also allowed to transfer to Syon (Deanesly, *Incendium Amoris,* p. 139). Another sister of Syon, Joan Sewell, signed herself as *reclusa* (ibid., p. 124), so clearly Syon was a strict house and special considerations may have been in effect. The only known instance of "reverse migration" save for those related to Syon occurred when Henry IV nominated an anchoress named Maude, the daughter of John Wilmyndoun of Fisherton, Wiltshire, to become a nun at Wilton, the famed Benedictine nunnery. The Close Roll entry suggests that the king was under some pressure to appoint someone: ". . . as it pertains to the king to nominate a nun by reason of his coronation, and he did nominate a damsel, who died before she was there received, as he is informed" (*CCR 1402–05,* p. 410).

Alnwick, the Westminster anchorite, and Thomas Fyschebourne, formerly recluse at St. Germain's, St. Albans, Hertfordshire. If indeed Alnwick had promoted the foundation of Syon in his nocturnal meeting with Henry, he now found himself drawn into its development. First asked by Henry to participate in a conference of monks and theologians called to mediate certain difficulties of rule and organization within the new community, he later left his cell completely and came to Syon as confessor-general (the abbess was to be administrative head and the confessor-general spiritual leader). He remained at this post for one year only. Early in 1418 he returned to his cell, exhausted by his adventure (*tedio et senio confectus ad cellam suam, unde egressus fuerat, reversus est*). In 1420 a recluse within the monastery of Westminster dispensed four pounds (in alms?) for the king. It was probably Alnwick, back in his anchorhold.[93] At Syon he had been replaced by another former recluse, Thomas Fyschebourne, who also had received the king as penitent. A man of social position, onetime steward to the abbot of St. Albans, Fyschebourne had both built an anchorhold for an anchoress near St. Germain's Chapel and retired into another himself. By 1418 he had left his own cell, at least temporarily, to serve as royal commissioner to Pope Martin V. His task: to obtain the papal bull approving the newly founded Bridgettine monastery. Successful in his mission, he was installed as confessor-general at the first fully canonical election at Syon, where he remained until his death in 1428.[94]

Clearly, Henry V surrounded himself with the advice and the presence of anchorites in the establishment of new monasteries. Bending ecclesiastical policy for his most estimable causes, endowing reclusoria at luxurious levels, the king's involvement and respect for recluses was marked. Anchorites were his confessors. His monastic foundations were ascetic in nature, and there seems to have been a shared identity between them and the more classic

93. Knowles, *Religious Orders*, 2:178, 179; Amundesham, *Chronica monasterii S. Albani*, 1:27; Devon, *Issues of the Exchequer*, p. 363. Although it is possible that John London was the anchorite serving the king, it is unlikely. London is never mentioned in this context.

94. *CCR 1413–19*, p. 46 Amundesham, *Chronica monasterii S. Albani*, 1:27.

recluses of his time. This is a good example of the centrality of the English recluse to the important religious movements of the day—whether the asceticism of the twelfth century, the growth in numbers of female religious in the thirteenth, the mysticism of the fourteenth, or the expansion of the strict orders in the fifteenth. Many late medieval recluses had ties to establishments involved in the production and dissemination of the important devotional writings of the period, almost all of which were devoted to the exaltation of the solitary life. Margery Pensax, the recluse at St. Botulph's, Bishopsgate, whom Henry IV had first endowed, left her copy of Hilton's *Scale of Perfection* to Syon on her death; John Kyngeslowe, the first recluse at Sheen, bequeathed *The Chastising of God's Children* to Sheen when he died.[95]

Recluses continued to be endowed and supported by the royal families in the last hundred years of Roman Catholic England. The reign of Henry VI brought no change in royal policy. Henry VI not only continued all previous royal commitments but accepted the anchorite foundation at Richmond, Yorkshire, as his own when he assumed control over the lordship that had endowed it and moved forward independently by establishing a cell for a female recluse in 1443 at St. Margaret's, Westminster, at a pension rate of six marks yearly.[96] In 1449 Emma Cheyne, the widow of the Bury St. Edmunds recluse, became a royal pen-

95. Clay, "Further Studies," p. 79. Later recluses both at St. Botulph's and at Sheen also left manuscripts. See also Joyce Bazire and Eric Colledge, eds., *The Chastising of God's Children and the Treatise of Perfection of the Sons of God* (Oxford: Basil Blackwell, 1957), p. 37. The connections of solitaries to the mystical movement in England is especially notable in the late fourteenth century, when every one of the major figures was or had been a recluse or hermit. Many of their works were directed to other solitaries, giving the mystical movement in England a different tone than on the Continent. The major English mystics were Julian of Norwich, herself an anchoress, the anonymous author of the *Cloud of Unknowing* (ed. Phyllis Hodgson, EETS, o.s. 218 [1933]) who was a solitary and addressed the work to another solitary, plus Hilton and Rolle. The Monk of Farne, a man named John Whiterig whose work is more newly identified and is considered by some scholars to be of high mystical quality, also was a hermit.

96. Sir Harris Nicolas, ed., *Proceedings and Ordinance of the Privy Council of England*, 7 vols., Record Commission (London, 1834–37), 5:282.

sioner.[97] Henry also may have established another reclusory at Sheen—this one for a woman.[98]

One anchorite commitment was terminated during this reign. The Lancastrian foundation at Whalley came to an end around 1443 when the incumbent fled from the reclusorium and the monks of Whalley used the opportunity to push for the conversion of the cell and its endowment to other purposes. The recluse, Isolda de Heton, enclosed in 1436, was a widow with a minor child who found herself still tied to the world in a variety of ways. Most important, she was attempting to retain certain rights pursuant to her son's wardship and marriage. In addition, her servants at Whalley seem to have been unchaste, the subject of some local scandal, an irritation to the Cistercian monks and perhaps to her as well. Whitaker, the historian of Whalley, suggests that her vow was taken "in the first fervours of sorrow, which soon wore off, so that the widow grew weary of her confinement" and there may be truth here also. She did indeed depart, most likely because of her concerns about her son, for documents indicate that she went into hiding with him.[99] No charge of sexual laxity was made against her but the combination of events enabled the monks of Whalley to petition the king successfully:

97. See my chapter 2 and its note 20 for more discussion of Emma. She received a pension of "4d. a day from the petty custom of London, as Christina Huchin, deceased, had of late." As in previous reigns her pension was determined by money available from recent vacancies.

98. Joan Grenewood, the anchoress at the royal reclusory at St. Botulph's, Bishopsgate, is said by A. B. Emden, A Biographical Register of the University of Oxford to A.D. 1500, 3 vols. (Oxford: Clarendon Press, 1957), 1:615–616, to have been enclosed at Sheen previously. If so there would have had to be a second cell there, for the original reclusory was designated for chaplains and at this time was inhabited by John Dygoun, an Oxford graduate who is the first known scribe of De Musica Ecclesiastica, better known as De Imitatione Christi. Grenewood was Dygoun's widowed sister and together they bequeathed several devotional books to Magdalen College, Oxford, and to Exeter College. See André Wilmart, Auteurs spirituels et textes dévots du Moyen Âge latin (1932; reprint, Paris, 1971), pp. 420, 422, and Clay, "Further Studies," p. 78n.

99. T. D. Whitaker, An History of the Original Parish of Whalley, 4th ed., 2 vols., rev. and ed. J. G. Nichols and P. A. Lyons (London: Routledge and Sons, 1872), 1:101, 2:96–97, 101–102; "The Last Ancress of Whalley," in Historic Society of Lancashire and Cheshire 64, n.s. 28 (1912): 268–272. Dugdale, Monasticon, 5:645–646.

To the Kyng owre Sovereign Lord. &c.
Be hit remembyrd that the plase and habitacion of the seid recluse is within place halowed, and nere to the gate of the seyd monastre, and that the weemen that have been attendyng and acquayntyd to the seyd recluse have recorse dailly into the seyd monastre, for the livere of brede, ale, kychin, and other thyngs for the sustenacyon of the seyd recluse accordyng to the composityon endentyd above rehersyd; the whyche is not according to be had within such religyous plases. And how that dyvers that had been anchores and recluses in the seyd plase aforetyme, contrary to theyre own oth and professyon, have broken owte of the seyd plase, wherein they were reclusyd, and departed therfrom wythout eny reconsilyatyon. And in especyal how that now Isold of Heton that was last reclusyd in the seyd plase, at denomynatyon and preferment of owre Sovereign Lord and Kyng that nowe is, is broken owte of the seyd place, and hath departyd therfrom contrary to her own oth and professyon, not willyng nor entendying to be restoryd agayn, and so livying at her own liberte by this two yere and more, like as she had never bin professed. And that divers of the wymen that have been servants ther and attendyng to the recluses afortym have byn misgovernyd, and gotten with chyld withyn the seyd plase halowyd, to the grete displeasuance of hurt and disclander of the abbeye aforeseyd, &c. Please hyt your Highness of our espesyal grase to grant to your orators the abbat, &c.[100]

Henry granted the monks' request and the funds endowing the reclusorium became the foundation of a chantry for the souls of Duke Henry, Henry VI, and others. But 1443 was also the year when Henry gave six marks to the new recluse at St. Margaret's, Westminster, and Emma Cheyne's pension came even later. The termination of the reclusorium at Whalley was hardly a symptom of institutional decay, as some would have it, but rather a well-documented account of an event that, human frailty being what it is, was likely to have occurred from time to time. The situation seems not to have affected royal gift-giving patterns. The anchorite's cell at St. Margaret's endured through most of the remaining period of the Middle Ages. Caught in the vicissitudes of the Lancastrian-Yorkist wars, the women who lived there emerged at the

---

100. Printed both in Whitaker, *Whalley*, 2:102–103, and "The Last Ancress of Whalley," p. 270, citing *Whalley Coucher* as source.

end of that period with their endowment intact. Their grants were paid by the sheriffs of various counties in various reigns but move untouched from Henry VI to Edward IV to Richard III to Henry VII. The writ that instituted the pension had stated: "Grant, for life to Cecily Norton, widow, of Westminster, recluse, of six marks yearly, out of the issues of the counties of Cambridge and Huntingdon, provided that this grant not grow into a precedent."[101] It did indeed grow into a precedent. A later anchoress at Westminster was a woman named Alice Rippas who received plenary remission from the pope in 1469 and was in arrears with her parish guild dues in 1476. Richard III confirmed her grant (ca. 1483), the money to come from the issues of Nottingham; Henry VII, in 1486, preferred that the revenues of Southampton should bear the charge for her upkeep.[102] The recluse cell at St. Margaret's, Westminster, had become a permanent royal commitment. Its incumbents were remembered in the wills of the faithful. One of them received a bequest of one-half mark in 1465 (in a will also remembering the anchoress in the royal reclusorium at St. Botulph's); another received 3s. 4d. in 1503 and then five shillings in 1505. After that no more is heard.

In 1480 the petition of one Elizabeth Katherine Holsted to be admitted to the anchorage at St. Peter's, St. Albans, was supported by Edward IV, by his queen, and also by "diverse magnates dwelling in the king's household." In the next generation the privy purse of Elizabeth of York noted expenditures of two marks for the anchoress of St. Michael's, St. Albans, for the year 1503 (probably a portion of an annuity) and alms gifts of twenty pence and 3s. 4d. to two other female recluses, one of whom was the anchoress at St. Peter's who had known her parents' patronage.[103]

101. *CPR 1441–46*, p. 177. Subsequent notices reconfirm the grant (*CPR 1452–61*, pp. 80, 293). The notice for 1456 (p. 293) identifies Cecily only as widow, all other entries calling her both widow and recluse.

102. *CPL*, 12:699; Clay, "Further Studies," p. 81n; "Anchorites in Faversham Churchyard," *Archaeologia Cantiana* 11 (1877): 32–33; *CPR 1485–94*, pp. 61, 75.

103. H. R. Riley, ed., *Registra quorundam abbatum monasterii S. Albani, qui saeculo XV^mo floruere*, 2 vols., RS 28, pt. 6 (1872–73), 2:202; Nicholas Harris Nicolas ed., *Privy Purse Expenses of Elizabeth of York* (London: William Pickering, 1830), pp. 102, 67; Clay, *Hermits and Anchorites*, p. 110.

Elizabeth, daughter of Edward IV, wife of Henry VII, mother of Henry VIII, was clearly in the beneficent royal mode described in these pages, and her son, in his turn, would respond similarly up to the final moments before his break with Rome and the dissolution of the monasteries. Payments to the recluse at Sheen regularly appear on Henry VIII's accounts. In 1521 a routine alms grant included "ancres" among its recipients. Henry's queen, Catherine of Aragon, gave one mark to John Benton, anchorite of Marlborough, and twenty shillings to the anchoress of Stamford. The cell at St. Botulph's remained active, still enjoying royal support. When Henry needed information from the anchorite at Canterbury in the closing days of his struggle for a divorce, he approached the anchorite as cautiously and as respectfully as Henry III had done in approaching Loretta some 270 years earlier. After the Dissolution, one of the books Henry requested for his personal library out of the confiscated monastic collection of Bardeney abbey was a copy of the *Ancrene Riwle*.[104]

These later notices enrich the picture of royal support of anchorites by establishing the role of the queen as well as the king, reinforcing the notion that this support was routine and an expected component of royal charity. It was a tradition dating back at least to the reign of Stephen. Its expression was influenced by the particular values of the king, which were in themselves the product of personality factors, family expectations, and social norms. Dynastic shifts could intensify or diminish the levels of that support, but in general the great noble families, as the next chapter will develop more fully, shared the same orientations as the monarchy. Clearly, royal involvement with anchorites was continuous throughout the Middle Ages. The patterns of royal support laid down in the twelfth and thirteenth centuries endured and some anchorites always could depend on their sovereign for their daily bread.

104. *LP*, 2:2:1449; *LP*, 3:2:1535, 1543, 1545; *LP*, 4:3:2732; Marc Fitch, ed., *Index to Testamentary Records in the Commissary Court of London*, 2 vols., Historical Manuscripts Commission Joint Publication 13 (London: HMSO, 1974), 2:123; J. R. Liddell, " 'Leland's' Lists of Manuscripts in Lincolnshire Monasteries," *English Historical Review* 54 (1939): 92.

6

Aristocratic and Gentry Support

The aristocratic and gentry response to the needs of anchorites was similar in style to the monarchal. The behavior of the upper classes, in this as in other situations, can be seen as a reflection of the royal style, while the king's actions are largely those of the nobility writ large. King, baron, and landed gentleman shared the same values and attitudes and expressed them through the same legal, institutional, and private mechanisms. As expected, the far-ther down the social scale one goes, the less generous the level of support. But the point of view remained constant: the anchorite was a worthy and awe-inspiring religious. Moreover, that point of view held throughout the period and can be substantiated for the sixteenth century as for the twelfth. I propose to analyze the aris-tocratic contribution first, followed by that of the gentry, in order to note differences between the two groups and allow for compar-isons with other studies based on aristocratic/gentry distinctions. The similarities between the two groups, however, far exceed dif-ferences. These similarities demonstrate the fundamental per-ception that this book seeks to prove: widespread anchoritism, supported (at the very least) by all social groups for whom rec-ords exist.

ARISTOCRATIC SUPPORT

Even as the king supported recluses out of the yearly revenues of his lands, so did his feudatories from theirs. Information concern-ing contractual arrangements has survived in most instances as a result of the feudal practice of escheat. The occasional return of granted lands to royal control provides the opportunity to examine the promises and the obligations of the king's chief tenants, for these baronial commitments were recorded on the royal rolls during the period of escheat and so survived along with the royal records. In almost all cases aristocratic support of anchorites was less ample than royal support. Whereas the king thought in terms of daily pennies, even in the twelfth century, and later in multiples of pennies, barons thought in terms of a penny or two a week. During the second half of the twelfth century recluses in Hertfordshire and Yorkshire received grants of about one and a half pence weekly from William de Mustral and Robert Lacy.[1] Two pence weekly were provided by the earl of Arundel,[2] by William, count of Poitou, and by Thomas of St. Walric[3] to recluses in Sussex, Essex, and Middlesex. Two and a half pence per week, a relatively high rate of payment for the nobility, were paid to recluses in the gift of the earl of Gloucester. In contrast, William de Curci was committed to only thirty-six pence for the year for his Oxfordshire recluse, and Robert of St. Remigius paid no more than six pence a year to an anchorite in Bedfordshire.[4]

Like the king, the greater lords can be found supporting more than one recluse. William d'Aubigny, the earl of Arundel, supported one from the receipts of the honor of Petworth and another from the honor of Arundel. The honor of the earl of Gloucester succored anchorites at Warham and Bradenstoke and also other *inclusis*.[5] Richard de Reviers, earl of Cornwall, paid fixed alms of

1. PR 9 Henry II (1163), p. 23; PR 10 Henry II (1164), p. 37; PR 11 Henry II (1165), p. 17.

2. PR 27 Henry II (1181), pp. 145, 146; PR 28 Henry II (1182), p. 91; PR 29 Henry II (1183), p. 106 and others.

3. William, count of Poitou: PR 9 Henry II (1163), p. 23; PR 10 Henry II (1164), p. 38. Thomas of St. Walric: PR 4 Richard I (1192), p. 9; PR 5 Richard I (1193), p. 132; PR 6 Richard I (1194), p. 225.

4. William de Curci: PR 34 Henry II (1188), p. 4; PR 1 Richard I (1189), p. 7. Robert of St. Remigius: PR 7 Richard I (1195), p. 36. Gloucester: PR 1 John (1199), p. 36.

5. PR 32 Henry II (1186), p. 200; PR 33 Henry II (1187), p. 15; PR 34 Henry II (1188), p. 13.

£4. 11s. 9d. to *inclusis et monachis.*[6] William de Vesci allowed £7. 3s. 4d. for clothes for three anchorites and twenty prebendary brothers in a one-and-a-half-year period and provided them with alms as well.[7] Not "overmighty" subjects, these nobles yet imitated the royal flair as benefactors of many. In fact, in their own regions their largesse might have seemed greater than that of the king because its distribution was concentrated and its local impact stronger.

The thirteenth century shows the rate of noble support rising. The earl of Chester, Ranulph de Blundeville, paid Winmark, the recluse of Frodsham, the royal rate of one penny per day.[8] Most nobles were content to grant less than that, even if giving more than they previously had. Alienore, countess of Salisbury, gave the recluse of Culing, Wiltshire, twenty shillings per year. William de Warenne, earl of Surrey, supporting at least three anchorites, paid twenty shillings annually to Margaret, enclosed within the hospital of St. Leonard in Grantham, Lincolnshire; three quarters of wheat to Muriel, at Campsall, Yorkshire; and 13 shillings plus a tree for firewood to the recluse of Dorking, Surrey.[9] John de Lacy, earl of Lincoln, gave the Pontefract recluse one-half mark in money and nine quarters of corn each year, and the lord of Kearsney Manor in Kent paid Mariun 33s. 4d.[10] In the next century Sir Robert de Holand supported Aline with thirty shillings annually from the proceeds of his lands in Lancashire, and Thomas, duke of Gloucester, granted forty shillings yearly to a woman recluse out of the issues of the manor of Kneesall.[11]

6. PR 22 Henry II (1176), p. 153; *PR 23 Henry II* (1177), p. 9; *PR 24 Henry II* (1178), p. 16.

7. *PR 31 Henry II* (1185), p. 9; *PR 32 Henry II* (1186), p. 202.

8. *CCR 1272–79,* p. 209.

9. *CR 1231–34,* p. 37 (for Culing). *CR 1247–51,* pp. 130–131, 426; *CLR 1251–60,* p. 281 (for Grantham). *CR 1237–42,* p. 232; *CPR 1232–47,* p. 435 (for Campsall). *CR 1237–42,* p. 214; *CLR 1226–40,* p. 488 (for Dorking).

10. *CR 1237–42,* p. 258; *CInqpm 1272–91,* no. 605. Not all recluses in the gift of aristocrats were doing so well. William de Kentwell of Suffolk paid only six shillings per year for two sisters enclosed at Sudbury (*CLR 1245–51,* p. 172; *CInqM 1, 1219–1307,* p. 37). In general there is always considerable variation in these grants.

11. For Holland see my chapter 3 and its notes 47–48; *CInqM 6, 1392–99,* pp. 206–207.

These grants were all for the life of the recluse. Other aristocratic patrons established permanent foundations and the anchorites who lived in them can be charted over centuries. In the late thirteenth century the lords of Richmond, Yorkshire, endowed a reclusorium in perpetuity: "John, late earl of Richmond, son of the duke of Brittany, by letters patent dated at Richmond on Wednesday before Michaelmas A.D. 1274, granted in frank almoin to the anchorite in the said chapel [St. Edmund's] two quarters of wheat payable yearly at Michaelmas at Richmond castle by the hands of the bailiffs there."[12] The lordship of Richmond was held throughout the fourteenth century by the dukes of Brittany, save for a thirty-year period (1342–72) when it passed into the hands of John of Gaunt. Between 1399 and 1425 it was held by Ralph Neville, earl of Westmorland, after which John, duke of Bedford, a son of Henry IV, gained control for the next ten years. In 1435 Henry VI took possession. Subsequently the lordship devolved on Edmund Tudor, Henry VI's half-brother, next on Henry Tudor, the future Henry VII, and ultimately on Henry Fitz Roy, the illegitimate son of Henry VIII.[13] Each of these men, all great nobles and several of royal blood, inherited the Richmond anchorite foundation with the lordship. By the beginning of the fifteenth century the two quarters of wheat frequently were commuted to a cash payment of twenty shillings, and it was this amount of money that Henry VI granted to Margaret Askham in 1439 "who forty years and more has been the anchorite immured in St. Edmund's chapel, Richemond...." In 1446 she was replaced by another woman, Alice Howorth, who in turn was granted twenty shillings by Henry VI.[14] There is no reason to assume that the foundation did not continue on until the Dissolution, but the data cease here.

The Pontefract reclusorium, first funded by the Lacys in the thirteenth century, also was a permanent commitment, although

12. CPR 1436–41, p. 289.
13. These data from Frederick M. Powicke and Edmund B. Fryde, eds., *Handbook of British Chronology*, 2d ed. (London: Royal Historical Society, 1961), pp. 445–446.
14. CPR 1436–41, p. 289; CPR 1441–46, p. 457.

the evidence does not indicate that it was initially planned as such. Nonetheless, anchorites there received pensions first from the Lacys, then from the Lancasters both as nobles and as monarchs, and subsequently from later monarchs as well. These Yorkshire foundations (the gentle Fitzwilliam family established a further one at Doncaster) give some sense of the continuity of that kind of spirituality that had made the North so hospitable to the Cistercians in the previous century. But Yorkshire was not the only place where noble families endowed reclusoria. Foundation charters survive telling us of Whalley in Lancashire and Droitwich in Worcestershire. The Whalley foundation was established by Henry, duke of Lancaster; Droitwich by Thomas Beauchamp, earl of Warwick.

Will data further expand the group known to have been involved with anchorites. Since wills figure extensively as a source of data in this and the following chapters it will be useful to pause and set down the criteria that have governed the use of testamentary material. A will[15] bequest was a final bequest. It was made at a time and in a situation in which the testator was under considerable emotional pressure and in the presence (and perhaps under the influence) of other men, at the very least of the cleric who was writing it down. Almost all testamentary bequests were one-time gifts—gestures. Occasional wills provided the equivalent of an endowment for a fixed number of years or until the death of the recluse, but such wills are rare.[16] Typically will bequests provided small grants of money to specific anchorites or to all the recluses within a city, county, or diocese. Such bequests were made to an-

15. The term *will* is used interchangeably with *testament* in this study. Technically, *will* describes a document that devises real property and *testament* one that makes bequests of personal property alone. While some medieval testators did prepare both will and testament, a greater number prepared only one instrument for both purposes. Even when two documents were written, there was often overlapping of function in them. See Ernest F. Jacob's "Introduction" to *Chichele*, 2:xix–xxi.

16. Particular references to such wills are made below (see my chapter 6, note 27) and in chapter 7 on merchants where the elaborate sixteenth-century will of Robert Jannys of Norwich is discussed (see chapter 7, note 39). Chapter 7 also cites a similar case in the will of William Brown of Stamford, Lincolnshire (see chapter 7, note 46).

chorites in a percentage of wills. Ten percent of wills calendared at the London Court of Husting in the ten-year period between 1351 and 1360 (14 of 142) and 9 percent of those calendared for the twenty years between 1366 and 1385 (27 of 301) contained bequests for anchorites; of testators whose wills were proved at the prerogative court of Archbishop Chichele between 1414 and 1443, 5 percent (16 of about 300) left bequests for anchorites; 11 percent of a series of Exeter clerical wills of the first half of the fifteenth century did so.[17] Twenty-one percent of all clerical wills of Norwich between 1370 and 1532 and 18 percent of all lay testaments from the same period in Norwich made bequests to anchorites. Almost 8 percent of the townsfolk of St. Albans made bequests to anchorites in the first half of the fifteenth century; 52 percent of the mayors of York made such bequests in the years 1385–1446.[18]

York mayors aside, a bequest to an anchorite was made by a minority within that minority of the English population leaving a written testament. As such it suggests special involvement: for instance, a local proprietary responsibility to a town anchorite; a family tradition to anchorites in general or to anchorites at specific sites; a clerical or lay magnate's largesse to all the anchorites in his diocese or county; a London merchant's responsibility to his city's recluses; a gift to a known individual—a relative, a friend, a confessor, an anchorite whose fame for prophecy or sanctity was widespread.

Anchorites were also among the "pious and charitable" causes that typically received the residues of estates but remain unspecified in most wills. The will of Bishop Anian II of St. Asaph, Wales,

17. F. C. Hingeston-Randolph, ed., *Register of Edmund Stafford, Bishop of Exeter, 1395–1419* (Exeter, 1856), pp. 379–423; Lacy, *Exeter Reg.* 4:1–63.

18. For Norwich: Norman P. Tanner, *The Church in Late Medieval Norwich 1370–1532*, Pontifical Institute of Mediaeval Studies, Studies and Texts 66 (Toronto, 1984), p. 223; for St. Albans: "Abstracts of Wills: Archdeaconry of St. Albans, Register 'Stoneham,' " *Herts Genealogist and Antiquary* 1–3 (1895–99); for York mayors, BIHR Reg. 1–4, and see my chapter 7, note 33. Percentages have not been calculated for wills in the *Testamenta Eboracensa* series because the data are incomplete. Wills are printed both selectively and partially. Wills containing anchorite bequests are printed without these grants at times and with them at others.

in 1288 left a hundred cows for pious uses and these he did describe as being monasteries, lepers, and anchorites (*inclusi*).[19] But lacking record of disbursements, we cannot know to what degree anchorites benefited from other estate dispersals. This was part of the unrecorded understanding that formed the basis of the relationship between testator and executor. The 1417 will of Richard Hals, treasurer of Exeter cathedral, spoke of the verbal instructions that Hals had given his executors with respect to the deployment of the residue of his estate once his debts had been paid.[20] Executors were a man's intimates. They routinely included his priest (now his lawyer), his wife if he was married, fellow clergy if a priest, his brother, his friends. These people would answer to his unspecified almsgiving, knowing his desires, concerns, and religious commitments. Some anchorites were surely included in this category.[21]

Another problem for this study is that testamentary data are unevenly available. For some areas of the country there is an abundance of information; in other areas almost no testamentary materials survive.[22] For yet other regions there are wills but no pattern of bequests to anchorites. When no such gifts appear in a series of wills it is hard to determine if we are dealing with a lack of anchorites or the absence of a local pattern to provide in this way. Certainly some people and groups sufficiently supported anchorites through personal alms and the boxes of fraternal and parish guilds (which took over some of these functions in the later Middle Ages). Grants may be hidden just under the surface of wills that seem empty of bequests. Anchorites sometimes received

19. C. Eveleigh Woodruff, ed., *Sede Vacante Wills*, Kent Archaeological Society, Records Branch 3 (1949), p. 116.

20. Hingeston-Randolph, *Reg. E. Stafford*, pp. 416–417.

21. Such inferences, of course, cannot be "counted." But even beyond the ambiguity of these kinds of donations, some estates failed to provide any residue, and even may have had trouble paying out detailed gifts. For the probate record of one man for whom only two-thirds of his legacies could be paid due to inadequate funds, see *Chichele*, 4:252–253.

22. For example, only eighty wills survive from Chester from the earliest of times to those proved in the 1540s (Douglas Jones, *The Church in Chester, 1300–1540*, Chetham Society, 3d ser., 7 [1957], p. 96).

long-term annual gifts as part of anniversary arrangements, which might be part of a will or a separate document. A person could have adequately provided for anchorites in other ways during his lifetime. Henry, duke of Lancaster, left a will bare of any reference to anchorites when he died in 1361, yet just four months previously he had endowed the reclusorium at Whalley—this in addition to his other commitments to recluses. All these alternate forms of endowment and support, both overt and hidden, suggest that the evidence of wills can be used positively when and where available but that absence of such evidence is not an argument against concern or provision for anchorites. I have therefore drawn such conclusions as are deducible from the evidence, but I have not interpreted the lack of will data in a locale or in a specific social group.[23]

One further concern is the modern distinction between "pious" and "charitable" bequests. The medieval testator considered a gift to a church, a monastery, or the friars to be no more efficacious in working for his salvation than a bequest for the poor, for bridges, for lepers, for highways, for widows, for orphans, or for dowerless young maidens. A will was thus an opportunity to make an individual statement of some kind; it was an opportunity to favor one group over another. While all orders of friars received gifts in routine fashion in medieval wills, one man might leave a larger gift for the Carmelites, another to the Preachers, as others to the Minors or Augustinian friars. One bishop, Thomas Bitton of Exeter (d. 1307), left bequests for thirty-nine leprosaria in his diocese. Archbishop Courtenay (d. 1396) bequeathed a substantial gift to every anchorite in his province, but nothing for any lepers. John Mersdon, the rector of a Leicestershire church, made bequests for the repair of thirteen bridges in 1425; eight years later the bishop

23. Barrie Dobson, "The Residentiary Canons of York in the Fifteenth Century," *Journal of Ecclesiastical History* 30 (1979): 168, speaks of similar problems in reading the wills of residentiary canons of York: "There can be no doubt that before their deaths many residentiaries had made important gifts never recorded in their testaments. It was also common for the canons of York to leave a very considerable degree of discretion in disposing of their goods to their executors. The absence of a particular bequest to a particular purpose may accordingly be quite misleading."

of Worcester, Thomas Polton, left nothing in the category of public works. Both of these wills, however, did remember anchorites.[24] These wills do not make a social statement of any kind beyond that all these categories for giving existed and all were deemed worthy of support. They reveal only an individual consciousness that put one group or need before another in the testator's mentality—a function of his own experience or sense of obligation.

All these categories of needy causes were lumped together as "pious and charitable" by the medieval testator. While the exploration of medieval social attitudes and behavior through the window of the will has often proceeded by the assignment of bequests into "pious" and "charitable" categories,[25] the separation of piety from charity is a modern differentiation developed within an intellectual framework that divides life into religious and secular spheres. Medieval men thought of their bequests as pious *and* charitable. They advised their executors to dispose of the residue of their estates for pious and charitable uses. The words were cumulative, not disjunctive. Piety and charity were one and the same.[26]

This is not to imply that medieval testators made no distinctions with respect to their grants. In some wills that made both pious and charitable bequests, religious gifts were separated from social betterment gifts, suggesting that differences were perceived. Some wills included gifts to anchorites among the "religious"

24. William H. Hale, ed., *Account of the Executors of Richard, Bishop of London, 1303 and of the Executors of Thomas, Bishop of Exeter, 1310*, Camden Society, n.s. 10 (1874), p. 9; for Courtenay, see my chapter 3, note 78; for Mersdon, *Chichele*, 2:333; for Polton, *Chichele*, 2:485–495.

25. Most especially in recent years by Wilbur K. Jordan in his monumental works *Philanthophy in England, 1480–1660* (New York: Russell Sage Foundation, 1959) and *The Charities of London, 1480–1660* (London: George Allen & Unwin, 1961). As correctives to Jordan see the work of John A. F. Thompson, "Piety and Charity in Late Medieval London," *Journal of Ecclesiastical History* 16 (1965): 178–195; John M. Jennings, "The Distribution of Landed Wealth in the Wills of London Merchants, 1400–1450," *Mediaeval Studies* 39 (1977): 261–280; and Allison K. McHardy, "Some Late-Medieval Eton College Wills," *Journal of Ecclesiastical History* 28 (1977): 387–395.

26. McHardy, "Late-Medieval Eton Wills," p. 389, handles the issue with subtlety by making "civic and charitable causes" one of her categories of "bequests which can be considered 'religious' in intention."

grants, along with bequests to churches, religious houses, secular clergy, and friars; other wills listed bequests to recluses in that portion of the testament devoted to the "enclosed poor," that is to lepers, prisoners, and the poor in hospitals and almshouses. This difference in perception shows some confusion as to what an anchorite was; it also shows that two separate categories could exist for some testators. But distinctions in grouping do not necessarily connote anything beyond an orderly mind. In the Hustings data twenty-one of fifty-three testators grouped bequests to anchorites along with other religious grants, nine testators classified them with grants to the poor, and twenty-three listed all their bequests in random fashion.

For the purpose of this study all grants, whether classifiable as religious or secular, have been considered as equivalents. Any order or coherence to be extracted from wills by analysis depends not on distinguishing separable tendencies or motives but rather on the regularity of the overall charitable response of the testators. Will evidence has been used in conjunction with other data where possible and alone when necessary. Naturally the former situation gives a more richly colored picture. I was fortunate to be able to begin with the royal family because the tapestry of that support was woven with many colored strands. At times this will be true for other social groups, most specifically for the aristocracy, to whom it is time to return.

In a rare early thirteenth-century will written in 1220, Agnes de Condet, wife of Walter Clifford, ancestor of the earls of Cumberland, not only left twelve shillings to each anchorite in Canterbury and a mark to the hermit of "Hoppa" but also two packloads of wheat annually to the anchorites of St. Andrews, Wickhamborough, for as long as they lived—a tactic, it seems, to guarantee an already ongoing commitment after her death. In 1268 William Beauchamp bequeathed four shillings for every anchorite in Worcester and parts adjacent.[27] In the fourteenth and fifteenth centuries, such illustrious names as Stafford, Roos, Scrope, Beauchamp,

27. C. W. Foster and Kathleen Major, eds., *The Registrum antiquissimum of the Cathedral Church of Lincoln*, 11 vols., Lincoln Record Society (1931–68), 1:292–293; Nicholas Harris Nicolas, ed. *Testamenta Vetusta* 2 vols. (London, 1826), 1:50–51.

and Neville, to say nothing of Lancaster, appear among wills containing bequests for anchorites. These wills of powerful families add another dimension to this study, for in addition to indicating the continuation of anchorite support by the aristocracy into these later years, they suggest that patterns of support through generations may have been the practice in aristocratic circles as well as in the royal line.

Three members of the aristocratic Roos family, Lady Beatrice and her sons John and William, wrote their wills in the brief period between 1392 and 1414.[28] John wrote his as he was preparing for a pilgrimage to Jerusalem in 1392. In this he was following in the footsteps of both his father, Thomas Lord Roos, and his uncle, William Lord Roos. Like them he was not to survive the journey. He died at the age of twenty-six, without heirs, at Paphos on the island of Cyprus on the return leg of his trip.[29] John's will, to be supervised by Ralph Neville and Richard le Scrope among others, was brief and almost completely personal. He desired to be buried opposite the sepulchre of St. Aelred at Rievaulx; he remembered his wife, his mother, sister and aunt, and his immediate entourage. The parish church received vestments, two clerics his missal and his "legenda." The only extraneous gifts were grants of twenty shillings to each of three anchorites living at Helmsley, Byland, and Beverly, in the area of his lordship, as well as ten shillings to the hermit of Harum.

His brother William succeeded to the patrimony as seventh Lord Roos of Helmsley in 1393 on John's death. William was closely associated with Henry IV and Henry V, serving them both as privy councillor. From 1404 he was Henry IV's most substantial supporter in the northern Midlands and he was justice of oyer and terminer during the Lollard rebellion.[30] His will, dated 22 February 1412, was written well before his death in September 1414.

28. John Roos: Gibbons, *Early Lincoln Wills*, pp. 20–21; William Roos: *Chichele*, 2:22–27; Beatrice Roos: *Test. Ebor.*, 1:375–79.

29. John de Trokelowe, *Johannis de Trokelowe . . . chronica et annales . . . A.D. 1259–1296, 1307–1324, 1392–1406*, ed. Henry T. Riley, RS 28, pt. 3 (1866), pp. 164–165; *Test. Ebor.*, 1:201n.

30. *Chichele*, 2:674.

It is an unusual document in several respects. His burial directions stated that on his death his body was to be taken without delay (*sine dilacione*) for burial at either Canterbury, Belvoir, or Rievaulx, whichever was closest to the place of his death, and moreover that this was to be done in as secret a manner as possible (*secreciori modo quo poterit*). The burial was to proceed attended only by the prior and conventuals of the house (it was in fact Belvoir) without convocation of any other prelates or expense of bringing magnates or other men. With such stern provisions, the document harmonizes with the wills of other religious men of the time who flirted with notions sometimes perceived as "Lollard."[31]

But William Lord Roos was no Lollard. Nothing could be more orthodox than his bequest of four hundred pounds to pay for ten chaplains to say daily masses in the chapel at Belvoir for a period of eight years for his soul and the souls of his relatives. Roos also left a hundred pounds to be distributed among chaplains and hermits, male priest-recluses, known and named, honest men, serving God assiduously and devotedly, so that they might especially pray for him.

Lady Beatrice, the mother of both these men, wrote her will in 1414. The wife, the mother, and the sister-in-law of men who died on pilgrimage, her own will was traditional in format, remembering leprosaria in the York suburbs, the poor in hospitals, needy tenants, mendicants, parish churches, and convents in addition to two female anchorites at Leak (near Helmsley) and Nun Appleton who were granted forty shillings each. Lady Beatrice and her son John left bequests for recluses within their lordship for whom they felt some commitment, whether legal or moral. William, in contrast, remembered recluses in his search for honest and worthy chaplains to provide the most efficacious of masses. Close to two Lancastrian kings who were involved with solitaries, William made an obvious choice.

---

31. For "Lollard" wills, see Kenneth B. McFarlane, *Lancastrian Kings and Lollard Knights* (Oxford: Clarendon Press, 1972), pp. 207–220. See also Malcolm G. A. Vale, *Piety, Charity, and Literacy among the Yorkshire Gentry, 1370–1480*, Borthwick Papers, no. 50 (York: St. Anthony's Hall Publications, 1976), pp. 203, 206.

Lady Beatrice was the daughter of Ralph, earl of Stafford, by Margaret, daughter and heir of Hugh, Lord Audley, earl of Gloucester. Other Staffords and Audleys appear in these records. Lady Elizabeth Stafford's will of 1405 made a bequest of twenty shillings for William Whityng, the anchorite at Sherborne, Dorset; in 1480 the will of Anne, duchess of Buckingham, daughter of Ralph Neville and widow of Humphrey Stafford, requested that on her death her body be carried "as secretly as conveniently" to the church at Plessy, where it was to be buried modestly, "setting all pomp and pride of the world apart." Each priest at Syon and in the charterhouses of London and Sheen was to have twenty pence to pray for her soul and the souls of her husband and children in five masses with five *diriges*. The "Anker in the Wall beside Bishopsgate, London [was to] have 6s. 8d. to pray in twenty masses for the souls before mentioned, and to say twenty *diriges* for them." In 1521 the March accounts of the duke of Buckingham allowed for one mark for the servant of the anchorite of Marlborough, who had brought gifts to the duchess and to her daughter-in-law, Lady Stafford. One presumes the gifts of two simnels (a mid-Lenten fruitcake) and holy wax were the offerings of the anchorite to his patronesses. As for the Audleys, in the early fourteenth century Lady Catherine de Audley was herself the Ledbury anchoress; in 1400 Elizabeth Lady Audley left a mark to the anchoress of Hereford.[32]

The Stafford and Audley wills were written by women. Joel Rosenthal has noted that aristocratic women were "somewhat more likely than were their husbands to offer money for the relief and release of prisoners, the marriage of poor but virtuous girls, and the support of anchorites and hermits."[33] That these gifts often appeared together in wills this study will confirm. But why women were the exemplars of this kind of generosity within the nobility (and within the gentry as well) is unexplained in general.

32. Frederic W. Weaver, ed., *Somerset Medieval Wills*, 3 vols., Somerset Record Society 16, 19, 21 (1901–05), 2:304; Nicolas, *Testamenta Vetusta*, 1:356–357; *LP*, 3:1:500–501; Weaver, *Somerset Wills*, 2:300.
33. Joel Rosenthal, *The Purchase of Paradise* (London: Routledge and Kegan Paul, 1972), p. 118.

In the specific case of the Staffords, it can be argued that each of the women who remembered anchorites in her will was subject to influences outside the Stafford family. If for the moment Lady Beatrice is considered a Stafford, there are eight Stafford wills extant in the ninety-five years between 1385 and 1480, four of men, four of women. Three of the women left bequests for anchorites, none of the men did.[34] Lady Beatrice was under Roos influence, however; Duchess Anne was a Neville and granddaughter of John of Gaunt; Lady Elizabeth was under the sway of a clerk named William Ekerdon.[35] Thus, for these women at least, the Stafford connection may not have been a significant factor and might explain the relative indifference of the family men to solitaries.

Yet another possibility can be considered. The accounts of the duke of Buckingham that show Lady Stafford receiving the appreciative gifts of the anchorite at Marlborough also note a payment of 6s. 8d. to John Glade, a hermit, "formerly the Duke's servant."[36] Men had resources by which to make grants during their lifetimes. The hermit's payment is quite likely to have been a regular pension. Women had less opportunity to endow persons on their own and this might account for their use of wills to express this kind of piety more frequently than men.

In a family such as the Scropes, however, the use of the will to ensure the livelihoods of anchorites was definitely a male prerogative. Scrope men wrote wills over a period of three generations during which their involvement with recluses was clear. There are five anchorite wills from this family in the period 1382–1455.[37] One of these wills, written in the year 1400, belonged to Richard le Scrope, first lord Scrope of Bolton, the head of the elder branch

34. Earl Henry (1385): Nicolas, *Testamenta Vetusta*, 1:118–119; Anne Stafford: *Chichele*, 2:596–597; Humphrey Stafford: *Chichele*, 2:620–624; Duke Humphrey: Nicolas, *Testamenta Vetusta*, 1:296; Humphrey, earl of Devon: Weaver, *Somerset Wills*, 2:196–197.

35. For William Ekerdon, see my chapter 8.

36. *LP*, 3:1:500.

37. Geoffrey le Scrope (1382): Foster, *Lincoln Wills*, 1:11–19; Richard le Scrope (1400): *Test. Ebor.*, 1:272–278; Stephen le Scrope (1405): *Test. Ebor.*, 3:31–37; Henry le Scrope (1415): Rymer, *Foedera*, 9:272–280; John le Scrope (1455): *Test. Ebor.*, 2:184–193.

of the family and mentioned previously as supervisor for John Roos's will. In his own will Richard made bequests of one mark each for anchorites at Richmond, Burneston, Kirkby Wiske, and Wath. The cadet branch of the family was settled in Masham. The will of Henry le Scrope, the first Lord Masham, does not survive but that of his brother, Geoffrey le Scrope, does. In 1382 Geoffrey, first cousin to Richard and a canon of the Cathedral church of Lincoln, left bequests for five anchorites, three in Yorkshire and two in Lincoln. The anchorite of Hampole received twenty shillings, the anchorite at the church of the Holy Trinity of Lincoln also twenty shillings plus a furred tunic and cloak, anchorites at St. Paul's, Stamford, and at Kirkby Wiske (on his cousin's list) 13s. 4d. each, and the anchorite at Doncaster half that amount. In 1406 Stephen le Scrope, the second Lord Scrope of Masham and nephew to Geoffrey, bequeathed twenty shillings each to the anchorite of Kirkby Wiske and to Robert, recluse of Beverly. He also left twenty shillings to Elizabeth of Hampole, who was probably the servant of the former anchorite of Hampole (now presumably dead).[38] Stephen's first son and heir, Henry le Scrope, succeeded him to the barony in 1407. Henry's own remarkable will was written on 23 June 1415, just six weeks before he was summarily detained and executed as privy to the plot of the earl of Cambridge and Sir Thomas Gray against Henry V. In this will Henry made bequests to seventeen anchorites, to one hermit, and to Elizabeth, formerly servant to the anchorite of Hampole. These grants ranged in value from one hundred shillings to one mark. In addition he granted one-half mark to every anchorite and recluse in York and its suburbs, one-half mark to every anchorite and recluse in London and its suburbs, and one-half mark to any other anchorite, male or female, who could be identified within three months. Named anchorites included John London, anchorite at Westminster, who received one hundred shillings as well as Scrope's own rosary; Robert, the recluse of Beverly, who received forty shillings (and was remembered in Henry's

38. Hope Emily Allen, *Writings Ascribed to Richard Rolle, Hermit of Hampole, and Materials for His Biography* (Modern Language Association of America, 1927; reprint, New York: Kraus, 1966), p. 507.

father's will); the anchorite of Wath (also noted in Richard le Scrope's will); and the anchorite of Kirkby Wiske (who had been mentioned by every one of the previous Scrope testators). To this evidence of family concern must be added the grants of Geoffrey, Stephen, and Henry to the anchorite of Hampole and then to her servant Elizabeth.

Henry's will is deeply religious in tone. The anchorites are listed after a large number of gifts to a wide variety of old and new religious houses and parish churches. The poor are to be remembered on Henry's burial day, but there are no other gifts of "charitable" significance. Books represent a second striking aspect of this will. Twenty-nine individual books were bequeathed to thirteen different beneficiaries out of a library of indeterminate size—many beneficiaries getting their choice of volumes. Six books were specified as French, one was English. An autograph of Rolle's *Judica Me Deus* was owned by Scrope as well as Rolle's *Incendium Amoris*. *The Prick of Conscience* was the English book. Scrope's library, including these volumes of contemporary devotional writings, were among his most carefully bestowed treasures. Granted to his friends and members of his family, they appear in the will following his bequests to every anchorite in the entire country.

Henry Scrope's brother John inherited the attainted barony, becoming fourth Lord Scrope of Masham. He died in 1455. His will is different in conception from those of earlier Scropes in that it is the will of a man whose religious and charitable horizons were in the main bound by the city of York and its suburbs. He made bequests to the local conventual houses, to the four orders of friars in York, to every parish church, every leprosarium, and every almshouse in the city and suburbs as well as to the two guilds of which he was a member. He also left grants to three anchorites living in York at that time, one at All Saints, Fishergate, one at the house of nuns called Clementhorpe, and one at St. Margaret's, Walmgate. The amounts of money granted were small. Leprosaria and almshouses received twelve pence per household; the guilds and the anchorites each received 3s. 4d. The direct line of wills stopped here. The will of Thomas, son and heir of John, does not exist. The will of his son Thomas, the sixth baron of Masham, was written in 1492.[39] His only bequests were for chantry priests and for religious houses, both of regulars and of friars, in the city of York. All else he left to his wife. Traditional religiosity continued but the grand gesture was gone.

So the Scrope men, unlike the Staffords, assumed responsibility for anchorites. The regularity and consistency with which the Scrope men accepted that charge indicates more than chance. The Scrope wills cannot be random accidents, and in each case save that of Geoffrey (and as a clergyman other criteria enter the picture) the will belongs to the head of the family. Wills of the Masham barons requested that they be buried at St. Peter's, York, which was "their" church and where the chapel of St. Stephen was *"vulgariter vocata* Scrop Chapell."[40] Richard, Geoffrey, Stephen, and Henry all made bequests to the Premonstratensian abbey of Coverham, near Masham in Richmondshire, the burial place of Geoffrey's father, Sir Geoffrey le Scrope, a chief justice of the king's bench. Otherwise, the Scrope wills are more different than similar—a good illustration of the lack of consistency in noble testaments. But precisely because each will is fairly idiosyncratic, the regularity of the Scrope gifts to anchorites becomes more meaningful.[41]

The Beauchamps were another family with long-term commitments to anchorites. But in their case wills are not the only data to describe them. William Beauchamp already has been mentioned as a thirteenth-century testator who left four shillings to every anchorite in Worcester and parts adjacent.[42] In the late fourteenth century Thomas Beauchamp, earl of Warwick, built and endowed an anchorite's cell situated in the convent of the Augustinian friars, a house also of his foundation, at Droitwich in Warwickshire. Thomas established the anchorite's cell and re-

39. Eric E. Barker, ed., *Register of Thomas Rotherham*, vol. 1, CYS 69 (1976), pp. 80–81.

40. From John le Scrope's will, *Test. Ebor.*, 2: 185.

41. See Rosenthal, *Purchase of Paradise*, pp. 115–116, for somewhat similar observations.

42. The reclusorium established by Peter of Wick-by-Pershore (see my chapter 2 and its note 57) also belongs to the Beauchamp milieu, as Peter was a member of the Beauchamp *familia*.

tained the right of presentation for himself and his heirs: all inhabitants of the cell were to be men, either Augustinians already or prepared to assume the Augustinian habit and submit themselves to the obedience of the prior.[43] Thomas Beauchamp was one of the Lords Appellant accused of treason in 1397, and he pleaded that he had acted trusting in the holiness and wisdom of "the Abbot of Saint Albones and of the Recluse of Westmynstre, that saide it was lawfulle that he dede."[44] Warwick was not alone in seeking the advice and counsel of a Westminster anchorite or in the hope that invocation of his name might protect him. But for a Beauchamp to claim such a reason as justification and support was not a false note. A broad perception of the anchorite as a holy person ran in the family.

In 1416 Isabella Ufford, the countess of Suffolk, wrote her will. She was Warwick's sister, the fifth daughter in that Beauchamp family. In the will she is territorially identified with Norfolk and Suffolk, making bequests to all the houses of friars in both shires and also to four conventual houses there. She also left twenty shillings to Julian of Norwich, establishing her relationship with a renowned mystic, now an anchoress. In the next generation both Richard Beauchamp (son of Thomas and now himself earl of Warwick) and his wife Elizabeth were involved with prominent anchorites. Elizabeth was one of several fashionable ladies who were under the sway of Thomas Fyschebourne during his anchoritic period.[45] Richard was influenced by two anchoresses. One was a clairvoyant named Dame Emma Rawgton who lived in an anchor-

43. Treadway R. Nash, *Collections for the History of Worcestershire*, 2 vols. (London, 1799), 1:331–332.

44. John Silvester Davies, ed., *An English Chronicle*, Camden Society, o.s. 64 (1856), p. 11. Adam of Usk said of Thomas on this same occasion that "like a wretched old woman, he made confession of all contained therein, wailing and weeping and whining that he had done all, traitor that he was, submitting himself in all things to the king's grace" (cited by May McKisack, *The Fourteenth Century, 1307–1399* [London: Oxford University Press, 1959], p. 482).

45. *Chichele*, 2:94–97; John Amundesham, *Chronica monasterii S. Albani, a Johanne Amundesham, monacho*, ed. Henry T. Riley, 2 vols., RS 28, part 5 (1870–71), 1:21. See also Knowles, *The Religious Orders in England*, 3 vols. (1948–59; reprint, Cambridge: Cambridge University Press, 1971), 2:180.

hold in York; the other resided at Winchester. Both women gave the earl advice.

The accounts of Richard for the year 1421[46] attest to a payment of 13s. 4d. for the expenses of two men, one of them the chaplain of Guy's Cliff, to visit a Winchester anchoress on Richard's behalf, presumably to get her advice. A few months later when the earl was in London for a session of Parliament the Winchester anchoress was brought to London. Richard spent £2. 6s. 8d. for the costs of her transport, for keeping her in London for three days, and for offering her a suitable gratuity. She was brought to London in order that the busy lord might be able to consult with her personally. One wonders what was the issue for which her guidance was critical. Obviously she left her cell to accommodate her aristocratic friend. Her advice and her presence must have been deemed of the highest value.

Emma's role in Richard's life is better recorded.[47] She was a prophetess and at least two of her visionary experiences concerned Richard Beauchamp. When Henry VI became king in his infancy Emma made it be known "that it had been shown to her by Our Lady that he ought to be crowned in France as well as in England, and also that no person was better fitted to be his guardian than Richard Beauchamp, Earl of Warwick." Soon thereafter Richard did become a member of the council that ruled for the child king and from 1428 to 1436 he was the king's tutor. A man of honor and integrity, Richard had been one of Henry V's most trusted supporters and his choice for these positions was both natural and reasonable. Yet if Dame Emma's vision was not the cause of these events, neither did it hurt his position.

At about the same time, in the first year of Henry VI's reign (1422–23), Emma had another look into Beauchamp's future. Richard lacked a male heir and Emma's prophetic gifts now focused on that concern. It would please God, said Emma, if Richard would found a chantry in the chapel of the hermitage of Guy's

46. Charles Ross, "The Estates and Finances of Richard Beauchamp, Earl of Warwick," *Dugdale Society Occasional Papers* 12 (1956): 3–22.

47. John Rous, *Rows Rol* (London: William Pickering, 1845), no. 50; Clay, *Hermits and Anchorites*, p. 155.

Cliff, situated on the western bank of the Avon about a mile and a quarter from the town of Warwick. Guy's Cliff contained both a cave and a well and thus was a natural locale for a solitary. The place long had been associated with the Warwicks. As a religious site it was at least as old as the fifth century, when it was known as Gibcliff and was chosen by St. Dubricius, archbishop of Caerleon, as a place of devotion. There the saint had built an oratory dedicated to St. Mary Magdalen. In the tenth century the famous warrior Guy of Warwick had spent the last years of his life there after returning from pilgrimage, living in a cell with another hermit. In the fourteenth century Thomas Beauchamp, Richard's grandfather, procured the patronage of the hermitage from the priory of Warwick and changed its name to Guy's Cliff in honor of Sir Guy, and subsequently notice appears in royal and ecclesiastical records of hermit activity there. This Thomas Beauchamp in his will of 1369 left his son Thomas (the founder of Droitwich) the sword and hauberk of Guy of Warwick. To his son William he left a relic, a bone "which Thomas, earl of Lancaster, gave me when I was baptised."[48] It was the chaplain of Guy's Cliff, perhaps himself a hermit, who had journeyed to Winchester to visit the anchoress there for his patron. This then was the religious and emotional tone of the Beauchamp world. To found a chantry at Guy's Cliff as Dame Emma instructed was well in keeping with the family's mentality.

The foundation was to consist of two priests who were to perform divine service in perpetuity for the souls of the king and the founders. John Rous, an Oxford graduate, historian, and antiquarian, was chaplain there from 1444 until his death in 1491.[49] It is

48. Rous, *Rows Rol,* "Introduction," unpaginated; Edward Edwards, ed., *Liber monasterii de Hyda,* RS 45 (1866), pp. 122–123; there is also a romance of *Guy of Warwick,* ed. Julius Zupitza, EETS, e.s. 25, 26 (1875–76; reprinted as one vol., 1966); CPR 1330–34, p. 543; Rowland A. Wilson, ed., *Registers or Act Books of the Bishops of Coventry and Lichfield: Book 5 Being the Second Register of Bishop Robert de Stretton, A.D. 1360–1385,* William Salt Archaeological Society, n.s. 8 (1905), pp. 280, 285, 289; Gibbons, *Early Lincoln Wills,* p. 30.

49. Alfred B. Emden, *A Biographical Register of the University of Oxford to A.D. 1500,* 3 vols. (Oxford: Clarendon Press, 1957), 3:1596–1597.

from his work that some of the information concerning the foundation comes. Writing of Richard Beauchamp, Rous said:

Thys lord was maister of kyng herre the syxt in hys tender age and with the helpe of the land crownyd him twies at Westmystre as for kyng of England and at paris for kyng of fraunce he made certen there a fore was uncerten at Gybclif a chauntre of ij prystis that God wold send hym Eyre male. he did hyt by the styrryng of a holy anchoras namyd Em Rawghtone dwellyng at all halows in the northestrete of york and fore hyt to her apperyd our lady vii tymes in on yer. . . .[50]

Emma's vision became worth reporting for posterity when two years afterward Richard's son and heir was born on 22 March 1425.

At the end of the fifteenth century a work on the life of Richard Beauchamp was commissioned. *The Pageants of Richard Beauchamp, Earl of Warwick*[51] consists of fifty-three pencil drawings portraying episodes ("pageants") in his life. One of these drawings (no. 47) conflates Emma's two prophecies. The drawing shows the young Henry VI being crowned at St. Denis while the legend recites the role of Richard in his upbringing as predicted by Emma and further describes Emma's promotion of Guy's Cliff as a place of pilgrimage. It is believed that the *Pageants* was commissioned by Anne, Beauchamp's fourth daughter, countess of Warwick in her own right and widow of Richard Neville, the kingmaker, and that it was left unfinished at her death in 1493. The inclusion of the prophecies of Emma Rawgton, anchorite of York, in this memorial of Richard Beauchamp speaks in a rare and meaningful way of the Beauchamp connections with the recluses of their time.

The early commitments of the Lancaster family to anchorites already have been chronicled as evidence of royal almsgiving, but other members of the family continued this tradition on their own. Thomas and Joan Beaufort as well as Prince Humphrey, duke of Gloucester, the youngest son of Henry IV, show in their wills and other papers their personal commitments. Humphrey

50. Rous, *Rows Rol*, no. 50.
51. William, earl of Carysfort, ed., *The Pageants of Richard Beauchamp, Earl of Warwick*, Roxburghe Club (Oxford, 1908).

was identified quite closely with St. Albans, where both he and his wife were members of the fraternity of the abbey, a religious guild that also numbered the local anchorites in its membership. When he died he was buried at St. Albans, having endowed the church with properties by which the costs of his anniversary could be supported in perpetuity. The schedule detailing approved disbursements for that event showed alms payments for the local anchoresses living at St. Peter's and St. Michael's. Once a year, on the day of Humphrey's anniversary celebration, each anchoress was to receive twenty pence and presumably she added her prayers to those of the conventuals in aid of his soul. Thomas Beaufort, duke of Exeter, third child of Gaunt and Catherine Swynford, in 1426 left ten pounds to John London, the Westminster anchorite, and twenty shillings each to three female anchorites, two in London and one at St. Albans. Joan Beaufort, Gaunt and Catherine's fourth child, married Ralph Neville, earl of Westmorland, and his 1420 will made a bequest of twenty shillings to every anchorite in the bishoprics of York and Durham, one of whom was the anchoress at Richmond and already receiving the support of Neville as lord of Richmond. Neville appointed Thomas Beaufort, his "dearest brother," to supervise this will.[52] Anne, duchess of Buckingham, was the child of Joan and Ralph and her will already has been mentioned as a Stafford document. In 1480 she remembered the anchorite in the wall at Bishopsgate as her uncle Thomas Beaufort had done fifty-four years earlier.

Aristocratic charity was both a private act and a social one that was controlled and conditioned by a vast network of family relationships. Yet individuals had freedom within that network, especially with respect to their wills. If we look at the fourteen Roos, Scrope,[53] Beauchamp, Stafford, and Lancastrian wills that benefit anchorites in the period 1392–1480 (nine written by men and five by women), the following patterns emerge: nine made bequests to

---

52. Amundesham, *Chronica monasterii S. Albani*, 1:66; Dugdale, *Monasticon*, 2:202; *Chichele*, 2:355–364; *Wills and Inventories*, pp. 68–74.

53. The will of Geoffrey le Scrope is not included in this analysis. It is classified as a clergyman's will by the criteria that govern this study and no wills are counted twice.

the poor, thirteen to convents, and twelve to friars. Other kinds of charitable bequests were relatively infrequent. Four remembered the poor in hospitals; four, lepers; three, prisoners; three, public works; two, poor scholars; one, poor maidens. Most of the "charitable" grants were concentrated in the wills of four men: Gaunt, Beaufort, Richard Scrope, and John Scrope. In general, save for bequests to the poor, the orientation of these wills is "religious" as differentiated from "charitable." In comparison with the wills of other members of the aristocracy, in which only one in three left money for alms,[54] this group of testators is significantly more sympathetic to the needs of the poor. Otherwise, charitable grants are limited, and anchorites figure as worthy religious in the contexts of aristocratic wills.

THE GENTRY

The "country gentry" of medieval England ranked beneath the aristocracy in the social hierarchy. They were consequential members of the general community and men of substance at home. Knights and esquires, *milites et armigeri*, they held land, held office, and bore coats of arms.[55] They sat for their counties in Parliament and served as sheriffs, commissioners, coroners, and local justices at home. The patterns of their support of anchorites were similar to those of the aristocracy, although the vision of the gentry was narrower, at times even parochial. While not completely unknown among the gentry, the grand sweep of a Scrope or Ne-

54. Rosenthal, *Purchase of Paradise*, p. 103, reports that among wills leaving an appreciable number of bequests, only one in three left money for alms. Even if we eliminate Gaunt's and Beaufort's wills from our group (because Rosenthal does in his), our figure would still be seven out of twelve.

55. The criteria for determining the group were taken to afford a basis of comparison with the study made by Malcolm Vale and discussed in *Piety, Charity, and Literacy among the Yorkshire Gentry, 1370–1480*, Borthwick Papers, no. 50 (York: St. Anthony Hall's Publications, 1976). Rosenthal's study, *The Purchase of Paradise*, uses the criterion of parliamentary peerage to determine the "aristocracy" (pp. 4–6). Such individuals as appear in both studies or can be included by both definitions (Lord Philip and Lady Elizabeth Darcy; Lord Bardolf) here have been considered gentry.

ville will bequest was rare. This section examines the anchorite foundation of the Fitzwilliams of Yorkshire, spanning the years from the later thirteenth century to the Dissolution; the religious involvements of the Stapletons of Norfolk and Yorkshire in the late fourteenth and fifteenth centuries; and those of the Willoughbies of Nottinghamshire, for whom data are fullest in the sixteenth century. Finally, I consider the wills of the gentry as a group.

Charters of Thomas Fitzwilliam and his son William show that about 1270 they established a reclusorium for two female anchoresses at Doncaster Bridge, Yorkshire.[56] The master of the hospital of St. Edmund, to which the anchorage was attached, acted as custodian of the lands that guaranteed the endowment and the security of the recluses. The initial grant for eight quarters of grain was to be paid annually to two anchoress sisters, Anabel and Helen de Lisle, and afterward to their successors in four installments: two quarters each at Christmas, Easter, Pentecost, and Michaelmas. In 1328 the man then in control of the Doncaster endowment, Thomas de Cresacre, was given the overview of a grant of pavage to one Geoffrey de Bolton, hermit, by Edward III. The road to be paved was in front of the anchoresses' house. It is unclear whether the work being done was to benefit the anchoresses (or their retinue) or if the mention of them is merely by way of identifying the site. The Patent Roll states that the king has permitted a

grant, for stopping up certain pits near the king's high road (*regia strata*) before the door of the house of recluses (*reclusarum*) near Doncastr', and for repair of the pavement there, of pavage for three years to Geoffrey de Bolton, hermit, who out of charity undertook that work, viz. 1d. for every cart with iron tire (*ferro ligata*) laden with goods for sale, ½d. for every millstone, and ½d. for every horseload of goods for sale; these tolls are to be laid out by view and testimony of Thomas de Cresacre.[57]

If the purpose of the royal grant was to aid the recluses, this is a nice example of how many efforts came together: the original

56. See my chapter 2, notes 55–56, 61.
57. CPR 1327–30, p. 315.

209

grant from a local family; a hermit willing to undertake road work that would benefit a fellow solitary; the king supporting both endeavors and assuring that the road will be attended.

Many efforts continued to feed this foundation. In 1348 Lady Isabel Fitzwilliam, the widow of a later William Fitzwilliam, lord of Elmley and Sprotbrough, bequeathed a robe "of her order" to the incumbent, Lady Joan; wills of 1360, 1382 (that of Geoffrey le Scrope), and 1402 further presented the recluses there with small gifts of money. In the mid-fifteenth century John Fitzwilliam, then lord of Sprotbrough, restructured the duties of the master of the hospital and his assistant and placed different income-bearing properties in their hands. The assistant was given certain priestly duties and the charge of a new foundation for a pauper. The master of the hospital received the charge of the recluses. The lands and properties pertaining to the recluses' endowment, "Ancresse House" and "Ancresse Inges," became his responsibility, and he was exhorted by Lord John "concerning the performance of his priestly duties, and such provision for the anchoresses and other inmates as may reverently and honourably be fitting."[58]

The involvement of the Fitzwilliams with the anchorite household clearly did not end at its foundation. Rather, such a foundation marked only the beginning of responsibility and concern. An establishment of this nature demanded overseeing to ensure that both substance and detail were in order. The archbishop's involvement with this particular foundation has been discussed earlier.[59] For the family the right of nomination to vacancies remained an important privilege. This foundation first enclosed two sisters, the daughters of Jordan de Lisle. In 1294 a new anchoress entering the reclusorium, probably replacing one of the original sisters, was also surnamed "de Insula." There may have been some kind of family connection between the Fitzwilliams and de Lisles making

58. *Test. Ebor.*, 1:51; Richard S. Ferguson, ed., *Testamenta Karleolensia*, Cumberland and Westmorland Antiquarian and Archaeological Society, Extra Series 9 (1893), p. 30; Foster, *Lincoln Wills*, 1:17; Gibbons, *Early Lincoln Wills*, p. 103; Norman Smedley, "An Incised Stone from the Free Chapel of Ancres, Near Doncaster," *Yorkshire Archaeological Journal* 37 (1948–51): 509–510.

59. See my chapter 3, notes 72–73.

the reclusorium a family preserve and nicely blending piety and family objectives. One of the anchoresses in the fifteenth century, a woman named Margaret Tattersal, also is thought to have had a family connection, for Tattersals had intermarried with Fitzwilliams toward the end of the fourteenth century.[60]

The interaction between family members who endowed a reclusorium and members who became recluses would have reinforced the family commitment. A "family" reclusorium would have provided a natural retreat for kin of ascetic bent—precluding the alternative of a conventual choice. Moreover, it would have kept the idea and the ideal of voluntary poverty much in the forefront of the family consciousness. Lady Joan Wombell, a Fitzwilliam daughter, left a small bequest to the anchoress of Beeston, Yorkshire, in her 1454 will just at the time that her brother was rearranging the responsibilities of master and assistant at Doncaster and creating an additional endowment to support an indigent man. The Stapleton family, who will be discussed next and who were related to the Fitzwilliams by marriage, had a family member who was an anchoress. Recluses were not "other people" in these family constellations, they were family members.[61]

The concern of the Fitzwilliam family for the anchorite establishment and similar pious foundations was genuine and mirrored a background of knowledge and deep belief. When William Fitzwilliam wrote his will as lord of the manor in 1474, it was characterized, according to Malcolm Vale, by a theological erudition that separated it from others of his class in terms of scholarship if not of faith. In a lengthy Latin preamble William "considered the 'lacrimose and ever-mutable human condition . . . in this vale of tears' and speculated in a learned manner upon invisible essences

60. Smedley, "Incised Stone," pp. 505–507.
61. *Test. Ebor.*, 2:178. A member of the Scrope family may have been an anchorite as well. Thomas Scrope, alias Bradley, may have been a son or bastard grandson of Richard le Scrope, lord of Bolton. An anchorite of the Carmelite friary in Norwich for perhaps twenty years (1426–46), he later returned to active life, becoming bishop of Dromore (Ireland) and auxiliary bishop of Norwich. He translated the Lambeth Rule. See J. Bale, *Scriptorum Illustrium Maioris Bryannie Catalogus* (Basel, 1557), pp. 629–630; *CPL*, 9:241; Powicke and Fryde, *Handbook of British Chronology*, p. 317.

and human frailty."[62] When William wrote his will he was surely in charge of the Doncaster anchorites as well as the recently founded poor man's house. That the anchorite foundation lasted to the Dissolution is known from a document of 1543 describing a local chaplain as "channtreprest of the ancrisse."[63] Perhaps there was only one anchoress there in the final days of the reclusorium.

The Fitzwilliam involvement with anchorites goes beyond concern for those for whom they bore direct responsibility. The anchorite of Hampole, who appeared in the Scrope family wills, was probably one of these additional dependents, and her saga, though unique in many aspects, elucidates the religious atmosphere in Yorkshire in the second half of the fourteenth century and the connections between families involved with recluses. The anchorite of Hampole was Margaret de Kirkeby. She began her religious life as a nun of Hampole,[64] a small Cistercian convent (not far from Doncaster) which had been founded by the ancestor of the Fitzwilliam family, William de Clarefai, in the twelfth century. The Fitzwilliam connection to the nunnery was continuous throughout its life cycle. Records of donations over the years are one indicator; the members of the family who were buried in the nuns' church there, a second; the return of the house to the Fitzwilliams at the surrender, a third. Margaret came to Hampole as a young girl and it was probably while there that she first met and came under the influence of Richard Rolle, the hermit of Hampole. She became his disciple and subsequently asked ecclesiastical permission to leave the convent and become an anchoress. It was for Margaret that Rolle wrote his greatest (and probably final) work, *The Form of Living*, during the last year of his life in 1349. He also may have written the *English Psalter* for Margaret while she was still a nun at Hampole. With Rolle as spiritual director, Margaret

62. Vale, *Piety*, pp. 17–18. William's words recall similar remarks made by Henry of Lancaster more than a hundred years earlier.

63. Smedley, "Incised Stone," p. 511.

64. For much of what follows on Margaret de Kirkeby, see Allen, *Writings Ascribed to Richard Rolle*, pp. 34–36, 187–188, 256–268, 502–512. Allen's analysis depends on her identification of Margaret de Kirkeby with Margaret le Boteler. C. E. Whiting, "Richard Rolle of Hampole," *Yorkshire Archaeological Journal* 37 (1948–51): 11–13, questions Allen's identification and suggests two Margarets.

asked for and received permission to be enclosed. She was to live in three different anchorholds in Yorkshire over more than a fifty-year span.

The site of her initial enclosure was at East Layton, probably chosen because Rolle was then living there. East Layton, a small township, lay partly in the parish of Melonsby, and at the time of Margaret's enclosure in December 1348 the lords of the manor at Melonsby were the Fitzwilliam-related Stapletons. The Scropes and the Nevilles also had territorial connections there. In January 1356 Margaret was transferred to a new reclusorium because she could neither see the sacrament nor hear mass at Layton. Episcopal license was granted to her to move to a house by the parish church of Ainderby, where the circumstances of her enclosure would be more fitting, and she was absolved from her vow to remain perpetually at Layton. Ainderby was a manor of the Scropes. Some years later she again was allowed to move, this time back to Hampole, where she had begun as a nun and first known Rolle. What cell she occupied there is unknown, as are the reasons for this final and unusual second move. Perhaps she desired to end her life nearer the place of its beginning; perhaps she hoped to be a magnet for the first stirrings of a Rolle cult. In any event Geoffrey le Scrope's will establishes her there by 1382. She died sometime between 1401, when she was mentioned in another will, and 1405 when her servant Elizabeth was remembered in that of Stephen le Scrope. For this period of twenty years she was only a few miles away from the Doncaster anchoresses and quite clearly part of a general community of people committed to both the mystical and reclusive aspects of asceticism, people among whom the Fitzwilliams, the Scropes, and the Stapletons figure largely.

There were Stapletons both in Norfolk and in several locations in Yorkshire. It was in Norwich that Lady Emma Stapleton, the daughter of Sir Miles Stapleton, lived as the anchoress enclosed at the Carmelite friary for twenty-one years between 1421 and 1442. She must have been considered a person of some consequence because she was placed under the spiritual guidance of one of their more learned friars, a man named Adam Hemlyngton who had received a doctorate in theology from Oxford. Her father was probably the Sir Miles Stapleton who was one of the executors of the will of Lady Isabel Ufford, countess of Suffolk, the Beauchamp daughter who had remembered Julian of Norwich in her will of 1416. A Michael and an Edmond Stapleton each received forty pounds as a bequest from Isabel, an amount equal to that which she left to her "treasured nephew," so the Stapletons were clearly esteemed by Isabel. Isabel's grant to the anchoress Julian takes us into the spiritual center of the Norwich mystical movement and suggests some of the influence under which Emma may have been raised.[65]

In Yorkshire there were Stapletons at Bedale, Carlton, and Wighill. Many were called Miles or Brian (as were their Norfolk cousins), making identification somewhat precarious. The connections between the various branches of the family seem to have been close. When Sir Brian Stapleton of Wighill and Carlton died in 1394, he asked his nephew, Sir Miles Stapleton of Ingham (about twenty miles from Norwich), to be one of his executors, also bequeathing to him his great rosary of amber. When Miles died in 1414, his manor came into the possession of the Yorkshire family, so we can see that the various branches constituted one extended family.[66]

The will of Sir Brian Stapleton of Wighill is another in that series in which the testator wallowed in his unworthiness, and Stapleton spoke of both his body and his soul as "caitiff."[67] Yet his funeral was both highly public and very grand, given his station. This combination of fashionable—even Lollardlike—prose coupled with traditional—even conservative—religious practices surfaces periodically among the aristocrats and gentry. In this will

65. Clay, *Hermits and Anchorites*, p. 137; Emden, *Oxford*, 2:906; *Chichele*, 1:94-97.

66. *Test. Ebor.*, 1:198-201; Allen, *Writings Ascribed to Richard Rolle*, p. 528. See also Henry Harrod, "Extracts from Early Wills in the Norwich Registers," *Norfolk Archaeology* 4 (1855): 321-322.

67. Vale, *Piety*, p. 11, points out that Brian Stapleton's stepdaughter was married to the "Lollard" knight Sir William Neville. See McFarlane, *Lancastrian Kings*, pp. 176, 215, where he suggests (on this will evidence) that Stapleton may have been an unsuspected Lollard Knight. McFarlane's three indicators of Lollard sympathy are emphasis on the testator's unworthiness, contemptuous language toward the body, and strict injunctions against funeral pomp (pp. 210-211).

Stapleton remembered friars at Beverley, Doncaster, Pontefract, and Richmond among others—all places where anchorites are known to have been living and supported by the Scropes, Lancasters, and Fitzwilliams; he bequeathed to his niece an alabaster image of the Virgin "qui fust al ankerer de Hampoll." It is unclear whether this image belonged to Margaret of Kirkeby or to Rolle himself. Margaret was living as an anchoress at Hampole in 1394 and would have known Brian Stapleton from her days at East Layton where the Stapletons were lords of the manor. She could have given him this statue of the Virgin in her lifetime which he now passed on as a treasured possession to his niece. It is also possible that the "ankerer" meant was Rolle, now dead for forty-five years. In either case the bequest identifies Brian as a part of their milieu. His will further establishes that context in appointing Richard le Scrope, lord of Bolton, as supervisor and Sir John Depeden, lord of Helagh, as executor as well as legatee. As already noted, Scrope's will of 1400 made bequests to four anchorites, also leaving personal gifts to Brian Stapleton, the son, heir, and namesake of the man whose will he supervised. The will of Sir John Depeden, Brian's executor, was written in 1402 and was also a document with bequests to anchorites. He left a grant for every recluse, "vocato Ankers," in the whole of Yorkshire—a significant gesture for a member of the gentry.[68]

The next generations of the Stapleton family continued to express concern for anchorites and appreciation of the mystical-devotional literature of the period. The will of Brian's son and heir does not survive but that of his son's wife Agnes takes us into a household in which devotional books loomed large. While anchorites are not mentioned in her 1448 testament, most significant is her library (which she divided among various nunneries) containing a *Prick of Conscience*, a *Chastising of God's Children*, *Vice and Virtues*, a French *Lives of the Saints*, and "[her] book called 'Bonaventure,'" most probably some version of the pseudo-Bonaventuran *Meditationes Vitae Christi* (possibly the English translation by Nicholas Love called the *Myrrour of the Blessed Lyf*

68. *Test. Ebor.*, 1:277, 297.

of Jesu Christ) among other volumes.[69] The wills of Agnes's son and daughter-in-law, Sir John and Lady Margaret Stapleton, also survive. In 1455 John left a mark to every anchorite within the city of York. After his death Margaret took a widow's vow and moved into the nunnery of Clementhorpe. At her death in 1466 she remembered the anchoress who was part of that establishment as well as two other York anchoresses. John's and Margaret's wills take us to a time when the fire of the early mystical movement seems burned out. These wills are proper and orthodox, but like the will of John le Scrope (written in the same year as that of John Stapleton) they are limited in vision to the city of York. Scrope's bequests were to the same three anchoresses mentioned by Margaret Stapleton, and although John Stapleton's will made a general bequest to anchorites these three may have been all that were then enclosed in York. These wills terminate the period in which the connections of these families and recluses can be traced.[70]

The gentry did continue to support anchorites beyond the middle of the fifteenth century. Will evidence and household accounts continue to identify sites and inhabitants as well as individuals who provided support. The Pastons of Norwich considered gifts to anchorites as part of the usual affairs of their lives. A list of expenses for John Paston's funeral in 1466 allowed forty pence for the anchoress of Carrow, and in Margaret Paston's will of 1481 two female and one male anchorite were granted similar bequests. In 1471 Margaret Purdance, also of Norwich, left bequests for the anchoresses at Carrow priory and the Dominican friary. In 1475 Sir Oliver Mannyngham, about to leave on a pilgrimage to Rome, left a grant of 33s. 1d. for Lady Alice Darby, the anchoress of St. Clement's, York, in the event he did not return.[71]

69. John W. Clay, ed., *North Country Wills*, 2 vols., SS 116, 121 (1908–12), 1:48–49; for the literature see Elizabeth Salter, *Nicholas Love's "Myrrour of the Blessed Lyf of Jesu Christ,"* ed. James Hogg, Analecta Cartusiana 10 (Salzburg, 1974), p. 17.

70. *Test. Ebor.*, 2:181–183, 271, 184–193.

71. James Gairdner, ed., *The Paston Letters 1422–1509*, 4 vols. (Westminster: Archibald Constable, 1900–01), 2:266–267; Dawson Turner, "The Will of Margaret Paston," *Norfolk Archaeology* 3 (1852): 160–176; for Margaret Purdance: *Norfolk Archaeology* 4 (1855): 35, and Walter Rye, *Carrow Abbey* (Norwich, 1889), p. xix;

In 1516 Richard Peke of Wakefield, Yorkshire, left forty pence to his local anchoress who lived in the churchyard at St. John's, one of several grants made at this time to that anchoress. The accounts of the Lestranges of Hunstanton show the anchoress of Coxford, Norfolk, receiving a grant of two shillings in November 1537 (after the first surrendering of the monasteries).[72]

The Willoughbies of Nottinghamshire also were supporters of anchorites and extant wills and household accounts suggest the range of that support. Sir Hugh Willoughby's will of 1444 (John Scrope was executor) is the first piece of evidence of family involvement and in it he bequeathed one-half mark to the anchoress of Nottingham. In 1515 a later Willoughby will, that of Lady Jane Hastings, daughter of Sir Richard Wells, Lord Willoughby, provided for three London anchorites[73] at a time when the head of the family, Sir Henry Willoughby, was routinely supporting solitaries at home. On his account books are grants for two anchoresses and seven hermits, several of whom received repeated gifts.[74] The anchoresses were at Polesworth in Warwickshire and at St. Albans. The anchoress at Polesworth lived at the convent in a cell off the south aisle of the church which had been built in the thirteenth century. Quite possibly the anchorage had been occupied continually since then. At the Dissolution the anchoress there was Benedicta Burton, a woman of considerable education, and it may have been to her that the Willoughbies granted eight pence as a "rayward" from time to time during the 1520s; the anchoress of St. Albans received only four pence as her "rayward" in 1523.

---

for Mannyngham: Thomas Madox, *Formulare Anglicanum* (London, 1702), p. 437. Mannyngham's "bequest" comes in the form of a quadripartite indenture and was to take effect only if his daughter predeceased him.

72. For Wakefield, *Test. Ebor.*, 5:75; see also BIHR Reg. 9, fol. 5; BIHR Reg. 10, fol. 47. Daniel Gurney, "Extracts from the Household and Privy Purse Accounts of the Lestranges of Hunstanton from A.D. 1519 to A.D. 1578," *Archaeologia* 25 (1834): 494, 524.

73. *Test. Ebor.*, 2:130–134; Clay, *North Country Wills*, 1:73–75.

74. *Historical Manuscripts Commission: Report on the Manuscripts of Lord Middleton, preserved at Wollaton Hall, Nottinghamshire* (London: HMSO, 1911), pp. 327–391, for what is analyzed below.

Such a reward was a gratuity and usually was differentiated from alms and from payments for merchandise or services in these family accounts. Alms tended to be penny grants and were dispensed either in anonymous fashion as individual pennies or through almoners in amounts that were approximately equivalent to a penny per day. Other grants and gifts are called rewards and cover a wide variety of offerings ranging from one pence for maidens who give the lord a "powsay," to four pence for friars just passing by, to four to eight pence for soldiers—the higher figure more likely for those individuals designated by the accounts-keeper as "yowre sowgearse" (your soldiers) as compared to those who "belonged" to a friend. A church offering was four pence; alms for poor scholars, one; guild payments are found both at four and at twelve pence. There were two grants for highway repair and one for the relief of prisoners, ranging from two to four pence. Grants to hermits ranged from four to twelve pence for those who were known, but an unknown one received only two pence as alms at the gate. The grants to anchorites then were part of a system of bestowal of small amounts of money on many individuals most of whom would have anticipated not only a grant in a given set of circumstances but also the amount. Anchorites and hermits were part of the group receiving these payments, but it remains unclear (as with the Lestrange accounts) to what degree the gifts were regular, especially in the case of anchorites whose immobility prevented them from appearing in their own behalf for this charity.

The scope of these disbursements raises the question of the nature of the individuals likely to support anchorites and the general patterns of thought and feelings that prompted such generosity.[75] A more complete description of gentry wills may shed some light. Fifty-eight wills or will fragments have been identified whose writers can be classified as members of the gentry. The wills range in time from 1301 to 1520 but mainly are fifteenth-

75. Nigel Saul, also using wills, recently has explored the religious attitudes of some gentry: "The Religious Sympathies of the Gentry in Gloucestershire, 1200–1500," *Transactions of the Bristol and Gloucestershire Archaeological Society* 98 (1980): 99–109.

century testaments.[76] Twenty-four of the fifty-eight were written by women, a much higher percentage of female wills than normal. Thirty-two of these wills have been analyzed fully (others are fragments). Divided into two groups, the sample contains thirteen Yorkshire wills and nineteen drawn from nine other counties.[77] Table 8 displays the distribution of conventional gifts in these wills.

The analysis indicates a group of people who used their wills in typical medieval fashion to purchase masses and prayers from organized religious groups. The "charitable" impulse is minimal but gifts to the poor are more frequent than we might expect. Vale finds that only one in three of the Yorkshire gentry gave a grant for the poor in their wills[78] (and his sample includes all but one of our testators). The figures in table 8 show that our Yorkshire testators remembered the poor almost 50 percent of the time, with a higher percentage for the testators in the miscellaneous group and an overall average of two out of three. In this distribution of gifts the gentry wills parallel those of the aristocracy.

The gentry then viewed anchorites as part of the religious establishment and perhaps as part of a family commitment. Of the thirty-two wills six made general bequests to anchorites. All others made bequests to individuals at specific sites, often known and named. In the miscellaneous group of wills the anchorites received grants ranging from fifty shillings to four pence; in Yorkshire the range of the gift was more contained: John Stapleton's grant of a mark for each was the highest; most grants were for one-half and one-quarter of that amount. One of the most unusual wills of the group was that of Sir Thomas Cumberworth, of Som-

---

76. One known thirteenth-century will is not included in the analysis: the will of Sir Nicholas de Mitton of Bredon, Worcestershire (courtesy of Father Michael Sheehan), Worcestershire, Record Office, MS 713, fol. 334v. Mannyngham's document is not included either because it is not a true will and because the gift to the anchoress was a secondary bequest.

77. There are three from Norwich, two each from London, Lincoln, Bedfordshire, Exeter, and Somerset, and one each from Hampshire, Shropshire, and Cheshire.

78. Vale, *Piety*, p. 24.

TABLE 8

DISTRIBUTION OF ALMS: GENTRY WILLS (1301–1520)

	Yorkshire (13)	Miscellaneous (19)	Total (32)
Poor	6	15	21
Friars	10	16	26
Convents[1]	10	13	23
Public works	3	1	4
Prisoners	0	2	2
Lepers	1	2	3

1. Includes both male and female orders of which female orders much predominate and male orders are usually the newer and stricter houses. Malcolm G. A. Vale, *Piety, Charity, and Literacy among the Yorkshire Gentry, 1370–1480* (Borthwick Papers, no. 50. [York: St. Anthony Hall's Publications, 1976]), p. 20, makes similar comments relative to the Yorkshire gentry in general.

erby, Lincolnshire.[79] Written in 1451, it is rich in detail and bestows an unusual collection of relics and devotional books. He called his body "wrecchid" and desired that it be buried wearing only a sheet; there were instructions that he not be buried while still alive; most of his relics were to go to his chantry in Somerby church, which also received two of his religious books; other devotional books, including a Latin psalter (Rolle?), Walter Hilton's *De Vita Contemplativa et Activa*, and a volume of *De Vita Christi* (again some version of the *Meditationes Vitae Christi*) were granted to clerical friends, while a copy of the *Canterbury Tales* was bequeathed to his nephew's wife. Many religious houses and their superiors received grants of money and beads, and while there is no absolute separation between the old and the newer orders in this will, the Carthusians were treated more handsomely than other groups. Those individuals who came to Cumberworth's

79. Andrew Clark, ed., *Lincoln Diocese Documents 1440–1544*, EETS, o.s. 149 (1914), pp. 44–57.

funeral were to be repaid at the following rates: an abbot would receive a noble (6s. 8d.); a prior or prioress, 3s. 4d.; canons and nuns, 12d.; priests and friars, 4d.; clerks, 2d.; each "pore childe & woman," 4d. The rates changed for some at his month-mind (the service thirty days after his death), when abbots, priors, prioresses, canons, and nuns could double their rewards for coming; priests, friars, and clerks received the same gratuity but poor men only one pence. The anchoress at the "grese fote" in Lincoln was to have his roll of prayers, six yards of blanket, six yards of linen and three times the amount of alms that a prioress received.[80] This was the value Thomas Cumberworth placed on the vocation of the solitary recluse.

80. The "grese steps" or "Greestone Stairs" is the name still applied to a flight of stairs that ascend from the lower to the higher city. The church of the Holy Trinity-at-the-Stairs (*ad gressus*) stood there and it was long the home of a female recluse. Geoffrey le Scrope remembered the anchoress Isabel who lived there with his most lavish gift in 1382. By the time Cumberworth wrote his will the anchoress was a woman named Matilda. A will of 1502 left twelve pence to the "ankers at the Greese Foot," showing the cell still active then (John Mirk, *Myrc's Duties of a Parish Priest*, ed. Edward Peacock, EETS, o.s. 31 [1868], p. 90).

7

Merchant and Other
Lay Group Support

Merchant support of anchorites cannot be examined from as many directions as support by royal families, the aristocracy, or the gentry. Although anchorites were probably most common in those communities where merchants were most common, little save testamentary data exists by which to chart merchant support of anchorites. A rare document indicates that the burgesses of Richmond possessed the right of presentation to the town anchorhold, which was at the parish church. In 1490 that right was in dispute, with both the Grey Friars of Richmond and the Premonstratensians of Easby making claim for it. The dispute was settled in favor of the burgesses: ". . . the Bailiffe and the xxiij Burges of the grete inqueste of Richmund shall have the nominacion and fre election of the seid Ancores for euermore, from tyme to tyme when it happyns to be void, as they have had withouten tyme to mynde."[1] The right of presentation was in itself a desirable possession, but whether it carried with it any obligation is not specified. The advowson of the cell at Allhallows, London, was also in the gift of the city. In 1532 Alderman Robert Champneys made a request to the mayor and commonality that he be given the next voidance "after the decease of the anchorite." This was granted to him provided that he selected a proper and virtuous

1. *Test. Ebor.*, 2:114–115.

person for occupancy.[2] But again there is no sense of obligation here; rather a perquisite of office is being exploited.

A sense of obligation to anchorites, however, is discoverable in many merchant wills, and although wills provide only one kind of testimony for support, they are numerous enough in this group to enable us to find some important patterns. Norman Tanner has calculated that 18 percent of all lay wills probated in Norwich between 1370 and 1532 (largely a merchant group) made bequests for anchorites and hermits. That percentage grew during the period under review: whereas only 8 percent of wills made such a bequest between 1370 and 1439, 18 percent did so between 1440 and 1489, 21 percent between 1490 and 1517, and fully 25 percent between 1518 and 1532. Among York mayors in the period 1370–1440, more than half left bequests for anchorites.[3] London merchants of the same periods were also making bequests to anchorites, and I have used their wills to develop a profile of such merchant testators, a profile that has then been tested against observations of merchants from other periods and other locales. It serves as well for comparison with other social groups.

Fifty-three wills containing bequests to anchorites are found among those enrolled at the London Court of Husting between the years 1342 and 1413.[4] The Hustings Court (which still exists, although no longer for probate purposes) was in the Middle Ages a civil court to which citizens of London had access as one of their customary rights. A citizen of London was defined as an individual whose morality could be established, whose financial position was secure, and whose political loyalty to king and city was assured. All wills of such persons who bequeathed real prop-

2. VCH London, 1:588; Clay, "Further Studies," p. 84.

3. For Norwich, see Norman P. Tanner, The Church in Late Medieval Norwich, 1370-1532, Pontifical Institute of Mediaeval Studies, Studies and Texts 66 (Toronto, 1984), p. 223. For York see discussion in my chapter 7 below.

4. CWCH, 2 vols. The dates 1342-1413 represent the outside limits of the dates of enrollment. These wills actually were written between the years 1341 and 1408. When the wills are discussed individually their date of composition is employed. When the series is discussed or is being compared to other series that list wills according to probate dates, the enrollment dates are used.

erty within the boundaries of the city were subject to the jurisdiction of the Hustings Court. The Hustings rolls thus record the wills of a class of people identified both by citizenship and by possession of transferable real property.[5]

These fifty-three wills contain the only bequests to anchorites on the calendar (which spans the years 1258–1688). Fifty of the fifty-three individuals who wrote these wills were male. Three were women and the wives of citizens. Nine of the fifty men had been aldermen. Guild memberships of the testator or spouse are noted in forty-eight wills. Thirty-two persons were members of merchant companies (drapers, mercers, grocers, fishmongers, vintners, skinners) and twelve more were associated with guilds that Sylvia Thrupp classifies as of upper-middle rank (chandlers, brewers, glovers, painters, scriveners). Citizens, possessors of real property, aldermen, members of a major guild—these testators were affluent, established members of the merchant class of London society.[6]

Beyond their gifts to anchorites these fifty-three testators distributed grants to all the other pious and charitable categories deemed appropriate for medieval benefactions. The wills of these merchants outline a consistent portrait of generous and concerned individuals, and this generosity was bestowed equally on persons and groups falling into both "pious" and "charitable" classes. The wills that compose the Hustings sample indicate that their principals were members of a group that shared attitudes and behavior. The communality of their gifts to anchorites, which I have used as the basis for inclusion here, emerges as but one aspect of a highly developed sense of social awareness and responsibility.

The bequests to anchorites took both general and specific forms, but the general gift predominates. Forty-three testators made general bequests: to every anchorite in London and its

5. CWCH, 1:xx–xxiii, xlii; Mary Bateson, ed., Borough Customs, 2 vols., Selden Society 18, 21 (1904–06), 2:cxxxviii–cxl; Sylvia L. Thrupp, The Merchant Class of Medieval London (Ann Arbor: University of Michigan Press, 1962), pp. 2–3, 15.

6. Thrupp, Merchant Class of Medieval London, pp. 6, 13, 32, 45, for rankings of "upper-middle." Some members of lesser companies were also quite wealthy and in the fourteenth century had more status than they would a hundred years later (ibid., p. 33).

suburbs, to female recluses in London, to recluse anchorites in the city, to anchorites and recluses of London, to every anchorite and hermit in London, to "poor ankers." Thirteen individuals made bequests to specific anchorites, three wills containing both specific and general grants. Eleven anchorite sites were named. Brother John Ingram at Le Swannesnest near the Tower received four bequests. Two anchorites shut up together at St. Lawrence, Jewry received three. The anchorites at St. Giles without Holborn were mentioned in two wills, as was the anchorite of St. Peter of Cornhill and an anchorite at Westminster.[7]

Virtually all of these testators made bequests to their burial churches, as custom decreed. Other churches also were remembered in their wills, St. Paul's being singled out in twenty-two instances. Religious women—convent nuns at Clerkenwell, Haliwell, Kilburn and elsewhere, Poor Clares, and the sisters of the Hospital of St. Katherine by the Tower—were frequently mentioned. Whereas the details of gifts to abbeys and priories tend to be generalized in the calendar to "various religious orders," the Carthusians were carefully noted in seven of the twenty-five wills written after 1370.

Seven wills of the sample contained bequests for pilgrimages, either to fulfill a vow made in the testator's lifetime or an additional "good work" for the salvation of his soul. Friars were mentioned in the wills of thirty-one testators (58.5 percent) and, Chaucer's gibes notwithstanding, the frequency of gifts to friars increased as the period advanced.[8] Parish and merchant guild fraternities were mentioned in twenty wills (37.7 percent). They contained fourteen gifts that could be called "religious" (for an altar

7. CWCH, 2:147, 189, 218, 228, for John Ingram; CWCH, 2:107, 147, 197, for St. Lawrence Jewry; CWCH, 2:148, 158, for St. Giles without Holborn; CWCH, 1:483, 638; 2:260, 398 for St. Peter of Cornhill and Westminster.

8. Of the thirty-five wills written after 1368, twenty-three (65.7 percent) made bequests for one or more groups of friars; in the interval between 1381 and 1408, twelve of thirteen wills (92.3 percent) did so. John A. F. Thomson, "Piety and Charity in Late Medieval London," Journal of Ecclesiastical History 16 (1965): 189, notes a continuing trend in this direction throughout the extended period of his study. Gifts for the friars were more common in 1529–30 than in 1401–49. See also my table 9, note 3.

light, a chaplain, a missal, masses), illuminating the guild's function as a quasi-ecclesiastical organization. Eight wills delivered gifts, via guilds, that had social implications. These grants were earmarked for the almsboxes of the merchant guild fraternities and rightly belong to a discussion of gifts for the poor. Bequests to the poor, to lepers, and to prisoners are at high levels. Gifts for public works—which for these Londoners meant London Bridge above all else—were fewer but still considerable. The poor in hospitals were mentioned in twenty-nine wills (54.7 percent), lepers in thirty-three (62.3 percent),[9] prisoners in twenty-five (47.2 percent), public works in seventeen (32.1 percent).

If the Hustings figures are compared to those generated by John A. F. Thomson in his "Piety and Charity in Late Medieval London," their significance can be appreciated.[10] Thomson used the wills of all London testators proved at the Prerogative Court of Canterbury during specified intervals. Five registers of the Canterbury Court were culled by Thomson: two from the first half of the fifteenth century, Marche and Luffenam 1401–49; one from later in that century, Logge 1479–86; and two from the immediate pre-Reformation period, Bodfelde 1523–25 and Jankyn 1529–30. The first comparison focuses on the Marche and Luffenam data because they most clearly match the Hustings information in time. Where Thomson only reported overall figures, I have made approximations relative to Marche and Luffenam alone. Although the time span of the Hustings data is not identical

9. Twenty-eight wills made grants to lepers living in hospitals, five other wills to lepers "around London" or to lepers "near London." For examples, see *CWCH*, 2:144, 189.

10. Thomson, "Piety and Charity," pp. 184–190. I use the same counting technique as Thomson did. Thus I count a will as making a bequest to friars or lepers or prisoners as long as one unit is mentioned, and such a will is weighted equally with a will that may have made grants to several units within the category. Other studies have utilized different counting styles. John M. Jennings, "The Distribution of Landed Wealth in the Wills of London Merchants, 1400–1450," *Mediaeval Studies* 39 (1977): 261–280, weighted repetitive gifts, and W. K. Jordan in his many works weighted by using the amounts of bequests. Each style of counting has limitations. I have chosen to count by wills because that technique describes attitudes reasonably well and because all other techniques are likely to subject the data to greater distortion. No one counting pattern, however, is the answer for all investigative problems or approaches.

226

with that for the Canterbury data, nothing in this work or that of Thomson suggests that the time discrepancy invalidates the comparison in any meaningful way (see table 9).

Table 9 indicates that the Hustings testators in the anchorite-favoring group were a substantially more generous group than those in Marche and Luffenam, making bequests to the poor, to prisoners, to friars and monks at levels two and even three times that of the control group. The impact of the comparison is heightened when we recognize that Thomson's data already are weighted by his use of full wills proved in an ecclesiastical court. By law all wills were under church jurisdiction. Properly, a will, whether of

TABLE 9
PIOUS AND CHARITABLE BEQUESTS OF LONDON TESTATORS

Recipient	Hustings wills with anchorite grants (1342–1413)	Marche and Luffenam (1401–1449)
Poor in hospitals	54.7%	23.4%[1]
Lepers	63.3%	——
Prisoners	47.2%	29%[2]
Public works	32.1%	15%
Friars	56.6%	30%[3]
All conventual orders	90.6%	25.8%[4]

1. Thomson's figure includes gifts for the religious who maintained the hospitals as well as gifts directed to the poor and is thus inflated as compared to the Hustings figure, which does not reflect any religious gifts.

2. Includes 3.5 percent for freeing prisoners and 25.5 percent for their immediate relief.

3. This figure is an approximation. Thomson gives an overall count of 35.5 percent here, noting as well that the comparative popularity of the friars was increasing toward the time of the Reformation. Thus, his figure has been adjusted downward for this earlier period to accommodate the later swell.

4. This figure is the sum of Thomson's overall averages for monks (15.1 percent) and for nuns (10.7 percent). Higher than appropriate, because a will containing gifts for both monks and nuns is here counted twice, some of the overage is absorbed by the inverse of the phenomenon explained in note 3 above. The possessioner orders were more popular in the earlier period than later.

movable or immovable goods, first was probated at the appropriate level of the ecclesiastical court system.[11] Subsequently, those portions of a will relevant to the disposal of real property were enrolled in the civil courts of those communities where citizens had access to such courts. The data of the Hustings rolls are derived from wills or will fragments enrolled primarily to ratify the devise of real property in a civil court. The notation on the roll of a religious or charitable gift not connected to the distribution of that devise was at best of secondary interest to the clerks of that court. That the Hustings data are incomplete testifies even more dramatically to the extraordinary extent of charitable response seen among these testators.

In fact the poor were remembered by members of the Hustings group even more routinely than the table indicates. For conformity with Thomson's calculations, table 9 tallies only those gifts to the poor that were channeled through hospitals. In all, 73.6 percent of the Hustings testators (thirty-nine wills) made bequests for the poor in some fashion. If the data relative to burial day disbursements also had been available, the "poor statistic" probably would have approached the 100 percent mark, for that information typically provides the nucleus of grants to the poor in a statistical analysis of medieval wills.[12]

However general the response of the Hustings testators to the plight of the poor, as a group the testators remained emotionally distant. The great majority of their gifts went to an anonymous class—the hospital poor—whose existence impinged only marginally on a testator's life. A few individuals did bridge that gap. Two requested that marriage portions for poor maidens (young women without dowries) be provided; three remembered poor relations, among them some family orphans; one will contained a bequest

11. See Ernest F. Jacob's introduction to *Chichele*, 2:x–xv.

12. For example, Malcolm G. A. Vale, *Piety, Charity, and Literacy among the Yorkshire Gentry, 1370–1480*, Borthwick Papers, no. 50 (York: St. Anthony Hall's Publications, 1976), p. 24, reports that his examination of the wills of 148 members of the Yorkshire gentry who died between 1370 and 1480 shows that only 47 (1 in 3) made any provision for the poor. Of these, only 34 provided for poor other than their own tenants or servants, and most of these bequests were to paupers gathered at their funerals.

for the poor women and widows living in "Lymstrete." Two merchants remembered the poor of their working days. In 1346 John Hammond, a pepperer (or grocer), left sixty shillings for clothing for the porters of Soperslane as well as twelve pence to each of them and to every other laborer connected with his business. He also left twenty marks to be distributed among poor merchants who had traded with him. In 1369 John Not, also a pepperer, remembered the porters in a similar way. His executors were directed to "purchase cloth of Candelwykstrete, whereof to make coats and hoods for distribution among the porters of Soperslane who customarily served the pepperers."[13]

There is also concern for those newly poor. In 1408 John Wodecock, a mercer, bequeathed twenty pounds to the box of the "Art or Mystery of the Mercers of London in aid of charity... and a further sum of twenty marks to be distributed among those of the suit and livery of the Fraternity of the Art of the Mercers who have become poor." Earlier, in 1349, Hugh Robury, a glover, had acknowledged the same sentiment: "The residue of [my] goods to be divided among those who, having been reduced from affluence to poverty, are ashamed to get a livelihood by begging, and those poor men who come up from the rural districts to the City of London to get a living by selling brushwood, timber, heather, &c."[14] One function of the "box" of the fraternal craft guild was similar —it provided aid to a brother fallen on hard times, and the seven testators in addition to John Wodecock who left money to the boxes of these guilds may have expected that their gifts would be so used.[15]

But without question the preponderance of gifts to the poor in London took the form of gifts to the poor in hospitals. Some wills provided grants in general fashion (as they had with anchorites) to

13. *CWCH*, 1:516; 2:145.
14. *CWCH*, 2:398; 1:642.
15. Thrupp, *Merchant Class of Medieval London*, p. 30; Toulmin Smith and Lucy T. Smith, eds., *English Gilds, Their Statutes and Customs, A.D. 1389*, EETS, o.s. 40 (1870), p. xxxvi. For a parallel discussion of how fourteenth-century devotional societies of Venice became philanthropic institutions in the later fourteenth and fifteenth centuries, see Brian Pullan, *Rich and Poor in Renaissance Venice* (Cambridge, Mass.: Harvard University Press, 1971), pp. 63–66.

the inmates of all the hospitals in London and its suburbs; others were more specific, naming up to half a dozen different establishments. Yet the sense of general disbursement remains, as it does with gifts to lepers and prisoners. Most donors made grants to a great many units, many of which must have been relatively unknown to them but were a part of their gift-giving consciousness. The anonymity of the city is felt in these wills. The anchorites were not likely to be individually known. The poor and lepers also were part of a separate and distant world.

The anonymity of the city limits our vision of the testators as well. Rarely is it possible to find connections among them. Occasionally there is a clue. Geoffrey Patrick, a scribe, in an unusual will of 1371 made grants to at least six anchorites at five sites, four of whom (all male) he knew by name. One of these was Brother John Ingram at Swannesnest near the Tower. In 1380 a woman named Cecilia Rose, the widow of Thomas Rose, a clerk, made a bequest to every female recluse in the city and suburbs, and also to Brother John Ingram. She then left to Cecilia (her baptismal goddaughter?), a "daughter of *Geoffrey Patrick, her late clerk,*" a sum of money and other gifts. These are similar wills of two individuals tied together both by friendship and professional relationship.[16]

John Hammond and John Not, the pepperers who shared a concern for the laborers who served their businesses, were connected by more than that sentiment and their guild memberships. Both provided for their burial in the same church, St. Mary Bothawe. Hammond made bequests to John Not and to his wife Cecilia as well as to their two sons. In addition, Hammond left money to establish a chantry for Adam de Salesbury, once a pepperer himself and the first husband of Hammond's wife Agnes. In turn, John Not also would provide funds for a chantry for Adam de Salesbury as well as for John Hammond.

The wills of two drapers again suggest friendship and common interests. William Holbech, in a testament dated 1365, made a bequest to a kinsman, Thomas Holbech. Twelve years later, in 1377,

16. CWCH, 2:147, 288 (italics mine).

the draper John de Benyngton left funds for a chantry for the good of the soul of Thomas Holbech.[17] The connection is fragile. One cannot even be sure that the two references are to the same person. Yet both testators were drapers, and drapers were an unusual group among the anchorite testators. Of the fifty-three Hustings testators, forty-eight have known guild membership. These guild members represented only fourteen of the more than fifty different guilds current at this time.[18] Moreover, almost one-quarter of the forty-eight testators were drapers. There are eleven drapers, six fishmongers, five mercers, five pepperers, three each vintners, chandlers, and brewers, two each skinners, painters, glovers, scribes, and saddlers, and one potter and one apothecary in the Hustings group.

Nothing in the general sample accounts for this preponderance of drapers in the anchorite-favoring group. On the Hustings rolls there are fewer drapers in this period than fishmongers. In the fifteen years between 1358 and 1372 the calendar lists the wills of twenty-five fishmongers, fifteen drapers, thirteen mercers, nine goldsmiths, eight pepperers, eight chandlers, and seven vintners among others. An analysis of the guild memberships of aldermen of the second half of the fourteenth century gives twenty-nine fishmongers, twenty-seven drapers, twenty-two mercers, fifteen pepperers, twelve goldsmiths, and so forth.[19] Other statistical data make the same point. The drapers were among the major guilds of the period but always seem to have had fewer members than the fishmongers and were most equal with the mercers.[20]

17. Ibid., pp. 103, 196.
18. Guild memberships are noted in the rolls for forty-six of the fifty men; the guild memberships of the former husbands of the women are noted in two of three instances. May McKisack, *The Fourteenth Century, 1307–1399* (London: Oxford University Press, 1959), p. 376, says that at least fifty guilds were listed in the late fourteenth century. Thrupp, *Merchant Class of Medieval London*, p. 77, remarks that fifty-one crafts participated in a municipal council of 1376.
19. This data was drawn from appendix A of Thrupp, *Merchant Class of Medieval London*, pp. 321–377, which gives biographic information for London aldermen.
20. Thrupp, *Merchant Class of Medieval London*, p. 41. George Unwin, *The Gilds and Companies of London* (New York: Barnes and Noble, 1964; orig. ed., 1908), p. 77, describes the membership of a Common Council of London called in 1351: ". . . a summons was issued to the thirteen chief misteries, in consequence

Examination of these draper wills does not disclose any personal interrelationships save the tenuous Holbech connection mentioned above. Five of the six draper wills written between 1369 and 1400 did make bequests to the almsbox of the Fraternity of St. John of the Tailors of London. The Tailors fraternity was also a grantee in the 1345 will of a mercer and in the 1373 will of the wife of a saddler. In both of these wills the grant was for a religious purpose. It is quite likely that the Fraternity of the Tailors was a common meeting ground for many of these testators. It is even possible that anchorites were an alms responsibility of the guild itself—guilds sometimes undertook such obligations.[21] Whether or not the Fraternity of the Tailors is a clue to the drapers' predilections, they were favorably disposed to anchorites to a degree quite disproportionate to their numbers, and their wills, when abstracted from the larger sample, provide evidence that they dispensed charitable donations generally at levels that exceeded those of other members of the Hustings group (see table 10).

The drapers expanded the pious and charitable mood of the Hustings testators to its ultimate expression.[22] Their wills inten-

---

of which the Grocers, Mercers, and Fishmongers each elected six members; the Drapers, Goldsmiths, Woolmongers, Vintners . . . each elected four members; and the Ironmongers two members."

21. For example, the Trinity Guild of King's Lynn in Norfolk gave regular support to anchorites and hermits. The anchorite of All Saints, South Lynn, received twenty shillings per year from the guild for at least thirty-five years. See H. Harrod, *Report on the Deeds and Records of the Borough of King's Lynn* (King's Lynn, 1870), p. 30. Thrupp, *Merchant Class of Medieval London*, pp. 30–31, describes the Tailors fraternity as one of the two most prominent in London, to which many persons belonged who were not members of the trade—some of whom were not even citizens. The fraternity employed several priests and by the end of the period (1500) had two chapels of its own in which special indulgences were offered to regular worshipers. The fraternity also had accumulated shares in the spiritual profit accruing from the prayers and pious works of eight religious houses, and members could claim remission of a seventh part of all penances imposed on them.

22. In a study of Montpellier, Katherine Reyerson has noted some similarities there (Katherine Reyerson, "Changes in Testamentary Practice at Montpellier on the Eve of the Black Death," *Church History* 47 [1978]: 253–269). Although her focus is on other issues, Reyerson indicates in passing that recluses were the recipients of grants in 54 percent of the wills of inhabitants of Montpellier between the

TABLE 10
COMPARISON OF DRAPER WILLS TO ALL HUSTINGS
ANCHORITE-FAVORING WILLS

Recipient	Draper Wills (11)	All Anchorite Wills (53)
Poor[1]	90.9%	73.6%
Lepers	81.8%	62.3%
Prisoners	63.7%	47.2%
Public works	45.5%	32.1%
Friars	63.7%	56.6%
All conventual orders	90.9%	90.6%

1. This figure includes both grants to the poor in hospitals and all other grants for the poor, as discussed in the text. Thus this figure differs from its companion figure in table 9.

sify the coloring of this group of people who, in their last testaments, responded to the needs of many social groups to a degree far beyond what general evidence suggests might have been the case. The common thread of concern for anchorites was not an unrelated tie. Even as aristocrats and gentry who supported anchorites showed a greater sensitivity to the poor, these merchants expressed that motif more dramatically and more conclusively. The awareness of the plight of the poor—in all their manifestations—was ever present in the city. Late fourteenth-century London merchants, especially drapers, attempted to mitigate that poverty in their final testaments along with their gifts to anchorites.

years 1200 and 1345. The testators are indentified as "merchants, drapers, changers, and legal specialists, those holding the title of bourgeois and their wives, daughters, and widows." Although the percentage of wills with such grants drops just before the Black Death, it still remains high: 36 percent for the year 1348. Moreover, gifts to recluses are the most commonly mentioned bequests during the extended period, by far outdistancing gifts for friars, churches, hospitals, and chantries.

THE FIFTEENTH AND SIXTEENTH CENTURIES

While all mention of anchorites disappears from the Hustings enrollments after 1413,[23] sixteen wills outside these enrollments testify to the continuing use of bequests to provide for London anchorites after this period. During the years 1415–1528 only 2 wills (dated 1415 and 1442) made general bequests to all the anchorites in London and its suburbs; after 1442 all wills made specific bequests only. The later wills suggest fewer anchorites, with those remaining personally known to the testator who desired their prayers. Six sites are repeatedly named, four housing women and two housing men. By 1503 Hugh Browne, a mercer, could write: "To each of the two Ankers, and to every of the two Ankeresses in the City of London and Westminster to pray for my soul III s. and IIII d." and, although there were more than four anchorites in London at this time, the will establishes the changed mood.[24]

While London anchorites were fewer in number in these last days of English orthodoxy, those yet embracing this rigorous *conversatio* still retained the respect that their predecessors had known. Less anonymous than their fourteenth-century counterparts, they remained possessed of the charisma long associated with their ascetic and mystical vocation, and the wills of late medieval London merchants who have made their presence known to us create a pattern that verifies the Hustings indicators. Seven of the sixteen wills recording bequests to London anchorites in the fifteenth and sixteenth centuries were written by merchants and an eighth by the widow of a merchant. Seven of these testators belonged to guilds of the highest rank (mercers, skinners, grocers). Three had been aldermen and mayors of London, as also had been the second husband of Jane, Viscountess Lisle, whose 1500 will forms part of the group. Seven of these eight wills are complete (that of Hugh Browne alone is a fragment) and permit an analysis of greater subtlety than that afforded by the Hustings

23. See my appendix 3 for discussion of this phenomenon.
24. C. Eveleigh Woodruff, ed., *Sede Vacante Wills*, Kent Archaeological Society, Records Branch 3 (1949), p. 9.

enrollments.[25] Moreover, they allow for further comparison with Thomson's evaluations (see tables 11 and 12).

Table 11 makes evident that the general patterns of almsgiving established for the fourteenth-century merchants who made bequests to anchorites and who thus appeared in the Hustings sample are paralleled in later merchant testaments. Table 12 lists the amounts of grants to anchorites along with the amounts bequeathed for lepers, prisoners, friars, and other regular objects of these merchants' concern. Here we can note the substantiality of the bequests to anchorites, for gifts to anchorites are compared to grants for *institutions*, such as leprosaria, hospitals, prisons, and friaries. The gift to the individual anchorite in his individual household is contrasted to a gift for a group of variable yet not insignificant size. The comparative extent of the bequests to anchorites indicates that the will sample has meaning. These testators not only remembered anchorites in their wills, they were all very favorably disposed to them. They were not constrained to remember recluses, as one feels they were with the friars (gifts to friars were so commonplace in medieval wills as to imply a social pressure close to obligation). Rather, a voluntary decision was enhanced by a positive desire, and this quality unified the group.

The practice in this study has been to count by category, not by numbers within a category or by the amounts of money dispensed, even when that information is available (see note 10 for this chapter). Most of these testators did, however, make grants to several units within each category if more than one unit existed. In addition, money grants, while most often equal to each unit within the category, could be variable—preferences frequently were ex-

25. These wills may be found: Robert Markele: *Chichele*, 2:218–221; John Welles: *Chichele*, 2:615–620; William Gregory: James Gairdner, ed., *The Historical Collections of a Citizen of London*, Camden Society, n.s. 17 (1876), pp. xlii–xlix; John Boteler: Margaret McGregor, ed., *Bedfordshire Wills Proved in the Prerogative Court of Canterbury, 1383–1548*, Bedfordshire Historical Record Society 58 (1979), pp. 19–21; John Emlyn: Philip E. Jones, ed., *Calendar of Plea and Memoranda Rolls of the City of London, A.D. 1458–1482* (Cambridge: Cambridge University Press, 1961), pp. 132–135; Jane, Viscountess Lisle: Woodruff, *Sede Vacante Wills*, pp. 127–145; William Butler: McGregor, *Bedfordshire Wills*, pp. 142-147.

TABLE 11

ANALYSIS OF WILLS OF LONDON MERCHANTS WHO BEQUEATHED TO ANCHORITES (1420–1528)

	Poor	Hospital poor	Lepers	Prisoners	Public works	Guilds	Poor maidens	Friars	Convents
Robert Markele (1420)	x	x	x	x		x	x	x	
John Welles (1442)	x		x	x	x	x		x	
William Gregory (1465)	x	x		x	x	x	x	x	x
John Boteler³ (1465)	x	x				x		x	x
John Emlyn (1475)	x			x		x		x	
Jane, Viscountess Lisle (1500)	x	x	x	x	x	x	x	x	x
William Butler³ (1528)	x	x	x	x	x	x	x	x	x
Percentage	100	71.4	57.1	85.7	57.1	100	57.1	100	57.1
Thomson average percentage	—¹	20²	—	29	12.2	—	10.3	35.6	20²

1. General bequests to the poor were "extremely common," according to John A. F. Thompson, "Piety and Charity in Late Medieval London," *Journal of Ecclesiastical History* 16 (1965): 183.

2. Approximate.

3. These men may have been related, but were not in direct descent.

TABLE 12

BEQUESTS TO LONDON ANCHORITES
COMPARED TO BEQUESTS TO OTHER GROUPS

	Anchorites	Hospitals (Poor)	Prisons	Friaries	Leprosaria
Markele	General: 2s. to each	(ls.)[1]	(ls.)[1]	10s.	3s. 4d.
Welles	General: 20s. to each		40s.	40s.	40s.
Gregory	Four: 6s. 8d. each	20s.	@ 23s.[2]	@ 37s.[2]	
Boteler	One: 3s. 4d. (Hermit: 3s. 4d.)	5s.		3s. 4d.	
Emlyn	Male: 1s. Female: ½s.		3s. 4d.	1s. 8d.	
Lisle	Two: 13s. 4d. to each	10s.	@ 42s.[2]	13s. 4d.	13s. 4d.
Butler	Male: 10s.	20s.[3]	@ 25s.[2,3]	20s.	

1. These are individual bequests: 1s. to each bedridden person in hospitals and to each prisoner.

2. These figures are averages.

3. Plus additional grants of food four times yearly, for two to five years.

pressed with regard to the friars. For example, Markele, Welles, Gregory, and Butler each made bequests to all of the five orders of friars with houses in London: the Franciscans, the Dominicans, the Augustinians, the Carmelites, and the Crutched friars. Markele and Welles treated all the orders equally; Gregory gave the Minors five marks, the Preachers and Austins three marks each, the Whitefriars two marks, and the Crutched friars only one; Butler also was partial to the Minors, then to the Crutched friars, lumping the White, Black, and Austin friars at the bottom of his scale. Boteler, Emlyn, and Lisle made bequests to the four main groups of friars only. Boteler and Lisle treated them all equally,

237

but Emlyn made extra provisions for the Augustinians, who were in charge of his obit, a memorial mass held yearly on the anniversary of death.

Prisons also were treated variably. Save for Emlyn, whose grant was payable to Ludgate prison only, the other testators made bequests for prisoners at all of the five major London prisons: Newgate, Ludgate, Marshalsea, King's Bench, and the Fleet. In addition, Gregory and Lisle remembered inmates of the ecclesiastical prison at Westminster and those in the two Counters (debtors' prisons). Lisle treated each unit equally, as she had the friars, while Gregory made distinctions in his bequests as before. He granted thirty shillings each to Ludgate, Newgate, and each of the Counters, twenty pence to each *prisoner* at Westminster (for prayers), and one mark each to the prisons of King's Bench, Marshalsea, and the Fleet. He made a further bequest of ten pounds to acquit prisoners "out of Ludgate and Newgate moost needefull," at his executors' discretion. As to leprosaria, Markele made a general bequest "to each of them"; Welles named three; Lisle, four; Butler, six; all made equal grants to each house.

Although the group is small, the consistency of response of these seven testators is remarkable. Table 11 meets or surpasses the expectations created by table 9 in every category of gifts save convents. Of higher municipal status than the Hustings group (where only one in five could claim aldermanic position), this group was more generous to prisoners and public works. In comparison with Marche and Luffenam, this anchorite-favoring group of testators generated rates of benefaction three, four, and even five times higher. Although this group is too small to be statistically valid, the higher rates are meaningful and will be confirmed below in my discussion of York merchants. In general these wills of late medieval merchant testators reveal a grand sense of noblesse oblige and a measure of communal responsibility that we see much less frequently among the aristocracy. I have next analyzed the wills of a control group of London citizens in order to plumb the origins of that responsibility and to question how much of it derived from a mentality that favored anchorites and how much from high municipal status and wealth.

238

The register of Archbishop Henry Chichele 1414–43 contains the wills of seventeen London citizens, all of them possessing *bona notablia* as well as sufficient status to have their wills proved *coram domino.*[26] Three of these Londoners made bequests to anchorites. The wills of Robert Markele and John Welles already have been analyzed as part of the late medieval London group. A further testator who left bequests to anchorites was William Neel, who, while qualifying as a London citizen, made most of his charitable bequests (including his grants to recluses) in Chichester, and so was outside the parameters of tables 11 and 12. The fourteen other testators in the Chichele London group include some major figures of the day: Richard Whittington, William Waldern, John Coventry, Thomas Knowles, Robert Oteleye, and the archbishop's two brothers, Robert and William. All of these men had been mayors except William Chichele, and he had been both alderman and sheriff. The wills in the Chichele register can thus be used to explore the role of high municipal status in gift giving. Table 13 compares the figures obtained by the analysis of these wills with the results of the earlier will analyses. We are able to compare this group, whose wealth and position gave them access to the archbishop himself in the probate of their wills, to the Marche and Luffenam group, for instance, whose members had to be satisfied with the archbishop's deputies in Ivy Lane. We can also compare the Chichele group, in which 45 percent (eight of seventeen) were aldermen, to the Hustings group, in which seventeen percent (nine of fifty-three) were aldermen. Finally we can compare two groups of essentially equal status.

Table 13 indicates that the social concern reflected in wills benefiting anchorites is in London, at least, related to wealth and high municipal position. The comparison of Chichele to Marche

26. See *Chichele* for William Neel (1418), 2:149–153; John Reynolds (1418), 2:169–170; Robert Markele (1420), 2:218–221; Richard Whittington (1423), 2:240–244; William Waldern (1424), 2:276–278; William Chichele (1426), 2:339–341; John Wyssyngsete (1427), 2:364–366; Edmund Chymbeham (1428), 2:376–377; John Coventry (1429), 2:402–406; Robert FitzRobert (1434), 2:505–515; Thomas Knowles (1435), 2:519–526; Alice Galiot (1435), 2:553–554; Robert Oteleye (1437), 2:549–553; Robert Chichele (1438), 2:564–568; John Darell (1438), 2:568–571; William Rauff (1440), 2:571–572; John Welles (1442), 2:615–620.

TABLE 13

CHICHELE DATA COMPARED TO MARCHE AND LUFFENAM AND
ANCHORITE-FAVORING TESTAMENTS

Recipient	Chichele register London citizens (1414–43)	Marche and Luffenam (1401–49)	Hustings (anchorite-favoring) (1342–1413)	Late medieval (anchorite-favoring) (1420–1528)
Hospital poor	29.4%	23.4%	54.7%	71.4%
Lepers	35.3%	—	62.3%	57.1%
Prisoners	41.2%	29%	47.2%	85.7%
Public works	41.2%	15%	32.1%	57.1%
Poor maidens	35.3%	10%	—	57.1%
Friars	41.2%	30%	56.6%	100%
All conventual	58.8%	25.8%	90.6%	57.1%

and Luffenam in the categories of public works, poor maidens, and convents indicates a substantially more active philanthropic role for the Chichele testators. Yet when compared to the Hustings group—a group of lesser municipal status—the Chichele citizen group falls behind in every category save public works, that category most connected to their sense of office. When compared to the late medieval group of anchorite-favoring testators, an equally high status group, the Chichele group falls behind even more markedly.

Several of the individual testators within the Chichele sample were nonetheless extraordinarily generous. The wills of Richard Whittington and Robert Chichele meet all the expectations for wills that benefit anchorites, although no anchorites are specified. The will of John Coventry is creative and free in a way that makes the regular bequests of the anchorite-favoring testators to the hospital poor look unimaginative—safe gifts of proven value when the heavenly accounts might be tallied but lacking any deep involvement with the problems of the poor. Coventry made a bequest of one hundred pounds for the relief of the poor of London; those within a radius of twenty miles were to be paid in the amount of twelve pence each to aid them in their payment of the king's tallage and to assist them in their harvest-service and collection of grain in the autumn. Both of these grants were in addition to gifts to the poor on Coventry's burial day and gifts to poor maidens, poor prisoners, and the poor of the mercers guild. Clearly it would be inappropriate to suggest that widespread generosity and concern for the welfare of others among London merchants were characteristic only of those who made bequests to anchorites. But the conclusion remains inescapable that the individuals who specifically mentioned anchorites and whose wills have been examined here were unusually concerned about the welfare of others. Was this concern peculiar to Londoners or was it connected to a more broadly conceived "merchant" mentality? To answer that question I turn my attention to York.

York was the second city of England during much of this period. At best a third of London's size (highest estimates place its population peak at 12,000 compared to London's 35,000), it was nonetheless the administrative capital of the North and the see of the Northern Province. Like London, York boasted multiple sites for anchorites in the fourteenth and fifteenth centuries and also a merchant class committed to their support. The probate registers of the York Consistory Court (the court of the diocese) provide wills attesting to that support and these wills make possible a comparison with testaments of merchants in London. The results of an analysis of thirty-two merchant wills written between 1361 and 1535 bear little resemblance to the results of a similar analysis of Yorkshire gentry wills (see table 8) but great resemblance to figures for London merchants (see table 15 below). One hundred percent of the York merchant wills provide grants to the poor; 84 percent to the hospital poor; 81 percent to lepers; 100 percent to friars; 59 percent to convents; 63 percent to prisoners. In comparison with London testaments the York wills rarely mention "poor maidens," although individual gifts for dowries are common and poor widows, poor clerks, and even poor fathers are specified.

As in London most York merchants making bequests to anchorites made them generally to all the anchorites in the city even as they made other general gifts to lepers and almshouses. The anonymity that characterized the London wills is less pervasive here (certainly in any given period the York merchants were at least acquainted with one another) but is nonetheless common in much of the giving. The poor are disembodied even when living in maisondieux (the name given to poorhouses in the North) of a testator's own establishment. Lepers are in their hospitals, prisoners in their cells, anchorites by parish churches.

Wills making specific bequests indicate that there were two active anchorite sites circa 1360, seven between 1380 and 1415, five between 1420 and 1480, and only one after 1510. The anchorites within these cells received repeated grants: the anchoress at St. Cuthbert's received seven grants between 1388 and 1416; the anchoress of All Saints, North Street (Dame Emma Rawgton of the Beauchamp connection), five grants between 1430 and 1436; the anchoresses of All Saints, Fishergate, eight grants between 1428 and 1465; the anchoresses at the convent of St. Clement, eleven grants between 1449 and 1483 (all these in addition to those grants made generally). The anchoress of St. Mary's Bishophill, Senior, the lone recluse known for the sixteenth century, received eight grants between 1520 and 1533. Turned out of her cell in 1543, some years after the Dissolution, she continued to receive support from York merchants in their wills. In 1549 Mistress Haiton "that was the ancres" received a one shilling bequest. Three years later "Mother Johanne of Bishophill" was granted 6s. 8d. for her prayers, still considered of value.[27]

The specific grants also provide clues to possible connections between testators and possible influences on them. One of the early wills in the York series was written by John Croxton in 1394. Croxton left bequests to an anchoress at Wath and two at West Heaton; he left a grant for an anchoress at Thorganby as well as for her maid; he remembered two York anchoresses, one at St. John the Baptist's, Hungate, and the other at St. Cuthbert's. Even earlier York wills, those of John de Gysburne (1385), Henry de Yarum (1388), and William Durem (1390), had left grants for the Hungate anchoress, Yarum also rewarding the St. Cuthbert woman and Gysburne the recluse at Layerthorpe Bridge. In addition Yarum left a bequest to a priest recluse at St. Martin's Chapel, Aldwark, as did a later testator, Agnes de Santon (1400), who also mentioned the St. Cuthbert anchoress in her will.[28]

St. John's, St. Cuthbert's, St. Martin's Chapel, Layerthorpe Bridge are all very close to one another and represent four of the six known anchorite sites in York in the late fourteenth century. Nearby was St. Saviour's church, in which parish St. Martin's Chapel lay. The rector of St. Saviour's from the 1390s to 1433 was Adam Wigan, a man of education (most probably an Oxford scholar of Balliol) and local respect. His will of 1433 left grants for

27. See D. M. Palliser, *The Reformation in York 1534-1553*, Borthwick Papers, no. 40 (York, 1971), pp. 27-28, for Mistress Haiton.

28. Names of all testators have been spelled in conformity with the *Index of Wills in the York Registry 1389-1514*, Yorkshire Archaeological Society, Record Series 6 (1889), and the *Index of Wills, etc. from the Dean and Chapter's Court at York A.D. 1321-1636*, Yorkshire Archaeological Society, Record Series 38 (1907). John Croxton: BIHR D/C Reg. 1, fol. 111, also printed in *Test. Ebor.*, 1:184-186; John de Gysburne: BIHR Reg. 1, fol. 15; Henry de Yarum: BIHR Reg. 1, fol. 57; William Durem: BIHR Reg. 1, fol. 20; Agnes de Santon: BIHR Reg. 3, fol. 75. (Wills are footnoted only the first time they are mentioned in the text.)

six anchorites, all women, three in the city and three dispersed in the county. Locally, anchoresses at All Saints, North Street, at Fishergate, and at Walmgate received two shillings each. An anchoress at Pontefract received two shillings, one at Beeston 3s. 4d., and an anchoress at Thorganby 6s. 8d. The Thorganby anchoress was identified by name and her grant was more substantial than that of the others. Wigan also left a bequest for John Raventhorpe, a chaplain residing with his servant within St. Martin's Chapel, probably in the quarters formerly occupied by the priest-anchorite. In turn Raventhorpe in his will requested that he be buried at St. Saviour's and that his vestments and altar be given to St. John's, Hungate, in the event St. Martin's Chapel ceased to exist.[29]

A Thorganby anchorite bequest shows up in two other York merchant wills of this period—this is somewhat surprising because the village was some distance southeast of the city. In 1436 Thomas Bracebrigg left bequests for the same three York anchoresses given grants by Wigan as well as for the Thorganby recluse; in 1458 Richard Wartere left bequests for three York anchoresses (including two of the three mentioned by Wigan and Bracebrigg) as well as one at Thorganby "in patria," desiring all to pray for him. Both Bracebrigg and Wartere are tied to St. Saviour's. Bracebrigg was a parishioner and was buried there along with his family. In 1410 he was granted a license to provide in mortmain an annuity for Adam Wigan's use in the church. Wartere left a bequest of twenty-one pounds for rebuilding St. Saviour's tower and roof. Two more testators had Hungate-St. Saviour's connections. Richard Russell, a parishioner of St. John's, Hungate, left one hundred shillings to the churchwardens of St. Saviour's and gifts to the poor of that parish in his 1435 will along with large grants to the

---

29. Adam Wigan: BIHR Reg. 3, fol. 363, also printed in *Test. Ebor.*, 2:25–26; John Raventhorpe: BIHR Reg. 3, fol. 358. In the event Raventhorpe seems to have predeceased Wygan by some two months. For Wigan see Alfred B. Emden, *A Biographical Register of the University of Oxford to A.D. 1500*, 3 vols. (Oxford: Clarendon Press, 1957), 3:2107. St. Martin's Chapel was torn down some time after Raventhorpe's death. See Angelo Raine, *Mediaeval York* (London: John Murray, 1955), p. 91.

anchoresses at Walmgate and All Saints, North Street, and to another at St. Helen's, Fishergate. John Bolton in 1445, making bequests generally to anchorites in York, asked to be buried at St. Saviour's, although it was not his parish church.[30]

This melange of data is highly suggestive. A disproportionate amount of anchorite-related behavior in York at this time was centered in the area of St. Saviour's. In the late fourteenth century four of six known anchorite sites in York were concentrated here. Beginning in the 1390s Adam Wigan, who would leave money for six anchorites in his will, began his tenure as parish priest of St. Saviour's, a tenure that would last for almost forty years. By the time of his death the anchorite sites in the immediate vicinity no longer seem to have been occupied[31] and anchorites living outside the neighborhood became the recipients of grants from Wigan and others in his milieu. Successive anchorites in Thorganby received grants from York merchants with St. Saviour's-Hungate connections in 1394, 1436, and 1458. There was some relationship between the site at Thorganby and the Wigan group. All the testators who were part of this connection save for John Bolton made specific grants for individual anchorites, naming them and clearly knowing them. Richard Russell, in the most elaborate of these wills, left five marks each (66s. 8d.) to the Walmgate anchoress and to one at St. Helen's, Fishergate (a site known only from this will), and forty shillings to Dame Emma Rawgton. These large bequests were not to be bestowed outright but rather doled out to the recluses by the executors of his estate as needed.

These connections and the implications of these attitudes are valuable because they indicate that even within a community in which the granting of bequests to anchorites might be a common and even expected form of testamentary practice there might be deeper meanings in the exercise of such practice for some of the

---

30. Thomas Bracebrigg: BIHR Reg. 3, fol. 487; Richard Wartere: BIHR Reg. 4, fol. 115; *CPR 1408–13*, p. 189; Richard Russell: BIHR Reg. 3, fol. 439, also printed in *Test. Ebor.*, 2:52–57; John Bolton: BIHR Reg. 2, fol. 107.

31. St. Cuthbert's was torn down and rebuilt in the early fifteenth century. The last reference to an anchorite cell there is in a will written in 1416: Emma Eston, BIHR Reg. 3, fol. 605.

testators than for others, meanings often obscured by simple counting techniques. In order to explore these meanings further, I examined the sequence in gift giving of the York merchant wills in a manner similar to that used earlier with the London Hustings wills. Analysis of the thirty-two York testaments indicated that twelve placed grants to anchorites among religious grants or among personal bequests; thirteen merchants placed their bequests to anchorites in a sequence so that the grant served as a bridge between religious grants and grants to the poor or as a bridge to personal grants; three placed anchorites in the midst of bequests to the enclosed poor; four wills were random. Examples of a "religious" sequence include John Croxton's will, which ran: personal bequests, anchorites, nunneries, further anchorites, nunneries; Thomas Bracebrigg's will: rectors and chaplains, chapels, anchorites, priories, anchorite, hermit, nunneries, poor; and Margaret Blackburn's will (1435): friars, anchorites, chaplains. Wills that used the anchoritic bequest to shift from one conception to another included that of William Bowes (1437): burial day bequests, grant to the cathedral fabric, anchorites, maisondieux, prisoners, lepers; that of Robert Howme, Jr. (1433): friars, chantries, anchorites, lepers, poor; and that of John Norman (1525): friars, tombstone provisions, anchoress, maisondieux, prisoners. Two wills placed anchorites with gifts to the enclosed poor: William Helmeslay's (1404): friars, lepers, anchorites, maisondieux, prisoners; and John Carré's (1487): lepers, prisoners, anchoresses, maisondieux, poor maidens, poor.[32]

York merchants who made bequests for anchorites were likely to have perceived those bequests as religious. This was especially true of those testators who made specific bequests: all the testators of the St. Saviour nexus belong to the group who placed their bequests to anchorites among their religious grants, and these testators are quite clear that anchorites are enclosed by choice and as a form of religious expression. Other testators are some-

32. Margaret Blackburn: BIHR Reg. 3, fol. 415, also printed in *Test. Ebor.*, 2:46–51; William Bowes: BIHR Reg. 3, fol. 580; Robert Howme, Jr.: BIHR Reg. 3, fol. 365; John Norman, BIHR Reg. 9, fol. 327, also printed in *Test. Ebor.*, 5:213–215; William Helmeslay: BIHR Reg. 3, fol. 215; John Carré, *Test. Ebor.*, 4:26–30.

what more ambiguous in orientation. Their concern for anchorites apparently either triggered or was triggered by concern for
others enclosed less willingly. Yet overall, the religious motif pre-
vailed somewhat more so than in London. In addition, like London merchants, the York testators who favored anchorites and
desired their prayers were a more philanthropic group than those
of their peers who did not remember anchorites. That conclusion
was among the results of a second analysis of York merchant wills.

The wills of a group of York merchants who lived from the mid-
fourteenth to the mid-fifteenth centuries provided the data for
this second analysis. The merchants represent all those persons
who served as mayor in York between 1368 and 1440 whose wills
are extant and who died by 1445 (to coincide roughly with the
Chichele register). Twenty-seven wills were found for men who
had been mayors between these dates. Two of them, the wills of
Nicholas Blackburn, Jr. (1448) and Richard Wartere (1458), were
eliminated because their probate dates were beyond the time
frame. Blackburn's will contained no bequests to anchorites but
Wartere's did. This left the wills of twenty-five men who
represented the elite of a York merchant aristocracy. Not only
aldermen and mayors, at least seventeen of the twenty-five had
been representatives of York in Parliament (as also had been
Blackburn and Wartere). They were a group of men who knew
each other well, who married into each other's families, who were
each other's executors and friends. More than half of them (thirteen of twenty-five) left bequests for anchorites.[33]

Ten of these thirteen wills contained general bequests. These
ranged from Robert de Howm's 1396 gift of twenty shillings for
every anchorite in the city[34] to his son's grant of one shilling for
each anchorite in 1433. Three wills were specific—those of John
de Gysburne, Thomas Bracebrigg, and Richard Russell. Russell's
grants were unusually high, but the other specific grants were well

33. For mayors listed from 1396 see R. B. Dobson, ed., *York City Chamberlains'
Account Rolls 1396–1500*, SS 192 (1980), pp. 208–210. For earlier mayors see Francis Collins, ed., *Register of the Freemen of the City of York*, 2 vols., SS 96, 102
(1897–1900), vol. 1, passim.

34. Robert de Howm: BIHR Reg. 1, fol. 100.

within the parameters of the general wills. The distributions of specific gifts are displayed in tables 14 and 15. Table 14 describes the anchorite-favoring wills internally, showing how meaningful the anchoritic grant was to the testator.[35] Table 15 compares the York mayoral anchorite-favoring testators with the non-anchorite-favoring mayoral testators (columns B and C) as well as with London data.

Table 14 indicates that the bequests to anchorites in each will are proportionately significant when compared to grants to groups (such as lepers in houses or prisoners). The great variety in the patterns of these gifts (even within the context of a sample drawn so narrowly) shows how personal these wills were and how free men felt to dispose of their alms according to their own peculiar tastes. In general the friars were remembered well. Large grants for anchorites were usually accompanied by more generous grants for others as well.

Table 15 shows that York mayors who made gifts to anchorites were more generous than their colleagues who did not. The projections of the London analysis are both strikingly confirmed and reinforced. The two groups of York mayors are more equal in numbers, wealth, and status than any other comparisons I have been able to provide and it is legitimate to consider their testaments a pattern. In every category the testators remembering anchorites responded more frequently than did the group that ignored them: with regard to lepers and prisoners at rates three and four times higher. As compared with London testaments, the paralleling of column A with B and column C with D indicates that merchant London testators in general responded in higher percentages for the relief of prisoners and for public works than did their York counterparts but at lower levels for the relief of lepers. Friars were considerably less important to the Chichele testators than to York merchants as were the hospital poor.

The hospital poor may represent a special case for York. The city was dotted with maisondieux (fourteen were suppressed at the

35. Not earlier footnoted, Thomas Smyth: BIHR Reg. 3, fol. 27; John Northeby: BIHR Reg. 2, fol. 619; William Girlyngton: BIHR Reg. 2, fol. 83, also printed in *Test. Ebor.*, 2:93–95.

Dissolution).[36] Three of the twenty-five testators of the mayoral group had established their own poorhouses. Both Robert de Howm, an anchorite-favoring testator, and his brother Thomas, a member of the non-anchorite-favoring group, founded maison-dieux. Robert's, a house for poor of both sexes with twenty beds and situated on Monk's Bridge, was endowed in his will with enough funds to enable it to pay each of its inhabitants one pence per day for one hundred years. John de Craven, also in the non-anchorite-favoring group, left arrangements in his 1416 will for his paupers on Layerthorpe Bridge: thirteen persons were to receive weekly grants, twelve of them at three pence weekly and the thirteenth at four pence in return for morning and evening prayers. These houses, among the others, were remembered in local wills, sometimes identified by their location, sometimes by their founder's name. Houses with few occupants were at times granted smaller sums than those with more beds. Nicholas Usflete (1443) left twelve pence to each house with twelve beds or more and six pence to houses with under twelve beds; William Ormeshede (1435), 3s. 4d. to each house of over sixteen beds and two shillings to those with fewer. Local custom and pattern surely affected the high rates of gifts to hospital poor in York.[37]

While local differences did affect testamentary grants in specific ways, the York data offer a clear picture of merchant anchorite-favoring testators and one that fully corresponds to the predictors of the London study. The York mayors who made bequests to anchorites were benefactors to religious institutions and the poor alike, and at very high levels. Compared with their equals in York, they were men of much broader generosity. Compared with their London counterparts, they were men of similar mood.

Merchants from other locales and times also fit this mold. John Bonde, a fuller from Norwich, left bequests to four anchorites, to the poor, to friars, to two hospitals (including St. Giles, established by Bishop Suffield), for bridge work, and for a pilgrimage to be

---

36. George Benson, *Later Medieval York* (York, 1919), p. 122.

37. Thomas de Howom: BIHR Reg. 3, fol. 254; John de Craven: BIHR Reg. 3, fol. 606; Nicholas Usflete: BIHR Reg. 2, fol. 58; William Ormeshede: BIHR Reg. 3, fol. 503.

TABLE 14

BEQUESTS TO YORK ANCHORITES COMPARED TO BEQUESTS TO OTHER GROUPS IN YORK MAYORAL WILLS

	Anchorites	Maisondieux	Leprosaria	Prisons	Friaries
John de Gysburne (MP) 1385 (ca. 1390)[1]	3 @ 13s. 4d. 1 @ 6s. 8d.	3 @ 40s.	4 @ 10s. 2 @ 5s.	3 @ 20s.	4 @ 20s. 13 @ 40s.
Robert de Howm 1396	General @ 20s.	6 @ 40s.[2]	York: £5[3] County: £10[3]	3 @ 40s.	4: average @ £24 22 @ 66s. 8d.
Thomas Smyth 1399	General @ 2s.	1 @ 6s. 8d.	4 @ 3s. 4d.		1 @ 20s. 3 @ 13s. 4d.
William de Helmeslay 1404	General @ 1s.	General @ 1s.	4 @ 1s.	3 @ 1s.	4 @ 6s. 8d.
John Northeby (MP) 1430 (1432)	General @ 3s.	General @ 3s. 4d.	1s. *per leper* @ 4 houses		4 @ 20s.
Robert Howme, Jr. (MP) 1433	General @ 1s.		General @ 4d. *per leper*		1 @ 20s. 3 @ 13s. 4d.
Richard Russell (MP) 1435	2 @ 66s. 8d. 1 @ 40s.	General @ 10s.	General @ 5s. *per leper*		4 @ £10

William Ormeshede (MP) 1435 (1437)	General women @ 1s. 8d.	General: average @ 3s.[4]	4 @ 6s. 8d.	3 @ 2s. 1 @ 1s.	4 @ 20s.
Thomas Bracebrigg 1436 (1437)	3 @ 6s. 8d. 1 @ 3s. 4d.	9: average @ 2s.	General @ 4d. per leper	3: average @ 3s. 5d. plus[5]	1 @ 10s. 3 @ 6s. 8d. plus[6]
William Bowes (MP) 1437 (1439)	General @ 2s.	General @ 2s.	4 @ 2s.	3 @ 2s.	1 @ 26s. 8d. 3 @ 20s.
Nicholas Usflete (MP) 1443	General @ 1s. 8d.	1 @ 3s. 4d.; Others average @ 9d.[7]			4 @ 6s. 8d.
William Girlyngton (MP) 1444	General @ 10s.	General: 40s. for distribution	4 @ 5s.	1 @ 10s. 1 @ 13s. 4d.	4 @ 40s.
John Bolton (MP) 1445	General @ 3s. 4d.		4 @ 6s. 8d.		4 @ 20s.

1. Year of probate enclosed in parentheses when different from year of writing.
2. Does not include endowment for own earlier established maisondieu.
3. For general distribution.
4. Three shillings four pence for each with over sixteen beds; two shillings for each with under sixteen beds.
5. Plus one pence per prison weekly for fifteen years.
6. Plus six pence for each individual friar.
7. Twelve pence for each with over twelve beds; six pence for each with under twelve beds.

TABLE 15

COMPARISON OF YORK AND LONDON MERCHANT WILLS (1361–1535)

	A	B	C	D
	Late-medieval London anchorite-favoring (7)	York anchorite-favoring (13)	York non-anchorite-favoring (12)	Chichele non-anchorite-favoring (14)
All poor	100%	100%	83%	79%
Hospitals	71%	85%	58%	21%
Lepers	57%	100%	33%	21%
Prisoners	85%	54%	25%	36%
Public works	57%	38%	17%	43%
Friars	100%	100%	100%	29%
Convents	57%	54%	42%	50%

made to the Holy Land—all this in 1248. In 1271 Nicholas de Weston, a burgess of Oxford, left bequests to nine anchorites in the region of Oxford in addition to gifts for the poor, many religious houses, five orders of friars, hospital poor, lepers, and four bridges. In 1394 William Snelleston of Lincoln remembered the poor, religious houses, prisoners, guilds, and three anchorites in his city. In 1415 John Plumpton of Norwich left bequests to hospital poor, lepers, prisoners, friars, and the famed anchoress Julian of Norwich and her maid. That same year Katherine Curson, the widow of a burgess of Bishop's Lynn, left small legacies to the friars, lepers, almshouse poor, the anchorite at All Saints in South Lynn, and the anchorite at the Preachers in Bishop's Lynn. In 1429 Roger Thornton of Newcastle-upon-Tyne, three times representative to Parliament, nine times mayor, chose John Lacy, the Dominican anchorite, as one of his chantry priests in a will providing one hundred marks for the reparation of Tyne Bridge, twenty pounds for the maisondieu of his own earlier establishment, plus gifts to all other houses of poor, lepers, and friars within the town and to convents in the region. John Brompton of Beverly (Yorkshire) made bequests in 1444 for friars, many convents of nuns, almshouse poor, and the poor in every other category, lepers as well, in addition to the two anchorites in Beverly. Agnes Grosewell of Boston (Lincolnshire) in an unusual will of 1488—unusual because she made it during her husband's lifetime (with his license) and also because *she* is called "goldsmith"—bequeathed to friars, to an orphanage, to guilds, to the poor, to the mending of highways, and to the anchoress of Boston "to have me specially remembyrd among hyr prayers."[38]

Three merchant testaments—one each from York, Norwich, and London—illustrate the richness of these wills. The writers were wealthy individuals of deep social commitment. The will of Thomas Bracebrigg of York (1436) began in the traditional fashion of the orthodox, providing grants for priests, candles, and masses along with grants to four anchorites and a hermit in this first, most "religious" portion of the document. Beyond the gifts to lepers, friars, and others noted in table 14 he left one hundred shillings to the poor, blind, lame, weak, and sick on his burial day, with forty shillings more to be distributed on the octave; fifty shillings for ten chaldrons of sea-borne coals to be given to the poor and needy in York and its suburbs, with a further 6s. 8d. allotted for their delivery to the homes of the poor; twenty shillings for wood—fallen branches—to be distributed to the poor, especially those in his parish of St. Saviour; twenty shillings for

---

38. John Bonde: William Hudson and John C. Tingey, eds., *Selected Records of the City of Norwich*, 2 vols. (Norwich, 1910), 2:358–359; Nicholas de Weston: Herbert E. Salter, ed., *Cartulary of Oseney Abbey*, 6 vols., Oxford Historical Society 89–91, 97–98, 101 (1929–36), 2:562–565, and Anthony Wood, 'Survey of the Antiquities of the City of Oxford,' Composed in 1661–66, by Anthony Wood, ed. Andrew Clark, 2 vols., Oxford Historical Society 15, 17 (1889–90), 2:502–503; William Snelleston: Gibbons, *Early Lincoln Wills*, pp. 73–74; John Plumpton: *Chichele*, 3:412–413; Katherine Curson: *Chichele*, 3:404–406; Roger Thornton: *Wills and Inventories*, pp. 78–80, and E. Mackenzie, *A Descriptive and Historical Account of the Town and County of Newcastle upon Tyne*, 2 vols. (Newcastle-upon-Tyne, 1827), 1:151, 204–209, 298; John Brompton: *Test. Ebor.*, 2:96–105; Agnes Grosewell: Charles W. Foster, "Lincolnshire Wills Proved in the Prerogative Court of Canterbury," *Reports and Papers of the Architectural and Archaeological Societies* 41 (1932–33): 207–209.

forty pairs of men's shoes and ten shillings for twenty pairs for women; and lifetime pensions of one pence per week for five poor widows. Finally he ordered that on the onset of his final illness, when he took to his bed, his executors immediately were to order and distribute a thousand loaves of white bread, called farthing loaves.

The will of Robert Jannys (1530) of Norwich is separated from Bracebrigg's by almost a hundred years in time but not at all in tone. Also a mayor (he served both in 1517 and 1524), he left bequests for every friar in the city: twelve pence for priors and doctors, four pence for priests, two pence for novices. To the blind, lame, and sore—the bedridden poor—he gave four pence each, and the same to prisoners. Forty lined gowns were to be made and distributed to poor men and women on his burial day and again thirty days later; twenty poor maidens were granted twenty shillings each. Eighty poor men and women were to be granted a pension of one pence weekly for the next twenty years. Katherine Mann, the anchoress at the Blackfriars, was given a tenement for the term of her life, and "every ancre and ancres" within Norwich was to receive fourteen pence each three months for the next twenty years.[39]

Not least was the testament of Jane, Viscountess Lisle (1500). Counted a "merchant" will even though her third and last husband was an aristocrat, she associated herself in her will with her second husband, Robert Drope, a former mayor and alderman of London, asking to be buried next to him at St. Michael's Cornhill, the church connected to the drapers guild. She distributed one pence each to the poor in burial day alms, to the sum of twenty pounds. To each poor household in her ward of Cornhill, she bequeathed five shillings, to the sum of ten pounds, and also "likewise . . . amoung the poure householders and other more nede people dwelling and abidyin in the other XXIIII wards of London in every ward XXs. to be disposed by the most worshipfull woman dwelling in every of the same wards." She made bequests to Syon, to the Carthusians, to the Minoresses of London, to many other

---

39. Tanner, *The Church in Late Medieval Norwich*, pp. 248–252.

London nunneries, to the friars; to the "Anchor in London Wall," to pray, and to the "Anchoresse in London Wall," to pray. For the Observant Friars she provided bread, ale, and victuals. Three hundred shirts and smocks were to be made for poor folk and to be distributed—half to men, half to women. The marriages of poor maidens and poor widows were to be aided. Rochester Bridge and the highways of London were not forgotten. The Fellowship of the Drapers of London was to take charge of her obit. This was the will of a woman born in Hampshire who had made London her town. Surviving three husbands, she identified herself with her second husband, a draper, and wrote a will fully in keeping with the patterns exhibited by that group a hundred and more years earlier.[40]

Merchant anchorite-favoring testators were generous to many charitable entities as well as to the recluses who represented the essence of medieval spirituality. Responsibility to church and the less fortunate were defined social obligations for these men and women—obligations broadly conceived. In general these testators answered the needs of a wide and growing constituency: when new religious orders, new maisondieux, new guilds emerged as institutions, each entered all-embracing lists of suitable bequests. Each took its place alongside older, already approved benefactions without displacing them. The philanthropic net of these merchants was cast very wide. A pattern of accretion emerges here— if one charity was good, more were better. Many roads to heaven were surer than a few. Piety and charity merged with anxiety.

Yet we cannot read these wills without feeling that the desire to ease the soul into heaven was only a part of the motivation for the bestowal of gifts. The grants for masses, for church bequests, for candles to burn on altars, for religious of all kinds, are paralleled by grants for the poor that express more than that they too are conduits to heaven. The gifts to the poor indicate a concern for these people who were the underclass of the cities in which the testators thrived. We feel the poverty that was a part of medieval

40. She was married in turn to Master John Tregman, Robert Drope, and Edward Grey, Viscount Lisle (*CWCH*, 2:626).

urban life. I believe that the testator felt it too and was trying to alleviate it in some measure. Certainly grants for the poor, as well as grants for bridges and highways, would be "counted" on the day of final reckoning. Certainly such grants were routine and automatic. Certainly the language of these grants was composed of stock phrases, yet it does not detract from their poignancy and resonance. There is empathy in these wills. Robert de Howm would write:

> I bequeath for distribution to the poor, weak, lame, blind and needy continually lying in their beds in the city and suburbs of York and also to other men who through misfortune have lost their goods and have been brought to poverty. . . . I bequeath for distribution and division among poor fathers of families especially those from whom my servants have bought wool for my trade and also among other fathers of families who were once powerful and have come to great poverty. . . . I bequeath for poor debtors burdened with debt . . . for poor lepers . . . for buying thick woolen clothes for the poor . . . for buying shoes to be given to the poor. . . .[41]

These merchant testators who remembered anchorites were leaders of their communities, men and women of substance and social position. They were orthodox in their religion and in their concern for the poor. More than their peers who did not remember anchorites in their wills, they were likely to be generous to many persons and institutions. On the basis of their wills such persons were worthy of the leadership roles they played in their society.

YEOMAN AND ARTISAN SUPPORT

As the researcher moves down the social scale records grow fewer and those that remain are limited in scope. Eventually they fail altogether. Almost all data that tell of yeoman or artisan support for anchorites are testamentary.[42] A rare exception is the

41. BIHR Reg. 1, fol. 100.
42. Yeoman and artisan groups are defined negatively. They contain persons who lack identification as gentry or merchants.

256

charter of a man named Adam Sage who granted a rent of three shillings to be paid to his niece, Joan, each year. Joan was the anchoress at Kiddington, Oxfordshire, circa 1236, and the charter of her uncle is a tantalizing glimpse into a lost realm of probable family arrangements of this sort.[43]

Adam Sage owned land. The deed ratifying his grant was a proper legal document.[44] It was witnessed by five clerks and several laymen whose names suggest modest backgrounds: Philip Molendarius (miller), Adam Ianitor (doorkeeper), and Henry of Lectona, porter. The absence of other designations for Adam and the professions of his witnesses suggest that he be classified as a yeoman. That his niece was an anchoress is telling as to the social origins of some recluses; that an uncle was active in her support is indicative of the involvement of the extended family in the maintenance of a recluse.[45] Similar support has been noted for the gentry. Where the funds of the individual were not adequate for self-support, the family was likely to have been the first avenue of approach for long-term commitments. Three shillings was a considerable sum in the thirteenth century, especially for a person of modest means. While far below the royal rate of thirty shillings per annum, some aristocratic grants were in the three-shilling range and some even lower. So the grant of Adam Sage stands as a reasonable and significant gift.

Sage's deed stands almost alone in the evidence. The corrodial arrangements that supported Childlove at Faringdon, Berkshire, in the mid-thirteenth century also represent the efforts of persons in this class, and again a family member was providing for an anchoress. Lucas de Worth was Childlove's brother and it was he who purchased the corrody for her from Oseney abbey. Lucas was

43. Salter, *Oseney Cartulary*, 2:483.
44. On the gradual growth of the use of written records see M. T. Clanchy, *From Memory to Written Record: England, 1066–1307* (Cambridge, Mass.: Harvard University Press, 1979).
45. The aunt of the anchoress at All Saints, Fishergate (referred to frequently in the merchant portion of this chapter) left her niece a bequest. Both aunt and niece were probably of modest social status. The anchoress, Lady Isabel German, was in the cell at least from 1428 to 1448 and received grants not only from her aunt, Alice Haukesworth (BIHR Reg. 3, fol. 373), but also from others of moderate means.

a chaplain, and so technically his support of an anchoress belongs with that of the clergy, but (as with Geoffrey Scrope) surely family considerations played a major role in this transaction. While deeds of men like Sage and Worth surface only rarely, they probably were representative and not unique. But this is difficult to prove. What can be proved is that among those yeomen and artisans who wrote wills some remembered anchorites, just as the more affluent did. Moreover, a gift of a few pence from a poorer man can be interpreted as more meaningful than the gift from a richer man, both in absolute and comparative terms. In absolute terms, such grants represent only the tip of an iceberg: there are more poor than rich but the wills of the poorer are less likely to have survived. In comparative terms, the value of a few pence to the poorer man in contrast to the value of shilling gifts to the richer could indicate a deep and personal response to anchorites among these lesser folk.

Approximately one hundred wills or will fragments that bear gifts to anchorites from members of yeoman and artisan ranks have been identified for the period 1361–1543. Sixteen are from Faversham, Kent, seventeen from the St. Albans area, sixty more distributed for the most part in Lincoln diocese, Norwich, and Yorkshire. In general these wills are modest. Gifts are left to one anchorite in most cases, on occasion to two or to an anchorite and a hermit. The most typical grant for an anchorite is one shilling, always expressed as twelve pence. Some grant less, some more, a few make grand donations. In wills that dispose of sizable sums, anchorites reap proportionate shares. The will of William Brown of Stamford, Lincolnshire (1489), proved in the Prerogative Court of Canterbury, left twenty shillings to the anchoress in Stamford as one legacy in a testament that ordered the distribution of twenty pounds to the poor on Brown's burial day, again on the seventh day after his death, and again on the thirtieth. Brown's will further provided that a recluse in Stamford was to receive twenty shillings each year for the ten subsequent years "if any be closid there." Not only was this a grant of great generosity but it also implied that the testator's gift was directed at the vocation, not a specific individual. Any person enclosed in that cell would receive the grant. Another substantial bequest appeared in the

258

will of a Norwich woman who left five shillings to the anchoress at the Friars Preachers in 1481 along with a further grant of one shilling to the recluse's servant. A 1408 will from Durham diocese selected the local anchorite, John Lacy, the Dominican priest enclosed in the friary at Newcastle-upon-Tyne, to be the celebrant of mass for an entire year and for this provided him with eight marks—more a payment for services rendered than a bequest but still an indication of regard and identification with a perceived holiness. Another friar-recluse, an Augustinian at Northampton, received a bequest in 1510 in a will proved at Canterbury that said in part: "To the Freers Austens, to the prior xxs. & to the anker xs. & to every priest in the same place xijd. & to them that be no priests iiijd."[46]

At Faversham, Kent, there were two cells for recluses, one attached to the parish church and one a separate building in the churchyard. During the fifteenth and sixteenth centuries a series of female anchorites lived in the cell attached to the church. At least seventeen wills probated between 1465 and 1523 acknowledged the anchoress there. She received gifts from a mayor, a baker, the former vicar (now an anchorite himself and the builder and occupant of the reclusorium standing free in the churchyard), and others, both male and female. Her grants ranged from ten shillings to two pence. At times she had two attendants, at times one, for two wills contained bequests to her "women" as well as to her and two others only to one servant. Five testators specifically asked for her prayers. With one exception these wills were probated in the court of the archdeacon at Canterbury, marking them as the wills of persons of modest means, all of whose possessions were essentially located within the archdeaconry. One will had been proved in the Consistory Court and this will provided the major benefaction of ten shillings. With the exception of the former vicar, these testators were lay and of limited social status

46. William Brown: Foster, "Lincolnshire Wills Proved in the Prerogative Court of Canterbury," p. 206; Henry Harrod, "Extracts from Early Wills in the Norwich Registers," *Norfolk Archaeology* 4 (1855): 335; R. L. Storey, ed., *Register of Thomas Langley, Bishop of Durham, 1406–1437*, 6 vols., SS 164–182 (1948–67), 1:90–91; R. M. Serjeantson and H. Isham Longden, "The Parish Churches and Religious Houses of Northamptonshire: Their Dedications, Altars, Images, and Lights," *Journal of the British Archaeological Association* 70 (1913): 446.

and wealth, but they made wills and remembered the town anchoress.[47]

William Thornbury, the vicar-turned-anchorite, had his own resources and did not figure in any of these wills save as benefactor himself. A later male recluse at Faversham, however, did receive a will bequest. The first notice of this sixteenth-century anchorite comes from royal records. In 1533 the "ancker" of Faversham supplicated Thomas Cromwell. The next year both he and his sister, Ann Sawsten, submitted petitions to Cromwell. In 1541 (a late date for an anchorite bequest) one Raynold Lewknor left twenty shillings to the anchorite at Faversham, Sir William Crakynthorpe, a priest. Whether Ann Sawsten's brother and Sir William (who may be the same person) lived in the original reclusorium or in the newer one that Thornbury had built for himself is not evident. Since will data cease for the female anchoress in 1523, it is possible that a man had become resident in the church reclusory. Yet Thornbury's will provided that the funds sustaining him in his lifetime were to be used in part to continue maintenance on both the chapel and the parvise where he had lived—and so these should have remained viable properties, a cell endowed at least as far as its own physical plant was entailed.[48]

Three observations can be made here. The small community of Faversham sustained at least one recluse in the parish church in the late fifteenth and early sixteenth centuries. The occupants were recipients of modest grants from modest people, and occasionally the recluses received significantly larger sums. These grants continued for as long as there were recluses, and there were recluses there after Henry VIII's dissolution of religious houses.

Wills probated in the archdeaconry court of St. Albans give a similar picture of the support of members of a local community for its local anchorites. Anchoresses at St. Peter's and St. Michael's, parish churches of St. Albans, have been mentioned earlier as re-

47. Arthur Hussey, ed., *Testamenta Cantiana* (London: Mitchel Hughes and Clarke, 1907), pp. 128–129; "Anchorites in Faversham Churchyard," *Archaeologia Cantiana* 11 (1877): 24–39.
48. *LP*, 6:135; *LP*, 7:437–438; Hussey, *Test. Cant.*, p. 29.

cipients of grants from the Lancasters and others. Thomas Beaufort had left one of them twenty shillings in 1426. His nephew, Humphrey, duke of Gloucester, had provided twenty pence annually for each anchoress on the date of his anniversary. Elizabeth of York, Henry VII's queen, passing through town, gave the anchoress at St. Peter's 3s. 4d. in 1502, and Elizabeth's account books of the following year note a substantial gift of 26s. 8d. (two marks) to the St. Michael's recluse. A will of Richard Dicons, Esquire, written in 1520, left 3s. 4d. to each of the incumbents, and one may recall that an "ancres of Sent Talbonse" was on the account books of Sir Henry Willoughby in 1523.[49]

Between the years 1416 and 1451, twenty-two local testators of modest means also remembered these recluses who lived in cells that had been occupied at least as far back as the thirteenth century. Although there were at this time at least four occupied anchorholds in St. Albans, only the incumbents of St. Michael's and St. Peter's received testamentary gifts. The other two reclusoria were under the aegis of the monastery. One also was ancient and at this time housed Thomas Fyschebourne for a period. The other was an installation recently constructed for a female recluse. Neither of these cells was mentioned in any wills. The monastery presumably took care of its own. In the community of St. Albans there was clear understanding of which recluses to remember.

The 22 St. Albans wills with bequests for anchorites have been isolated from a series of 614.[50] Residents of St. Albans proper wrote 264 of these 614 and these include 20 with anchorite bequests. Seven wills of clergy account for 4 of these grants to anchorites, leaving 257 wills of lay members of the community supplying 16 anchorite bequests. From the outlying area also served by the archdeaconry court are 350 registered wills, only 2 containing bequests for the St. Albans recluses (1 lay will and 1 clerical). On this basis the support of these anchoresses by yeomen and artisans is seen to be a local function where *local* is narrowly defined.

49. Richard Dicons: McGregor, *Bedfordshire Wills*, p. 111.
50. Printed as "Abstracts of Wills, Archdeaconry of St. Albans: Register 'Stoneham,'" in *Herts Genealogist and Antiquary* 1–3 (1895–99).

To consider the St. Albans laity alone, of these 257 wills 103 left no charitable gifts at all. These testaments granted all possessions to a member of the family. Of the 154 other lay wills 98 restricted their "charitable" gifts to a cleric or local parish church—to its lights, fabrics, chapels, vicars, and chaplains—gifts so commonplace that they have not been analyzed in these chapters exploring gift-giving patterns. Only 56 wills dispensed other gifts, usually in addition to parish church bequests but on occasion in lieu of them and including, of course, anchorite bequests. The convent of St. Albans received gifts in 21 wills.[51] The nunneries of Sopwell and St. Mary de Pré, St. Albans dependencies, received 14 and 12, respectively, 8 of which were in the same wills. There was a tendency to think of the nunneries together and also in conjunction with the monastery, a pattern somewhat analogous (if less exaggerated) to the naming of all groups of friars in those communities that sustained several groups. Friars themselves were named in 15 wills, some testators naming one and some two units. As there were no friaries in St. Albans itself, it was the Minors of Ware who received 9 gifts and the Preachers of Dunstable and the Carmelites of Hitchin who each received 4. These three establishments ringed the area and served its needs. Minors at Aylesbury and Newgate, London, and Trinitarians at Hounslow (Middlesex) were each mentioned once as well. Bequests for mending the roadways were made in 10 wills. The poor were mentioned only twice for other than burial-related gifts.[52]

The only other kind of religious or charitable gift recorded in these data is a gift to an anchorite. The anchoress of St. Michael's received thirteen gifts, the anchoress of St. Peter's ten, seven wills naming them both. As with the nuns of Sopwell and Pré, the two anchoresses often were remembered in tandem, and some of the individual gifts may indicate a temporary vacancy in the other cell. In 1433 and in 1434 two men who were to be buried at

51. In determining these figures I have counted any bequest related to the convent as a gift, whether a grant to the house at large, or to a specific chapel or light there, or to any individual monk in whatever capacity.

52. The wills are printed in abstract form in the journal and burial details are lacking (if in fact they ever were written out). The place of burial, however, is noted.

St. Peter's left bequests only to the anchoress at St. Michael's, which seems surprising unless there was no one then in residence at the burial church. In general, however, the evidence of the wills indicates that the anchoress of St. Michael's was better known. Several testators referred to her by name; one remembered her "companions"; another mentioned two women by name who probably were those companions. One will named her male servant who bore the same last name as one of these companions. In addition, she alone received gifts from the two testators who lived outside the immediate vicinity of St. Albans.

The testators who made bequests to anchorites were predominately male, as were most testators in the register itself. As local villagers, at least nine of them were buried at St. Peter's and at least three others at St. Michael's. Thus, their identification with these recluses was both personal and immediate. Their wills were no more "charitable" than were the wills of the others who fall into the category defined by the fifty-six wills: wills dispensing religious-charitable gifts beyond the range of their own parish commitments. In absolute terms, for three of the St. Albans testators the anchorite gift is the *sole* religious-charitable bequest, as it is also in the two wills from outside the area. Five of the anchorite-favoring wills (out of sixteen) also contained bequests to Sopwell and Pré, four to St. Albans, and four to friars. Since there is one anchorite will for about every three and a half wills in this category (sixteen of fifty-six), this is about what we would expect on a purely statistical basis. Rather than a symptom of an unusually generous frame of reference, the anchorite gift for these testators *is* their charitable gift of choice. It takes the place of another one—quite different from the merchant group where such a gift emerged as part of a far-reaching charitable mentality. In this context we can note that there is no overlap between those wills containing bequests for anchorites and the ten that made grants for road repair.

The anchoresses of St. Albans were perceived as religious, not as anonymous poor. That four of the seven clergy wills provided for them indicates their status; it also indicates that the standards of the community must have encouraged such grants. A similar group of wills drawn from Lincoln diocese offers similar results: each will names one or two anchorites, almost always local, and the anchorite grant is often the sole charitable grant within the will. If not, it is joined by perhaps one other to a local convent, friary, or poorhouse. The interest in the anchorites in all these wills is direct and proprietary. Those who left money to the anchorites seem to have known them, and they could feel confident of having secured the anchorites' prayers.

Yeomen and artisans had fewer pennies to distribute in this way than members of higher classes. Yet their wills are not substantially different from those of the gentry. For those who looked beyond their immediate heirs, their families, some would remember recluses: in the community of St. Albans two out of seven would do so. It was not an inconsiderable proportion.

8

Clerical Support

The responsibilities of the hierarchy to anchorites have been treated in an earlier chapter. These were mandated responsibilities, involving no element of personal choice. Whether an individual bishop or canon, priest or abbot was particularly enthusiastic about solitary vocations, his procedural role was prescribed. Process carried him through appropriate steps.

Clergymen, however, shared with other members of medieval society the possibility of expressing positive sentiments for anchorites by offering them financial support. That some did so is another indication that an emotional attachment to anchorites was present at every level and in every group in medieval society. Chapter 3 discussed episcopal generosity as one aspect of the role of bishops. Here I will explore the role of other clerical institutions and individuals in the maintenance of recluses and consider the function of the clergy in influencing lay society.

Twelfth-century Pipe Rolls indicate that abbots as well as bishops assumed financial responsibility for some anchorites, even anchorites who were not originally of their own monastic house and who had no claim on their support through prior rights of communal sharing.[1] The abbot of Peterborough, for example,

---

1. The kinds of support granted in the arrangements of houses such as Westminster, Bury St. Edmunds, and the Dominican friaries are considered in chapter 3. Carmelites also had reclusoria for their own members, both nuns and friars, though not necessarily within their own houses. As professed religious in these orders, anchorites probably were supported, as Lyndwood allowed, by their brethren.

supported two female recluses at 8s. 8d. per year, one of them receiving an additional 5s. 6d. as a dress allowance; the abbot of Fécamp, in Normandy, paid out one pence per week (4s. 4d.) to the *inclusa* of Playden, Sussex, from the receipts of his English lands. In the thirteenth century Peter, prior of Holy Trinity, Aldgate, paid out 3s. 4d. each year to the anchorites of London. In 1235 the anchoress of St. Michael's, St. Albans, was granted a St. Albans corrody. In 1272 the abbot of St. Osyth's made an agreement with Cecily, the recluse of St. James, Colchester, promising to pay her five quarters of wheat annually. Two female recluses received beer and bread from Worcester priory in the thirteenth century and probably beyond. In the sixteenth century one anchoress lived there and the prior was at times concerned with her needs. Most extraordinary was the early fourteenth-century promise of the abbey of Bury St. Edmunds to distribute money, candles, and bread to forty-two anchorholds in Suffolk and its environs each year at Michaelmas. In the late fifteenth century the prioress of Pré gave alms to the anchoress at St. Peter's, St. Albans.[2]

Some clerical grants have a personal quality. That of Lucas de Worth for his sister Childlove has been mentioned in the previous chapter. In the thirteenth century the rector of St. Ebbe's, Oxford, endowed Basilia (enclosed in a cell within his own church) with the proceeds of a rent that was his own property. Henry Lexington, bishop of Lincoln, left a grant for Lina, the anchoress of St. John the Poor, in his will circa 1260. She was to receive four shillings yearly on the day of his anniversary for as long as she lived. The provision of so substantial a sum makes it likely that

2. *PR 34 Henry II* (1188), p. 6; *PR 23 Henry II* (1177), p. 105; Gerald A. J. Hodgett, ed., *Cartulary of Holy Trinity, Aldgate*, London Record Society 7 (1971), p. 122; Henry T. Riley, ed., *Chronica monasterii S. Albani: Gesta abbatum monasterii sancti Albani, a Thoma Walsingham, regnante Ricardo secundo, ejusdem ecclesiae precentore, compilata*, 3 vols., RS 28, part 4 (1867–69), 1:305; *VCH Essex*, 2:158; William H. Hale, ed., *Registrum sive liber irrotularius et consuetudinarius prioratus beatae Marie Wigorniensis*, Camden Society, o.s. 91 (1865), pp. cii, 120b, 124b; William More, *Journal of Prior William More*, ed. Ethel S. Fegan, Worcestershire Historical Society, (1914), p. 136; Antonia Gransden, "The Reply of a Fourteenth-century Abbot of Bury St. Edmunds to a Man's Petition to Be a Recluse," *English Historical Review* 75 (1960): 464; Dugdale, *Monasticon*, 3:360.

Lina had been in the gift of the bishop during his lifetime and had come to depend on his generosity.[3]

Other clerical anniversary arrangements were more modest, placing the gift in the category of a purchase of prayers by a well-spent penny. Sefrid II, bishop of Chichester 1180–1204, left two pence to each of four recluses; William de Kaynesham, canon of Chichester, one pence to each of two male recluses in 1237; Geoffrey de Glovernia, dean of Chichester, one pence to the recluse of St. Cyriac in 1247. In the late fifteenth century William Thornbury, the former vicar turned anchorite, arranged for his own anniversary payments. His schedule allowed four pence yearly for the anchoress at Faversham and two pence for her maid. Thornbury's grants were perpetual annuities and not tied to the life of any individual. The Faversham anchoress was included among the permanent officials of the church, and it was expected that there would be a recluse in residence.[4]

Testamentary evidence is a major source of information for clergy as for other social groups. Clergy, save for regulars and mendicants, could own property and write wills. I have accumulated seventy-eight clerical wills and will fragments with bequests for anchorites.[5] Eleven are from the thirteenth century and the remainder from the period 1360–1530. Included are the wills of one archbishop, nine bishops, one cardinal-priest, twenty-three middle-rank clergy (such as canons, diocesan officials, hospital masters), and forty-four lower rank clergy (those identified solely as priest, chaplain, or rector). Of the group written after 1360 the

3. Herbert E. Salter, ed., *Cartulary of the Hospital of St. John the Baptist,* 3 vols., Oxford Historical Society 66, 68–69 (1914–17), 2:244; Charles W. Foster and Kathleen Major, eds., *The Registrum antiquissimum of the Cathedral Church of Lincoln,* 11 vols., Lincoln Record Society (1931–68), 2:117–118.

4. Henry Mayr-Harting, ed., *Acta of the Bishops of Chichester, 1075–1207,* CYS 56 (1964), pp. 146–147; W. D. Peckham, ed., *Chartulary of the High Church of Chichester,* Sussex Record Society 46 (1946), pp. 142, 154; "Anchorites in Faversham Churchyard," *Archaeologia Cantiana* 11 (1877): 29–30.

5. Mainly from Devonshire, Kent, Yorkshire, Norfolk, Hertfordshire, and London and drawn from both published and unpublished sources. Tanner's analysis of Norwich wills indicates sixty clerical testaments with anchorite or hermit bequests between 1370 and 1532 (21 percent of all clerical wills). Of these sixty about fifteen are included in my sample.

wills of fifty-three individuals are complete and indicate that almost all made some provision for the poor save five from the St. Albans area. Thirty-one provided for convents (58 percent), thirteen specified lepers (25 percent), nine public works (17 percent), bridges most often. Thirty of the fifty-three testators left something to one or more groups of friars (57 percent). Of the twenty-three who did not, nine were canons or officials of cathedral churches (for whom the avoidance of giving to the friars may suggest an undercurrent of clerical competition) and eight lived in communities where there were no local groups of friars, five of these eight from St. Albans. Eleven of the fifty-three made bequests for prisoners (21 percent) and all eleven of these individuals lived in communities where there was a prison. Clerical giving was not an abstract phenomenon but was governed by personal tastes, prejudices, proximities, and local custom.

The interactions between one local anchoress and the clerical community that nourished her come to life in data from the cathedral city of Exeter. In the fifteenth century Alice Bernard lived in the anchorhold attached to the parish church of St. Leonard for more than forty years. Bequests for her have been found in ten wills, nine of them clerical. Studying these wills and other related documents we can sense the dynamics that lay behind the bequests and develop some feel for the *communitas* of the group whose center lay with the canons of the cathedral. The story begins on 18 May 1397 when the bishop of Exeter, Edmund Stafford, issued a commission to John Dodyngton, canon of Exeter, directing him to enclose Alice Bernard "in quodam domo in cimiterio ecclesie parochialis Sancti Leonardi extra portam australem" (in a certain house in the churchyard of the parish church of St. Leonard outside the south door). Three years later, on 26 March 1400, Dodyngton wrote his will, including in its terms a bequest of forty shillings for the anchoress of St. Leonard's along with a request for her prayers. Dodyngton's death occurred soon; the will was proved within a month. On 8 April of the same year, only two weeks after the writing of Dodyngton's will, Bishop Stafford gave Alice Bernard a license to choose a confessor with plenary powers.[6] We can conjecture that Dodyngton, after enclosing Alice, became her confessor. His death created a vacancy and Stafford allowed the anchoress to choose a successor herself. That she was a person of some consequence is clear from the number and size of the bequests she received over the next thirty-six years. During that period six canons of Exeter, one of Wells (who earlier had been beneficed in Exeter and licensed to preach publicly in both the cathedral and city of Exeter), two rectors, and a knight of the region left her testamentary grants.[7] Table 16 charts the data.

In 1436, the date of the last will mentioning Alice, she had been in her cell for almost forty years. How much longer she lived is uncertain, but the cell was empty eleven years later when Bishop Lacy commissioned the precentor of Exeter cathedral to examine Christine Holby, an Augustinian canoness of Kildare, who desired to be enclosed at St. Leonard's.[8] Since the precentor was instructed to enquire into the source and adequacy of the nun's endowment before enclosing her, the cell was obviously not endowed, which may account for the size as well as the consistency of Alice's gifts. Alice represents an anchorite for whom a fairly localized group of clergy felt responsibility over an extended period of time. That responsibility was freely undertaken and implied respect as well as response to perceived need. The will of Thomas Barton underlines that implicit respect.

Barton, who was rector of Ilfracombe as well as a canon of Exeter, wrote a lengthy, thoughtful, and discriminating will. His extensive funeral arrangements included directions for the meal to be served on his burial day: ". . . 200 persons are to be fed . . . in a suitable manner, on baked meats and roast with spiced drink not more than enough for poor men of that sort; lest they should

6. F. C. Hingeston-Randolph, ed., *Register of Edmund Stafford, Bishop of Exeter, A.D. 1395–1419* (Exeter, 1856), pp. 99, 179–189, 20.

7. For the wills of Dodyngton, Tyttesbury, Bonevylle, and Barton: Hingeston-Randolph, *Reg. E. Stafford*, pp. 379–380, 394–395, 390–393, 411–415; for the wills of Dunham, Bachiler, Fylham, and Orum: Lacy, *Exeter Register*, 4:3–4, 7–8, 32–33, 23–25; for Brita and Lerchedeken: *Chichele*, 2:501–503, 476–482.

8. See my chapter 3 and its note 49.

TABLE 16
TESTAMENTARY GIFTS: EXETER RECLUSE

Benefactor	Amount	Other Recluse Gifts
John Dodyngton (1400), canon of Exeter	40s.	Prayers for Stephen
Richard Tyttesbury (1406), canon of Exeter	40d.	Anchorites at Marham-church and Bodmin @ 40d.
Sir William Bonevylle (1407), knight	50s.	Hermit of St. Teath @ 20s.
Thomas Barton (1415), canon of Exeter	20s. and a robe	
Thomas Dunham (1425), rector of Lower Torrington	20s. and a book of English sermons	
Roger Bachiler (1427), rector of Churchstow	40d.	Anchorite at Wille @ 6s. 8d.
Reginald Brita (1430), canon of Wells	26s. 8d.	
Martin Lerchedeken (1430), canon of Exeter	3 canonical loaves per week for one year	
William Fylham (1435), canon of Exeter	3 canonical loaves per week for one year	
John Orum (1436), canon of Exeter	2 canonical loaves per week for one year	

gorge themselves." He specified that on his burial day, if not the day before, "there is to be a general distribution of alms to beggars and indigent people—1d. to each; but to the decrepit, the blind, and the helpless, unable to make a living, in Exeter, Credition, and Ilfracombe, 4d. each." He left twenty shillings to the priory of Cornworthy on account of its "extreme poverty"; twenty pounds for construction work at Credition church—but only if the parishioners or other canons contributed matching funds; he would support the construction of two new bridges if the parishioners were willing to contribute and to complete the work within one year. This was a man who demanded value for his money and one who took a rather wary view of some of his fellow men. But Alice's gift (which was greater than that given to the priory of Cornworthy) was recorded without qualification. In such a will that was high praise indeed.

The wills of the nine clergymen in this Exeter series form a coherent whole. All made bequests to the poor (Barton, Lerchedeken, and Brita emphasizing the lame, decrepit, paralytic, and bedridden); seven of the nine made bequests to friars, and another seven remembered poor scholars—in this case children studying at the local grammar school connected to the Hospital of St. John the Baptist, Exeter, and other local schools as well as poor clerks of Devonshire studying at Exeter and at more exotic places like Oriel Hall and Exeter College, Oxford. Five of the testators left sums of money for bridge work, four for prisoners, and three for lepers.

Such data are not representative of Exeter clergymen as a group. The registers of Edmund Stafford and Edmund Lacy record a series of clerical wills written between the years 1399 and 1455.[9] They contain seventy-two clerical wills of which eight provided bequests for anchorites. Thus, one testament in nine made a gift for a recluse as well as other charitable gifts. By comparison, of the remaining (non-anchorite-favoring) sixty-four clerical wills in these registers, only thirty-two remembered the poor (50 percent);

---

9. Hingeston-Randolph, *Reg. E. Stafford*, pp. 379–423; Lacy, *Exeter Register*, 4:1–63.

twenty, friars (31 percent); eight, lepers (12.5 percent); five, prisoners (8 percent); six, public works (9 percent); eight, poor scholars (12.5 percent). On the basis of these calculations Exeter clergy were not particularly concerned about those less fortunate than themselves. On that basis the anchorite-favoring wills became even more interesting because they indicate more than an accidental concurrence among the will makers.

The wills of the Exeter clergymen Lerchedeken, Fylham, and Orum deserve special mention in this context. These three men were all highly educated: Lerchedeken was an M.A. and licentiate of canon law who had been educated at Oriel College, Oxford; Fylham, was *sacre pagine professor*; John Orum, who was chancellor as well as canon of Exeter cathedral, was designated *sacre theologie professor*. Their wills alone contain bequests in kind.[10] Lerchedeken bequeathed three canonical breads per week not only to the anchoress but also to the inmates of both the king's and the bishop's prisons at Exeter, to the lepers at St. Mary Magdalen's, to the poor priests and scholars of St. John's, and to the Preachers and the Minors of Exeter. The anchoress and the lepers received bread alone; the others received a small money grant on the burial day, followed a month later by the onset of the bread dole. Fylham's will was similar. All the same groups save the bishop's prisoners were to receive identical grants of bread, and the money bequests varied only slightly. Orum left no money at all. Two loaves per week were to be supplied to the anchoress and three loaves for the friars, the king's prisoners, and the scholars of St. John's.[11]

10. Stafford's register includes the will of William Poundestoke (1411), a canon of Exeter (Hingeston-Randolph, *Reg. E. Stafford*, p. 404), which also contained bequests of four canonical loaves weekly for the friars of Exeter, both the Minors and the Preachers, in the manner described by Lerchedeken and the others, but there are no other similar wills in either Stafford's or Lacy's register.

11. In the sixteenth century another Alice, Alice Buttes, was living as an anchoress within the Hospital of St. John's. She is discovered when she appears on the pension lists after the Dissolution. It is possible that there was an anchorite at St. John's throughout this period as well, but if the site had been adequately subsidized the recluse would not have received testamentary grants and so would have slipped through the net of this enquiry (*LP*, 18:1:258).

These wills may represent an attempt to restructure patterns in almsgiving. One wonders if they reflect only the personal persuasion of these men of similar scholastic background. Certainly the men were friends as well as fellow canons of Exeter, and Fylham was one of Lerchedeken's executors. But friendship alone was not enough to prompt such a will. Roger Bolter, the precentor of Exeter cathedral, was also a friend of Fylham's. He and Fylham were each other's executors but Bolter's will contained no such gifts in kind.[12] In a will written in 1442 Michael Lerchedeken, nephew to Martin and one of his executors, a canon of Exeter cathedral as well as its treasurer, made only money bequests. He distributed funds to every group that had received gifts from his uncle save the anchorite (perhaps a bit of negative evidence for her death by then) but in all ways it was a standard will.[13] The canons of Exeter did not adopt a new pattern of giving. The wills of the nine clergymen do, however, describe a mosaic of intellectual and social interrelationships that tied the gift-givers together and without question the testators formed a small community of persons with compatible practices and ideas.

One of the executors of Sir William Bonevylle, the lone lay testator of table 16, was another canon of Exeter, William Ekerdon. Ekerdon himself left a bequest to a different anchorite—the monk recluse of Sherborne abbey—and it is time to take up that story, retracing some of our steps in the process. When John Dodyngton wrote his will in the year 1400, he not only bequeathed forty shillings to Alice Bernard, anchoress and his "spiritual daughter," but also a cup to one Matthew Stoke, the cup identified as having been the property of Stephen, a recluse. Dodyngton's will further directed that his obit be said for twenty years and that the two chaplains designated to say mass for him also were to pray for the souls of Archbishop Courtenay and the recluse Stephen. Mat-

---

12. Lacy, *Exeter Register*, 4:27–30.

13. Ibid., pp. 37–41. This will of another member of the family, Elizabeth Lercedekne, occurs in Stafford's register (Hingeston-Randolph, *Reg. E. Stafford*, p. 388) for the year 1406. She was a widow, vowed to celibacy, and left bequests to friars at Exeter and Plymouth, lepers at Plympton, Exeter, and Totnes, and to the Hospital of St. John.

thew Stoke, Courtenay, and the recluse Stephen are all threads in this narrative. Let us look at Stoke first.

Dodyngton granted the property of a recluse to Stoke. This would be a great honor, implying high regard for the man. Seven years later, in 1406, another well-placed member of the Exeter-based clerical community, John de Lydeford, archdeacon of Totnes, also made a bequest to Stoke in a context implying respect. In a will of critical tone, not unlike that of Barton, Lydeford left "to Matthew Stoke the same sum [40s], and my new long crimson coat, furred with pelury [fur used as lining or trimming], and a large hood of the same suit, well furred."[14] Lydeford's will was replete with specific, if conventional, admonitions: the canons and priests at his obit were to perform their services strictly; two priests who were to say mass for a year were to be of good conversation and reputation; the names of the poor to whom his executors would give money were to be ascertained diligently; and "poor penniless people, bedridden, and confined to their huts and cottages, unless they are really able to work, shall be remembered." Most pointed of all were his remarks about burial day feasting. He absolutely prohibited all banqueting on the occasion on the part of the canons and other ministers "all customs to the contary, when Canons of Exeter depart this life, notwithstanding." Yet this man with such severe attitudes left handsome gifts for Matthew Stoke, and Stoke's was the first personal bequest in the will.

Stoke's name appears in two other wills in Stafford's register. The will of John Govys (1416), rector of Holy Trinity, Exeter, and a vicar in the Cathedral church, contained a gift for him as did that of Thomas Clifford (1418), another canon of Exeter, who granted him a silver cup.[15] Clifford's will, moreover, appointed Stoke executor with wide-ranging discretionary powers. Matthew Stoke was none other than the rector of St. Leonard's, Exeter, the church of Alice Bernard's reclusion. He is known to have been in residence there in 1410; it would not be unlikely that he already was at St. Leonard's in 1400 when Dodyngton first granted him

14. Hingeston-Randolph, *Reg. E. Stafford*, pp. 389–390.
15. Ibid., pp. 415, 422.

Stephen's cup. What more fitting than for the overseer of one recluse to possess the cup of another? The date 24 August 1419 is the *terminus ad quem* to Stoke's tenure there, for in that year another man was presented to the benefice by the local patron.[16] We know that Stoke executed Clifford's will in February of that year and that is the final reference to him in these will series. He may have resigned; perhaps he died. Clearly, however, between the years 1400 and 1418 he was a highly regarded member of the clerical community at Exeter. Whether the anchorite of St. Leonard's benefited from his stature or he from hers is hard to know, but certainly we may assume that when Stoke was delivered the residue of Clifford's estate to distribute for pious causes, Alice was one of them.

Now for Stephen, the recluse, the grant of whose cup first brought Matthew Stoke to our attention. Who was Stephen and how did Dodyngton come into possession of his cup? Moreover, why would Dodyngton especially be concerned with the soul of Archbishop Courtenay as well as with Stephen's? John Dodyngton was the rector of Crewkerne, Somerset, as well as a canon of Exeter. There is record of Crewkerne as the home of solitaries as far back as the early twelfth century when a woman named Odolina, the *inclusa* of "Cruke," figured in the *Life* of Wulfric of Haselbury. Between 1176 and 1180 Henry II supported another female recluse there.[17] Then in 1396 William Courtenay bequeathed five marks (66s. 8d.) to the male recluse of Crewkerne, this in addition to another forty shillings that every recluse in the province received. Thus Dodyngton, as rector of Crewkerne, was at least nominally in charge of a recluse of special interest to Courtenay. That alone might have been sufficient to establish a relationship between Dodyngton and Courtenay (if there had not been one previously) and to make more comprehensible Dodyngton's concern for Courtenay's soul, for it is unusual to find the archbishop figuring in this way in such a will, although the diocesan bishop does on occasion. What is possible is that Stephen was the Crew-

16. Ibid., pp. 99, 319.
17. John, abbot of Ford, *Wulfric of Haselbury*, ed. Maurice Bell, Somerset Record Society 47 (1933), p. 90; *PR 22 Henry II* (1176), p. 10.

kerne recluse of Courtenay's will; that he died sometime between 1396 and 1400, that is, sometime between Courtenay's and Dodyngton's deaths; and that Dodyngton had come into the possession of Stephen's cup, which Dodyngton then bequeathed to Matthew Stoke on his own death. We know that the Crewkerne cell was available in 1402 when Sir Robert Cherde, a Cistercian monk of Ford abbey, was appointed to it[18] and it may have stood empty for a few years or even been occupied briefly by another recluse.

The Crewkerne connections do not yet lead us out of the maze. If another of Courtenay's gifts is followed, however, it takes us back to Exeter. Courtenay's will, we may remember, did not only provide for the Crewkerne recluse. Also specifically named as a legatee was the male recluse of Sherborne abbey. He was to receive forty shillings in addition to the common bequest. The singling out of these two men by Courtenay fully establishes their significance for him. The Sherborne recluse also was remembered by three other testators, one of whom was the aforementioned William Ekerdon, canon of Exeter and the executor of the will of Sir William Bonevylle (see table 17).

In 1396 the recluse of Sherborne was a man named Edmund Arthur. In that year he not only received Courtenay's will bequests but also the monies accruing from a sale of indulgences offered for his aid by the bishop of Salisbury. Indulgences for anchorites were rare and marked their recipients in a special way. During the previous year Arthur had received a bequest from Lady Alice West of Hampshire, who had asked for his prayers.[19] By 1405 there was a new recluse at Sherborne. In that year, in a will made while her husband was still living, Lady Elizabeth Stafford bequeathed twenty shillings to the monk enclosed at Sherborne, a man named William Whityng, as well as one hundred shillings plus other gifts to the canon of Exeter, William Ekerdon. She further left five marks and a cup to Edmund Elyot of Cheseburgh, a clerk.

18. See my chapter 3 and its note 42.

19. Christopher Wordsworth, "Wiltshire Pardons or Indulgences," *Wiltshire Archaeological and Natural History Magazine* 38 (1913/14): 31; Frederick J. Furnivall, ed., *Fifty Earliest English Wills*, EETS, o.s. 78 (1882), pp. 4–10.

TABLE 17

SHERBORNE RECLUSES

Benefactor	Amount	Other recluse gifts
1395: Lady Alice West of Hampshire	40s.	Br. Thomas, recluse at St. James in the Holte: 40s.
1396: William Courtenay, archbishop of Canterbury	40s.	Crewkerne recluse: 5m.; all recluses in province: 40s.
1405: Lady Elizabeth Stafford	20s.	
1413: William Ekerdon, canon of Exeter	6s. 8d.	

Both Ekerdon and Elyot were among Lady Stafford's executors. Eight years later Ekerdon's own will provided a half mark for William Whityng, recluse, as well as forty shillings for Elyot. Lady Stafford has earlier been described as a member of a noble family whose charitable will probably was written under the influence of a cleric.[20]

Ekerdon, who first came to notice as executor of Bonevylle's will, is one of the links between the two groups of testators. Ekerdon was rector of Long Bredy as well as a canon of Exeter. His parish was situated about forty-five miles east of Exeter and about twenty miles south of Sherborne in the county of Dorset in Salisbury diocese. Bonevylle's interests also were dispersed in this southern area. His will indicates his involvement with institutions and individuals both in and near places where he was a landowner as well as in the city of Exeter. Friars at Ilchester, Dorchester,

20. Frederick W. Weaver, ed., *Somerset Medieval Wills*, 3 vols., Somerset Record Society 16, 19, 21 (1901–05), 2:304–306; Hingeston-Randolph, *Reg. E. Stafford*, pp. 402–403; Lady Staffford's will contained bequests for the poor, for many groups of friars in this region, for many conventual houses, and for two young boys to attend school.

Salisbury, and elsewhere as well as those in Exeter received bequests from him. Bridges and highways in Somerset and Devon
benefited from his will. A new almshouse was to be established in
Exeter to care for twelve poor men and women. Many convents
in the broad region were enriched as well as St. John's Hospital in
Exeter. The hermit of St. Teath, Cornwall, was remembered
along with the anchoress of St. Leonard's.

While the knight's interests were appropriately regional, when
he addressed himself to the community of Exeter he responded in
the conventional ways of many Exeter clerical wills. His testament surely was influenced by clergy. In addition to William Ekerdon, three other clerks were executors. Certainly the clergy had
ample opportunity to propose their values to the laity and in some
cases must have been successful. The commitment to anchorites
that the clerical wills indicate could have reverberated beyond
what is known. It is clear that many if not most of the testators in
the two groups knew one another and their recluses and shared a
sense of community. A complicated set of personal relationships
has carried this inquiry in several directions but at least two of
them converged in William Ekerdon's testamentary request that
he be buried in Exeter cathedral next to John Dodyngton.

Clerical support for anchorites is clearly more similar than dis-
similar to support from other social groups. The element of personal decision is strong but certain patterns could be imposed or
suggested by outside forces, both clerical and nonclerical. Like the
royal family, bishops had to sustain "inherited" recluses. Geoffrey
le Scrope, canon of Lincoln and York, remembered "family" recluses. A canon of Exeter might have felt some pressure to support the recluse of St. Leonard's, a rector in St. Albans to reward
the recluses of St. Peter's and St. Michael's. If there were several
recluses in the community, good form may have decreed that all
be granted a stipend. But the personal element in the giving is
more pronounced. Especially when it came time to write a will,
no man was forced to remember a recluse. That some clergy chose
to do so remained a mark of favor. That clergy responded in the
same terms as lay social groups is another indicator of the ordi-
nariness of the anchorite bequest and by extension an indicator of

the role of the anchorite in medieval English society. From the beginning of this study I have attempted to demystify the anchorite, to proclaim his or her dual identity. Like any other medieval individual, the recluse was both a commonplace daily presence and a likely heavenly dweller. The response of the clergy to the anchorite underscores this dual identity: while, as clergy, they might be somewhat disposed to answer the needs of recluses, as individuals this response was not excessive but within the comfortable framework of the known and the typical.

Some clerics were able to influence their parishioners. The connection of Adam Wigan of St. Saviour's, York, to various anchorite testators has been explored in the previous chapter. Lady Stafford and Sir William Bonevylle were surely only two more among many who shared with their clerical advisors their decision to support local anchorites. Clerical persuasion could be brought to bear at many moments in a lifetime and clerical acceptance of an anchorite might promote more than an occasional will bequest. But the data do not take us to firm knowledge of that. As much to the point is that the conjunction between laity and clergy in the provisioning of anchorites brings us full circle. Anchoritism, both a lay and a clerical vocation, found its suppliers as well as its adherents at every point in the medieval social system.

Conclusion

Anchoritism was a significant religious phenomenon in medieval England and a wide range of persons were touched by it. From as early as the twelfth century independence from communal religious environments was regularly desired by individuals who nonetheless wanted to live a religious life. Such independence was tolerated by the hierarchy, and the social community at large was willing to undertake the support of these ascetics in separate and private establishments. English culture fostered or at least gave adequate room to such individuals, allowing them both the freedom and the capacity to respond to a personal religious calling. The anchorite movement in England resisted the "slide into cenobitism" seen elsewhere. Anchoritism ended as it had begun, as a movement of separate and separated persons. Perhaps England's freedom from heresy until the late fourteenth century better enabled it to tolerate independent ascetics, for suspicions of heresy always dogged the steps of free-acting religious on the Continent. Concern over possible heresy may lie behind the diffidence with which early English rules for anchorites approached overt mystical themes: excessive mystical fervor, especially among the undereducated and among women, might lead to heretical beliefs. The moderate regimes prescribed in these rules would diminish the likelihood of the hallucinatory states that more extreme ascetic practices encouraged. But this is not the full answer. English society displayed a willingness to bear with a situation that was by its nature vulnerable to distortion, and English society was successful in preserving, under cautious controls, a potentially disruptive way of life. The necessary energy was expended without complaint, century after century, to allow these independent religious their private way. This is a remarkable fact.

The religious hierarchy can be understood to have reconciled themselves to an indigenous religious response, one that had its own historical authenticity as derived from Scripture and legend. The motivations and expectations of the "general" public—not the lower classes about whom we know little but those who form the support groups—are of another order. Here we have seen that family and communal values played a role in determining the nature of that support. Most significant, especially in the earlier centuries encompassed by this study, was the support of the royal family. Both as a factor itself and as a model of appropriate behavior, the positive attitudes of the English monarchy toward the vocation were important and go far to explain the long-term survival of a vocation dependent on outside support. The meaning of such support to the royal family and to the other support groups —the aristocracy, the gentry, merchants, clergy—was complex, not monolithic. Different groups and different individuals within those groups approached anchoritism from varied perspectives. The capacity of the vocation to incorporate a range of symbolic meanings facilitated this many-sided vision, which in turn was another factor enabling its long-term survival. For Henry II, Henry III, and Henry V, support of anchorites was a personal response to a perceived holiness and a means of identification with the recluse: the royal penny made possible the chosen life. Participants and patron were joined together and shared virtue. Some royal persons further sought the advice of ascetics, seeing them as carriers of wisdom and endowed with certainty. Nor were the kings alone in this recourse. The aristocratic Beauchamps, among others, revered their prophetesses and their relics.

The response of an aristocrat such as Henry, duke of Lancaster, takes us to a more profound level of spiritual kinship. Identification for Henry of Lancaster was in terms of a life he could have led himself. His support of those who lived the reclusive life was an embracing of its values—not for others, but for himself. He was not joined to them because he supported them, but rather he supported recluses because he was already one with them. Feelings of this depth may lie behind the extraordinary will of Henry, Lord Scrope of Masham. For him also the anchoritic life represented the highest form of religious commitment that an individual could make, and his will affirmed that conviction. Other aristocrats invested anchorites with less intense emotional significance. Much anchorite support by aristocrats and gentry expressed patterns of behavior related to status and regional responsibility, and women shared in this responsibility. Local lords and ladies incorporated the needs and exemplified the values of an area. If anchorites were held in high esteem, the support of the aristocratic or gentry family would have been as natural as the payment of tithes. An element of competition may have been present in some situations. A local anchorite of some renown—as prophet, scholar, mystic, or ascetic—might have conferred some dignity on his patron as well.

Village or small town identification with the anchorite was immediate and constant. The anchorite was part of the routine life of the community: let us not forget the gossiping anchoress of Aelred and *Ancrene Riwle*. We can conjecture an England in which a village anchorite was a feature of religious life both commonplace and awe-inspiring; an England whose parish life was enhanced by the residence of one among them who had chosen this difficult way; an England in which the quality of daily life was enriched by the example of one so low who might become so high. Identification with the anchorite provided the villager with a private conduit to heaven and salvation. The anchorite was a close and visible symbol of holiness. Support for him, however minimal, was an indication of the patron's own worthiness.

The anchorite had less immediate impact on the merchant in the larger community. Urban support of anchorites was part of a generalized response that included substantial beneficence to many other institutions and groups dependent on charitable donation—here "charitable" begins to take on modern notions of gift giving not always tied into the religious system. The individual identification with individual anchorites that is a theme within the distribution patterns of giving in small communities is absent in a city the size of London (though somewhat more common in York). But typically merchants who made wills and included bequests for anchorites were merchants whose sense of overall public responsibility was more deeply felt than that of other merchants of their own time and community. Whether an innate response to the value of the reclusive life was the stimulus to such charity or whether anchorites were the lucky recipients of the overflow of generosity emanating from other sources cannot be determined from the data; nor is it wise to attempt such a distinction in what was surely a circular internal process. While the substantial amounts of money left to anchorites in merchant wills make it clear that these gifts represented an affirmation of the vocation by the merchant class, it remains true that for most merchants the anchorite was more a category of religious benefaction than a symbol of individual religious glory.

The response of the clergy was somewhat similar to that of the merchants. Here too those clergymen who supported anchorites were more broadly generous than their brothers who did not; their wills were mindful of the needs of many. Less overwhelmed by the "holiness" of the anchorite, less in need of spiritual credits themselves, clergymen reacted to anchorites in more down-to-earth terms than the laity did. Deeming the recluse worthy of support, clergy granted that support as one element of their philanthropy. To the cleric the anchorite way of life was one way, a religious way, a good way, but not automatically a better or the best way. Practitioners of such a life were entitled to financial aid and in need of it. The clergy recognized that obligation, answered it, and encouraged others in their circles of influence to respond in turn.

Analysis of the bequests made to one fifteenth-century recluse throws light on these subtly varying perspectives of anchorite support and anchorite perception. Julian Lampett was the anchoress at Carrow abbey, a small Benedictine convent in the suburbs of Norwich, for at least fifty-six years. Between 1426 and 1481 she received specific bequests in the wills of sixty-seven persons,[1] forty-nine of whom also left grants for the nuns and prioress

1. Most of these bequests are abstracted in Walter Rye, *Carrow Abbey* (Norwich, 1889), pp. xiv–xxiv.

of the abbey.[2] Nineteen of the sixty-seven wills were written by clergymen (one bishop, one archdeacon, and seventeen lesser clergy), twenty-two by merchants or their wives (three women), seventeen members of the gentle class (seven women), and nine by persons of indeterminate status (four women). Table 18 indicates the value of the gifts that Julian received compared to those granted to the prioress and nuns and displays that information according to social groups. It allows for a cross-cultural glance at the support of one particular anchoress who lived in a monastic setting.

Table 18 shows that the gentry were clearest about perceiving the anchorite as a unique religious individual. Seven of seventeen persons left grants to the anchoress alone; the remaining ten, who also remembered the nuns of the convent in their wills, were unambiguous in their acknowledgment of the greater worth of the anchoress—at least as expressed by the value of their bequests. The indeterminate group (yeomen, artisans) responded similarly if less absolutely and only one of nine testators ranked the prioress as worthier than the anchoress. Both merchants and clergy expressed greater variety in the distribution of their gifts. Balancing four clerical wills that remembered the anchoress alone were four others that ranked her no higher than a nun. Nine of the remaining eleven clerical wills ranked her above nuns and prioress. On average, these clergy expressed a positive view of the anchoritic vocation which granted the anchoress considerable status, but the clergy did not disregard alternative religious vocations. Merchants were least consistent in their responses. While four of twenty-two wills remembered the anchoress alone and eight more found her worthier than a prioress or nuns, ten ranked the anchoress only equal to the prioress. In all but two wills, however, she was seen as superior to the nuns and received bequests in various testaments at rates two, three, and even ten times that granted to them.

That Julian was a woman of some stature is indicated not only by the extent of these grants but also by the ways in which she

2. There are 146 wills with bequests referring to the abbey in some way during these years. Anchorites appear in 45 percent of these wills (65 of 146), sometimes alone and sometimes in conjunction with the prioress and/or nuns.

TABLE 18
Distribution of Gifts at Carrow Abbey by
Anchorite-favoring Testators (1426–1481)

	Clergy (19)	Mer-chants (22)	Gentry (17)	Others (9)	Totals (67)
Anchoress[1]	4	4	7	3	18
Anchoress > prioress > nuns	3	1	2	2	8
Prioress > anchoress > nuns	1	5	0	1	7
Anchoress = prioress > nuns	1	3	0	1	5
Anchoress > nuns[2]	6	7	8	2	23
Anchoress = nuns	2	1	0	0	3
Prioress > anchoress = nuns	2	1	0	0	3

1. Implies grant to anchorite alone or to her and her servants.
2. Includes grants specified as to nuns, to prioress and nuns, and to the convent.

was treated in some of these wills. In 1428 Sir Thomas Erpingham, a member of the household of John of Gaunt and then of
Gaunt's son Henry IV, granted five marks for distribution among
Norwich recluses and an additional grant of 23s. 4d. just for Julian,
whom he mentioned by full name. Sir William Phelip, called Lord
Bardolf and a member of Henry V's retinue, was Erpingham's
nephew and heir. In his 1438 testament he granted ten marks to
be distributed to the poor of Norwich according to the "assignment, will, and discretion" of Julian Lampett. In 1477 Lady Bardolf wrote a similar will. In 1472 Bishop Walter Lyhert left Julian
a bequest of twenty shillings, equivalent to what he left the
Carrow prioress; Julian was the only recluse in his diocese he
remembered.[3]

Anchorites were honored by the gentry, respected by the
clergy, and judged superior to nuns if not always to the prioress in

3. Erpingham: *Chichele*, 2:381; Lord Bardolf: *Chichele*, 2:600; Lyhert: Blomefield, *Norfolk*, 3:538.

the eyes of merchants; anchorite support was a constant among the various social groups but had different meanings in each setting. Looking at Julian through the prism of these varied responses, we see that the woman so highly regarded by the Bardolfs as to be the distributor of their posthumous alms was quite anonymous to the merchants of Norwich; the bishop of Norwich remembered only her among the many other anchorites of his diocese, but that gift did not exalt her beyond the prioress; women in the gentry and indeterminate groups without exception saw her as first-ranking, but the three merchant wives ranked the prioress above the anchoress in two cases and equal to her in the third.

The ability to sustain a range of meanings and a range of perception among its patrons was a strength to anchoritism and a major factor in its survival. Anchoritism was never dependent on the whim or agenda of any one particular social class. Signifying different things to different groups (and to different individuals within those groups), the vocation was able to remain flexible, to grow and change without threatening or undermining the basis of its support. This flexibility not only enabled anchoritism to survive vis-à-vis its patrons but also provided the means by which it was able to adjust to changing religious ideals without compromising its own integrity. Anchoritism was positioned for long term survival both because of the broad basis of its support and because the vocation incorporated within itself a multifaceted perception of its goals and meanings, one that was able to accommodate shifts in religious fashion while remaining true to its pristine vision. Striking about anchoritism is its centrality to every major religious trend in England in the Middle Ages: asceticism in the twelfth century, the absorption of large numbers of women in the thirteenth, mysticism in the fourteenth, and the growth of austere orders in the fifteenth century. Striking are the individual anchorites who both exemplified and advanced that centrality: the twelfth-century Wulfric of Haselbury, priest, prophet, and healer; the thirteenth-century countess Loretta of Hackington, welcoming the newly arrived Franciscans to England; the fourteenth-century Julian of Norwich, extraordinary mystic and writer; the fifteenth-century John Dygoun, scholar, living among the Carthusians, copying the books of the mystical movement; the sixteenth-century Katherine Mann, suspect because of her friendship with the soon-to-be martyred Thomas Bilney. Striking is a religious phenomenon so unique that it could be described by one set of criteria as constant throughout the entire four hundred years under review and by another as so flexible as to engage each new religious mentality as it emerged.

This plasticity extended to the patrons of anchoritism as well. Patrons were drawn from groups that were innately conservative and from groups that were consciously avant-garde. Conservative patrons saw their recluses as representing the best of the past in an unbroken continuum. Conservative patrons supported recluses along with convents, nurtured their own ascetic anchorite-prophets, maintained anchorites in their domains as their fathers and grandfathers had done. Avant-garde patrons saw themselves and their anchorites as in tune with the currents of the day. They encouraged new movements, embraced the *devotia moderna*, used the language of self-depreciation, championed, read, and owned the books of the expanding mystical and lay devotional movements.

One can say with caution that anchoritism responded to conservative (but contemporary) trends in the early and late centuries under analysis here and to avant-garde trends in the thirteenth and fourteenth centuries. The anchorite experience in England began for the purposes of this study in the early days of the Anglo-Norman period, with Christina of Markyate and Godric of Finchale. In their Lives one feels as well as visualizes the empty spaces of early twelfth-century England, hermits and anchorites in their rural ascetic abodes with a clientele of Anglo-Saxon gentry, a post-Conquest conservative response to a changing world. In the thirteenth century anchoritism had a new face. It grew quickly and gave way to organization and control, maturing under the aegis of a good and pious king and becoming a province of women. Anchoritism in the fourteenth century became part of the urban world, where there were new winds in the air and where anchoritism remained the calm eye of the storm, the absolute

287

center of the English mystical movement. In the fifteenth century anchoritism flourished as the mystical movements waned. Carthusians and Bridgettines, sharing with the anchorite motifs of withdrawal, asceticism, and contemplation, took the lead in protecting the literature of the recent past. Their ties to fifteenth- and sixteenth-century anchorites were many. In each period the anchoritic life represented an accommodation between the old and the new, between the conservative and the avant-garde. In each period an anchorite or his patron could have perceived himself as protecting the values of his forefathers or could see himself as on the threshold of a new world. The fourteenth century brought about a lasting change in the religious climate, a change that did not disappear after its first impetus was spent, for lay piety became a permanent factor on the religious scene. The anchorite of old, typically a lay woman, was an example of the new in even sharper terms than before. Now she became more than an object of esteem for the few, she became an exemplar for the many.

English anchorites and their patrons thus straddled two worlds. Both conservative and avant-garde, conventional and faddish, anchorites and their patrons were joined together by more than promises of prayers and promises of support, by more than patterns of testamentary bequests, by more than bookishness, by more than contempt for the physical self. They were bound together by a shared image of a world within which it was possible to reach God and uncover their inner selves. The anchorite's cell was the most likely site of that possible encounter. The cell, at the core of the solitary life, home to individual English anchorites, remained the desert of antiquity.

So anchoritism survived in England until it was wiped away with a stroke of the pen. At the Dissolution there were fewer anchorites than there had been a hundred years earlier, but the vocation had suffered ebbs and flows before and the future could not have been known. The late data, whether from wills, gentry accounts, or royal records, are suffused with the same timeless quality that pervaded the earlier evidence. In 1521 a new anchorhold was constructed in London for a woman named Margaret Elyote.

Attached to the Blackfriars, it became the subject of a legal action when the prior, anxious lest Margaret become a financial burden on the friary, refused her entry and Margaret saw no recourse save to take him to court. She won her suit after promising never to "claim meat, drink, or clothing" from the Dominican house, and within four days of the resolution of the case she was enclosed with all due ritual.[4] The meaning of this story lies as much in the commonplace tone of the court proceedings as in the information that new reclusoria were still being built. Anchorites had been forced to prove that they possessed adequate support before being enclosed ever since the thirteenth century. The Blackfriars litigation was a tale of "everything as usual," not a new mood in the wind.

Other new anchorholds were built in the sixteenth century. There were anchorites in old and new sites in London, in Lincoln, in Kent, in Norwich, and in Lynn as well as elsewhere. Christopher Warner desired his solitude at Canterbury, Katherine Mann received letters from Thomas Bilney at Norwich, Margaret Kydman, a nun, moved into Julian Lampett's cell at Carrow, Alice Buttes was at St. John's Hospital in Exeter, Simon Appulby at All Hallows, London Wall, Benedicta Burton at Polesworth in Warwickshire, Robert Barrett in the Austin friary of Northampton. These are but a few who are not lost in the mist of time and their liminal existence. They were safe, secure, and supported until the Dissolution.

Medieval English anchoritism was extraordinary in its endurance, in its high degree of stability, in its success in gaining and keeping the support of large numbers of the broad community from the king down to the parishioner of modest means. It was remarkable in its capacity to encounter change and remain inviolate, to reject heresy, to resist all pressure to communal life. With great success anchoritism challenged the society in which it emerged to be true to that society's ideals.

One measure of a culture is how well it treats the exceptional, how well it accommodates those who place demands on it when

4. Clay, "Northern Anchorites," p. 214. Margaret was enclosed by the suffragan bishop.

289

those demands are in congruence with its felt and stated values. In medieval England society fulfilled an unspoken but implicit promise to those who, nurtured in a religious system that sanctified solitude, accepted its challenge. Medieval England met the test of an honorable and healthy civilization. English anchoritism died by fiat and not for lack of the faithful.

appendix 1

APPENDIX 1

ANCHORITE DISTRIBUTION BY COUNTIES IN MEDIEVAL ENGLAND

Counties	Twelfth century					Thirteenth century					Fourteenth century					Fifteenth century					Sixteenth century[2]				
	F	M	I	T	S	F	M	I	T	S	F	M	I	T	S	F	M	I	T	S	F	M	I	T	S
Bedfordshire	2	1		3	3	1	2		3	3	1			1	1										
Berkshire	4	1		5	3	3	1	2	6	6															
Buckinghamshire																									
Cambridgeshire	1		6	7	7	4			4	3		2	2	4	4	1			1	1					
Cheshire						6			6	6	2	6		8	6	2		1	3	2	1			1	1
Cornwall																									
Cumberland																									
Derbyshire											1			1	1										
Devonshire	2			2	2		1		1	1	4	1		5	5	3	4		7	6	1	1		2	2
Dorset	7	1		8	3							2		2	2		1		1	1					
Durham												3		3	3		3		3	2			1	1	1
Essex	2	3		5	3	2			2	2	1			1	1	1			1	1					
Gloucestershire	1	2	2	5	5	6	2	2	10	10	2	1	3	6	5	1		1	2	2	2			2	2
Hampshire	7	2	2	11	5	4	2	4	10	10	1			1	1	1			1	1					
Herefordshire	1	1		2	2	6			6	4	4			4	4	2			2	2					
Hertfordshire	1	2		3	3	2	1		3	3	2			2	2	6	1		7	4	3			3	2
Huntingdonshire											3			3	2										
Kent						9		6	15	12	3		1	4	1	2	2	1	5	3	2	3		5	4
Lancashire						1			1	1	3	1		4	4	2			2	2	1			1	1

County	F	M	I	T	S	F	M	I	T	S	F	M	I	T	S	F	M	I	T	S	F	M	I	T	S
Leicestershire	1															3		2	2	1	4			4	3
Lincolnshire	1	1		2	2					1	13	13	9			16	12	9	6		4			10	6
Middlesex[1]	4	2	7	7	10	14	10	8		6	26	11	12	20	1	25	9	20	9	3	10	3		21	13
Norfolk	1	1		8	3	21	19	3	6		12	11	18	20	1	39	20	3	3		9	3		3	1
Northamptonshire	3	3	3	2		2	2	1			1	1	3			3	3	3	3					3	1
Northumberland				1		1	1						1	1	1	3	3								
Nottinghamshire	1	1		2	2	2	2	3			3	3	3	1	2	6	6	5			1				1
Oxfordshire	3	6	8	8	6	15	13	1			1	1									1				
Rutland																									
Shropshire			5	5	3	8	8	3	1		4	3	1	1		2	2	2	1		1	1		1	1
Somerset	2	3	1	1	2	1	1	1			4	3	1	2		3	3	3	1		1	1		1	1
Staffordshire			1	1	1	2	2	1			1	1	1		2	2	2				1	1		1	1
Suffolk	1	1	4	4		4	3		37	38	38	38	1	1		2	2								
Surrey	1	2	2	2	2	5	5	1	2	3	3	3	5	5		5	5	1			2	2		2	1
Sussex	3	8	5	5	1	12	11						2	2	1	3	3	3							
Warwickshire								1		1	1	1			1	2	2		1		1			1	1
Westmorland																									
Wiltshire	1	6	7	7		9	7	2			2	1	1	1	1	3	3	1	1		1	1		2	2
Worcestershire	2	6	9	2	1	12	9		1	1	1	1	1	1		1	1	1	1		1	1		2	2
Yorkshire	1	2	12	12	1	14	12	38	10	34	53	34	36	4	11	51	29	3	3	1	3	1		4	3
Unidentified	1	1	2		2	2	2	2		3	3	3	1	1		1	1	1							
Totals	48	30	18	123	37	198	175	96	77	214	171	110	66	28	204	129	37	27	4	68	49				

1. Includes London
2. To 1539

Legend: F = Female; M = Male; I = Indeterminate; T = Totals; S = Sites

appendix 2

English Anchorite Rules

Writings for anchorites range from the briefest of hortatory and didactic epistles to major ascetic treatises. There are thirteen extant English works.

1. *Liber confortatorius,* written by Goscelin, a Benedictine monk and famous hagiographer, for Eve, a former nun of Wilton, circa 1080. It exists in a unique manuscript of the late twelfth century, ed. C. H. Talbot, *Analecta Monastica* 3, *Studia Anselmiana* 38 (1955): 1–117. The work is long, running about 3,200 lines.

2. *Letters,* written by St. Anselm, first monk then abbot of Bec and later archbishop of Canterbury: two letters for the instruction of female anchorites, circa 1103–1107, ed. F. S. Schmitt, *Opera omnia,* 6 vols. (Edinburgh: Thomas Nelson and Sons, Ltd., 1946–61), 4:134–135, 5:359–362; as well as a third letter to a male recluse named Hugo while he was still at Bec, *PL* 158, cols. 1171–1175.

3. *De institutis inclusarum,* also known as *De vita eremita, ad sororem reclusam,* written by St. Aelred, abbot of Rievaulx, a Cistercian: an extended letter composed for his sister at her request, circa 1162, ed. C. H. Talbot, *Analecta Sacri Ordinis Cisterciensis* 1 (1951): 167–217. There is an English translation in *The Works of Aelred of Rievaulx I: Treatises; The Pastoral Prayer,* Cistercian Father Series 2 (Spencer, Mass.: Cistercian Publications, 1971), pp. 43–102. It is about 1,100 lines. Aelred's letter was the basis for later rules and widely dispersed, the

meditation forming its middle section a significant model of twelfth-century spirituality. It was twice translated into Middle English in the fourteenth century.

4. *Admonitiones,* written by Robert, a priest, for Hugo, an anchorite. This is published as an appendix to the Dublin Rule (see no. 6 below) but is an earlier and separate work according to Livario Oliger, its editor. It is in the main a treatise on the Eucharist and from internal evidence has been dated between the years 1140 and 1215, that is, between Gratian and the Fourth Lateran Council. About 210 lines.

5. *Ancrene Riwle,* written by an Augustinian canon for three sisters, circa 1220 (according to the most recent consensus). The author remains anonymous[1] but the work is the most famous piece of prose literature of the early Middle English period. Soon after its composition it was translated into French and subsequently into Latin, and the English version was revised. In its revised form the work is known as *Ancrene Wisse.* It exists in many manuscripts, five of which belong to the early thirteenth century, attesting to its immediate popularity. Many later compilers of didactic literature borrowed from it. Replacing the old Camden Society edition of James Morton (1853) are six editions of Middle English manuscripts (EETS 225, 229, 232, 249, 252, 267), a Latin edition (EETS 216), and two French editions (EETS 219, 240). All of these have been published since 1944. There is a modern English translation of the *Ancrene Wisse* manuscript by M. B. Salu, *The Ancrene Riwle (The Corpus MS: Ancrene Wisse)* (Notre Dame: University of Notre Dame Press, 1955) which runs about 8,000 lines.

6. *Regula reclusorum dubliniensis,* the Dublin Rule, written for male anchorites by an anonymous author. It draws from St. Benedict, Aelred, *Ancrene Riwle,* and Grimlaic (the ninth-century Continental rule for anchorites that is the earliest

---

1. Most recently Eric J. Dobson, *The Origins of Ancrene Wise* (Oxford: Clarendon Press, 1976), pp. 312–368, in masterful fashion concludes that the name of the author was Brian of Lingen.

known). Edited by Livario Oliger, "Regulae tres reclusorum et eremitarum Angliae saec. XIII–XIV," *Antonianum* 3 (1928): 170–183, the *Admonitiones* following, 183–190. Oliger dates it in the thirteenth century with the *Ancrene Riwle* (ca. 1220) the *terminus post quem* and 1312 (from the contents of the folio containing the unique manuscript) as the *terminus ante quem*. He thinks it likely that the manuscript dates to the beginning of the period rather than to its end. About 350 lines.

7. *Regula reclusorum Walteri reclusi*, circa 1280. Walter, an Augustinian canon who became a recluse after having lived a communal life for thirty years, wrote this work as advice for other recluses, essentially other male recluses who would have shared his experience. He was sixty years old at the time of writing and had then been enclosed for ten years. In many ways this is the most interesting of these documents because it speaks from the inside. Walter asks those who read it to keep their copy and make another for someone else, a kind of chain letter. It draws from Aelred and Grimlaic. Three manuscripts survive. Edited by Livario Oliger, "Regula reclusorum Angliae et quaestiones tres de vita solitaria, saec. XIII–XIV," *Antonianum* 9 (1934): 53–84, it runs about 930 lines. Three separate short treatises (discussing the superior merits of the solitary life as compared to the cenobitic) form an addendum to Walter's Rule in the manuscripts. The first treatise was written by St. Thomas Aquinas (d. 1274). The other two are anonymous but most probably of English provenance and are dated 1298 x 1323. The anonymous writers were religious, possibly themselves solitaries, and both knew the Aquinas writing, one specifically referring to it (see L. Oliger, "Regula reclusorum Angliae," *Antonianum* 9 [1934]: 243–259).

8. *The Lambeth Rule*, so called from the unique manuscript that survives, is a very short document, a charge rather than a rule proper. It was written for male lay recluses in English in the thirteenth century. The surviving manuscript derives from the fifteenth century. There are Latin and French versions as well. About seventy half-lines (see Livario Oliger, "Regula re-

clusorum Angliae et quaestiones tres de vita solitaria, saec. XIII–XIV," *Antonianum* 9 [1934]: 260–265).

9. *Letter of a Fourteenth-century abbot of Bury St. Edmunds.* A response to a monk's petition to become a recluse. The abbot is unnamed, the recluse is identified as *dominus L.* The short work, about fifty-five lines, draws from Aelred among others. Antonia Gransden, ed., *English Historical Review* 75 (1960): 465–467.

10. *Speculum inclusorum,* anonymous, but the author was certainly a priest and a religious, most probably a Carthusian and educated in the schools. Written shortly after the beginning of the second half of the fourteenth century, it exists in two manuscripts in its original Latin version and in a fifteenth-century Middle English translation. All the manuscripts belong to the fifteenth century. The *Speculum* was written for male recluses, but the Middle English translation, called *Advice to Recluses,* broadens the audience to include women. Not only draws from Aelred but suggests that its readers use Aelred's rule along with this one. The Latin version has about 1,875 lines. The English *Advice* has several lacunae and only 1,360 lines. The *Speculum* was edited by Livario Oliger, *Lateranum,* n.s. 4, no. 1 (Rome, 1938). The *Advice* is found in B.M. MS Harl. 2372. L. E. Rogers prepared an edition of it. It is unpublished and to be found in the Bodleian Library, Oxford (B. Litt., Oxford, 1933).

11. *Form of Living,* by Richard Rolle. Rolle, a fourteenth-century hermit and one of the most prolific writers of the mystical movement of that century, composed the *Form of Living* for an anchoress who was a disciple of his, a woman named Margaret de Kirkeby in all probability. Written circa 1348, shortly before his own death, it is in Middle English and one of his great affective works. Rolle, known as the Hermit of Hampole, also wrote the *Incendium amoris,* a series of discourses on subjects concerned with the life of solitaries (not necessarily anchorites) and may have been the author of the Latin

Cambridge Rule, a rule for hermits which borrowed extensively from Aelred. For the *Form of Living,* see Hope Emily
Allen, *English Writings of Richard Rolle, Hermit of Hampole*
(Oxford: Clarendon Press, 1931; repr. 1971, Scholarly Press),
pp. 85–119; for the *Incendium amoris* see the English translation by Clifton Wolters (Penguin Books, 1972); for the *Cambridge Rule* see Livario Oliger, "Regulae tres reclusorum et
eremitarum Angliae saec. XIII–XIV," *Antonianum* 3 (1928):
151–169, 299–312.

12. *The Scale (or Ladder) of Perfection,* by Walter Hilton, written
in the second half of the fourteenth century. Hilton was an
Augustinian canon who had spent a portion of his life as a
hermit. At least the first book of this major work was written
as a guide for an anchoress. There is scholarly disagreement
as to the intended audience of the second book, written some
years after the first. It may have been directed to meet "the
spiritual needs of all, *pusilli et magni*."[2] This is a mystical work
of significance and Hilton is considered a more experienced
(and higher level) mystic than Rolle. Evelyn Underhill, ed.,
The Scale of Perfection (London: Watkins, 1923), provides a
modernized version. Both books together run about 13,500
lines.

13. *Epistola ad quendam solitarium,* by Walter Hilton. Written for
a priest who had come under ecclesiastical censure. He abandoned his former life and became an enclosed solitary. The
letter is found in B.M. Royal MS 6 E III, fols. 120–123. Joy
Russell-Smith has translated it as "A Letter to a Hermit," *The
Way* 6 (1966): 230–241. Similar in teaching to the *Scale.* The
translation runs about 450 lines.

2. Joy Russell-Smith, "Walter Hilton," in *Pre-Reformation English Spirituality,*
ed. James Walsh (New York: Fordham University Press, 1965), p. 195.

appendix 3

TABLE A
TRANSFERENCE OF ALMS: GLOUCESTERSHIRE (1170–1198)

	Ralph of Tamewurda 10s.	Gilbert, cecus 40s. 5d.		Heilwise, foreigner 45s. 7½d.		John Pirun 45s. 7½	Adam, inclusus 10s.[1]
Henry II 1170	Ralph of Tamewurda 10s.	Gilbert, cecus 40s. 5d.		Heilwise, foreigner 45s. 7½d.		John Pirun 45s. 7½	Adam, inclusus 10s.[1]
1171	„	„		„		„	„
1172	„	„		„		„	60s.
1173–77	„	„		„		„	„
1177	William, cecus 10s.	„		„		„	„
1178–83	„	„		„		„	„
1184	„	Nuns: Ankerwyke 20s. 2½d.	Nuns: Cheshunt 20s. 2½	„		„	„
1185	„	Richard Gaweus 40s. 5d.		Reginald Lorimer 45s. 7½d.		„	„
1186–87	„	„		„		„	„
1188	„	„		„ 22s. 9d.	Wm. s. Reg. 22s. 9d.	„	„

Richard I 1189	Walter Haselton 5s.	"	William son of Reginald 45s. 7½d.	"	"	"	"	Hugh, focarius 45s. 7½d.
1190	"	John, chaplain 5s.	"	"	"	"	"	"
1191	"	"	"	"	"	"	"	"
1192–93	"	"	"	"	"	"	"	"
1194	"	"	"	"	?	Adam, clerk 22s. 9d.	"	"
1195	"	"	"	"	Adam, Queen's clerk 45s. 7½d.	"	"	"
1196	"	"	"	"	"	" 30s.	Thomas 30s.	"
1197	"	"	"	"	"	Harvey 30s.	"	Durandus, chaplain 45s. 7½d.
1198	"	"	"	"	"	Harvey Freschet 60s.	"	"

1. First year funds for less than full accounting year.

TABLE B
Transference of Alms: Surrey (1178–1199)

Henry II	John, almoner 30s. 5d.	Roger son of Codulf 60s. 10d.				John de Capella 60s. 10d.
1178–80						
1181	„	„				„
1182	„	„				„
1183	„	„				„
1184	„ 15s. 2½d. / William Schobete 15s. 2½d.[1]	„				„
1185	William Schobete 30s. 5d.[1]	„				„
1186	„	„				„
1187	„	Priest 15s. 2½d.	Poor house of St. James outside London 15s. 2½d.	Poor house at Swaffham 15s. 2½d.	Nuns of Huntingdon 15s. 2½d.	„
1188	„	Nicholas & son 60s. 10d.				„
Richard I 1189	„	„				Nicholas & John, converts 30s. 5d.
1190	Wischardus 30s. 5d.[1]	„				Thomas, cook 60s. 10d.
1191–93	„	„				„
1194	„	„				„
1195	„	„				„
1196	„	„				Fulcon Fermage 60s. 10d.
1197	„	„				„
1198	„	„				„
John 1199	„	„				„

1. Denotes funds in more than one column.

TABLE B

Transference of Alms: Surrey (1178–1199), *Continued*

Henry II 1178–80	Svein, keeper 30s. 5d.		Gilbert de Moretano 30s. 5d.		Gilbert: priest 30s. 5d.		
1181	"		" 6s. 6d.	Sick: Gildford 23s. 11d.	"		
1182	"		Nuns: Ankerwyke 30s. 5d.		"		
1183	"		Nuns: Ankerwyke 15s. 2½d.	Nuns: Garing 15s. 2½d.	"		
1184	"		Nuns: Ankerwyke 30s. 5d.		" 15s. 2½d.	William Schobete 15s. 2½d.[1]	
1185	"		Nuns: Ankerwyke 15s. 2½d.	Nuns: Greencroft 15s. 2½d.	William Schobete 30s. 5d.[1]		
1186	"		Marinus: clerk 15s. 2½d.	Nuns: Littlemore 15s. 2½d.	"		
1187	"		Gervase, scribe 30s, 5d.		"		
1188	"		Nicholas: convert 15s. 2½d.	John: convert 15s. 2½d.	"		
Richard I 1189	"		Nuns: Kilburn 30s. 5d.		"		
1190	"		Osbert: man of the Queen 30s. 5d.		Wischardus 30s. 5d.[1]		
1191–93	"		"		"		
1194	"		"		"	Emma wife of Robert 15s. 2½d.[2]	Chaplain: Lepers 30s. 5d.[2]
1195	"		"		"	" 30s. 5d.	" 60s. 10d.
1196	"		"		"	"	"
1197	"		"		"	"	"
1198	Chamberlain 15s. 2½d.	William Stiviton 15s. 2½d.	"		"	,	"
John 1199	Willam Stiviton 30s. 5d.		Richard Norrensus 30s. 5d.		"	"	"

1. Denotes funds in more than one column.
2. First year funds for less than full accounting year.

TABLE C
Transference of Alms:
Buckinghamshire and Bedfordshire (1159–1197)

Henry II 1159-63	Druard of Bedford 45s. 7½d.	Robert de Capella 60s. 10d.	Contractus de Loitona 30s. 5d.
1164	"	"	" 15s. 2½d. | Ralph de Hintona 15s. 2½d.
1165-67	"	"	Ralph de Hintona 30s. 5d.
1168	"	" 30s. 5d. [X]	"
1169	"	[X]	"
1170	"	[X] Robert f. Fulkonis 30s. 5d.	"
1171-81	"	Robert f. Fulkonis 60s. 10d.	"
1182	Nuns of St. James, Westminister 35s. 7d.	Sick: Queen's hospital outside London 10s.	"	Brothers of the Hospital of Witsand 30s. 5d.
1183	Nuns of St. James Westminister 22s. 9d.	Nuns: Stratford 22s. 9d.	"	"
1184	William Wassepoke 37s. 4½d.	Nuns: Ankerwyke 8s. 3d.	"	"
1185	Nuns: St. James, Huntingdon 45s. 7½d.		"	"	*Recluse:* St. Mary's 27s. 4d.[1]
1186	Nuns: St. James, Huntingdon 22s. 10d.	Bilandus 22s. 9½d.	"	" 3s. 10d. [X]
1187-89	Bilandus, keeper 45s. 7½d.		"	"	[X]
2 Richard I 1190	[X]	John Pedefer 14s. 5d.[1]	"	[X]
1191	[X]	John Pedefer 30s. 5d.	"	[X]
1192	[X]	"	"	[X]
1193-97	[X]	"	"	[X]

1. First year funds for less than full accounting year.

304

appendix 4

The Husting Rolls

The Husting Rolls cease to provide any evidence of anchorites after 1413. It is possible to infer from this that anchorites were no longer living in London after that time or had fallen from popularity, at least among merchants.[1] Wills outside the Hustings sample and other data help to dispel these ideas, but the absence of any anchorite data in the rolls after 1413 needs explanation. The answer lies more in the nature of the evidence than in the nature of the anchorite phenomenon. What changed was the data base itself: both the number and the character of the wills enrolled at Hustings underwent considerable alteration.

The Hustings enrollments begin as the briefest of legal entries. If they are examined from the year 1271 (when the series becomes regular) the pattern of enrollments quickly becomes apparent:

Rokesle (Richard de.)—Last will, whereby he gives and assigns to William and John, sons of Vivian de Rokesle, shops near Douegate, and to Avice his wife a house for life, all said tenements being in the parish of All Hallows de la Heyswarwe.

1. So Francis D. S. Darwin, *The English Medieval Recluse* (London: SPCK, 1944), pp. 64–65. John M. Jennings, "The Distribution of Landed Wealth in the Wills of London Merchants, 1400–1450," *Mediaeval Studies* 39 (1977): 277, makes a similar assumption with regard to prisons, hospitals, and education. Noting the very small numbers of bequests to those categories, he concludes "that these were not too popular as ends for these testators."

Paris (William de.)—Last will, whereby he gives and assigns to the nuns of St. Helen, London, certain rents in Westcheap. The residue of his rents in the city of London to be sold for payment of his debts.

Essex (Walter de.)—Last will, whereby he gives and assigns to Agnes de Orpington his capital messuage with two gates and a garden extending to la More.[2]

Derkin (John), apothecary.—Last will, whereby he assigns all his goods, movable and immovable, to be sold to pay his debts, and the residue to go in certain portions to his sons and servants *as in the testament of the said John is more fully and better contained.*[3]

Heremy (Mathilda de.)—Last will, whereby she gives and assigns to Agnes her daughter her house wherein she lived; remainder in default of heirs, to Nicholas, brother of the said Agnes; remainder for the good of the souls of the faithful. To Johanna de Marleberne a certain shop for life, *as in her testament is better and more fully contained.*[4]

These early entries make clear that London citizens, having secured the right of probate of the devise of real property in the borough court, took advantage of their prerogative and often did distinguish between their last will, devising real property, and their testaments, devising movables. Such few "pious and charitable" gifts noted in these early enrollments are tied directly to the disposal of real estate. It can be discovered that the nuns of St. Helen were endowed by William Paris because rents in Westcheap were the foundation of that support; the information that John Derkin provided for his servants comes directly as a result of their being beneficiaries of the sale of his real estate. Much data concerning chantries come from these first entries on the Hustings rolls— chantries being the frequent recipients of the proceeds of the real-estate transactions set in motion by these wills.

During these years it is rare to find an outright money grant enrolled. What are routinely listed are rents and the accruals of property sales and transfers. The sole exception to this pattern are grants for London Bridge. In the years 1300–16 small monetary

2. *CWCH,* 1:10.
3. Ibid., p. 13 (italics mine). The year is 1273 in this and the following citation.
4. Ibid., p. 14 (italics mine).

bequests for London Bridge began to be enrolled at Hustings. In amounts ranging from four pence to four shillings, with one woman bequeathing her gold wedding ring,[5] during these years almost one testator in five (101 of 525) left small sums of money to London Bridge. We can hardly do otherwise than conjure up a vision of preachers throughout the city intoning from their pulpits that London Bridge was falling down and that God-fearing parishioners should take heed. Although London Bridge did receive a steady trickle of bequests in later years (quite often as a secondary benefaction),[6] this intensive response was never repeated. London Bridge aside, the early enrollments at the Court of Husting fulfill the criteria established for enrollment but do not go beyond them.

Starting about the year 1325, more complete copies of wills begin to appear on the rolls. The more detailed will includes burial place data and bequests of both movable and immovable property. While a condensation, this will is clearly the framework into which details (presumably contained in the complete document probated in the ecclesiastical court) could be inserted. What we find here is one will, not two. In these comprehensive wills the first bequests to anchorites appear. The first anchorite will in the Hustings series comes in 1341, just at the point in the calendar when the fuller will, though still rare, becomes more prevalent. Between 1351 and 1400 such a will is likely to occur one-third to one-half of the time. These are the years of the anchorite grants. After 1400 the will selections enrolled get shorter again and less complex. Fewer and fewer contain broadly disbursed gifts, and those that do concentrate on the poor and the maintenance of highways. London Bridge, friars, prisoners, lepers all disappear from these wills as routine recipients of benefactions and are discoverable only in those increasingly rare enrollments still encompassing the larger and more complete will. Pilgrimage data also disappear from these wills at the moment when the anchorite bequests cease. That grants for pilgrimages still were being made can be attested by reference to the nine wills in the

5. Ibid., p. 153.
6. Jennings, "Distribution of Landed Wealth," p. 264.

Chichele register which made such provisions, by those in Norwich, and by wills elsewhere.[7]

For another example: John M. Jennings' study of London merchants, which drew all its data from the Hustings enrollments of the years after 1400, notes that prisoners (to note but one category) received bequests only twenty-two times in a reading of the 360 wills enrolled between 1400 and 1450.[8] The 53 Hustings wills of the anchorite group alone provided 25 wills with bequest to prisoners (plus 1 further testament that made a grant to the "ministers of various prisons") and 17 of these made grants to prisoners at more than one prison. Moreover, the percentage of these testators leaving grants for prisoners was rising as the period moved forward. Between the years 1341 and 1365, 8 of 22 anchorite-favoring wills (36.7 percent) made bequests to prisoners; between the years 1366 and 1408, 17 of 30 wills did so (56.7 percent). Table 15, giving the Chichele and Marche and Luffendam data relative to grants to prisoners at this time, reinforces the position of this study: that the Hustings data are so impoverished with regard to this kind of donation as to give a picture that is not only lacking but is essentially incorrect.

Another phenomenon was taking place simultaneously. The number of wills being enrolled was decreasing. Table D describes those data.

The declining rate in the numbers of testators whose wills were enrolled at the Court of Husting would result eventually in the total cessation of enrollments by 1688. As can be seen, there was already a ten-year period in the late fifteenth century when an average of only one will per year was being registered. Moreover, some of the testators who did enroll a will at Hustings enrolled more than one—so there are fewer testators involved than there are numbers

<hr>

7. *Chichele*, 2:74, 104, 124, 272, 385, 411, 485, 488, 539; Norman P. Tanner, *The Church in Late Medieval Norwich 1370–1532*, Pontifical Institute of Mediaeval Studies, Studies and Texts 66 (Toronto, 1984), pp. 85–90.

8. Jennings, "Distribution of Landed Wealth," p. 266.

TABLE D

Number of Wills Enrolled at the London Court of Husting (1271–1500)

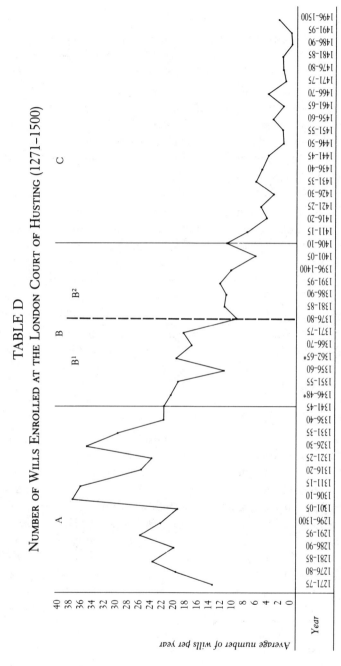

*The plague years 1349, 1350, and 1361 have been eliminated from the graph because of the distortion they render. There are 356 wills for 1349, 49 for 1350, and 127 for 1361. Otherwise these are raw figures. Population trends have not been weighted. The population of London, however, was rising throughout the fifteenth century. Estimated at 35,000 in 1377, it was about 50,000 in Henry VIII's reign (Russell, *British Medieval Population*).

of wills.[9] By custom all seven of the merchants who compose the late medieval group of London anchorite-favoring testators should have enrolled their wills at Hustings. In fact only three of them did—John Welles, William Gregory, and William Butler—and they had been both aldermen and mayors and may have felt that their civic positions demanded compliance.[10] Unlike the aldermanic wills of the fourteenth century which had been enrolled at Hustings in considerable detail, however, the wills enrolled for Welles, Gregory, and Butler were fragments. Welles's Hustings enrollment contains no ecclesiastical gifts at all. What are calendared are those portions of his will bearing on his sense of municipal status: he desired that the mayor, the sheriffs, and the swordbearer of the city as well as three wardens of the Grocers attend his obit for thirty years; he made a bequest for the purpose of building a standard in Westcheap, the boundary of his ward; he left money for the repair of the aqueduct conduit and London Bridge; he remembered the poor of his guild. The sections of his will enrolled at the Court of Husting were extracted and condensed from the body of his full will, which was probated in the prerogative court of Chichele. The unabridged will is a classic of the patterns developed in these pages for a merchant testator. Welles made bequests to the poor on his burial day and to poor householders in his ward; to the friars, to prisoners, and to every anchorite in the city and suburbs; to repair highways in addition to the public works mentioned above. The Hustings entry takes no notice of these grants.

Gregory's enrollments are even more instructive. No fewer than six separate wills of Gregory were entered in the Hustings rolls— each dealing with a separate real estate transaction.[11] His testament is another document and is found in Register Godyn. His testament provided extensively for the poor on his burial day, as well as for hospital poor and lepers. He left money for the immediate relief of prisoners as well as to free them, to four fraternities including the

9. For two wills of Thomas Mockying: CWCH, 2:448; for two wills of William Sevenoke: CWCH, 2:462; for three wills of Thomas Beaumond: CWCH, 2:533, 534-35; for three wills of Henry Frowyk: CWCH, 2:541-542, 579.

10. But that this was not always so has been seen.

11. CWCH, 2:499-500.

Tailors, to all five orders of friars in London, to the London Charterhouse and to Syon, to nuns in convents around London, to the Minoresses. As Jane Lisle would do thirty-five years later, he bequeathed money to provide "frise to make gownes and cotes, and lynnen cloth to make shertes and smokkes, and for c paire of shone, for puer men and women . . . and I biqueth ls [50s.] for to buy c quarters coles to be gyven to pouere men and women . . ." He also left money to send clerks to school, to mend foul ways and feeble bridges, and provided dowries for the marriages of poor maidens and widows of good name and fame. He made bequests to four named anchorites. None of this could be learned from the Hustings entries.

Butler's Hustings enrollment is a brief paragraph dated nine months later than his testament proved at Canterbury. Certain tenements, messuages, cottages, and a quitrent were to support a chantry, pay for his obit, and provide for the poor of St. Mildred in the Poultry by supplying them with twelve shillings yearly in charcoal. These grants had been established in the earlier will, along with a whole range of others (as table 11 indicated), Butler also providing cloth for shirts and sheets for the poor. The Hustings enrollment is not really a will. Rather, it is the publication of a legal notice relative to certain properties.[12]

The Hustings data can be divided into the three periods designated "A," "B," and "C" on table D. In the first period "A" wills are plentiful but brief—rarely more than an abstract of a real-estate transferral. There are no anchorite data in this period. In the "B" period the number of wills already is declining but a meaningful proportion of them are being enrolled more completely. *This period provides the anchorite data.* The gradual losses in numbers, however, already are affecting the totals. The period B^1 (1341–75) contains thirty-seven anchorite wills. The period B^2 (1376–1413), a period of equal length, contains just sixteen. The final period, "C," is again a period with no anchorite data. It is characterized both by falling numbers and by a reversion to briefer and more specific enrollments.

12. Ibid., pp. 544, 556, 557, 557–558, 567, 573.

Many London testators had ceased enrolling even the real-estate portions of their wills in Hustings. By 1419 wills could be pleaded which had not been enrolled and enrollment was no longer even called probate.[13] An analysis of the places of probate of the wills of London aldermen between 1380 and 1500 sheds light on the gradual abandonment of the Hustings enrollment. Between 1380 and 1400, thirty-eight of forty-one aldermen (92.7 percent) enrolled wills at Hustings; between 1401 and 1450, thirty-four of sixty-five did (52.3 percent); between 1451 and 1500, only fifteen of eighty-nine did (16.9 percent).[14] London aldermen, who were the most likely group to have availed themselves of city custom and partake of city obligations, chose to disregard this one in increasing numbers as the century wore on. Chichele's register provides a parallel example. Of the seventeen London citizens whose wills were proved there, fully ten have no comparable Hustings enrollments—and among these testators were the former mayors William Waldern, John Coventry, and Robert Oteleye, all members of the inner circle of wealth and power in their city in their time. If such could ignore the Hustings enrollment its significance surely had declined.[15]

The Hustings court underwent substantial change in the fifteenth century. While some conclusions can be drawn from information that was enrolled, in many instances that information became so selective as to provide a distorted view of the larger picture. To infer from those data, as some have done, that certain patterns of gift giving were changing or that former classes of beneficiaries not now in evidence were no longer in receipt of testamentary grants would be to argue on inconclusive grounds.

13. Ibid., p. 641.
14. Mary Bateson, *Borough Customs*, 2 vols., Selden Society 18, 21 (1904–06), 2:cxl, 195.
15. Thrupp's aldermanic list (Sylvia Thrupp, *Merchant Class of Medieval London* [Ann Arbor: University of Michigan Press, 1962] pp. 321–77) was checked against Hustings enrollments.

Bibliography

PRIMARY SOURCES

Anchorite Rules, Devotional and Didactic Literature
Aelred, St. *De institutis inclusarum*. Edited by Charles H. Talbot. *Analecta Sacri Ordinis Cisterciensis* 7 (1951): 167–217. Translated as "Rule of Life for a Recluse." In *The Works of Aelred of Rievaulx* 1. Cistercian Fathers Series, no. 2, pp. 43–102. Spencer, Mass.: Cistercian Publications, 1971.

———. *De sanctimoniali de Wattun*. PL 195, cols. 789–796.

———. Sermon 5. PL 195, cols. 241–243.

Ancrene Riwle. The Ancrene Riwle (The Corpus MS: Ancrene Wisse). Translated by Mary B. Salu. Notre Dame: Notre Dame University Press, 1955. For various editions of text in Middle English, Latin, and French, see Early English Text Society, o.s. 216–. 1944–.

Anselm, St. Letter 22: to Hugo. PL 158, cols. 1171–1175.

———. *Sancti Anselmi opera omnia*. Edited by Franciscus S. Schmitt. 6 vols. Edinburgh: Thomas Nelson and Sons, 1946–61.

Basil, St. *The Ascetic Works of Saint Basil*. Edited by W. K. Lowther Clarke. London: Society for Promoting Christian Knowledge, 1925.

Bazire, Joyce, and Colledge, Eric, eds. *The Chastising of God's Children and the Treatise of Perfection of the Sons of God*. Oxford: Basil Blackwell, 1957.

Benedict, St. *Holy Rule of St. Benedict*. St. Meinrad, Indiana, 1975.

Dublin Rule. See Oliger, Livario, ed.

Goscelin. *Liber confortatorius*. Edited by Charles H. Talbot. *Analecta Monastica 3, Studia Anselmiana* 38 (1955): 1–117.

Gransden, Antonia. "The Reply of a Fourteenth-century Abbot of Bury St. Edmunds to a Man's Petition to Be a Recluse." *English Historical Review* 75 (1960): 464–467.

Grimlaic. *Regula solitariorum. PL* 103, cols. 577–664.

Haeften, Benedict, ed. *Monasticarum disquisitionum libri xii: Quibus S. P. Benedicti regula et religiosorum rituum antiquitates varie dilucidantur.* Antwerp, 1644.

Hilton, Walter. *Epistola ad quendam solitarium.* B.M. Royal MS 6 E III, fols. 120–123. Translated by Joy Russell-Smith in "A Letter to a Hermit." *The Way* 6 (1966): 230–241.

_____. *The Scale of Perfection.* Edited by Evelyn Underhill. London: Watkins, 1923.

Hoccleve, Thomas. *Hoccleve's Regement of Princes.* Edited by Frederick J. Furnivall. Early English Text Society, e.s. 72. 1897.

Hodgson, Phyllis, ed. *The Cloud of Unknowing and the Book of Privy Counselling.* Early English Text Society, o.s. 218. 1933.

Julian. *Julian of Norwich's Showings.* Edited by Edmund Colledge and James Walsh. Classics of Western Spirituality. New York: Paulist Press, 1978.

Lancaster, Henry of. *Le Livre de Seyntz Medicines: The Unpublished Devotional Treatise of Henry of Lancaster.* Edited by Émile J. F. Arnould. Anglo-Norman Text Society. Oxford: Basil Blackwell, 1940.

Langland, William. *Piers the Plowman.* Edited by Walter W. Skeat. 2 vols. 1886. Reprint, London: Oxford University Press, 1969.

Mirk, John. *Instructions for Parish Priests.* Edited by Giles Kristensson. Lund Studies in English 49. Lund, 1974.

_____. *Myrc's Duties of a Parish Priest.* Edited by Edward Peacock. Early English Text Society, o.s. 31. 1868.

Oliger, Livario, ed. "Regula reclusorum Angliae et quaestiones tres de vita solitaria, saec. XIII–XIV." *Antonianum* 9 (1934): 37–84, 243–265. (Walter's Rule)

_____. "Regulae tres reclusorum et eremitarum Angliae, saec. XIII–XIV." *Antonianum* 3 (1928): 151–190, 299–320. (Dublin Rule)

_____. *Speculum inclusorum: Auctore anonymo anglico saeculi XIV. Lateranum,* n.s. 4, no. 1. Rome: Facultas Theologica Pontificii Athenaei Lateranensis, 1938.

Rogers, L. E., ed. *Advice to Recluses*. B.M. MS Harl. 2372. B. litt., Oxford, 1933. (Middle-English versions of *Speculum inclusorum*)

Rolle, Richard. *Form of Living*. In *English Writings of Richard Rolle, Hermit of Hampole*, edited by Hope E. Allen, pp. 85–119. 1931. Reprint, Scholarly Press, 1971.

_____. *The Incendium Amoris of Richard Rolle of Hampole*. Edited by Margaret Deanesly. Manchester: Manchester University Press, 1915. English translation: *The Fire of Love*, Translated by Clifton Wolters. Penguin Books, 1972.

Walter's Rule. See Oliger, Livario, ed.

Whiterig, John. *The Monk of Farne*. Edited by Hugh Farmer. Benedictine Studies. Baltimore: Helicon Press, 1961.

William of St. Thierry. *The Golden Epistle: The Works of William of St. Thierry* 4. Cistercian Fathers Series 12. Kalamazoo, Michigan, 1976.

Biography and Hagiography

Bale, J. *Scriptorum Illustrium Maioris Bryannie Catalogus*. Basel, 1557.

Bazire, Joyce, ed. *The Metrical Life of St. Robert of Knaresborough*. Early English Text Society, o.s. 228. London, 1953.

Carysfort, William, earl of. *The Pageants of Richard Beauchamp, Earl of Warwick*. Roxburghe Club. Oxford, 1908.

Elmham, Thomas of (Pseudo Elmham). *Tomae de Elmham Vita et Gesta Henrici Quinti*. Edited by Thomas Hearne. Oxford, 1727.

Horstman, Carl., ed. *Nova Legenda Angliae*. 2 vols. Oxford: Clarendon Press, 1901.

John, abbot of Ford. *Wulfric of Haselbury*. Edited by Maurice Bell. Somerset Record Society 47, 1933.

Kempe, Margery. *The Book of Margery Kempe*. Edited by Sanford Meech. Early English Text Society, o.s. 212. London, 1940.

Reginald. *Libellus de vita et miraculis S. Godrici, heremitae de Finchale, auctore Reginaldo monacho Dunelmensi*. Edited by Joseph Stephenson. Surtees Society 20. 1847.

Talbot, Charles H., ed. and trans. *The Life of Christina of Markyate: A Twelfth-century Recluse.* Oxford: Clarendon Press, 1959.

Taylor, Frank, and Roshell, John S., eds. and trans. *Gesta Henrici Quinti: The Deeds of Henry the Fifth.* Oxford: Clarendon Press, 1975.

Trokelowe, John de. *Annales Edwardi II.* Edited by Thomas Hearne. Oxford, 1729.

Zupitza, Julius, ed. *Guy of Warwick.* Early English Text Society, e.s. 25–26. 1875–76. Reprinted as one volume in 1966.

Cartularies, Chronicles, and Collections

Amundesham, John. *Chronica monasterii S. Albani, a Johanne Amundesham, monacho.* Edited by Henry T. Riley. 2 vols. Rolls Series 28, part 5. 1870–71.

Bedae (Venerabilis). *Opera Historica.* Edited by Charles Plummer. 2 vols. Oxford: Clarendon Press, 1899.

Busch, John. *Liber de reformatione monasteriorum.* Edited by Karl Grubbe. 2 vols. Halle, 1886.

Crawley-Boevey, A. W., ed. *Cartulary and Historical Notes of the Cistercian Abbey of Flaxley.* Exeter, 1887.

Davies, John Silvester, ed. *An English Chronicle.* Camden Society, o.s. 64. 1856.

Dugdale, William. *Monasticon Anglicanum.* Edited by John Caley et al. 6 vols. London, 1817–30.

Eccleston, Thomas of. *Tractatus de adventu Fratrum Minorum in Angliam.* Edited by Andrew G. Little. Manchester: Manchester University Press, 1951.

Edwards, Edward, ed. *Liber monasterii de Hyde.* Rolls Series 45. 1866.

Foxe, John. *The Acts and Monuments of John Foxe.* Edited by Josiah Pratt. 4th ed. 8 vols. London: Religious Tract Society, n.d.

Gairdner, James, ed. *The Historical Collections of a Citizen of London.* Camden Society, n.s. 17. 1876.

———. *The Paston Letters 1422–1509.* 4 vols. Westminster: Archibald Constable, 1900–01.

Hart, William H., and Lyons, Ponsonby A., eds. *Cartularium monasterii de Rameseia.* 3 vols. Rolls Series 79. 1884-93.

Hodgett, Gerald A. J., ed. *Cartulary of Holy Trinity, Aldgate.* London Record Society 7. 1971.

Knighton, Henry, ed. *Chronicon Henrici Knighton, vel Cnitthon, monachi Leycestrensis.* Edited by Joseph R. Lumby. 2 vols. Rolls Series 92. 1889-95.

Luard, Henry R., ed. *Annales monastici.* 5 vols. Rolls Series 36. 1864-69.

Mason, Emma, ed. *Beauchamp Cartulary Charters, 1100-1268.* Pipe Roll Society, n.s. 43. 1980.

Maxwell, Sir Herbert, trans. *The Chronicle of Lanercost, 1272-1346.* Glasgow: James Maclehose and Sons, 1913.

Paris, Matthew. *Matthaei Parisiensis, monachi sancti Albani, chronica majora.* Edited by Henry R. Luard. 7 vols. Rolls Series 57. 1872-83.

Peckham, W. D., ed. *Chartulary of the High Church of Chichester.* Sussex Record Society 46. 1946.

Riley, Henry T., ed. *Chronica monasterii S. Albani: Gesta abbatum monasterii sancti Albani, a Thoma Walsingham, regnante Ricardo secundo, ejusdem ecclesiae precentore, compilata.* 3 vols. Rolls Series 28, part 4. 1867-69.

Rous, John. *Rows Rol.* London: William Pickering, 1845.

Salter, Herbert E., ed., *Cartulary of Oseney Abbey.* 6 vols. Oxford Historical Society 89-91, 97-98, 101. 1929-36.

———. *Cartulary of the Hospital of St. John the Baptist.* 3 vols. Oxford Historical Society 66, 68-69. 1914-17.

Timson, Reginald T., ed. *The Cartulary of Blyth Priory.* 2 vols. Thoroton Record Society 27-28. 1973.

Trokelowe, John de, and Blaneforde, Henry de. *Johannis de Trokelowe et Henrici de Blaneforde, necnon quorundam anonymorum, chronica et annales ... A.D. 1259-1296, 1307-1324, 1392-1406.* Edited by Henry T. Riley. Rolls Series 28, part 3. 1866.

Walbran, John R., ed. *Memorials of the Abbey of St. Mary of Fountains.* Vol. 1. Surtees Society 42. 1863.

Wigram, S. Robert, ed. *Cartulary of the Monastery of St. Frideswide at Oxford.* 2 vols. Oxford Historical Society 28, 31. 1895-96.

Episcopal Registers, Pontificals, and Legislation

Archer, Margaret, ed. *Register of Philip Repingdon, 1405–1419.* 2 vols. Lincoln Record Society 57–58. 1963.

Bannister, Arthur T., ed. *Registrum Ade de Orleton, episcopi Herefordensis, A.D. 1318–1327.* Canterbury and York Society 5. 1908.

_____. *Registrum Caroli Bothe, episcopi Herefordensis, A.D. 1516-1535.* Canterbury and York Society 28. 1921.

Barker, Eric E. ed. *Register of Thomas Rotherham.* Vol. 1. Canterbury and York Society 69. 1976.

Barnes, Ralph, ed. *The Liber Pontificalis of Edmund Lacy, Bishop of Exeter.* Exeter, 1846.

Brown, William N., ed. *Register of Walter Giffard, Lord Archbishop of York, 1276–1279.* Surtees Society 109. 1904.

_____. *Register of William Wickwane, Lord Archibishop of York, 1279–1285.* Surtees Society 114. 1907.

_____. *Registers of John le Romeyn and Henry of Newark, Lord Archbishops of York, 1286–1299.* 2 vols. Surtees Society 123, 128. 1913–17.

Cambridge. Corpus Christi College. CCCC MS 79, fol. 72. Pontifical of Richard Clifford, Bishop of Worcester (1401–07) and London (1407–21). *Ordo* for the enclosure of anchorites.

_____. Trinity College. MS B. 11. 9, fols. 98v–116v. Pontifical of Henry Chichele, Archbishop of Canterbury (1414–43). *Ordo* for the exclosure of anchorites.

_____. University Library. MS Mm. 3. 21, fols. 189v–190v. Pontifical of John Russell, Bishop of Rochester (1476–80) and Lincoln (1480–94). *Ordo* for the enclosure of anchorites.

Clark, Andrew, ed. *Lincoln Diocese Documents 1440–1544.* Early English Text Society, o.s. 149. 1914.

Clercq, Carlo de, ed. *Concilia Galliae a. 511–a. 695.* Corpus Christianorum. Series Latina. Volume 148a. Turnhout, Belgium, 1963.

Collins, A. Jefferies, ed. *Manuale ad usum Percelebris Ecclesie Sarisburiensis.* Henry Bradshaw Society 91. 1958.

Constitutiones legitime seu legatine regionis anglicane cum subtilissima interpretatione domini Johannis de Athon ... necnon et constitutiones provinciales ... Paris, 1504.

Dahmus, Joseph H., ed. *The Metropolitan Visitations of William Courteney, 1381-1396: Documents Transcribed from the Original Manuscripts of Courteney's Register, with an Introduction Describing the Archbishop's Investigations.* Urbana: University of Illinois Press, 1950.

Deeds, Cecil, ed. *Episcopal Register of Robert Rede, Ordines Predicatorum, Lord Bishop of Chichester, 1397-1415.* 2 vols. Sussex Record Society 8, 11. 1908-10.

Dunstan, G. R., ed. *Register of Edmund Lacy, Bishop of Exeter, 1420-1455.* 4 vols. Canterbury and York Society 60-63. 1963-71.

Flower, Cyril T., and Dawes, Michael C. B., eds. *Registrum Simonis de Gandavo, diocesis Sarebiriensis, A.D. 1297-1315.* 2 vols. Canterbury and York Society 40-41. 1933-34.

Foster, Charles W., and Major, Kathleen, eds. *The Registrum antiquissimum of the Cathedral Church of Lincoln.* 11 vols. Lincoln Record Society. 1931-68.

Fowler, Robert C., ed. *Registrum Radulphi Baldock, Gilberti Segrave, Ricardi Newport, et Stephani Gravesend, episcoporum Londoniensium, A.D. 1304-1338.* Canterbury and York Society 7. 1911.

Frere, Walter H. *Pontifical Services Illustrated from Miniatures of the XVth and XVIth Centuries.* Vol. 1. Alcuin Club 3. 1901.

Gibbons, Alfred W., ed. *Ely Episcopal Records.* Lincoln: James Williamson, 1891.

Hale, William H., ed. *Registrum sive liber irrotularius et consuetudinarius prioratus beatae Marie Wigorniensis.* Camden Society, o.s. 91. 1865.

Hardy, Sir Thomas D., ed. *Registrum palatinum Dunelmense: The Register of Richard de Kellawe, Lord Palatine and Bishop of Durham, 1314-1316.* 4 vols. Rolls Series 62. 1873-78.

Henderson, William G., ed. *Liber pontificalis Chr. Bainbridge archiepiscopi Eboracensis.* Surtees Society 61. 1875.

_____. *Manuale et processionale ad usum insignis ecclesiae Eboracensis.* Surtees Society 63. 1875.

Hill, Rosalind M. T., and Robinson, David B., eds. *The Register of William Melton, Archbishop of York, 1317-40.* 2 vols. Canterbury and York Society 70-71. 1977-78.

Hingeston-Randolph, F. C., ed. *Register of Edmund Stafford, Bishop of Exeter, 1395–1419.* Exeter, 1856.

_____. *Register of John de Grandisson, Bishop of Exeter, A.D. 1327–1369.* 3 vols. Exeter, 1894–99.

_____. *Registers of Walter Bronescombe (A.D. 1257–1280), and Peter Quivil (A.D. 1280–1291), Bishops of Exeter, with some records of the episocopate of Bishop Thomas de Bytton; also the taxation of Pope Nicholas IV, A.D. 1291 (Diocese of Exeter).* London and Exeter, 1889.

Hobhouse, Edmund, ed. *Calendar of the Register of John de Drokensford, Bishop of Bath and Wells, A.D. 1309–1329.* Somerset Record Society 1. 1887.

_____. "Register of Roger de Norbury, Bishop of Lichfield and Coventry from A.D. 1322 to A.D. 1358." In *William Salt Archaeological Society* (now *Staffordshire Record Society, Collections for a History of Staffordshire*), o.s. 1. 1880.

Holmes, Thomas S., ed. *The Register of Ralph of Shrewsbury, Bishop of Bath and Wells, 1329–1363.* 2 vols. Somerset Record Society 9–10. 1896.

Jacob, Ernest F., ed. *Register of Henry Chichele, Archbishop of Canterbury, 1414–1443.* 4 vols. Canterbury and York Society 42, 45–47. 1937–47.

Kirby, T. F., ed. *Wykeham's Register.* 2 vols. Hampshire Record Society. 1896–99.

Lincoln. Lincolnshire Archives Office. Register 3. Dalderby Memoranda.

_____. Register 5. Burghersh Memoranda.

Lyndwood, William. *Provinciale . . . cui adjiciuntur Constitutiones legatinae d. Othonis et d. Othoboni . . . cum . . . annotationibus Johannis de Anthona.* Oxford. 1679.

Lyte, Sir H. C. Maxwell, and Dawes, Michael C. B., eds. *The Register of Thomas Bekynton, Bishop of Bath and Wells, 1433–1465.* 2 vols. Somerset Record Society 49–50. 1934–35.

Mansi, Johannes D., ed. *Sacrorum conciliorum nova et amplissima collectio.* 31 vols. Florence, 1759–98.

Mayr-Harting, Henry, ed. *Acta of the Bishops of Chichester, 1075–1207.* Canterbury and York Society 56. 1964.

More, William. *Journal of Prior William More*. Edited by Ethel S. Fegan. Worcestershire Historical Society, 1914.

Parry, Joseph H., transcr., and Bannister, Arthur T., ed. *Registrum Edmundi Lacy, episcopi Herefordensis. A.D. 1417–1420*. Canterbury and York Society 22. 1918.

Powicke, Frederick M., and Cheney, Christopher, R. *Councils and Synods, with Other Documents Relating to the English Church, II, A.D. 1205–1313*. 2 vols. Oxford: Clarendon Press, 1964.

Raine, James, ed. *Historical Papers and Letters from Northern Registers*. Rolls Series 61. 1873.

————. *Register or Rolls of Walter Gray, Lord Archbishop of York*. Surtees Society 56. 1872.

Riley, Henry T., ed. *Registra quorundam abbatum monasterii S. Albani, qui saeculo XVᵐᵒ floruere*. 2 vols. Rolls Series 28, part 2. 1872–73.

Smith, David M. "A Reconstruction of the Lost Register of the Vicars-General of Archbishop Thoresby of York." *Borthwick Institute Bulletin* 3:1. 1983.

Storey, R. L. *Register of Thomas Langley, Bishop of Durham, 1406–1437*. 6 vols. Surtees Society 164–182. 1948–69.

Swanson, R. N., ed. *Calendar of the Register of Richard Scrope, Archbishop of York, 1398–1405*. Borthwick Texts and Calendars: Records of the Northern Province 8. York, 1981.

Thompson, A. Hamilton, ed. *Register of William Greenfield, Lord Archbishop of York, 1306–1315*. 2 vols. Surtees Society 145, 149. 1931–34.

————. "The Registers of the Archdeaconry of Richmond, 1361–1442." *Yorkshire Archaeological Journal* 25 (1920): 129–268.

————. *Visitations of Religious Houses in the Diocese of Lincoln*. 3 vols. Canterbury and York Society 17, 24, 33. 1915–27.

Webb, John, ed. *A Roll of the Household Expenses of Richard de Swinfield, Bishop of Hereford, during Part of the Years 1289 and 1290*. Camden Society, o.s. 62. 1855.

Whitelock, Dorothy, et al., eds. *Councils and Synods with Other Documents Relating to the English Church I, A.D. 871–1204*. 2 vols. Oxford: Clarendon Press, 1981.

Willis Bund, J. W., ed. *Register of Bishop Godfrey Giffard, Sept.*

23rd, 1268 to August 15th, 1301. 2 vols. Worcestershire Histori-cal Society. 1902.

Wilson, Henry A., ed. *The Pontifical of Magdalen College.* Henry Bradshaw Society 39. 1910.

Wilson, Rowland A., ed. *The Registers or Act Books of the Bishops of Coventry and Lichfield. Book 4, Being the Register of the Guardians of the Spiritualities during the Vacancy of the See, and the First Register of Bishop Robert de Stretton, 1358–1385.* William Salt Archaeological Society, n.s. 10, part 2. 1907.

_____. *Registers or Act Books of the Bishops of Coventry and Lichfield: Book 5 Being the Second Register of Bishop Robert de Stretton, A.D. 1360–1385.* William Salt Archaeological Society, n.s. 8. 1905.

Wood, Alfred C., ed. *Registrum Simonis de Langham, Cantuarien-sis Archiepiscopi [1366–68].* Canterbury and York Society 53. 1956.

Wordsworth, Christopher. "Wiltshire Pardons or Indulgences." *Wiltshire Archaeological and Natural History Magazine* 38 (1913/14): 15–33.

Royal and Municipal Records

Brown, R. Allen, ed. *The Memoranda Roll for the Tenth Year of the Reign of King John, 1207–08, together with the Curia Regis Rolls of Hilary 7 . . . and Fragments of the Close Rolls of 16 and 17 John, 1215–16.* Pipe Roll Society, n.s. 31. 1957.

Dobson, R. B., ed. *York City Chamberlains' Account Rolls, 1396–1500.* Surtees Society 192. 1980.

Collins, Francis, ed. The Register of the Freemen of the City of York. 2 vols. Surtees Society 96, 102. 1897–1900.

Grace, Mary, ed. *Records of the Gild of St. George in Norwich, 1389–1547.* Norfolk Record Society 9. 1937.

Great Britain. Historical Manuscript Commission. *Ninth Report.* 3 vols. 1883–84.

_____. *Report on the Manuscripts of Lord Middleton, Preserved at Wollaton Hall, Nottinghamshire.* London: His Majesty's Statio-nery Office. 1911.

Great Britain. Record Commission. *Foedera, conventiones, litterae, et cujuscunque generis acta publica. . . .* Edited by Thomas Rymer. 20 vols. 1727-35.

_____. *The Great Rolls of the Pipe for the First Year of the Reign of King Richard the First, A.D. 1189-1190.* Edited by Joseph Hunter. London, 1844.

_____. *The Great Rolls of the Pipe for the Second, Third, and Fourth Years of the Reign of King Henry the Second, A.D. 1155, 1156, 1157, 1158.* Edited by Joseph Hunter. London, 1844.

_____. *Issue Roll of Thomas de Brantingham, Bishop of Exeter, Lord High Treasurer of England.* Edited by Frederick Devon. London, 1835.

_____. *Issues of the Exchequer; Being a Collection of Payments Made out of His Majesty's Revenue, from King Henry III to King Henry VI Inclusive.* Edited by Frederick Devon. London, 1837.

_____. *Proceedings and Ordinances of the Privy Council of England.* Edited by Sir Harris Nicolas. 7 vols. London, 1834-37.

_____. *Rotuli litterarum clausarum in turri Londinensi asservati.* Edited by Thomas D. Hardy. 2 vols. London, 1833-34.

Great Britain. Public Record Office. *Calendar of Chancery Warrants, A.D. 1244-1326.* London: His Majesty's Stationery Office, 1927.

_____. *Calendar of Entries in the Papal Registers Relating to Great Britain and Ireland: Papal Letters.* Edited by W. H. Bliss et al. London: His (Her) Majesty's Stationery Office, 1893-.

_____. *Calendar of Inquisitions Miscellaneous (Chancery).* London: His (Her) Majesty's Stationery Office, 1916-.

_____. *Calendar of Inquisitions, post mortem, and other analogous documents.* London: His (Her) Majesty's Stationery Office, 1898-.

_____. *Calendar of Memoranda Rolls (Exchequer) . . . Michaelmas 1326-Michaelmas 1327.* London: Her Majesty's Stationery Office, 1968.

_____. *Calendar of the Close Rolls.* London: His (Her) Majesty's Stationery Office, 1900-.

_____. *Calendar of the Liberate Rolls.* London: His (Her) Majesty's Stationery Office, 1916-.

_____. *Calendar of the Patent Rolls.* London: His (Her) Majesty's Stationery Office, 1891–.

_____. *Close Rolls of the Reign of Henry III.* London: His Majesty's Stationery Office, 1902–38.

_____. *Curia Regis Rolls.* London: His (Her) Majesty's Stationary Office, 1922–.

_____. *Letters and Papers, Foreign and Domestic, of the Reign of Henry VIII.* London: His (Her) Majesty's Stationery Office, 1862– 1932.

_____. *Register of Edward the Black Prince.* 4 vols. London: His Majesty's Stationery Office, 1930–33.

The Great Roll(s) of the Pipe . . . of the Reign(s) of King Henry the Second, King Richard the First, King John . . . Pipe Roll Society Publications 1–. London, 1884–.

Hudson, William, and Tingey, John C., eds. *Selected Records of the City of Norwich.* 2 vols. Norwich, 1910.

Jones, Philip E., ed. *Calendar of Plea and Memoranda Rolls of the City of London, A.D. 1458–1482.* Cambridge: Cambridge University Press, 1961.

Nicolas, Nicholas H., ed. *Privy Purse Expenses of Elizabeth of York.* London, 1830.

Percy, Joyce W., ed. *York Memorandum Book.* Surtees Society 186. 1969.

Wood, Anthony. *'Survey of the Antiquities of the City of Oxford,' Composed in 1661–66 by Anthony Wood.* Edited by Andrew Clark. 2 vols. Oxford Historical Society 15, 17. 1889–90.

Wills (see also Episcopal Registers)

"Abstracts of Wills. Archdeaconry of St. Albans, Register 'Stoneham.'" *Herts Genealogist and Antiquary* 1–3 (1895–99).

Blaauw, W. H. "Will of Richard de la Wych." *Sussex Archaeolgical Collections* 5 (1848): 164–192.

Burtt, Joseph. "Will of Richard de Elmham, Canon of the Church of St. Martin le Grand, London." *Journal of the British Archaeological Association* 24 (1867): 340–344.

Clay, John W., ed. *North Country Wills, Being Abstracts of Wills Relating to the Counties of York, Nottingham, Northumberland,*

Cumberland, and Westmorland at Somerset House and Lambeth Place. 2 vols. Surtees Society 116, 121. 1908–12.

Darlington, Ida., ed. *London Consistory Court Wills, 1492–1547.* London Record Society 3. 1967.

Duncan, Leland L. "The Will of William Courtenay, Archbishop of Canterbury." *Archaeologia Cantiana* 23 (1898): 58–67.

Ferguson, Richard S., ed. *Testamenta Karleolensia: The Series of Wills from the Pre-Reformation Registers of the Bishops of Carlisle, 1353–1386.* Cumberland and Westmorland Antiquarian and Archaeological Society, Extra Series 9. 1893.

Foster, Charles W., ed. *Lincoln Wills Registered in the District Probate Registry at Lincoln.* 3 vols. Lincoln Record Society 5, 10, 24. 1914–1930.

———. "Lincolnshire Wills Proved in the Prerogative Court of Canterbury." *Reports and Papers of the Architectural and Archaeological Societies* 41 (1932–33): 61–114, 179–218.

Furnivall, Frederick J., ed. *Fifty Earliest English Wills.* Early English Text Society, o.s. 78. 1882.

Gibbons, Alfred, ed. *Early Lincoln Wills.* Lincoln: J. Williamson, 1888.

Hale, William H., ed. *Account of the Executors of Richard, Bishop of London, 1303 and of the Executors of Thomas, Bishop of Exeter, 1310.* Camden Society, n.s. 10. 1874.

Harrod, Henry. "Extracts from Early Wills in the Norwich Registers." *Norfolk Archaeology* 4 (1855).

Hussey, Arthur, ed. *Testamenta Cantiana.* London: Mitchel Hughes and Clarke, 1907.

Madox, Thomas. *Formulare Anglicanum, or a Collection of Ancient Charters and Instruments of Divers Kinds . . . from the Norman Conquest, to the End of the Reign of King Henry the VIII.* London, 1702.

McGregor, Margaret, ed. *Bedfordshire Wills Proved in the Prerogative Court of Canterbury, 1383–1548.* Bedfordshire Historical Record Society 58 (1979).

Nicolas, Nicholas Harris, ed. *Testamenta Vetusta.* 2 vols. London, 1826.

Nichols, J., ed. *A Collection of All the Wills Now Known to Be Extant of the Kings and Queens of England. . . .* London, 1780.

Norwich. Norfolk and Norwich Record Office. Testament of Walter Suffield. Great Hospital Records 24/1/2.

Raine, James, ed. *Testamenta Eboracensia; or Wills Registered at York Illustrative of the History, Manners, Language, Statistics, etc., of the Province of York, from the Year 1300 Downwards.* Vols. 1-5. Surtees Society 4, 30, 45, 53, 79. 1836-84.

_____. *Wills and Inventories Illustrative of the History, Manners, Language, Statistics, etc., of the Northern Counties of England, from the Eleventh Century Downwards.* Vol. 1. Surtees Society 2. 1835.

Rye, Walter. *Carrow Abbey.* Norwich, 1889.

Sharpe, Reginald R., ed. *Calendar of Wills Proved and Enrolled in the Court of Husting, London, A.D. 1258-1688.* 2 vols. London, 1889-90.

Turner, Dawson. "The Will of Margaret Paston." *Norfolk Archaeology* 3 (1852): 160-176.

Weaver, Frederick W., ed. *Somerset Medieval Wills.* 3 vols. Somerset Record Society 16, 19, 21. 1901-05.

Woodruff, C. Eveleigh, ed. *Sede Vacante Wills.* Kent Archaeological Society, Records Branch 3. 1949.

Worcestershire. Worcestershire Record Office. Will of Sir Nicholas de Mitton. MS 713, fol. 334v.

Yorkshire. Borthwick Institute of Historical Research, York. Will Registry. Dean and Chapter Jurisdiction. Probate Registers 1-2.

_____. Borthwick Institute of History Research, York. Will Registry. York Consistory Court. Probate Registers 1-4, 9, 11.

SECONDARY WORKS

Allen, Hope Emily. *Writings Ascribed to Richard Rolle, Hermit of Hampole, and Materials for His Biography.* Modern Language Association of America, 1927; reprint, New York: Kraus, 1966.

"Anchorites in Faversham Courtyard." *Archaeologia Cantiana* 11 (1877): 24-39.

Arnould, Émile, J. F. "Henry of Lancaster and His *Livre des Seintes Medicines.*" *Bulletin of the John Rylands Library* 21 (1937): 352-386.

Auden, Henrietta M. "Shropshire Hermits and Anchorites." *Transactions of the Shropshire Archaeological and Natural History Society*, 3d ser. 9 (1909): 97–112.

Baker, Derek. " 'The Surest Road to Heaven': Ascetic Spiritualities in English Post-Conquest Religious Life." In *Sanctity and Secularity: The Church and the World*, edited by Derek Baker, pp. 45–57. Studies in Church History 10. Oxford: Basil Blackwell, 1973.

Barratt, Alexandra. "Anchoritic Aspects of *Ancrene Wisse*." *Medium Aevum* 49, no. 1 (1980): 32–56.

Bateson, Mary. *Borough Customs*. 2 vols. Selden Society 18, 21. 1904–06.

Benson, George. *Later Medieval York: The City and County of the City of York from 1100 to 1603*. York, 1919.

Bettelheim, Bruno. *The Uses of Enchantment: The Meaning and Importance of Fairy Tales*. New York: Alfred A. Knopf, 1976.

Besant, Sir William. *Survey of London*. 10 vols. London: Adam and Charles Black, 1902–12.

Blomefield, Francis. *An Essay towards a Topographical History of the County of Norfolk . . . and other Authentick Memorials*. 11 vols. London: William Bulmer, 1805–10.

Bolton, Brenda, "Mulieres Sanctae." In *Sanctity and Secularity: The Church and the World*, edited by Derek Baker, pp. 77–85. Studies in Church History 10. Oxford: Basil Blackwell, 1973. Reprinted in *Women in Medieval Society*, edited by Susan M. Stuard, pp. 141–158. Philadelphia: University of Pennsylvania Press, 1976.

———. "*Vitae Matrum*: A Further Aspect of the *Frauenfrage*." In *Medieval Women*, edited by Derek Baker, pp. 253–73. Studies in Church History, Subsidia 1. Oxford: Basil Blackwell, 1978.

Boudet, Marcellin. "La recluserie du Pont Sainte-Christine à Saint-Flour." *Revue de la Haute-Auvergne* 3 (1901): 335–355, 4 (1902): 1–43.

Brown, Peter. *The Making of Late Antiquity*. Cambridge, Mass.: Harvard University Press, 1978.

———. "The Rise and Function of the Holy Man in Late Antiquity." *Journal of Roman Studies* 61 (1971): 80–101.

Burton, Janet E. *The Yorkshire Nunneries in the Twelfth and Thirteenth Centuries.* Borthwick Papers, no. 56. York: Borthwick Institute of Historical Research, 1979.

Byrne, Mary. *The Tradition of the Nun in Medieval England.* Washington, D.C.: Catholic University of America, 1932.

Casagrande, Giovanna. "Note su manifestazioni di vita comunitaria femminile nel movimento penitenziale in Umbria nei secc. XIII, XIV, XV." In *Prime manifestazioni di vita comunitaria maschile e femminile nel movimento francescano della penitenza (1215-1447).* Analecta Tor XV/135 (Rome, 1982): 459-479.

Clay, Rotha M. "Further Studies on Medieval Recluses." *Journal of the British Archaeological Association,* 3d ser., 16 (1953): 74-86.

_____. *The Hermits and Anchorites of England.* London: Methuen, 1914.

_____. "Some Northern Anchorites." *Archaeologia Aeliana,* 4th ser., 33 (1955): 202-217.

Cheney, Christopher R. "The Earliest English Diocesan Statutes." *English Historical Review* 75 (1960): 1-29.

_____. *English Synodalia of the Thirteenth Century.* 1941. Reprint, London: Oxford University Press, 1968.

_____. *Hubert Walter.* London: Thomas Nelson, 1967.

_____. "Legislation of the Medieval English Church." *English Historical Review* 50 (1935): 193-224, 385-417.

_____. "The Medieval Statutes of the Diocese of Carlisle." *English Historical Review* 62 (1947): 52-57.

_____. "The So-called Statutes of John Pecham and Robert Winchelsey for the Province of Canterbury." *Journal of Ecclesiastical History* 12 (1961): 14-34.

_____. "William Lyndwood's *Provinciale.*" *Jurist* 21 (1961): 405-434.

Clanchy, M. T. *From Memory to Written Record: England, 1066-1307.* Cambridge, Mass.: Harvard University Press, 1979.

Constable, Giles. "Aelred of Rievaulx and the Nun of Wattun: An Episode in the Early History of the Gilbertine Order." In *Medieval Women,* edited by Derek Baker, pp. 205-226. Studies in Church History, Subsidia 1. Oxford: Basil Blackwell, 1978.

Corfield, Penelope. "Economic Growth and Change in Seventeenth-century English Towns." In *The Traditional Community under Stress*, pp. 31–72. Milton Keynes, The Open University Press, 1977.

Crompton, James. "Leicestershire Lollards." *Leicestershire Archaeological and Historical Society, Transactions* 44 (1968–69): 11–44.

Darwin, Francis D. S. *The English Medieval Recluse.* London: Society for Promoting Christian Knowledge, 1944.

Dauphin, Hubert. L'érmitisme en Angleterre aux XIᵉ et XIIᵉ siècles. In *L'eremitismo in Occidente nei secoli XI e XII: Atti della seconda settimana internazionale di studio, Mendola, 30 agosto–6 settembre 1962.* Publicazioni dell'Università cattolica del Sacro Cuore, Contributi Serie 3: Varia 4, pp. 271–310. Miscellanea del Centro di studi medioevali 4. Milan, 1965.

Déchanet, Jean-Marie. "La contemplation au XIIᵉ siècle." *Dictionnaire de spiritualité, ascétique, et mystique,* cols. 1948–1966. Paris, 1960.

Dobson, Barrie. "The Residentiary Canons of York in the Fifteenth Century." *Journal of Ecclesiastical History* 30 (1979): 145–173.

Dobson, Eric J. *The Origins of Ancrene Wisse.* Oxford: Clarendon Press, 1976.

Doerr, Otmar. *Das Institut der Inclusen in Süddeutschland.* Beiträge zur Geschichte des alten Mönchtums und des Benediktinerordens 18. Münster: Verlag der Aschendorffschen Verlagsbuchhandlung, 1934.

Doyere, Pierre. "Érémitisme en occident." *Dictionnaire de spiritualité ascétique, et mystique,* cols. 953–982. Paris, 1960.

Dugdale, Sir William. *The Antiquities of Warwickshire.* 2d ed. 2 vols. London: John Osborn and T. Longman, 1730.

Eliade, Mircea. *Occultism, Witchcraft, and Cultural Fashions.* Chicago: University of Chicago Press, 1976.

Emden, Alfred B. *A Biographical Register of the University of Oxford to A.D. 1500.* 3 vols. Oxford: Clarendon Press, 1957.

L'eremitismo in Occidente nei secoli XI e XII: Atti della seconda settimana internazionale di studio, Mendola, 30 agosto–6 settembre 1962. Publicazioni dell'Università cattolica del Sacro Cuore, Contributi Serie 3: Varia 4, Miscellanea del Centro di studi medioevali 4. Milan, 1965. For individual articles see H. Dauphin, H. Grundmann, and J. Hubert.

Fitch, Marc, ed. *Index to Testamentary Records in the Commissary Court of London*. 2 vols. Historical Manuscripts Commission Joint Publication 13. London: Her Majesty's Stationery Office, 1974.

Fowler, Kenneth. *The King's Lieutenant: Henry of Grosmont, First Duke of Lancaster, 1310–1361*. New York: Barnes and Noble, 1969.

Gairdner, James. "A Letter Concerning Bishop Fisher and Sir Thomas More." *English Historical Review* 7 (1892): 712–715.

Georgiana, Linda. *The Solitary Self: Individuality in the Ancrene Wisse*. Cambridge, Mass.: Harvard University Press, 1981.

Gibson, J. H. "Compton Church—The Oratory." *Surrey Archaeological Collections* 51 (1949): 154–155.

Gillingham, John. *Richard the Lionheart*. New York: Times Books, 1978.

Goffman, Erving. *Asylums*. Chicago: Aldine, 1962.

Gougaud, Louis. *Ermites et reclus: Études sur d'anciennes formes de vie religieuse*. Moines et monastères 5. Vienne: Abbaye Saint-Martin de Ligugé, 1928.

———. "La *Theoria* dans la spiritualité médiévale." *Revue d'ascétique et de mystique* 3 (1922): 381–394.

Grayson, Janet. *Structure and Imagery in Ancrene Wisse*. Hanover: University Press of New England, for the University of New Hampshire, 1974.

Grundmann, Herbert. "Deutsche Eremiten, Einsiedler und Klausner im Hochmittelalter (10.–12. Jahrhundert)." *Archiv für Kulturgeschichte* 45 (1963): 60–90. Reprinted and translated into Italian in *L'eremitismo in Occidente nei secoli XI e XII: Atti della seconda settimana internazionale di studio, Mendola, 30 agosto–6 settembre 1962*. Publicazioni dell'Università cattolica del Sacro Cuore, Contributi Serie 3: Varia 4, pp. 311–329. Miscellanea del Centro di studi medioevali 4. Milan 1965.

———. *Religiöse Bewegungen im Mittelalter: Untersuchungen über die geschichtlichen Zusammenhänge zwischen der Ketzerei, den Bettelorden und der religiösen Frauenbewegung im 12. and 13. Jahrhundert und über die geschichtlichen Grundlagen der deutschen Mystik*. Rev. ed. with suppl., "Neue Beiträge . . . "

Hildesheim: George Olms; Darmstadt: Wissenschaftliche Buch-gesellschaft, 1961.

Gurney, Daniel. "Extracts from the Household and Privy Purse Accounts of the Lestranges of Hunstanton from A.D. 1519 to A.D. 1578." *Archaeologia* 25 (1834).

Hallam, Elizabeth M. "Henry II as a Founder of Monasteries." *Journal of Ecclesiastical History* 28 (1977): 113–132.

_____. "Henry II, Richard I and the Order of Grandmont." *Journal of Medieval History* 1 (1975): 165–186.

Hallam, Herbert E. "Some Thirteenth-century Censuses." *Economic History Review*, 2d ser., 10 (1958): 340–361.

Hanning, Robert M. *The Individual in Twelfth-century Romance.* New Haven: Yale University Press, 1977.

Harrod, Henry. *Report on the Deeds and Records of the Borough of King's Lynn.* King's Lynn, 1870.

Holdsworth, Christopher. "Hermits and the Power of the Frontier." Unpublished.

Hubert, Jean. "L'érémitisme et l'archéologie." In *L'eremitismo in Occidente nei secoli XI e XII: Atti della seconda settimana internazionale di studio, Mendola, 30 agosto–6 settembre 1962.* Publicazioni dell'Università cattolica del Sacro Cuore, Contributi Serie 3: Varia 4, pp. 485–487. Miscellanea del Centro di studi medioevali 4. Milan 1965.

Index of Wills, etc., from the Dean and Chapter's Court at York, A.D. 1321 to 1636; with an Appendix of Original Wills, A.D. 1524 to 1724. Yorkshire Archaeological Society, Record Series 38. 1907.

Index of Wills in the York Registry, 1389 to 1514. Yorkshire Archaeological Society (until 1893 the Yorkshire Archaeological and Topographical Association), Record Series 6. 1889.

Introduction to the Study of the Pipe Rolls. Pipe Roll Society 3. London, 1884. Reprint, 1966.

Jennings, John M. "The Distribution of Landed Wealth in the Wills of London Merchants, 1400–1450." *Mediaeval Studies* 39 (1977): 261–280.

Johnston, Philip M. "An Anchorite's Cell at Letherhead Church." *Surrey Archaeological Collections* 20 (1907): 223–228.

_____. "Hardham Church, and Its Early Paintings." *Sussex Archaeological Collections* 44 (1901).

Jones, Douglas. *The Church in Chester, 1300-1540.* Chetham Society, 3d ser. 7. 1957.

Jordan, Wilbur K. *The Charities of London, 1480-1660.* London: George Allen and Unwin, 1960.

_____. *The Charities of Rural England, 1480-1660.* London: George Allen and Unwin, 1961.

_____. *Philanthropy in England, 1480-1660.* New York: Russell Sage Foundation, 1959.

Knowles, David. *The Monastic Order in England: From the Times of St. Dunstan to the Fourth Lateran Council, 940-1216.* 2d ed. Cambridge: Cambridge University Press, 1966.

_____. *The Religious Orders in England.* 3 vols. 1948-59. Reprint, Cambridge: Cambridge University Press, 1971.

_____, and Hadcock, R. Neville. *Medieval Religious Houses: England and Wales.* New York: St. Martin's Press, 1971.

Krause, John. "The Medieval Household: Large or Small? *Economic History Review,* 2d ser., 9 (1957): 420-432.

Labarge, Margaret W. "Henry of Lancaster and *Le Livre de Seyntz Medicines." Florilegium* 2 (1980): 183-191.

"The Last Ancress of Whalley," *Historic Society of Lancashire and Cheshire* 64, n.s. 28 (1912): 268-272.

Leclercq, Jean. "Deux opuscules médiévaux sur la vie solitaire." *Studia Monastica* 4 (1962): 93-109.

_____. "Le cloître est-il une prison?" *Revue d'ascétique et de mystique* 47 (1971): 407-420.

_____. "La contemplation dans la littérature chrétienne latine." *Dictionnaire de spiritualité, ascétique, et mystique,* cols. 1911-1948. Paris, 1960.

_____. " 'Eremus' et 'eremita': Pour l'histoire du vocabulaire de la vie solitaire." *Collectanea Ordinis Cistercensium Reformatorum* 25 (1963): 8-30.

_____. "Études sur le vocabulaire monastique du Moyen Âge." *Studia Anselmiana* 48 (1961): 80-144.

_____. "L'exhortation de Guillaume Firmat." *Analecta Monastica* 2, *Studia Anselmiana* 31 (1953): 28-44.

_____. *Otia Monastica: Études sur le vocabulaire de la contempla-tion au Moyen Age. Studia Anselmiana* 51 (1963).

_____. "Pierre le Vénérable et l'érémitisme clunisien." In *Petrus Venerabilis 1156-1956: Studies and Texts Commemorating the Eighth Centenary of His Death,* edited by Giles Constable and James Kritzeck, pp. 99-120. *Studia Anselmiana* 40. 1956.

Lemoing, F. *Ermites et reclus du diocèse de Bordeaux.* Bordeaux: Clèdes et Fils, 1953.

Liddell, J. R. "'Leland's' Lists of Manuscripts in Lincolnshire Monasteries." *English Historical Review* 54 (1939): 88-95.

Mackenzie, E. *A Descriptive and Historical Account of the Town and County of Newcastle-upon-Tyne.* 2 vols. Newcastle-upon-Tyne, 1827.

McCurry, Charles. "Religious Careers and Religious Devotion in Thirteenth-century Metz." *Viator* 9 (1978): 325-333.

McDonnell, Ernest W. *The Beguines and Beghards in Medieval Culture.* 1954. Reprint, New York: Octagon Books, 1969.

McFarlane, Kenneth B. *Lancastrian Kings and Lollard Knights.* Oxford: Clarendon Press, 1972.

McHardy, A. K. "Bishop Buckingham and the Lollards of Lincoln Diocese." In *Schism, Heresy and Religious Protest,* edited by Derek Baker, pp. 131-145. Studies in Church History 9. Cambridge: Cambridge University Press, 1972.

_____. "Some Late-Medieval Eton College Wills." *Journal of Ecclesiastical History* 28 (1977): 387-395.

McKisack, May. *The Fourteenth Century, 1307-1399.* London: Oxford University Press, 1959.

Maitland, Frederic W. "The Deacon and the Jewess." *Law Quarterly Review* 3 (1886): 153-165. Reprinted in Frederic W. Maitland, *Roman Canon Law in the Church of England,* pp. 158-179. London: Methuen, 1898.

Mayr-Harting, Henry. "Functions of a Twelfth-century Recluse." *History* 60 (1975): 337-352.

Morin, G. "Rainaud l'ermite et Ives de Chartres: Un épisode de la crise du cénobitisme au XIᵉ-XIIᵉ siècle." *Revue bénédictine* 40 (1928): 99-115.

Morris, Colin. *The Discovery of the Individual: 1050-1200.* New

York: Harper and Row, 1972.

Nash, Treadway Russell. *Collections for the History of Worcestershire.* 2 vols. London: John White, 1799.

Nichols, John. *History and Antiquities of the County of Leicester.* 4 vols. London: Nichols, Son and Bentley, 1795–1815.

Owen, Hugh, and Blakeway, John B. *History of Shrewsbury.* 2 vols. London, 1825.

Palliser, D. M. "A Crisis in English Towns? The Case of York, 1460–1640." *Northern History* 14 (1978): 108–125.

_____. *The Reformation in York 1534–1553.* Borthwick Institute of Historical Research. Borthwick Papers, no. 40. York, 1971.

_____. *Tudor York.* Oxford: Oxford University Press, 1979.

Palmer, C. F. R. "The Friar-Preachers, or Blackfriars, of King's Lynn." *Journal of the British Archaeological Association* 41 (1884): 79–86.

Palmer, J. J. N. "The Historical Context of the *Book of the Duchess*: A Revision." *Chaucer Review* 8 (1974): 253–261.

Pearce, Ernest H. *The Monks of Westminster.* Cambridge: Cambridge University Press, 1916.

Peers, C., and Tanner, Lawrence E. "On Some Recent Discoveries in Westminster Abbey." *Archaeologia* 93 (1949): 151–164.

Pegues, Franklin. "Royal Support of Students in the Thirteenth Century." *Speculum* 31 (1956): 454–462.

Philippe, Paul. "La contemplation au XIIIᵉ siècle." *Dictionnaire de spiritualité, ascétique, et mystique,* cols. 1966–1988. Paris, 1960.

Poole, Austin Lane. *From Domesday Book to Magna Carta, 1087–1216.* 2d ed. Oxford: Clarendon Press, 1955.

Power, Eileen. *Medieval English Nunneries c. 1275–1535.* 1922. Reprint, New York: Biblo and Tannen, 1964.

Powicke, Frederick M. "Loretta, Countess of Leicester." In *Historical Essays in Honour of James Tait,* edited by J. Goronwy Edwards et al., pp. 247–271. Manchester, 1933.

_____, and Fryde, Edmund B. *Handbook of British Chronology.* 2d ed. London: Royal Historical Society, 1961.

Pullan, Brian. *Rich and Poor in Renaissance Venice.* Cambridge, Mass.: Harvard University Press, 1971.

Raine, Angelo. *Mediaeval York*. London: John Murray, 1955.

Reyerson, Katherine. "Changes in Testamentary Practice at Montpellier on the Eve of the Black Death." *Church History* 47 (1978): 253–269.

Rosenthal, Joel T. "The Fifteenth-century Episcopate: Careers and Bequests." In *Sanctity and Secularity: The Church and the World*, edited by Derek Baker, pp. 117–127. Studies in Church History 10. Oxford: Basil Blackwell, 1973.

Ross, Charles. "The Estates and Finances of Richard Beauchamp, Earl of Warwick." *Dugdale Society Occasional Papers* 12 (1956): 3–22.

Russell, Jeffrey Burton. *The Devil: Perceptions of Evil from Antiquity to Primitive Christianity*. Ithaca: Cornell University Press, 1977.

———. *Lucifer: The Devil in the Middle Ages*. Ithaca: Cornell University Press, 1984.

———. *Satan: The Early Christian Tradition*. Ithaca: Cornell University Press, 1977.

Russell, Josiah C. *British Medieval Population*. Albuquerque: University of New Mexico Press, 1948.

Russell-Smith, Joy. "Walter Hilton." In *Pre-Reformation English Spirituality*, edited by James Walsh, pp. 182–197. New York: Fordham University Press, 1965.

Salter, Elizabeth. *Nicholas Love's "Myrrour of the Blessed Lyf of Jesu Christ."* Analecta Cartusiana 10. Edited by James Hogg. Salzburg: Institut für Englische Sprache und Literatur, Universität Salzburg, 1974.

Salzman, L. F. "A Litigious Anchorite." *Sussex Notes and Queries* 2 (1928/29): 135–137.

Sanders, I. J. *English Baronies*. Oxford: Clarendon Press, 1960.

Saul, Nigel. "The Religious Sympathies of the Gentry in Gloucestershire, 1200–1500." *Transactions of the Bristol and Gloucestershire Archaeological Society* 98 (1980): 99–109.

Serjeantson, R. M., and Longden, H. Isham. "The Parish Churches and Religious Houses of Northamptonshire: Their Dedications, Altars, Images, and Lights." *Journal of the British Archaeological*

Association 70 (1913).

Sheehan, Michael M. *The Will in Medieval England.* Toronto: Pontifical Institute of Medieval Studies, 1963.

Shepherd, Geoffrey. *Ancrene Wisse: Parts Six and Seven.* New York: Barnes and Noble, 1959.

Smedley, Norman. "An Incised Stone from the Free Chapel of Ancres, near Doncaster." *Yorkshire Archaeological Journal* 37 (1948–51): 503–513.

Smith, Toulmin, and Smith, Lucy T. *English Gilds, Their Statutes and Customs, A.D. 1389.* EETS, o.s. 40. London, 1870.

Southern, Richard W. *Western Society and the Church in the Middle Ages.* Baltimore: Penguin Books, 1970.

Stephens, William B. *Sources for English Local History.* London: Cambridge University Press, 1981. Revised and enlarged edition of *Sources for English Local History.* Manchester: Manchester University Press, 1971.

Talbot, Charles H. "Godric of Finchale and Christina of Markyate." *Month* (May 1963): 26–31.

Tanner, Norman P. *The Church in Late Medieval Norwich 1370–1532.* Pontifical Institute of Mediaeval Studies, Studies and Texts 66. Toronto, 1984.

―――. Popular Religion in Norwich with Special Reference to the Evidence of Wills, 1370–1532. Ph.D. diss., Oxford University, 1973.

Taylor, Arnold. "Royal Alms and Oblations in the Later 13th Century: An Analysis of the Alms Roll of 12 Edward 1 (1283–84)." In *Tribute to an Antiquary: Essays Presented to Marc Fitch by Some of His Friends,* edited by Frederick Emmison and Roy Stephens, pp. 93–125. Leopard Head Press, 1976.

Thompson, E. Margaret. *The Carthusian Order in England.* London: Society for Promoting Christian Knowledge, 1930.

Thomson, John A. F. "Piety and Charity in Late Medieval London." *Journal of Ecclesiastical History* 16 (1965): 178–195.

Thrupp, Sylvia L. *The Merchant Class of Medieval London.* Ann Arbor: University of Michigan Press, 1962.

Tillotson, John H. "Pensions, Corrodies, and Religious Houses: An Aspect of the Relations of Crown and Church in Early Fourteenth-century England." *Journal of Religious History* 8 (1974–75): 127–143.

Turner, Edward. "Domus Anachoritae, Aldrington." *Sussex Archaeological Collections* 12 (1860): 117–139.

Turner, Victor. *The Ritual Process*. Ithaca: Cornell University Press, 1969.

Unwin, George. *The Gilds and Companies of London*. 1908. Reprint, New York: Barnes and Noble, 1964.

Vale, Malcolm G. A. *Piety, Charity, and Literacy among the Yorkshire Gentry, 1370–1480*. Borthwick Papers, no. 50. York: St. Anthony Hall's Publications, 1976.

Vandenbroucke, François. "La contemplation au XIVe siècle." *Dictionnaire de spiritualité, ascétique, et mystique*, cols. 1988–2013. Paris, 1960.

Van Wintershoven, E. "Recluseries et ermitages dans l'ancien diocèse de Liége." *Bulletin de la société scientifique et littéraire du Limbourg* 23 (1906): 96–158.

Victoria Histories of the Counties of England. London and Oxford, 1900–.

Warren, Ann K. "The Nun as Anchoress: England 1100–1500." In *Distant Echoes: Medieval Religious Women* 1, edited by John A. Nichols and Lillian T. Shank, pp. 197–212. Cistercian Studies Series 71. Kalamazoo, Michigan, 1984.

Warren, Wilfred L. *Henry II*. Berkeley, Los Angeles, London: University of California Press, 1973.

Weinstein, Donald, and Bell, Rudolph M. *Saints and Society: Two Worlds of Western Christendom, 1100–1700*. Chicago and London: University of Chicago Press, 1982.

Whitaker, T. D. *An History of the Original Parish of Whalley*. 4th ed. 2 vols. Revised and edited by J. G. Nichols and P. A. Lyons. London: Routledge and Sons, 1872.

Whiting, C. E. "Richard Rolle of Hampole." *Yorkshire Archaeological Journal* 37 (1948–51): 5–23.

Williams, George. *Wilderness and Paradise in Christian Thought*. Cambridge, Mass.: Harvard University Press, 1962.

Wilmart, André. *Auteurs spirituels et textes dévots du Moyen Âge latin*. Études augustiniennes. 1932. Reprint, Paris, 1971.

Wood-Legh, Katherine. *Church Life under Edward III*. Cambridge: Cambridge University Press, 1934.

Wylie, James Hamilton. *History of England under Henry IV*. 4 vols. London: Longman's Green, 1884–98.

————, and Waugh, A. T. *The Reign of Henry V*. 3 vols. Cambridge: Cambridge University Press, 1914–29. Vols. 1 and 2 by J. H. Wylie; Vol. 3 completed by A. T. Waugh.

INDEX

Abbots
control over anchorites in early
canon law, 54–55
creation of own "internal" recluses, 55, 68–70; improper, 90
custodial care of anchorite, 16–
17, 72, 156n
delegated to investigate and enclose, 63–64n, 66–67, 83
delegated to oversee probationary anchorites, 72
imprisonment of disobedient religious, 92
intermediaries through whom patronage is dispensed, 156n
legal actions against, 73
legal actions of, 62
licensing religious to migrate to
reclusoria, 65–67, 70–71, 74,
83–84, 90
patronage rights to reclusorium,
62
retiring to hermitages, 55
support for anchorites, 265–266
See also Priors
Adam, anchorite of Gloucester, 134,
139
Adam le Cat, 153
Adinton, Hugh of, clerk, 73
Admonitiones, 295
Advice to Recluses, 297
Aelred, St., abbot of Rievaulx:
ambivalence over solitary life,
102n; letter to the nun of Watton, 92n–93n; Rule of, *De Institutis Inclusarum*, 42–43, 103–

104, 106–109, 282, 294–295,
296
Agde, council of, 54
Agnes, anchoress of Kirkburton,
Yorkshire, 117
Ainderby, Yorkshire, reclusorium at,
78n, 213
Aldermen. *See* London, aldermen
Aldrington, Sussex, rector of church
of, 64–65
Ale, 45, 255
Alfwen, anchoress, 33
Alice, anchoress, wood for, 158
Alice, anchoress of Hereford, 157
Alice, anchoress of Pilton, Devon-
shire, 77n
Alice, anchoress of St. Budhoc, Ox-
ford, 116
Alice, widow, 163
Aline, anchoress of Wigan, Lanca-
shire, 73–74, 169, 188
Allen, Hope Emily, 212n
All Hallows-on-the-Wall (Allhal-
lows), London, reclusorium in:
advowson of cell, 222; priest-
anchorite of, 24, 64n, 255
All Saints, Fishergate, York, ancho-
resses of, 201, 242, 244, 245,
257n
All Saints, North Street, York, anchoresses of, 242, 244, 245; prophecies of anchoress at, 203–
206
All Saints, King's (South) Lynn, anchorite of, 232n, 252
Almoners, 44, 140, 218; details of

339

disbursements lost, 156
Alms for anchorites, 42, 44–45; more available in larger communities, 39–40; non-contractual, 44–45; wills used to continue, 45, 190, 266–267
Almshouses. *See* Hospitals
Alnwick, William, Westminster anchorite, 177–77; reverse migration of to Syon, 179–180; three other contemporary William Alnwicks, 177n–178n
Amesbury priory, 145, 146n
Anchoresses
　gossiping, 108–109
　ideal models of chastity, 104n
　married, 28–29
　more common than male recluses, 19–20, 22
　mystics, 13, 41, 203
　needing protection from their chaplains, 60–61
　predominately lay, 22, 22–25
　prophetesses, 203–206
　social origins of, 25–26
　widows, 27, 165–167, 169n, 182, 182n, 184, *See also* Anchorites; Nuns
Anchorite letters and rules, 13, 31–33, 41, 42–43, 56, 68–69, 94, 97, 102–110, 112–115, 282, 294–298; absence of on Continent, 102n–103n; moderation as theme of, 106, 107. See also *specific rules*
Anchorites
　advisors, 111, 163, 178, 203–206, 281
　almsgiving of, 42–43, 110, 180
　Anglo-Saxons, 25
　arbitrators, 110
　authors, 24
　bequests of, 181, 182n

build own cells, 30, 62, 64, 68, 75, 116, 158–159 (*see also* Reclusoria)
carriers of religious values, 3, 15, 17, 286–288
chaplains, 48–49, 50
clothing of, 106–110
confessors (penitencers), 24, 69–70, 170, 177, 180; earning money from being, 42; prohibited from being, 58, 59
copyists, 24, 287; earning money from, 42
custodians of vestments and other goods, 58, 60, 110–112
daily schedules, 106–108
dependence upon patronage, 2, 15–16, 17, 41–44, 72–75, 90–91; provided by family members, 46, 210–211, 257
dietary allowances for, 48–50
dietary restrictions for, 79, 106–107
esteem of, 16, 82, 87, 88, 96–97, 123, 146–149, 156, 180, 186, 200–201, 234, 269, 271, 282, 288
exemplars, 1–3, 15–16, 151, 288
famous, imparting status upon sites, 164n
gifts of, 199
heretics, 79–81, 110
hospitality of, 32–33, 107, 108 (*see also* Visitors)
indulgences for, 42, 51, 80, 81–82
intercessors, 16, 17, 43, 49, 50, 110, 147–149, 151, 177n, 197, 204–207, 253, 259, 264, 268
married persons, 27–29
migration from reclusoria, 178–180, 211n
mystics, 13
Normans, 25–26n

numbers of, 18–20
orthodoxy of, 79, 80n
perceived as religious, 194–195, 201, 208, 246–247, 263
perceived in company with poor, 159, 195, 246–247
possessions of, allowed to have, 90
private masses for, 49, 77, 174
probation for, 28–29, 54–55, 71–72
prophets, 110, 203–206
providing masses, 49, 64, 170, 198, 252, 259
relationships with outside world, 98n, 110–113, 120–121, 162–163, 166–167, 180, 182
self-supporting, 42–43, 75, 90; dower rights used for, 73n, 165, 166, 169
sex ratios of, 19–20
sexual misbehavior of, 58, 60–61; denied, 81
social status of, 22–29
teachers, prohibited from being, 106, 112–113
translators, 24
travel of, 158n, 204 (see also Episcopal licenses; Papal licenses)
vow of, 99
See also Canons; Friars; Monks; Nuns; and individual religious houses and orders
Anchoritism,
advanced form of religious life, 22–23
ascetic vocation, 7, 9, 16, 101, 104–109, 113–118, 122, 213, 286–287
contemplative vocation, 8, 9, 11, 90, 100–101, 114–115, 120–122, 286–288
countrywide phenomenon, 36–41
feminine vocation, 20–22, 286–287
growing phenomenon, 20–22, 61, 286–287
as imprisonment, 7, 8, 92–95, 99–100, 121–122
lay vocation, 22–29
liminality of, 95–97
open to all social groups, 25–27
permanence of vows, 7, 8, 54, 69, 70, 116–118
responsive to changing religious ideals, 40–41, 122, 181, 286–289
rural phenomenon, 37, 41, 90, 287
superior to monasticism, 97, 101, 284; ambivalence about, 102n, 284
symbolic pilgrimage, 7, 13–14
urban phenomenon, 37–41, 90, 287
Anchorholds. See Reclusoria
Ancrene Riwle, 31–33, 36, 43, 103–104, 106–109, 112, 114, 165, 282, 295, 296; French version of, 165; Henry VIII requests copy of, 185; lands where written, 154; written for three sisters, 33
Andre, chaplain, 152n
Angrum, Alice de, anchoress of St. Mary, Walmgate, Yorkshire, 34–35, 68
Anian II, bishop of St. Asaph, Wales, 86, 191–192
Ankerwyke priory, 145, 146n
Anne, queen, wife of Richard II, 170
Anniversary grants, 42, 193, 207, 266–267

Annora, anchoress of Iffley, Oxfordshire. *See* Mortimer, Annora de
Anselm, St., archbishop of Canterbury, letters of, 56, 103, 104–
105, 294
Anthony, St., 9
Apothecaries, 231
Appulby, Simon, priest-anchorite
at All Hallows, London Wall,
24, 64n, 198, 207, 289
Aquinas, Thomas, St., 296
Arden priory, nun of, enclosure of,
34, 68
Ardland, Gloucestershire, Dean forest: anchoresses at, 159; former
hermit enclosed at, 16, 150,
152, 156n, 159
Aristocracy, 281–282
anchorites, 25–26n, 165–167,
169, 198, 211n
bequests of, 18, 19, 195–203 passim, 207, 208, 214
endowed reclusoria of, 46–47,
49, 173–174, 189–190
family pressures of to support recluses, 196, 202, 207
pensions granted, 51, 134, 135n,
146n, 149, 151, 169, 187–188;
less ample than royal, 51, 134,
187, 257; rise of value in, 188
similarity to monarchy, 186
site commitment of, 189–190
wills of: idiosyncratic nature of,
202, 207; religious orientation
of, 208; responsive to poor,
208, 233; written by women,
198–199, 207
Arthur, Edmund, anchorite at St.
Mary le Bowe, Sherborne abbey, 82, 276
Artisans. *See* Yeomen
Arundel, Thomas, archbishop of
Canterbury, 70

Arundel, William d'Aubigny, earl
of, 134, 187
Arundel, Sussex, Dominican friary
of, reclusorium at, 70, 78n
Asceticism, 9, 101–118, 122; moderation as theme of, 106, 107,
177, 286
Ashurst, Gloucestershire, reclusorium of, 111
Askham, Margaret, anchoress of
St. Edmund's Chapel, Richmond, Yorkshire, 189
Assinis, Sara de, anchoress of
Loose, Kent, 84–85
Audley, Catherine de, anchoress of
Ledbury, Herefordshire, 169,
198
Audley, Elizabeth, 198, 199
Augustinian canons, 66, 71, 222,
296, 298. *See also* Canons; *and
individual houses*
Augustinian (Austin) friars, anchorites, 190, 202, 237, 238,
259, 289. *See also* Friars; *and
individual orders and houses*
Aylesbury, Buckinghamshire, Fran-
ciscans of, 262
Ayleston, Joan de, anchoress of Not-
tingham, 170–171, 177

Bacon, 166
Bainbridge, Christopher, arch-
bishop of York, 76n
Bakers, 259
Baldock, Ralph, bishop of London,
117
Baldwin, blind man, 144
Banbury, Lincolnshire, prison of,
81
Bardeney abbey, 185
Bardolf, Lord (Sir William Phelip),
208n, 285–286

Bardolf, Lady, 285–286
Barking abbey, nun of, 178
Barley, 166, 174
Barrett, Robert, priest-anchorite at Austin Friary, Northampton, 289
Bartholomew, St., 13
Barton, Elizabeth, nun, 111, 121
Barton, Thomas, canon, 269–271 274
Basil, St., 102
Basilia, anchoress at St. Ebbe, Oxford, 266
Bath and Wells diocese, bishops of: Beckington, Thomas, 79; Bowet, Henry, 71; Drokensford (Droxford), John de, 78; Stafford, John, 79
Bavarian Rule, 31n
Beatrice, anchoress at Doncaster Bridge, Yorkshire. See Hodesack, Beatrice de
Beauchamp, 202–206, 281
  Anne, countess of Warwick, 206
  Elizabeth, wife of Richard, 203
  Richard, earl of Warwick, 158n, 203–206, 242
  Thomas, earl of Warwick, first patron of Guy's Cliff, 205;
  Thomas, earl of Warwick, founder of Droitwich reclusorium, 190, 205
  William de, 18–19, 195, 202
  See also Suffolk, Isabella Ufford, countess of
Beaufort
  Joan, wife of Ralph Neville, earl of Westmorland, 206, 207
  Thomas, duke of Exeter, 206, 207, 208, 261; supervisor of Ralph Neville's will, 207
Becket, Thomas, 147
Beckington, Thomas, bishop of Bath and Wells, 79

Bede, 55
Bedford, John, duke of, 189
Bedford, anchorite at St. Mary's, 134
Bedford, anchorite of, 140n
Bedfordshire: anchorite in, 187; gentry wills of, 219n
Beer, 49, 266
Beeston, Yorkshire, anchoress of, 211, 244
Beguines, 21; unknown in England, 22, 38–39
Bek, Thomas, bishop of Lincoln, 79
Belvoir priory, 197
Benedictine
  anchorites, 34, 66–69, 177
  convents, royal grants for, 145n, 146n
  hospitality, 32
  obedience, 69, 102
  rule, 23; basis for organization of anchorite life, 106–107
  See also Convents; Monks; Nuns; and individual houses
Bennyngton, John de, draper, 231
Benton, John, anchorite of Marlborough, Wiltshire, 185
Bernard, Alice, anchoress at St. Leonard, Exeter, 268–274
Bernard, St., 102n
Besant, Walter, 176
Bettelheim, Bruno, 10, 11
Beverly, Yorkshire: anchorites at, 34, 39, 175, 196, 253; friars of, 215; recluse of, 200
Bilney, Thomas, 110, 287, 289
Bingham, Robert, bishop of Salisbury, 20–21, 26n, 59–60, 72
Birkenhead priory, prior of, 64n
Bishop's Lynn, Norfolk. See King's Lynn
Bishops. See Episcopal; and individuals by diocese and name

Bishopsgate, London Wall, recluso-rium 198, 207, 255

Bitton, Thomas, bishop of Exeter, 193

Blackburn, Margaret, 246

Blackburn, Nicholas, Jr., merchant, 247

Blackfriars. *See* Dominicans

Blood-letting, 106

Blundus, John, messenger, 162

Blyth, Nottinghamshire, anchoress of, 44n, 46, 74–75, 111, 168–169

Bocking, Edward, 121

Boclaud priory, prioress of, 131

Bodfelde register, 226

Bodmin, Cornwall, anchoress of, 179

Boleyn, Anne, 121

Bolle, William, priest-anchorite of Chichester cathedral, 64–65, 68, 86, 87

Bolter, Roger, precentor, 273

Bolton, Geoffrey de, hermit, 209

Bolton, John, merchant, 245

Bolton, Richard Lord Scrope of. *See* Scrope family

Bonde, John, fuller, 249

Bonevyll, William, 273, 277–278, 279

The Book of Margery Kempe. See Kempe, Margery

Books, 181, 182n, 201, 215–216, 220

Boston, Lincolnshire: anchoress of, 253; Carmelite friary of, reclu-sorium in, 24

Boteler, John, merchant, 237, 238

Bourne, John, priest-anchorite at Dominican Friary, Arundel, Sussex, 70, 78n

Bowes, William, merchant, 246

Bowet, Henry, bishop of Bath and Wells, 71

Bracebrigg, Thomas, merchant, 244, 246, 247, 253–254

Bradenstoke. Wiltshire, anchorites of, 187

Bradley, Thomas. *See* Scrope, Thomas

Brampton, Northamptonshire, an-choress of, 73

Braose, William de, daughters of, 165, 166

Bread: for anchorites, 44, 45, 46, 47, 168, 266, 272; for poor, 254, 255, 272

Breknow, archdeacon of, 131

Brentano, Robert, 16n

Brewers, 224, 231

Bridges: bequests for, 193, 226, 249, 252, 255, 268, 271, 278, 306–307, 311; indulgences for, 81n. *See also* Public works

Bridgettines, 288. *See also* Syon abbey

Bristol, Gloucestershire
  anchoress of, 61–62; in castle, 157
  population of, 22

Brita, Reginald, canon, 271

Britford, Wiltshire, anchorites of, 159, 162, 165n

Brittany, dukes of, 189

Brokas, Katherine, widow, 27n

Brompton, John, merchant, 253

Broughton, Lincolnshire, recluso-rium in, 70–71

Brown, Peter, 10, 11, 96

Brown, William, 45, 190n, 258

Browne, Hugh, mercer, 234

Buckingham, Anne, duchess of, 198, 199, 207

Buckingham, duke of, 198, 199

Buckingham, John, bishop of Lin-coln, 81

Buckinghamshire, lack of anchorites in, 36
Buckinghamshire and Bedfordshire farm, 145
Buckland, Somerset, reclusorium in, 66
Burdell, Havise de, 153
Burguignon, 140, 144n
Burial day feasting, 274
Burneston, Yorkshire, anchorite of, 200
Burton, Agnes, anchoress, 63
Burton, Benedicta, non-anchoress of Polesworth abbey, 217, 289
Bury, Richard, bishop of Durham, 78
Bury St. Edmunds, anchorite of, 27; his widow, 181–182
Bury St. Edmunds abbey
alms for forty-two reclusoria, 18, 44, 168
Letter of a Fourteenth-century Abbot, 68–69, 103, 104, 106
reclusorium at, 68–69, 90, 265n, 266
Butler, William, merchant, 237, 238, 310, 311
Buttes, Alice, anchoress at Hospital of St. John, Exeter, 272n, 289
Byland, Yorkshire, anchorite of, 196
Byrne, Mary, 104n

Cambrai, Simon of, *inaneus*, 154
Cambridge Rule, 298
Cambridgeshire, reclusoria in, 168
Cambridgeshire and Huntingdonshire farm, 145
Campsall, Yorkshire, anchoress of, 188
Candles, grants of, 44, 48, 49, 68, 266
Canonesses, as anchoresses. *See* Nuns

Canons
anchorites, 23, 66, 71, 120
bequests of, 18, 193n
confessors, prohibited from being, 59
delegated to enclose anchorites, 63
grants for, 145, 145n–146n, 148
See also Convents; Monks
Canterbury, Kent: anchorites of, 18, 111, 121, 195; Dominican friary in, 111, 121, 185, 289
Canterbury archdiocese
archbishops of, 150: Anselm, St., 56; Arundel, Thomas, 70; Chichele, Henry, 27n–28n, 76n, 239, 247, 312; Courtenay, William, 80, 81, 82, 87, 176, 193, 273–276; Grant, Richard, 84; Kilwardby, Robert, 85; Langham, Simon, 82; Langton, Stephen, 21, 57, 58, 84, 89; Mepham, Simon "Stephen", 88, 89; Rich, Edmund, St., 84–85, 88–91; Savoy, Boniface of, 85; Walter, Hubert, 150n
Oxford Council (1222) of, 57, 89
Perogative Court of, wills of, 191, 226–228, 239–241, 258
support for anchorites, 84
Canterbury diocese, 58, 59; archdeaconry and consistory courts of, 259
Canterbury Tales, 220
Carlisle, Cumberland, 81n
Carmelites, 237, 262
anchorites, 24; marched in procession 158n; reverse migration of, 211n
friaries containing reclusoria, 24, 41, 211n, 213
guardianship of anchorites, 41, 213
reclusoria for own friars, 265n

Carré, John, merchant, 246
Carrow priory: anchoresses of, 216, 283–286; nuns and prioress of, 146n, 283–286
Carthusians, 288
anchorites, 24, 287
bequests for, 148, 198, 254; greater than that for other orders, 220–221; noted on Husting rolls, 225
houses of, 177n, 178, 179n, 198; reclusoria in, 27–28, 58, 178
monks: contemplatives, 101; intercession of, 177n, 198; migration of to Syon, 179n; mystical writing for, 114n–115n; petition of to become anchorite denied, 179n
Casagrande, Giovanna, 94n–95n
Catherine of Aragon, queen, wife of Henry VIII, 185
Cave, North, Yorkshire, anchoress of, 63
Cecily, anchoress of St. James, Colchester, 266
Cells. See Reclusoria
Cestreton, Adam de, clerk, 116
Champneys, Robert, alderman, 222
Chandlers, 224, 231
Chantries, foundation of, 183, 204–205, 230
Chaplains. See Priests
Charters: for bequests, 217n, changing status of hermit, 16–17, 150n; for corrodies, 45–46; for endowed reclusoria, 46–50, 119; for maintenance, 44–45, 75, 84–85, 257; necessity of to guarantee support, 43–44, 47–48
Chastising of God's Children, 181, 215
Chaucer, 174, 225

Cheney, Christopher R., 57n, 89
Cherde, Robert, monk-anchorite at Crewkerne, Somerset, 71, 276
Chertsey abbey, monk of, 70
Cheesburgh (Cheselbourne?), Dorset, priest of, 276
Cheshire, gentry will of, 219n
Cheshunt priory, 145, 146n
Chester, Edward, earl of. See Edward I
Chester, Ranulph de Blundeville, earl of, 188
Chester, Robert, 154
Chester: anchorite of, 76; hermit of, 170; reclusoria in, 39; wills of, very rare, 192n
Chester-le-Street, Durham, reclusorium in, 32
Cheyne, Emma, widow, 27, 181, 183
Chichele, Henry, archbishop of Canterbury: pontifical of, 76n; prerogative court of, 191, 239; registers of, 27n–28n, 239–241, 247, 312
Chichele, Robert, merchant, 239
Chichele, William, merchant, 239
Chichester, anchorites of, 239; at St. Cyriac, 267
Chichester diocese
bishops of: Reade, Robert, 64–65, 86, 87; Sefrid II, 267; Wich, Richard, 60, 85, 98n, 111–112
cathedral of: canon of, 267; dean of, 267; dean and chapter of, 64–65; reclusorium at, 32n, 64–65, 68, 86
Childlove, anchoress of Faringdon, Berkshire, 46, 257, 266
Chorleton, John de, Dominican anchorite, 64n
Chistiana, anchoress of Market Harborough, Leicestershire, 157

Christina of Markyate. *See* Markyate, Christina of
Cistercians
anchorites, 71, 119, 212, 276
bequests for, 148
concern over superiority of ascetic life, 102n
Clarefai, William de, 212
Clay, Rotha Mary, 8, 64n
Clementhorpe priory: anchoresses of, 201, 216, 242; widow at, 216
Clergy. *See* Priests
Clerkenwell priory, 146n, 225
Clifford, Richard, bishop of Worcester and London, 76n
Clifford, Thomas, canon, 274–275
Clifford, Walter, 195
Close Rolls, data lacking in, 156n
Clothing: for anchorites, 44, 50, 134, 157, 158, 165, 188, 200, 210, 266; for poor, 229, 254, 255, 256, 311
Cloud of Unknowing, 181n
Cluniacs, 148
Coal, 253, 311
Colchester, Essex, reclusorium at, 134, 135; at St. James, 73, 266
Coldstream priory, 83–84
Collys, Walter, precentor, 74
Colyford, Beatrice of, anchoress, 64n
Compton, Surrey, reclusorium at, 29, 32, 106n
Condet, Agnes de, 18, 195
Constantinople (*in Trullo*), council of, 54–55
Constitutiones of St. Edmund Rich, 88–89
Contemplative life, 8, 9, 11, 12, 93, 94, 96, 100–101, 108; changing perceptions of for anchorites, 114–123, 286–288. *See also* Mysticism

Convents
bequests for, 87, 148, 192, 197, 201, 202, 203, 208, 215, 225–226, 241, 242, 246, 252–255, 262, 268, 271, 277, 278, 283–286
in control of anchorites on Continent, 30n
corrodial grants of, 45–46, 265–266
grants for, 145–146, 154
imprisonment within: real, 92–93; symbolic, 93–94
liminality of, 95–96
migration from (*see* Monks; Nuns)
patronage rights to reclusorium, 62, 222
probation of anchorites in, 54–55
reclusoria in, 24, 29, 45, 46, 50, 55, 66, 68–71, 119, 120, 178, 216, 217, 265n, 273, 283–286, 289
reclusoria under control of, 16–17, 49, 50, 261
setting for a contemplative life, 100–101
tithes for, 130
See also Friaries
Converts, 145, 164
Cookham, Berkshire, anchorite of, 139, 149, 151
Coquet, island of, 55
Corbridge, Angus of, 144
Corbridge, John of, hermit, 81n
Corbridge, Thomas, archbishop of York, 84
Cordwaner, Alice le, anchoress of St. Mary, Walmgate, Yorkshire, 35
Cormeille convent, 130
Corn, 46, 84–85, 188. *See also* Grain; Wheat

Cornwall, Richard de Reviers, earl of, 187–188
Corrodies, 45–46, 168–169, 254
Courtenay, William, archbishop of Canterbury, 80–82, 87, 119, 176, 193, 273–276
Coventry, John, merchant, 239, 241, 312
Coventry, Warwickshire, priest-anchorite of, 118
Conventry and Lichfield diocese: bishop of, Northburger, Roger, 71; registers of, 24n
Coverham abbey, 202
Coxford, Norfolk, anchoress of, 217
Crakynthorpe, William, priest-anchorite of Faversham, Kent, 260
Craven, John de, merchant, 249
Crediton, Devonshire, 271
Cresacre, Thomas de, 47–48, 83, 93
Crewkerne, Somerset, reclusorium at, 71, 79, 275
Crompton, James, 175n
Cromwell, Thomas, 121, 260
Crowland, Lincolnshire, 13
Croxton, John, merchant, 243, 246
Crutched friars, London, 237
Culing, Wiltshire, anchoress of, 188
Cumberland, lack of anchorites in, 36
Cumberworth, Thomas, 219–221
Curci, William de, 187
Curson, Katherine, widow, 252
Cuthbert, St., 13

Dalby, William, hermit of, 169n
Dalston, Cumberland, 81n
Danegeld, 146n
Dante, 10
Darby, Alice, anchoress of Clementhorpe priory, 216

Darcy, Elizabeth, 208n
Darcy, Philip, 208n
De Imitatione Christi, anchorite-scribe of, 182n
De Institutis Inclusarum. See Aelred, St.
de la More, Mathilda, anchoress, 159
de la Tudel, John, 162
Denney abbey, 79
Depeden, John, 215
Derby, earl of, 151
Derwentwater, Cumberland, 13
Desert, as symbol of the anchorite experience, 8–14, 40, 93, 288
Devil, 9, 10, 23, 74, 94, 97, 99, 101
De Vita Christi, 220
De Vita Contemplativa et Activa, 220
Devonshire
    clerical wills of, 267n
    farm of, 145
    reclusorium in, 46
Devotia moderna, 287
Devotional writings, 181, 201, 220, 287. See also Mysticism; Books
Dicons, Richard, 261
Dissolution of the monasteries, 243, 248, 260, 272n, 288–289
Divine Comedy, 10
Dobson, Barrie, 193n
Dobson, Eric J., 165
Dodyngton, John, canon and rector, 268–269, 273–278
Doerr, Otmar, 99n, 102n–103n
Dollebeare, Walter, rector, 37
Dominicans, 237, 262
    anchorites, 24, 64n, 69, 70, 71, 78n
    confessors, 69–70
    houses containing reclusoria, 24, 24n, 69, 78n, 121, 216, 252, 254, 259, 265n, 289

Doncaster Bridge, near Sprotburgh, Yorkshire
anchoresses of, 72, 83–84, 209, 210–211, 213; alms for, 44n; bequests for, 51, 200, 210; indulgence for, 51; legal actions of, 47–48, 73
endowed reclusorium at, 34, 47–48, 51, 83–84, 190, 209–212; custodian of, 209, 210
friars of, 215
Dorchester, friars of, 277–278
Dorking, Surrey, anchorite of, 188
Dornford, Oxfordshire, anchorite of, 157
Dorset, hermit of, 170
Dover castle, reclusorium at St. Mary's Chapel of, 115, 156n, 157, 158
Down, West, Devonshire, 28, 71
Drapers, 224, 230, 254–255; preponderance of among Hustings sample, 231–232
Droitwich, Worcestershire, Austin friary of, endowed reclusorium in, 190, 202
Drokensford (Droxford), John de, bishop of Bath and Wells, 78
Drope, Robert, draper, 254
Dublin castle, anchorite of, 157
Dublin Rule, 13, 33, 103, 107, 109–112, 295–296
Dubricius, St., archbishop of Caerleon, 205
Dunstable, Bedfordshire: Dominicans of, 262; infirm of, 145
Durem, William, merchant, 243
Durham, anchoress in, 75
Durham diocese
anchorites of, 19, 207
bishops of: Bury, Richard, 78; Flambard, Raoul, 56; Poore, Richard, 58–60, 75, 89

legislation for, 59
peculiars of in York diocese, 59
support for anchorites, 84
yeoman will of, 259
Dygoun, John, monk-anchorite at Sheen reclusorium, 24, 182n, 287

Easby abbey, 222
Ecclesiastical
councils and synods, 54–55, 57, 89
legislation, 18, 21, 88
prisons, 80, 81, 238, 272
See also Episcopal
Eccleston, Thomas de, 166
Edward I: alms of, 51; limitations of anchorite patronage, 167–169; as Prince Edward, earl of Chester, 46, 168–169
Edward II: concern for Aline, anchoress of Wigan, 73–74; limitations of anchorite patronage, 167–168, 169; support for hermits, 169n
Edward III, 174: almoners of, 44; coin minted by, 175n; grant of pavage, 209–210; grants to anchorites and hermits, 169–170; protection for anchorite, 118–119; relationship with Henry, duke of Lancaster, 171
Edward IV, 184–185
Edward, the Black Prince, earl of Chester, 170, 171, 174
Ekerdon, William, canon, 199, 273, 277–278
Ela, anchoress at Massingham, Norfolk, 33, 61, 86
Eleanor, queen, wife of Henry III, 46, 168–169
Eliade, Mircea, 10, 11

Elizabeth of Hampole, servant, 200, 201
Elland, Yorkshire, anchoress of, 44n
Elltoft, Elizabeth, anchoress at Doncaster Bridge, Yorkshire, 72
Elmham, Richard, canon, 18
Ely diocese, support for anchorites, 57, 84
Elyot, Edmund, priest, 276–277
Elyote, Margaret, anchoress at Dominican friary, London, 288–289
Emlyn, John, merchant, 237, 238
Emma of Skepeye, anchoress of St. Mary, Dover castle, 115
Enclosure
    complicated process, 15, 98
    extended durations of, 15, 35, 52, 56, 78n, 84, 134, 135, 154, 211n, 213, 232n, 268, 269, 283
    fleeing from, 80–81
    guaranteed support a precondition of, 35, 41, 43–44, 53, 62–63, 72–75, 89, 288–289
    interdict interfering with, 155
    inviolable, 7, 8, 54, 69, 70, 101, 116–118
    licenses for, 35, 43–44, 63, 89, 90
    petitions for, 28, 35, 62, 63, 64, 71, 74, 75–76, 115–120, 169, 184
    probation before, 28, 53, 71–72, 77
    rites for, 56, 76–77, 97–100
    symbolic imprisonment, 7, 8, 92–95, 99–100, 121–122
    without proper licensing, 56, 61, 62, 83; concern over, 90
    without sufficient support, 58, 59–60, 74–75; concern over, 90–91
    See also Episcopal, enclosure; Reclusoria

England: bequests for anchorites of, 148, 200; London only major city in, 38–39; orthodoxy of, 21–22, 79
English Psalter, of Richard Rolle, 212
Episcopal
    alms, 44, 51, 53
    appointment of confessors for anchorites, 77
    appointment of priest-anchorites as penitencers, 24n, 69–70
    bequests for anchorites, 19, 85–87, 88, 267
    enclosure, 53, 55, 63, 65, 64n, 97, 99; delegated to others, 53, 63, 66, 71, 97, 99, 119, 268, 289n
    guardianship of anchorites, 47–48, 52, 53, 56–57, 61, 62, 74–75, 77–84, 88–91; historical development of, 53–57
    indulgences, 51, 53, 80–82
    investigation of potential anchorites: concern over fitness, 28–29, 35, 53, 62–63, 66–68, 71, 72, 74; concern over support, 41, 43–44, 58, 62–63, 72–74, 75, 269
    legislation, 18, 21, 57–61, 88–91
    licenses: for building reclusoria, 64, 75, 116; for changing cells, 70, 77–78, 213; for choosing confessors, 77, 268–269; for choosing a prelate to seclude, 78n; for dietary relaxations, 79; for enclosing anchorites, 35, 43–44, 63–71, 89–90; for entrance into reclusoria, 35, 63, 64, 116–117; for leaving reclusoria in old age, 78–79; for migration of religious to reclusoria, 65–71, 212; for reverse migration, 179; for private

masses, 77; for widows vows, 27n
pontificals, 76–77, 97
prisons, 80, 81, 238, 272
provision of reclusoria, 53, 75–76, 78, 116
rites for anchorites (*see* Enclosure, rites for)
rites for widows, 27n
support for anchorites, 46, 53, 57, 74–75, 84–85, 88, 135n, 266–267
wills, 85–87, 266, 227
Epistola ad quendam solitarium, 103, 298
Erpingham, Thomas, 285
Escheats, 134, 135n, 146n, 149, 151, 174, 187
Essex, anchorites of, 187
Essex and Hertfordshire farm, 130n, 142–143, 144–145, 152n
Eston, Emma, 245n
Eu, Alice, countess of, 166
Eucharist, 107, 295
Eve, anchoress, former nun of Wilton abbey, 103, 294
Eve, anchoress of Preshute, Wiltshire, 155
Exeter
  almshouse for, 278
  friars of, 272, 273, 277–278
  gentry wills of, 219n
  Holy Trinity, 274
  Hospital of St. John the Baptist, 278; poor priests of, 272; poor scholars of, 271, 272; reclusorium at, 272n, 289
  prisons of, 272
  St. Leonard, rector of, 274–275; reclusorium of, 74, 268–278 passim
  St. Mary Magdalene, leprosarium, 272

schools of, 271
Exeter College, Oxford, 182n, 271
Exeter diocese
  bishops of, 46, 59: Bitton, Thomas, 193; Briwer, William, 46; Grandisson, John, 28, 77n; Lacy, Edmund, 66n, 74, 75, 120, 271; Stafford, Edmund, 27n, 71, 119, 179, 268–269, 271
  cathedral of: canons of 268–278; precentors of, 74, 269, 273; treasurer of, 192; vicar of, 274
  clerical wills of, 191, 268–269, 271–278; bequests in kind, 272; not particularly philanthropic, 272
  registers of, 117
  support for anchorites, 84

Farina, 48
Faringdon, Berkshire, anchoress of, 46, 257
Farlington, Hampshire, Joanna, anchoress of, 158
Farne, 13; Monk of. *See* Whiterig, John
Faversham, Kent: anchorites of, 259–260, 267; wills of, 258–260
Fécamp abbey, Normandy, 266
Fellowship of the Drapers of London, 255
Fergant, Richard, 144
Finchale, Durham, hermitage at, 56, 287
Firmat, Guillaume, 94
Fish, 49; allowed for anchorites, 52
Fisherton, Wiltshire, anchoress of, 179n
Fishmongers, 224, 231
Fitzwalter, William, 56
Fitzwilliam family
  connections with Hampole priory, 212

endowment of reclusorium at Doncaster Bridge, 47, 190, 209–211; family members anchoresses of, 210–211; legal actions to force payments, 47–48
Isabel, 210
John, restructure of endowment, 210
Thomas, endower of reclusorium, 47–48, 209
William (13th cent.), endower of reclusorium, 47–48, 209
William (15th cent.), pious preamble of will of, 211–212
See also Clarefai, William de; Wombell, Joan
Flambard, Raoul, bishop of Durham, 56
Flaxley abbey: abbot of, 16; control of Ardland hermitage in sixteenth century, 159n
Folkton, Alice de, anchoress at St. Nicholas, Hedon, Yorkshire, 62–63, 72, 116
Fontevrault abbey, 145, 146n, 148
Food: for anchorites, 45–50 passim, 166, 168–169; for friars, 255; for poor, 269
Ford abbey: abbot of, 71; John of, 56; Robert Cherde, monk of, migration of, 71, 276
Forest infractions, pardons for, 146n
Form of Living, 70, 103, 212, 297–298
Foxe, John, 79–80n
Franciscans, 37n–38n, 110, 116, 222, 225, 237, 255, 262, 272, 286
Franke, Beatrice, nun-anchoress at Winterton, Lincolnshire, 65n, 66–67, 120
Frankfurt, council of, 54–56

Fraternity of the Art of the Mercers, London, 229
Fraternity of St. John of the Tailors of London, 232
Frere, Walter H., 76n
Freschet, Harvey, 150
Friaries
bequests for: aristocratic, 197, 201, 202, 203, 208, 277; clerical, 87, 271–273; gentry, 215; merchant, 225–226, 237–238, 242, 246–256 passim, 310; yeoman, 262
custodial care of anchorites, 39, 40
frequency of and variations in gifts for, 193, 235–238; increasing as period advances, 225
reclusoria in, 29–30, 69–70, 78n, 121, 202–203, 211n, 213, 216, 252, 289
Friars
alms for, 159, 218
anchorites, 24, 66, 71, 158n, 203, 259, 289; confessors, 24n, 69–70; dispensation from guaranteed support, 90; subject to obedience of prior, 203
arrival in England, 21, 110, 166, 286
confessors for anchorites, 213
Frodsham, Chester, anchoress of, 188
Fuel. *See* Wood
Fullers, 249
Funerals, hurried and without pomp, 197, 220
Fylham, William, canon, 272–273
Fyschebourne, Thomas, anchorite of St. Germain, St. Albans, 180, 203, 261

Gardens. *See* Reclusoria
Gateshead, Durham, anchoress of at St. Mary's, 75; new reclusorium at, 78
Gaunt, John of. *See* Lancaster
Geoffrey, abbot of St. Albans, 55
Gentry, 283
  anchoresses, 25–26, 210–211, 213–214
  bequests of, 19, 210–221 passim, 261; extent of for poor, 219, 228
  criteria for inclusion as, 208
  endowed reclusoria of, 47–49, 209
  similarity of patronage to aristocracy, 208, 219
  widows, 28n, 216
  wills of, analysis of gifts in, 218–219, 228n, 284; extent of women in sample, 219, 284
Gerald, archdeacon of Breknow, 131
German, Isabel, anchoress of All Saints, Fishergate, York, 257n
Ghent, Simon of, bishop of Salisbury, 64n
Giffard, Walter, archbishop of York, 44, 51, 62, 116
Giffard, William, bishop of Winchester, 56
Gilbert, chaplain, 129, 140
Gilbert, rector, 63
Gildford, infirm of, 144n
Glade, John, hermit, 199
Gloucester, Humphrey, duke of. *See* Lancaster
Gloucester, anchorite of, 134, 139, 149
Gloucester, honor of, anchorites in gift of, 153, 187
Gloucester, Isabella of, 153
Gloucester, Thomas, duke of, 188

Gloucestershire farm, 145
Glovernia, Geoffrey de, dean of Chichester, 267
Glovers, 224, 229, 231
Godric, St., hermit of Finchale, Durham, 56, 287
Godstow abbey, 146n
Godwin, hermit, 153
Godwin, priest-anchorite of St. Aedred, Winchester, 140, 144
Godyn register, 310
Goffman, Erving, 95
Golden Epistle, 114n
Goldsmiths, 231, 253
Goldwell, James, bishop of Norwich, 78
Goscelin, 103, 104, 114, 294
Grain, 46, 51, 209. *See also* Corn; Oats; Rye; Wheat
Grandisson, John, bishop of Exeter, 28, 77n
Grandmont convent, 148
Grant, Richard, archbishop of Canterbury, 84
Gray, William, bishop of Lincoln, 65n, 66–67
Greenfield, William, archbishop of York, 35, 47–48, 83–84
Gregory, William, merchant, 237, 238, 310–311
Grenewood, Joan, widow, anchoress of St. Botulph without Bishopsgate, London, 182n
Gregory IX, pope, 178
Grimlaic, 30n, 112, 295, 296
Grocers. *See* Pepperers
Grosewell, Agnes, goldsmith, 253
Guilds
  alms of, 44, 192
  anchorites members of, 184, 207
  bequests for, 201, 225, 229, 232, 252, 253, 310

charitable and religious functions of, 225–226, 229, 232, 310
grants for, 218
in London, 224, 231–232
patrons of anchorites, 44, 192, 232
procession of, anchorite in, 158n
rankings of, 224
Guy's Cliff, Warwickshire, chaplains of, 204–206
Gysburne, John de, merchant, 243, 247

Hackington, Kent, anchoress of, 110, 121–122
Haiton, Joan, anchoress of St. Mary Bishophill, Senior, York, 242–243
Haliwell priory, 225
Hallam, Elizabeth, 147n
Halls, Richard, treasurer of Exeter cathedral, 192
Hammond, John, pepperer, 229, 230
Hampole, Yorkshire: anchoress of, 200, 201, 212; Elizabeth of, servant of anchoress, 200, 201; priory of, Margaret de Kirkeby nun of, 70, 212
Hampole, Hermit of. See Rolle, Richard
Hampshire: gentry will of, 219n; levels of anchorite activity in, 36
Hanning, Robert, 93n–94n
Hardham, Sussex
anchorite of, 46
church of, 32n
priory, priors of, 44–45, 46
Hartland abbey, abbot of, 72
Harum, Yorkshire, hermit of, 196
Haukesworth, Alice, 257n
Haverholme convent, 145n

Harvey, focarius, 130n, 140, 144n
Harvey, vintner, 129
Haselbury Plucknett, Somerset, reclusorium at, 56. See also Wulfric of Haselbury
Hawton, Nottinghamshire, reclusorium at, 78n
Heaton, West, Yorkshire, anchorites of, 243
Hecham, Norfolk, anchoress at, 157
Hedon, Yorkshire, reclusorium at, 62, 116
Helmeslay, William, merchant, 246
Helmsley, Yorkshire, anchorite in, 196
Hemlyngton, Adam, Carmelite friar, 213
Henderson, William G., 76n
Henerebarwe, Roger de, priest-anchorite, 118
Henry, son of Henry II, 147
Henry I, 127
Henry II, 150, 155, 159, 275, 281
analysis of patronage detailed on Pipe Rolls, 128–149
anxiety about death, 147–148
change in patronage patterns, 144–146
grant of hermitage, 16–17
growth of support for anchorites during reign, 146–147
monastic foundations of, 147n
will of, 147–149
See also Royal patronage
Henry III, 130, 135, 177
esteem for anchorites, 156, 165
patronage for anchorites, 18, 115–116, 155–167: compared to that for university students, 164–165; escheat practices, 85, 166; geographic extent of, 176; grants (clothing, food, money, reclusoria, wood), 18, 20, 44,

115, 116, 157–159, 162, 165; limited in later years, 159, 167; pardons of debts, 158; pensions, 116, 135, 157–159, 162–163
relationships with individual anchorites: Annora, 159, 165–166; Joan Malewn, 162; Loretta, 121–122, 166–167, 185; Nicholas, 73
respect for asceticism of anchorites, 165–75
will of, 147n
See also Royal patronage
Henry IV, 187, 196, 206, 285
anchorite patronage of, 171–172, 176–177; geographically widespread, 176; inheritance of, 171–175
nomination of anchoress to be nun, 179n
promise to found three religious houses, 178
Henry V, 177–181, 196, 200, 204, 285
attitudes toward ascetics positive, 180–181, 281
foundation of Sheen and Syon, 50–51, 119–120, 178
relationship with Westminster anchorites, 163, 177–178, 180
Henry VI, 27–28, 47, 181–184, 189
relationship with Richard Beauchamp, 204–206
termination of Whalley reclusorium, 182–183
Henry VII, 184, 185; as Henry Tudor, 189
Henry VIII, 7, 121, 185, 189, 260
almoners of, 44
request for copy of Ancrene Riwle, 185
Henry Fitz Roy, 189

Henry of Coquet, St., 55
Hereford
anchorites of, 157, 198; at St. Audoneus, 149, 151, 154; at St. Peter, 72; at St. Sepulchre, 139, 154
churchyard of, 130
infirm of, 130
priory, 130
Hereford diocese
bishops of: Lacy, Edmund, 72; Orleton, Adam de, 64n; Swinfield, Richard, 43, 64n, 75; William, 16
legislation of, 59
registers of, 117
Herefordshire farm, 130–134, 135, 139, 145, 149, 152n, 153–154; anchorites of, 149, 153–154
Heresy, 21, 79–81, 110, 280; "not a problem in England," 53
Hermitages, 16, 55, 152, 170, 204–205
Hermitism, attitudes about, 102n
Hermits, 56, 80n, 93n–94n, 205
allowed to have possessions, 90
alms collectors, 152
ascetics, 175, 205
become anchorites, 16
bequests for, 86, 148, 175, 195–200 passim, 223, 225, 232, 246, 253, 258, 267n, 278
chaplains, 16, 152, 159n, 170, 175, 197, 205
confessors, prohibited from being, 59
freedom to move about, 8, 152
grants for, 76, 169n, 170, 199, 217–218, 232n
heretics, 175n
links between anchorites, 37, 41, 287
indulgences for, 81

mystics, 181n
pensions for, 152, 153, 170, 199
road and bridge work, 81n, 175, 209–210
self-supporting, 151–152
servants of, 152
support of by King John, 151–153
vows of, 77
Hertford castle, chaplain of, 152n
Hertfordshire, clerical wills of, 267n
Heton, Isolda de, widow, anchoress of Whalley, 182–183
Higham Ferrers, Northamptonshire, anchorite at, 149, 151
Hildesheim, anchoresses of, 26n, 31n
Hilton, Walter, 103, 104, 115, 122, 181, 220, 298
Hitchin, Hertfordshire, Carmelites of, 262
Hoccleve, Thomas, 42
Hodesack, Beatrice de, nun-anchoress at Doncaster Bridge, Yorkshire, 48, 63n, 83–84
Holand, Robert de, 73, 188
Holbech, Thomas, draper, 230, 231, 232
Holbech, William, draper, 230, 232
Holby, Christine, nun-anchoress of St. Leonard, Exeter, 74, 269
Holdsworth, Christopher, 95
Holsted, Elizabeth Katherine, anchoress of St. Peter, St. Albans, 184
Holy Trinity, Exeter, 274
Holy Trinity, Huntingdon, reclusoria of, 82
Holy Trinity (ad gressus), Lincoln, anchoresses of, 200, 221
Holy Trinity priory, Aldgate, London, prior or, 44, 266
"Hoppa," hermit of, 195

Horarium (monastic), 107
Hospitallers, 130, 131
Hospital of St. John the Baptist, Exeter, 271, 273, 278; reclusorium in, 272n, 289
Hospitals, reclusoria in, 29, 169, 188, 209, 272n, 289. See also Infirm; Poor, in hospitals
Hotham, Beatrice de, anchoress of St. Peter, Leicester, 82
Hoton, Gilbert de, 163
Hounslow, Middlesex, Trinitarians of, 262
Howm, Robert de, merchant, 247, 249, 256
Howme, Robert, Jr., merchant, 246
Howom, Thomas, merchant, 249
Hoton, John, abbot of Thornton abbey, 66–68
Howorth, Alice, anchoress of St. Edmund's chapel, Richmond, Yorkshire, 189
Huchin, Christina, 182n
Hugo, anchorite, 103, 295
Hulle, Margaret, prioress of Stainfield priory, 65n, 67–68
Hungerford, Isolda de, anchoress of St. Romald, Shrewsbury, 36n
Huntingdon, reclusoria at Holy Trinity, 82; at St. John, Baptist, 79
Husting, Court of. See London

Iffley, Oxfordshire, Annora, wife of Hugh de Mortimer, anchoress of, 156, 165–166
Ilchester, Somerset, friars of, 277
Ilfracombe, Devonshire: poor of, 271; rector of, 269
Imprisonment, as asceticism. See Anchoritism, as imprisonment
Incendium amoris, 13, 201, 297

Indentures. *See* Charters

Indulgences, 78: for anchorites, 42, 51, 80–82, 276; for hermits, 81n

Infirm (sick) of: Dunstable, 145; Gildford, 144n; Hereford, 130; Maldon, 130; Rochester, 145n; St. Albans, 130; "super montem", 140; Winchester, 140; Windsor, 130, 138

Ingram, John, monk-anchorite of 'Swannesnest', near the Tower of London, 118, 225, 230

Insula, Sybil de, anchoress, 63n, 210. *See also* Lisle

Interdict, 151, 155

Ironmongers, 232n

Isabel, anchoress of Holy Trinity (*ad gressus*), Lincoln, 221n

Isabella, queen, wife of Edward II, 35, 169, 170n

Isolda N., anchoress of St. Peter, Leicester, 119

Ivo, hermit at Knaresborough, Yorkshire, 152

Jankyn register, 206

Jannys, Robert, mayor of Norwich, 190n, 254

Jay, William le, 167

Jennings, John M. 226n, 305n, 308

Jerome, St., 93

Jews, 158, 167

Joan, anchoress of Crewkerne, Somerset, 79

Joan, anchoress of Doncaster Bridge, Sprotburgh, Yorkshire, 210

Joan, anchoress of Kiddington, Oxfordshire, 257

Joan, anchoress of St. John the Evangelist, Blyth, Nottinghamshire, 117; alms for, 44n; corrody for, 46, 168–169; ill-

ness of, 74–75; reclusorium used as safe deposit, 111

Joanna, anchoress of Farlington, Hampshire, 158

John, king of England, 128, 129, 138, 150n, 156n
  analysis of patronage patterns, 151–155
  concern for poor, 154–155
  general disinterest in anchorites, 151, 155
  interest in hermits, 151–153

John of Ford, 56

Jordan, W. K., 226n

Judica Me Deus, 201

Julian of Norwich, anchoress, 13, 41, 181n, 203, 214, 252, 286

Juliana, anchoress of Worcester, 158

Juliana, anchoress of Worcester diocese, 62

Kaynesham, William de, canon, 267

Kearsney manor, Kent, lord of, 188

Kempe, Margery, her anchorite-confessor, 24n, 69; her *Book*, 37

Kent
  clerical wills of, 267n
  farm of, 145
  levels of anchorite activity in, 37
  reclusoria in, 289

Kentwell, William de, 188n

Kiddington, Oxfordshire, anchoress of, 257

Kilburn, Middlesex, anchoresses of, 33

Kilburn priory, 101, 145, 145n, 225

Kildare priory, canoness of, 74, 269

Kilwardby, Robert, archbishop of Canterbury, 85

Kingston upon Hull, charterhouse, migration of monk of, 179n

King's (Bishop's) Lynn, Norfolk
anchorites in, 39, 40, 172, 252,
289; at All Saints (South Lynn),
252; Dominican friary, 24n,
69, 252
Trinity Guild of, 44, 232n
Kirkburton, Yorkshire, reclusorium
at, 117
Kirkby Wiske, Yorkshire, anchorite
of, 200, 201
Kirkeby, Margaret de, anchoress,
118; migrations of, 70, 78n,
213; relationship to Richard
Rolle, 212–213, 297
Kirkstall abbey, abbot of, 63n
Knaresborough, Robert of, St., her-
mit, 152–153
Knaresborough, Yorkshire, hermits
of, 169n
Kneesall manor, Nottinghamshire,
188
Knighton, Henry, 79
Knights of the Garter, 171
Knowles, Thomas, merchant, 239
Kydman, Margaret, nun-anchoress
of Carrow abbey, 289
Kyngeslowe, John, priest-anchorite
of Sheen, Surrey, 119, 181

Lacy, Edmund, bishop of Hereford and Exeter, 24n, 66n, 72,
74, 75, 269; clerical wills from
registers of, 271–278; pontifical of, 76–77
Lacy, John, Dominican-anchorite
at Newcastle-Tyne, Northumberland, 24, 69, 252, 259
Lacy family, 171
Alice de, wife of Thomas, earl
of Lancaster, 174
Henry de, earl of Lincoln, 169n,
174
John de, earl of Lincoln, 188

Pontefract reclusorium of, 46–
47, 173–174, 189–190
Robert, 187
Lakenby, Margaret, anchoress of
Pontefract, Yorkshire, 34
Lamberton, William de, bishop of
St. Andrews, 83–84
Lambeth Rule, 103, 211n, 296–297
Lampett, Julian, anchoress of Car-
row abbey, 283–286
Lancaster, Lancashire, Dominican
reclusorium at, 69
Lancaster, 171–181, 190, 206–208
Blanche of, wife of John of
Gaunt, 174–175
Henry, duke of, 171–174, 183,
281; author of Le Livre de
Seyntz Medicines, 173, 212n;
endower of Whalley recluso-
rium, 49, 174, 190; relationship
with Edward III, 171; will of,
175n, 193
Humphrey, duke of Gloucester,
anniversary arrangements of,
206, 261
John of Gaunt, duke of, 174–
175, 189, 199, 285; children of,
206–207; contacts with reli-
gious enthusiasts, 175n; will
of, 19, 172, 208
Thomas, earl of, 174, 205
See also Buckingham; Beau-
fort; Henry IV; Henry V; Henry
VI; Westmorland, earl of
Lancastrian rebellion, 73, 169, 174
Langham, Simon, archbishop of
Canterbury, 82
Langland, William, 42
Langton, Stephen, archbishop of
Canterbury, 21, 57, 58, 84, 89
Latimer, Alice de, anchoress, 169
Layerthorpe Bridge, York: maison-
dieu at, 249; reclusorium at,
243

Layton, East, Yorkshire, reclusorium at, 70, 78n, 213, 215
Leak, Yorkshire, anchoress at, 197
Leclercq, Jean, 93
Ledbury, Herefordshire, anchoress of, 169, 198
Legal actions, 44-45, 47-48, 62, 72-73, 289
Legenda. See Synodal Statutes of an Unknown Province
Leicester
  anchorites in, 175; at St. Peter's, 79, 82, 119, 176
  Lollardy in, 79-80
Leicester, Loretta, countess of, anchoress of Hackington, Kent, relationship with Henry III, 121-122, 165, 166-167, 185; support of friars, 110, 166, 286
Leicestershire, rector in, 193
Lemoing, F., 102n-103n
Lench, Payne de, anchoress of Ardland, Gloucestershire, 158-159
Lent, restrictions during, 108, 109
Lepers, bequests or grants for: aristocratic, 197, 201, 208; clerical, 86, 192, 193, 268, 271-272; merchant, 226, 238, 242, 246, 252, 253, 256, 310; royal, 148, 153
Lercedekne, Elizabeth, widow, 273n
Lerchedeken, Martin, canon, 271-273
Lerchedeken, Michael, canon, 273
Lestrange family, accounts of, 217
Letherhead, Surrey, reclusorium in church of, 32
Letter of a Fourteenth-century Abbot of Bury St. Edmunds, 68-69, 103, 106, 297
Letter of Walter Hilton. See Epistola ad quendam solitarium
Lewknor, Raymond, 260

Lexington, Henry, bishop of Lincoln, 266-267
Liber confortatorius, 103, 104, 114, 294
Liber Vitae, 127
Lina, anchoress at St. John the Poor, Lincoln(?), 45, 266-267
Lincoln, earl of. See Lacy
Lincoln
  anchorites in, 39, 252, 289; at hospital, 169; at St. John the Poor, 266
  gentry wills of, 219n
  population of, 38
Lincoln diocese
  anchorites in, 264
  bishops of, 45: Bek, Thomas, 79; Buckingham, John, 81; Gray, William, 65n, 66-67; Lexington, Henry, 266-267; Repingdon, Philip, 119; Russell, John, 76n
  cathedral church, canon of, 200
  wills of, 258, 264
Lincolnshire, levels of anchorite activity in, 36, 37
Linen, for underclothes, 52; bequest of, 221
Lingen, Brian of, 295n
Lisle, Anabel and Helen de, anchoresses of Doncaster Bridge, Yorkshire, 209, 210
Lisle, Jane Viscountess, 234, 237, 238, 254-255
Lives of the Saints, 215
Le Livre de Seyntez Medicines, 173
Logge register, 226
Lollard rebellion, 196
Lollardy, 79-82, 119, 175n, 214n. See also Piety; Wills
London, John, monk-anchorite of Westminster, 178n, 180n, 200, 207

London, Middlesex
aldermen of, 222, 224, 234, 239, 254, 310; abandonment of Hustings enrollment by, 312; guild memberships of, 231
anchorite activity in, 36–37, 224–225, 234
anchorites of, 19, 39, 44, 78n, 159, 170, 175, 198, 207, 217, 223–238 passim, 266, 310; at All Hallows-on-the-Wall (Allhallows), 24, 222, 255, 289; Bishopsgate, London Wall, 198, 207, 255; Dominican Friary, 288–289; St. Botulph without Bishopsgate, 176, 181; St. Dunstan, 116; St. Giles without Holborn, 225; St. Lawrence, Jewry, 34, 225; St. Margaret Pattens, 157–158; St. Peter, Cornhill, 27–28, 117, 225; 'Swannesnest' near the Tower of London, 119, 225; Tower of London, 158
citizens of, 239; criteria for, 223–224
Charterhouse, monks of, 177, 198, 311
Clerkenwell priory, nuns of, 146n, 225
Court of Husting, 19, 235, 239, 241, 247; analysis of wills of, 191, 195, 223–233; criteria for enrollment at, 223–224, 306–307; gradual cessation of enrollment at, 308, 312; limitations of rolls, 227–228, 305–312
friars, five orders of in, 311
guilds of, 224, 231–232, 234, 310–311; Drapers, 231–233; Mercers, 229; Pepperers, 310; Tailors, 232, 310
Haliwell priory, 225

hermits of, 170, 175, 225
House of Converts, master of, 116
Holy Trinity priory, Aldgate, 44, 266
Jews of, 158, 167
leprosaria of, 238
London Bridge, 226, 306–307, 310
mayors of, 234, 239, 254, 310
merchants of: generality of bequests of, 224–225, 229–230; high status of group, 224, 234, 238; preponderance of drapers in Hustings group, 230–232, 255
Newgate, Franciscans of, 262, 311
Poor Clares of, 225, 254, 311
population of, 38
prisons of, 238
St. Katherine by the Tower, 225
St. Martin le Grand, 18
St. Michael, Cornhill, 254
St. Mary Bothawe, 230
St. Paul, 175, 225
wills of: clerical, 267n; gentry, 219n; merchant, 195, 223–241
London diocese
bishops of, 27n, 59: Baldock, Ralph, 117; Clifford, Richard, 76n
registers of, 117
support of anchorites, 57, 84
Long Bredy, Dorset, rector of, 277
Loose, Kent, reclusorium at, 84–85
Love, Nicholas, 215–216
Lucas, John hermit of Shelford, Cambridgeshire, 81n
Luffenham register, 226, 238, 239–240
Lydeford, John de, archdeacon, 274
Lyhert, Walter, bishop of Norwich, 86, 285

Lyle, Richard, cannon-anchorite, 120
Lyndwood, William, 88–91, 265n
Lynn, Norfolk. *See* King's Lynn, Norfolk
Lyre convent, 130

McFarlane, Kenneth B., 214
McHardy, A. K., 194n
Magdalen College, Oxford, 182n
Maidens, poor. *See* Poor, maidens
Maisondieux. *See* Poor, endowments; York, maisondieux
Maldon, Essex: anchorite of, 134, 138, 139, 149; infirm of, 130
Malet, Maud, anchoress of St. Dunstan, London, 116
Malewn, Joan, anchoress of Britford, Wiltshire, 162
Malmesbury, Wiltshire, reclusorium at, 116
Mann, Katherine, anchoress at Dominican Friary, Norwich, 110, 254, 287, 289
Mannyngham, Oliver, 216, 219n
Marche register, 226, 238, 239–240
Margaret, anchoress of Bodmin, Cornwall, migration to Syon, 179
Margaret, anchoress of Hereford, 154, 155
Margaret, anchoress of St. Edward, Norwich, 46
Margaret, anchoress of St. Leonard, Grantham, Lincolnshire, 188
Margery the Anchorite (Margeria le Auncre), 73n
Marhamchurch, Cornwall, reclusorium at, 72
Mariun, anchoress at Kearsney, Kent, 188
Marius, priest, 140
Markele, Robert, merchant, 237, 238, 239

Market Harborough, Leicestershire, anchoress of, 157
Markyate, Christina of, recluse, 33, 93–94n; *Life* of, 37, 41, 127, 287
Marlborough, Wiltshire
anchorites of, 149, 185, 198, 199; at St. Mary's, 155
poor of, 149
Martha, widow, 167
Martin V, pope, 180
Mary the Egyptian, St., 9
Masham. *See* Scrope family
Massingham, Norfolk, anchoresses of, 33, 61, 86
Matilda, anchoress of Holy Trinity (*ad gressus*), Lincoln, 221n
Matilda, anchoress of St. Peter, Leicester, 79–81, 87, 110, 176
Maxtox priory, prior of, 118
Mayors, 191, 223, 234, 239, 247–249, 252, 254, 259
Mayr-Harting, Henry, 110
Meaus, Beatrice de, anchoress of St. Peter, Cornhill, London, 117
Meditationes Vitae Christi, 215, 220
Medmenham abbey, former monk of, 118–119
Melsa, John of, and Beatrice, 63
Melton, William, archbishop of York, 117
Members of Parliament, 247, 252
Mental hospitals, 95–96
Mepham, Simon "Stephen", archbishop of Canterbury, 88–89
Mercers, 224, 229, 231–232n, 234
Merchants, 233n, 284, 286
anchorite-favoring: charitable responses of 224, 232–233, 238, 247, 248, 249–253, 255, 283; high status of, 224, 234, 238, 247, 256; positive attitudes of, 39, 235, 283

patronage largely known through wills, 222–223
rights of presentation to reclusoria, 222
wills of, 168, 195, 223–255; general bequests predominate, 224–225, 242, 283, 286
Mersdon, John, rector, 193
Middlesex: levels of anchorite activity in, 36–37; patronage for anchorites of, 187
Miliana, anchoress of Steyning, Sussex, 44–45, 72, 86
Mirk, John, 91n
Monasteries. See Convents
Monk of Farne. See Whiterig, John
Monks
anchorites, 22, 24, 90, 118–119, 162–163, 177n–178n; confessors, 24n, 70, 163, 177–178; migration to anchoritic life, 65–66, 68–69, 70–71, 90; petition to migrate denied, 179n; probation for, 54–55; properly under episcopal control, 90; reverse migration of, 178–180; supported by monastery, 69, 90; under obedience of own superior, 68–69
bequests for, 148 (see also Convents)
confessors, 49, 69; prohibited from, 59
entrance into community, 47
See also Canons; Friars; Nuns; and individual orders
Montpellier, 232–233n
Le Morte d'Arthur, 32
Moretano, Gilbert de, 144n
Mortimer, Annora de, anchoress of Iffley, Oxfordshire, 165–166, 169
Moxby priory, 145n

Moys, Cecilia (Lucie), anchoress of Marhamchurch, Cornwall, 58, 71–72, 77
Muchelney, Somerset, vicar of, 78
Murder, pardons of fines for, 146n
Muriel, anchoress of Campsall, Yorkshire, 188
Murymouth, John, monk-anchorite of Westminster abbey, 163n, 170, 178n
Muscegros, Agnes, anchoress at North Cave, Yorkshire, 63, 117
Mustral, William de, 187
Myrrour of the Blessed Lyf of Jesu Christ, 215–216
Mysticism, 12, 40–41, 101, 114, 115, 122–123, 213: anchorite connections to, 181n, 286–288; growth of in fourteenth century, 40, 95, 115; limited in early rules, 114–115; literature of, 122, 181n, 215–216, 287; Norwich in center of movement, 214

Neel, William, merchant, 239
Neville, Ralph. See Westmorland, earl of
Neville, Richard, earl of Warwick, 206
Neville, William, "Lollard" knight, 214n
Newcastle-upon-Tyne, Northumberland
Dominican friary of, reclusorium at, 24, 69, 252, 259
maisondieu of, 252
Tyne Bridge, 252
Newham, Adam of, 131n
Newnham, Gloucestershire, anchorite of, 131, 135, 139, 151, 154
Newnham abbey, abbot of, 64n

Newton, Matilda, abbess of Syon, anchoress, 178–179
Nicholas, anchorite of Crediton, Devonshire, 46
Nicholas, anchorite of Westminster abbey, 116, 162–163
Nicholas, ostiary, 144
Noble, coin, 175
Norfolk: clerical wills of, 267n; levels of anchorite activity in, 36–37, 168
Norman, John, merchant, 246
Northburger, Roger, bishop of Coventry and Lichfield, 71
Northampton
    Lollardy in, 79–81
    reclusoria: Austin friary, 289; Domincan friary, 259, 289; St. Peter, 79, 81
    St. James, prison, 80
Norton, Cecily, widow, anchoress of St. Margaret, Westminster, 184
Norton priory, 71
Norwich
    anchorites of, 13, 39, 40, 41, 46, 86, 110, 216, 223, 254, 285; at Carmelite friary, 158n, 211n, 213; Carrow priory, 216, 283–286, 289; Dominican friary, 216, 254, 259; St. Edward, 46
    Carrow priory, 146n, 283–286
    hermit of, 223
    Julian of, 13, 41, 181n, 203, 214, 252, 286
    population of, 38
    St. George, guild of, 158n
    St. Giles, hospital, 249
    wills of, 284–286; clerical, 191, 222, 267n; gentry, 219n; merchant, 191, 222, 249; providing annuities, 190n, 254; yeoman and artisan, 258, 259

Norwich diocese
    bequests for anchorites of, 19, 86
    bishops of, 98n: Goldwell, James, 78; Lyhert, John, 86; Suffield, Walter, 19, 33, 60–61, 85–86, 98n; Wakering, John, 86
    support of anchorites, 84
Not, John, pepperer, 229, 230
Nottingham, anchoress of, bequest for, 217
Nottingham, anchoress seeking reclusorium in, 116
Nottingham, Joan, anchoress of, 170, 177
Nottingham and Derbyshire farm, 145n
Nun Appleton, Yorkshire, anchoress of, 197
Nuns, 58–59
    anchoresses, 34, 68, 74, 120, 178–179, 212, 289; rarity of, 22, 24–25
    bequests for, 148, 225
    disobedient, 92n–93n
    grants for, 140, 145
    ideal models of chastity and virture, 104n
    migration to anchoritic life, 65n, 66–68, 74, 83–84; petition for, 117, 120
    See also Convents
"Nuns of the forest," 138

Oats, 49, 166, 174
Ockam, Peter of, 167
Odolina, anchoress of Crewkerne, Somerset, 275
Oil, 49. See also Candles
Oriel College, Oxford, 272
Orleans, council of, 54
Orleton, Adam de, bishop of Hereford, 64n

Ormeshede, William, merchant, 249
Orum, John, canon, 272–273
Osbert, *homo regine*, 154
Oseney abbey, 46, 257
Oteleye, Robert, merchant, 239, 312
Otery, Richard de, vicar of St. Calixtus, 28
Oxford, anchorites of, 18, 168, 252; at St. Bodhuc, 116; St. Ebbe, 266
Oxford Council (1222), 57, 89
Oxford University, 182n, 205, 213, 243, 271, 272
Oxfordshire: levels of anchorite activity in, 36; pensions for anchorites in, 83; hermit in, 170

The Pageants of Richard Beauchamp, Earl of Warwick, 206
Painters, 224, 231
Palmer, Anna, anchoress of St. Peter, Northampton, 81
Papal licenses: for change of cells, 70, 77–78; for migration to anchoritic life, 66; denial of, 179n; for pilgrimage and travel, 77–78; for plenary remission, 77, 184; for private confessors, 77
Papworth, Elena de, 154
Paris, Matthew, 159
Paston, John, 216
Paston, Margaret, 216
Patrick, Geoffrey, scribe, 230
Paucamatus, 140, 144n
Paul of Thebes, St., 9
Peas, 48
Pegues, Franklin, 164
Pekard, Richard, priest-anchorite of Dominican friary, Lancaster, 69

Peke, Richard, 217
Penrith, Cumberland, 81n
Pensax, Margery, anchoress of Hawton, Nottinghamshire and St. Botulph without Bishopsgate, London, 78n, 176, 181
Pepperers, 224, 229, 231–232, 234
Perugia, anchorites of, 30n
Peter, priest, 140
Peter, prior of Holy Trinity, Aldgate, London, 266
Peter the Venerable, 102n
Peterborough abbey, 265–266
Pevesia, Berkshire, anchorite of, 134, 138, 139
Phelip, William. *See* Bardolf
Philip, abbot of Hartland abbey, 72
Piety, penitential quality of in upper classes, 173, 197, 198, 211–212, 214, 220, 287; Lollardlike, 214
Pilgrimages, 77–78, 196, 205, 216; bequests for, 225, 249–252. *See also* Anchoritism, symbolic pilgrimage
Pilton, Devonshire, 77n
Pipe Rolls, 127; analysis of, 128–130; continuity of lacking in later reigns, 156; limitations of, 150n, 155n, 156n
Playden, Sussex, anchoress of, 266
Plumpton, John, merchant, 252
Plymouth, Devonshire, lepers of, 273n
Plympton, Devonshire, friars of, 273n
Poitou, William, count of, 134, 138, 187
Polesworth abbey, reclusorium of, 68, 217, 289
Polsloe priory, 145n, 146n
Polton, Thomas, bishop of Worcester, 86

Pontefract, Yorkshire
anchoresses at, 34, 78, 175, 244
endowed reclusorium at the
chapel of St. Helen, 46–47,
173–174, 177, 188, 189–190
friars of, 215
Pontificals. *See* Episcopal, pontificals
Poor, 86, 87, 149, 150, 159, 208,
226–230, 241–249 passim
on burial day, 87, 201, 221, 228,
241, 246, 254
endowments for, 154, 210, 248–
249, 252, 254, 278
fathers, 242, 256
in hospitals, 159, 197, 208, 226–
230 passim, 242, 246–256 passim
households, 254, 310
maidens (dowerless), 148, 208,
228, 241, 246, 254, 255, 311
merchants, 229, 241, 256
orphans, 253
priests, 242, 271, 273
relations, 228
scholars, 208, 218, 271, 272,
277, 311
servants, 154, 228n
tenants, 197, 228n
widows, 229, 242, 254, 255, 311
work-related, 229, 256
Poor Clares, London, 225, 254
Poore, Richard, bishop of Salisbury
and Durham, 58–59, 75, 89
Potters, 231
Poundestoke, William, canon, 272n
Prates, Richard, Vicar General, 71
Premonstratensians, bequests for,
148
Preshute, Wiltshire, anchoress of,
155
Prick of Conscience, 201, 215

Priests
anchorites, 48, 49, 50, 56, 64–65,
82, 91, 118, 119, 170, 180,
182n; confessors, 24, 111, 180;
providing masses, 49, 64, 170,
198, 252, 259, 260
bequests for anchorites, 18, 19,
85–87, 191–192, 259, 261, 267–
268, 269, 271–273, 277
chantry priests, 197, 205–206;
salaries of, 177
chaplains or confessors for anchorites, 77, 78, 174, 212
delegated to enclose anchorites,
63–64n, 71
delegated to oversee probation
of anchoresses, 28, 72
influence on others when writing wills, 192, 199, 277–279
supervising anchorites, 56, 105;
sexual misbehavior of when,
58, 60–61, 89, 91, 98n
support for anchorites, 257–258,
265–267; one element in philanthropy, 283
university students, 164–165
wills of, 191–192, 243–244, 267–
278
See also Abbots; Canons; Friars;
Hermits; Monks; Poor, priests
and scholars; Priors
Prioresses
alms of, 266
bequests for, 284
imprisonment of disobedient
nuns, 92
licenses for migrations of nuns,
65n, 67, 74, 83–84
pension for, 131
Priors
alms of, 44, 45
anchorites, 46
consent to build reclusorium, 55

delegated to enclose anchorites, 63–64n, 118
grant for, 73
legal action against, 44–45
support for anchorites, 46
Prisoners, bequests for: aristocracy, 208; clerical, 268, 271–272; gentry, 218; merchant, 238, 242, 246, 252, 254, 256, 310; women likely to provide, 198
Prisons, 80, 81, 92–93, 238, 272
Probation, 28–29, 54–55, 71–72
Provinciale, 88–91
Pruet, William, priest-anchorite of Restormel, Cornwall, 170
Public works, 208, 226, 241, 268, 272, 310. *See also* Bridges; Road repair
Purdance, Margaret, 216
Purgation, 11, 113–115

Ralph, *apostolicus*, 139
Randleston, Suffolk, anchorite of, 134, 135
Raventhorpe, John, chaplain, 244
Rawgton, Emma, anchoress of All Saints, North Street, York, 203–206, 242, 245
Read, Robert, bishop of Chichester, 64–65, 86, 87
Reclusoria
access to adjoining church or chapel, 48, 64, 98n
altars within, 31, 99
building of, 20–21, 30, 46, 62, 64, 68, 75, 78, 116, 118, 158–159, 180, 288–289; repair or expansion of, 158, 162
demolished due to inadequate endowment, 21, 60–61, 72
depositories for valuables, 58, 60, 110, 111–112; broken into for, 111
distribution countrywide, 36–41

dimensions of, 31–34, 36n, 64, 106
doors of: blocking of in enclosure rite, 92, 98; construction of, 78, 98n
endowed, 21, 24, 46–50, 51, 119, 173–174, 178, 189–190, 202–203, 209–211, 260; dissolution of endowment, 182–183
famous sites, desire of anchorites to be enclosed within, 164n
gardens, 31, 50, 73n, 78, 98n; anchorite paying rent for, 50
guest rooms, 32, 33
inherited by younger companions, 34
inherited by servants, 26
multiple households, 33–35, 174, 188n, 209, 225; common on Continent, 30n
no egress from, 71
presentation to, 30, 49, 55, 61–62, 64–65, 115–116, 119, 169, 202–203, 210, 222; limited by overview of bishop, 49, 61; rights of interested parties, 63, 64–65, 66, 74, 116
provision of: by anchorites, 28, 30, 35, 64, 75; by bishops, 53, 75–76, 116
sepulchres within, 106
sevants quarters, 32–33
single households, 30
site commitments, 84–85, 128–129, 134, 184, 189–190
symbolic of desert, 8–9, 288
symbolic grave, 93n, 99n
symbolic prison, 8, 93–95, 100
symbolic street corner, 110
windows, 31–32, 60, 61, 98n
See also Enclosure
Reginald the Mason, 168
Reginald, priest, 140
Relics, 205, 220, 281

Repingdon, Philip, bishop of Lincoln, 58
Restormel, Cornwall, William Pruet, priest-anchorite at, 170
Reyerson, Katherine, 232n–233n
Rich, Edmund, St., archbishop of Canterbury, 84; "canon" of, 88–91
Richard, anchorite of Hardham, Sussex, 46
Richard, anchorite of St. Sepulchre, Hereford, 131, 139, 154
Richard I, 16, 17, 128, 129, 138, 149–151
Richard II, 170, 174; assumption of wife's commitment, 50, 170; confessed to Westminster anchorite, 163, 170
Richard III, 184
Richard of St. Victor, 12
Richard, Walter, anchorite of St. Lawrence, Jewry, London, 82
Richmond, Yorkshire
  anchorites of, 175, 200, 207
  burgesses of, 222
  friars of, 215, 222
  lords of, 189
  reclusoria: endowed, 47, 84, 181, 189; in parish church, 222
Riplay, George, Carmelite anchorite of Boston, Yorkshire, 24
Rippas, Alice, anchoress of St. Margaret, Westminster, 184
Road (highway) repair: alms for, 218; bequests for, 253, 255, 262, 278, 310, 311; grant of pavage for, 209; hermit's work, 16, 81n, 175, 209–210; indulgences for, 81n
Robert abbot of Tewkesbury, 33
Robert, anchorite of Dornford, Oxfordshire, 157
Robert, priest, author of treatise, 103, 295

Robert, priest, custodian of anchoresses, 56, 105
Robert, recluse of Beverly, Yorkshire, 200
Robert, sumetarius, 131
Robes. See Clothing
Robury, Hugh, glover, 229
Roche abbey: abbot of, 63, 63n, 83; anchoress of Dover castle visiting at, 158
Rochester, Kent: bridge of, 255; infirm of, 145n
Rochester diocese, John Russell, bishop of, 76n
Roger, chaplain, 131, 152n
Roger, hermit of Markyate, 93n–94n
Rolle, Richard, 13, 103, 104, 115, 123, 181n, 201, 220, 297–298; relationship with Margaret de Kirkeby, 70, 212–213, 297
Romeyn, John, archbishop of York, 51, 63, 117
Romsey abbey, 163
Roos, Beatrice, 196–199 passim
Roos, John, 196, 200
Roos, William, 196–197
Rose, Cecilia, widow, 230
Rosenthal, Joel, 198, 208n
Rotherham, Thomas, archbishop of York, 72
Rous, John, chaplain of Guy's Cliff, 205–206
Royal patronage
  enclosure, support for, 35, 169, 184
  exemplar for society, 127–128, 156, 281
  pensions, 50–51, 78n, 116, 128, 129–157 passim, 162–163, 176; continued from reign to reign, 128–129, 170–171; limitations of funds for, 130–135, 138n, 163n, 182n

rates of anchorite support, 50–51, 134, 157, 162, 163, 166, 170–171, 177, 181, 189, 257
site commitments, 128–129, 162, 184
See also *individual kings by name*
Russell, John, bishop of Rochester, 76n
Russell, Richard, merchant, 244, 245, 247
Rutland, lack of anchorites in, 36
Rye, 48, 49, 174

Saddlers, 231, 232
St. Aedred, Winchester, anchorite of, 140
St. Albans, Hertfordshire
anchorites of, 46, 217; at St. Michael, 184, 207, 260–263, 266; at St. Peter, 184, 207, 260–263, 266, 278. *See also* St. Albans abbey
archdeaconry court of, 260, 261
guild of, 207
infirm of, 130
wills of, 191, 258, 260–264, 268, 278
St. Albans abbey, 207, 262
abbots of, 55, 180, 203
anchorites under aegis of, 55: at St. Germain, 180, 261; near St. Germain, 180, 261
dependent convents: St. Mary de Pré, 262, 266; Sopwell, 262
monks of, 55, 177
St. Andrews, Wickhamborough, Kent, anchorites of, 195
St. Andrews diocese, William de Lamberton, bishop of, 83–84
St. Asaph, Wales, diocese, Anian II, bishop of, 86, 191
St. Audoneus, Hereford, anchoress at, 149, 151, 154

St. Bodhuc, Oxford, anchoress of, 116
St. Botulph without Bishopsgate, London, anchoresses of, 78n, 181, 182n, 184, 185
St. Calixtus, West Down, Exeter, vicar of, 28
St. Clement, York. *See* Clementhorpe priory
St. Cuthberth, York, anchoresses of, 242, 243, 245n
St. Cyriac, Chicester, anchorite of, 267
St. Dunstan, London, anchoress at, 116
St. Ebbe, Oxford, anchoress of, 266
St. Edmund, Doncaster Bridge, Sprotbrugh, Yorkshire, hospital, reclusorium at, 47, 209–211
St. Edmund, Richmond, Yorkshire, chapel, reclusorium in, 189
St. Edward, Norwich, anchoress of, 46
St. Edwin, Sherwood Forest, Nottinghamshire, hermit-chaplain of, 152
St. George, Norwich, guild of, 158n
St. George, Shrewsbury, Shropshire, reclusorium at, 36n
St. Germain, St. Albans, Hertfordshire, chapel, anchorite of, 180; reclusorium near St. Germain, 180
St. Giles, Norwich, hospital, 249
St. Giles without Holborn, London, anchorites of, 225
St. Gregory, Sudbury, Suffolk, anchoresses of, 33
St. Helen, Fishergate, York, anchoress at, 245
St. Helen, Pontefract, Yorkshire, chapel, anchoresses of, 173–174, 177, 189–190

St. James, Colchester, Essex, anchoress of, 73, 266
St. James, Northampton, prison of, 80, 81
St. James, Westminster, hospital, nuns of, 146n
St. John, Chester, collegial church, anchorites of, 71
St. John, Wakefield, Yorkshire, anchoress of, 217
St. John the Baptist, Hungate, York, anchoresses of, 243, 244
St. John the Baptist, Huntingdon, reclusorium at, 79
St. John the Evangelist, Blyth, Nottinghamshire, chapel, anchoress at, 168–169
St. Katherine by the Tower, London, hospital, nuns of, 224
St. Lawrence, Jewry, London, anchorites of, 34, 82, 225
St. Leonard, Exeter, reclusorium at, 74, 268–274
St. Leonard, Grantham, hospital, anchoress of, 188
St. Margaret, Walmgate, York, anchoresses at, 201, 244, 245
St. Margaret, Westminster, anchoresses of, 181, 183–184, 234
St. Margaret Pattens, London, anchoress of, 156n, 157–158
St. Martin le Grand, London, canon of, 18
St. Martin's Chapel, Aldwark, York, priest-anchorite of, 243, 244
St. Mary, Bedford, anchorite at, 134
St. Mary, Dover castle, anchoresses of, 115, 156n, 157, 158
St. Mary, Gateshead, Durham, reclusorium at, 78
St. Mary, Marlborough, Wiltshire, anchorite of, 155
St. Mary, Walmgate, York, reclusorium at, 35

St. Mary Bishophill, Senior, York, anchoress at, 242–243
St. Mary Bothawe, London, 230
St. Mary de Pré priory, 262
St. Mary le Bowe, Sherborne abbey, anchorite of, 82, 198, 273, 276
St. Mary Magdalene, Exeter, leprosarium, 272
St. Michael, Bristol, Gloucestershire, anchoress of, 62
St. Michael, Cornhill, London, 254
St. Michael, St. Albans, anchoresses of, 184, 207, 260–263, 266
St. Nicholas, Hedon, Yorkshire, anchoress of, 62–63, 116
St. Osyth abbey, abbot of, 73, 266
St. Paul, London, 175, 225
St. Paul, Stamford, Lincolnshire, anchorite at, 200
St. Peter, Cornhill, London: anchoress at, 117, 225; widow at, 27–28
St. Peter, Hereford, reclusorium at, 72
St. Peter, Leicester, reclusorium at, 79–81, 82, 110, 119, 176
St. Peter, Northampton, reclusorium at, 79, 81
St. Peter, St. Albans, Wiltshire, anchoresses of, 184, 207
St. Peter, York, 202
St. Reinold, Cologne, anchorite statutes of, 30n
St. Remigius, Robert of, 187
St. Romald, Shrewsbury, Shropshire, reclusorium at, 36n
St. Saviour, York, 243–246, 253
St. Sepulchre, Canterbury, priory of, 167
St. Sepulchre, Hereford, reclusorium at, 131, 139, 154
St. Teath, Cornwall, hermit of, 278
St. Thierry, William of, 114n
St. Walric, Thomas of, 187

St. Wyennus, Dalston, Cumberland chapel, hermit of, 81n
Sage, Adam, yeoman, 257, 258
Salesbury, Adam de, pepperer, 230
Salisbury, Alienore, countess of, 188
Salisbury, Margaret, countess of, 169n
Salisbury, Wiltshire, friars of, 278
Salisbury (Sarum) diocese, 276
  bishops of, 82: Bingham, Robert, 20–21, 26n, 59–60, 72; Ghent, Simon of, 64n; Poore, Richard, 58–59, 89
  legislation of, 58–60, 72
  Manual, 99–100
  pontificals of, 76n
  support of anchorites, 57, 84
Salt, 48
Santon, Agnes de, 243
Sarah, anchoress of Hecham, Norfolk, 157
Sarum. See Salisbury
Satan. See Devil
Savoy, Boniface of, archbishop of Canterbury, 85
Sawsten, Ann, 260
Scale of Perfection, 103, 104, 115, 181
Scherman, Emma, anchoress of Pontefract, Yorkshire, 78
Schevyngton, Lancashire, 73–74
Scholars, poor. See Poor, scholars
Schools, 271
Sclune and Pyum, Jews of London, 158
Scribes (scriveners) 224, 230, 231
Scrope family
  Geoffrey le, canon, 200–202, 207n, 210, 213, 221, 258, 278
  Henry of Masham, 178, 200–201, 281–282
  John of Masham, 201, 208, 216, 217

Richard le, archbishop of York, 69, 178
Richard of Bolton, 196, 199–202, 208, 211n, 215
Stephen of Masham, 200, 201, 213
Thomas of Masham, 201–202
Thomas (alias Bradley), anchorite of Carmelite friary, Norwich, 211n
Sefrid II, bishop of Chichester, 267
Servants, of anchorites, 31, 33, 49, 50, 69, 100
  bequests for, 200, 201, 213, 243, 252, 259, 263, 267
  conversing with anchorites, 33, 98n, 107–108
  grants for, 198
  need for, 15
  private room for, 32
  released from jury duty, 166
  sharing anchorite's quarters, 33
  sleeping outside the reclusorium, 33
  succeeding to cell, 26
  unchaste, 182–183
Severn Stoke, Worcestershire, reclusorium at, 128–129, 139, 145n, 151
Sewell, Joan, nun, 179n
Sheehan, Michael M., 86n, 219n
Sheen, Surrey, Carthusian monastery of
  bequests for, 181, 198
  foundation of, 50, 178
  intercession of monks requested, 177n
  reclusorium at, 24, 50, 119, 178; support of Henry VIII, 185
  second reclusorium (?) at, 182
Shefeld, Robert de, hermit of Chester, 170
Shelford (Great and Little), Cumberland, 81n

Sheppey, Kent, minster of, 146n
Sherborne abbey, anchorites at St. Mary Le Bowe, 82, 198, 273, 276
Sherman, Emmota, anchoress at Pontefract, Yorkshire, 34
Sherwood Forest, Nottinghamshire, chapel-hermit at, 152
Shipster, Margaret, anchores at St. Peter, Hereford, 72, 120
Shoes, 254, 256, 311
Showings, of Julian of Norwich, 13
Shrewsbury, Shropshire, reclusoria of, 36n, 39
Shropshire: gentry will of, 219n; reclusorium near Shrewsbury, several rooms in, 32
Skinners, 100
Sick. *See* Infirm; Poor, hospitals
Simon, *pictavensis*, 131
Site commitments. *See* Reclusoria
Sites. *See* Reclusoria
Skinners, 224, 231, 234
Smith, Sidney, 154
Snaith, Yorkshire, anchorites of, 175
Snelleston, William, merchant, 252
Somerby, Lincolnshire, gentry will of, 219-220
Somerford, Christine of, anchoress of Malmsbury, Wiltshire, 116
Somerset, gentry wills of, 219n
Sopwell priory, 262
Southampton farm, 145n
Southhill (*Cornwall?*), rector of, 37
Speculum inclusorum, 13, 39-40, 43, 103, 104, 115
Sprotbrugh, Yorkshire. *See* Doncaster Bridge
Stafford, Edmund, bishop of Exeter, 24n, 27n, 71, 119, 179, 268-269; registers of, 271-279

Stafford family, 198-199, 207; Elizabeth, 198, 276-277. *See also* Buckingham, Anne, duchess of; Roos, Beatrice
Stafford, John, bishop of Bath and Wells, 79
Stainfield priory, migration of nun of, 65n, 66-68, 120
Stamford, Lincolnshire, anchorites of, 45, 185, 200; will of, 190n, 258
Stapleton family, 209, 211, 213
Agnes, library of, 215-216
Brian (of Wighill), Lollardlike will of, 214-215
Emma, anchoress at Carmelite friary, Norwich, 213-214
John, will of, 216, 219
Margaret, widow's vow of, 216
Miles (of Norwich), father of Emma, 213-214
Stedham, Sussex, anchorite of, 134, 149
Stenton, Doris, 154
Stephen, anchorite of Crewkerne, Somerset, 273-276
Stephen, king of England, 127, 134, 139, 146n, 185
Stephen the Saracen, 140, 144n
Steyning, Sussex, anchorites of, 44, 86, 87
Stiviton, William de, 130n
Stoke, Matthew, rector, 273-276
Stratford-at-Bow priory, 145, 146n
Stratton, Norfolk, anchorite of, 86
Strong, Beatrice, probationary anchoress, 28-29, 71
Sudbury, Suffolk, anchoresses at St. Gregory's, 33, 188n
Suffield, Walter, bishop of Norwich, 19, 33, 60-61, 85-86, 98n
Suffield, Norfolk, anchorite of, 86
Suffolk, Isabella Ufford, countess of, 203, 214

Suffolk, thirty-seven reclusoria in, 168, 266
Surrey, William de Warenne, earl of, 188
Surrey farm, 130n, 144, 145
Sussex, levels of anchorite activity in, 36, 83
Svein, *valtrarius*, 130n, 144
'Swannesnest' by the Tower of London, anchorite of, 119, 225, 230
Swepestone, Richard, priest-anchorite of St. Lawrence, Jewry, 82
Swinderby, William, hermit, 175n
Swinfield, Richard, bishop of Hereford, 43, 64n, 75
Sybil, anchoress receiving indulgence, 82
Synodal Statutes of an Unknown Province, 59; as the *Legenda*, 89
Syon abbey, 178–181, 198, 254, 311

Tanner, Norman P., 223, 267n
Tattersal, Margaret, anchoress at Doncaster Bridge, Sprotburgh, Yorkshire, 211
Templars, 130–131, 140, 145n
Tertullian, 93
Testamenta Eboracensa, limitations of use of wills in, 191n
Tewkesbury abbey, annals of, 62, 111
Thetford priory, 145n
Thomas, anchorite of Worth, Somerset, 78, 98n
Thomas, chamberlain, 150
Thomson, John A. F., 226–227, 235
Thorgansby, Yorkshire, anchoresses of, 243, 244, 245
Thornbury, William, priest-anchorite of Faversham, Kent, 259, 260, 267

Thornham, Norfolk, anchorite of, 85
Thornton, Roger, merchant, 252
Thornton abbey, abbot of, 66–68
Thorpe, William, 80n
Thrupp, Sylvia, 224
Toledo, council of, 54–55
Torrington, Great, Devonshire, priest-anchorite of, 24n
Totnes, Devonshire, lepers of, 273n
Towns, reclusoria in, 37–41, 282
Treadway, William, priest-anchorite of Great Torrington, Devonshire, penitencer, 24n
Tregman, John, 255n
Trinitarians, 262
Trinity Guild, King's Lynn, 44, 232n
Trullan synod. *See* Constantinople, (*in Trullo*), council of
Tudor, Edmund, 189
Tudor, Henry. *See* Henry VII
Turner, Victor, 95
Twye, Stephen of, 163
Tyler, Wat, 163n, 170
Tynemouth priory, 55

Ufford, Isabella, countess of Suffolk. *See* Suffolk
Usflete, Nicholas, merchant, 249
Usk, Adam of, 203n

Vale, Malcolm G. A., 173, 208n, 211–212, 214, 220
Vannes, council of, 54
Venice, devotional societies in, 229
Vesci, William de, 188
Vice and Virtues, 215
Villages, reclusoria in 37–41, 282
Vintners, 224, 231–232n
Visitors, 98n, 107, 108, 121. *See also* Anchorites, hospitality; Reclusoria, guest rooms

Wakefield, Yorkshire, anchoress of, 217

Wakering, John, bishop of Norwich, 86

Waldern, William, merchant, 239, 312

Walter, anchorite and author of *Rule*, 24, 97, 102–104, 106n, 107, 109–112, 164n, 296

Walter, Hubert, archbishop of Canterbury, 150n

Wardesale, Maude, anchoress of St. Peter, Leicester, 176

Ware, Hertfordshire, Franciscans of, 262

Warham, Herefordshire, anchorites of, 187

Warner, Christopher, anchorite of the Dominican Friary of Canterbury, Kent, 110–111, 120–121, 185, 289

Wartere, Richard, merchant, 244, 247

Warwick, earls of. *See* Beauchamp

Warwick, Guy of, hermit, 205

Wath, Yorkshire, anchorite of, 200, 201, 243

Watton priory, 92n–93n

Welles, John, merchant, 237, 238, 239, 310

Wells, Somersewt, canon of, 269, 271

Westminster: anchoresses of at St. Margaret, 181, 183–184, 234; ecclesiastical prison of, 238

Westminster abbey, anchorite-monks of, 68, 162–163, 177n, 179–180, 203: bequests for, 200, 207, 235; royal confessors, 24n, 70, 111, 163, 177–178; two reclusoria for, 177–178n

Westmorland, Ralph Neville, earl of, 213; bequests of, 19, 207;

daughter of, 198, 199, 207; patronage of as lord of Richmond, 189, 207; supervisor of will of John Lord Roos, 196

Westmorland, lack of anchorites in, 36

Weston, Nicholas de, merchant, 168, 252

Whalley, Lancashire, endowed reclusorium of, 49, 50, 174, 175, 190, 193; multiple buildings of, 33n, 36n; dissolution of, 182–183

Wheat, 45, 47–48, 49, 73, 157, 165, 166, 174, 189, 195, 266; monetary value of, 157n

Whitaker, T. D., 185

Whiterig, John, the Monk of Farne, 13, 181n

Whittington, Richard, merchant, 239, 241

Whityng, William, anchorite of Sherborne abbey, 198, 276

Wich, Richard, bishop of Chichester, 60, 85, 98n, 111–112

Wick-by-Pershore, Worcestershire, Peter of endowed reclusorium of, 48–49, 61, 202n

Wickhamborough, Lincolnshire, anchorites of, 45, 195

Wickwane, William, archbishop of York, 74

Widows
    vows of, 27–28n, 77, 216, 273n
    wills of, 216, 230, 231n, 234, 252, 273n
    See also Anchoresses, widows; Poor, widows

Wigan, Adam, rector, 243–245, 279

Wigan, Lancashire, anchoress of, 73–74, 169, 188

Wilderness themes, 9–13

William, pardoned, 167

William, *arbalastarius*, 140
William, bishop of Hereford, 14
William, hermit of Dalby, 169n
William, *pottarius*, 144
William, priest-anchorite of Ardland, Gloucestershire, 16–17, 150, 152, 156n, 159n
William, prior of Blyth priory, 168
Williams, George H., 11, 94
Willoughby family, 209
  Henry, analysis of accounts of, 217–218
  Hugh, 217
  Jane Hastings, 217
Wills
  analysis and limitations of the use of, 175n–176n, 190–195, 226n, 235
  definition of, 190n
  lack of consistency in, 86–87, 202, 248
  Lollardlike, 197, 214
  most ample after 1350, 168
  pious and charitable grants of, 193–194, 224
  probate of, 223–224, 227–228
  providing annuities, 45, 190, 195, 254, 258, 266
  residues of, 192
  unevenly available, 37n, 192
  written in close proximity to death, 147
  written by women, 198–199
Wilmyndoun, Maude, anchoress, 179n
Wilton abbey, nuns of, 50, 103, 179n, 294
Wiltshire: farm of, 130n, 156n; hermit of, 170
Winchester, Hampshire
  anchoress of brought to London, 158n, 204
  anchorites in, 22; at St. Aedred, 140

  farm of, 130n, 140–144
  infirm of, 140
Winchester, Henry of, convert, 164
Winchester diocese, bishops of, 59: Giffard, William, 56; Wykeham, William, 82
Windsor
  anchorite of, 159
  farm of, 65, 138, 139, 156n
  infirm of, 130, 138
Wine: allowed for anchorites, 52; grants of, 163, 165, 168
Winmark, anchoress of Frodsham, Chester, 188
Winterton, Lincolnshire, reclusorium at, 66–67
Wiz, Juetta de, anchoress of Ardland, Gloucestershire, 159n
Wodecock, John, mercer, 229
Wombell, Joan, 211
Women, religious lives of, 21–22
Wood: for construction, 158–159, 170; for fuel, 44, 48, 49, 68, 157, 159, 162, 165–166, 170, 188, 253
Woolmongers, 232n
Worcester, anchorites of, 18–19, 158, 195, 207
Worcester diocese
  anchorite of, 62
  bishops of, 62: Clifford, Richard, 76n; Polton, Thomas, 86
  support of anchorites, 57, 84
Worcester priory: anchoresses of, 33, 45, 46, 266; prior of, 45, 266
Worcestershire: levels of anchorite activity in, 36; farm of, 145
Worth, Lucas de, priest, 257–258, 266
Worth, Somerset, anchorites of, 34, 78, 98n
Wotton, Oxfordshire, anchoress of, 157

Wragmire, Cumberland, hermit of, 81n
Writtle, Essex, anchorites at, 128, 129, 140, 145, 149, 151, 153
Wulfa, anchorite, 55
Wulfric of Haselbury, priest-anchorite of Haselbury Plucknett, Somerset, 37, 56, 62, 98, 110, 127, 275, 286
Wulstan, *caretarius*, 130n, 140, 144n
Wyclif, John, 119, 174
Wykeham, William, bishop of Winchester, 82
Wylie, James H., 176

Yarum, Henry de, merchant, 243
Yeomen and artisans
  anchorites, 257
  bequests of, 168
  defined negatively, 256n
  patronage local, 261, 264
  wills of, 258–263, 284
York, Elizabeth of, wife of Henry VII, 184–185, 261
York, Yorkshire
  anchorites of, 39, 200, 216, 242, 245, 247; at All Saints, Fishergate, 201, 242, 244, 245, 257n; All Saints, North Street, 206, 242, 244; Clementhorpe priory, 201, 216, 242; Layerthorpe Bridge, 243; St. Cuthbert, 242, 243, 245n; St. Helen, Fishergate, 245; St. John the Baptist, Hungate, 243, 244; St. Martin's Chapel, Aldwark, 243, 244; St. Margaret, Walmgate, 201, 244, 245; St. Mary Bishophill, Senior, 242–243; St. Mary, Walmgate, 35
Clementhorpe priory, 216
  hermit of, 170
  hospitals (maisondieux) of, 201, 248–249
  lepers of, 197, 201
  mayors of, 191, 223, 247–249
  merchant wills of, 242–249; anchorites as religious in, 246–247
  population of, 38; decline in 39n, 241
  residentiary canons of, 193n
  St. Peter, 202
  St. Saviour, 243–246, 253, 279
York archdiocese
  archbishops of, 44: Bainbridge, Christopher, 76n; Corbridge, Thomas, 84; Giffard, Walter, 44, 51, 62, 116; Greenfield, William, 35, 47–48, 83–84; Melton, William, 117; Romeyn, John, 51, 63, 117; Rotherham, Thomas, 72; Scrope, Richard le, 69, 178; Wickwane, William, 74
  registers of, 116–117
  support of anchorites, 57, 84
  vicar general of, 28n
York diocese: anchorites of, 19, 207; Consistory court of, 242
Yorkshire
  anchorites of, 19, 44, 215
  farm of, 145, 156n
  levels of anchorite activity in, 36–37, 39
  wills of, 258, 267n

Designer: U.C. Press Staff
Compositor: Freedmen's Organization
Printer: Thomson-Shore, Inc.
Binder: John H. Dekker & Sons
Text: 10/13 Elante
Display: Elante

DATE DUE

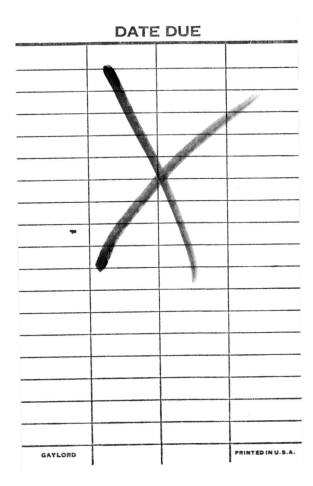